sh

# Sport and the Irish

*Histories, Identities, Issues*

edited by
**Alan Bairner**

University College Dublin Press
Preas Choláiste Ollscoile
Bhaile Átha Cliath

First published 2005
by University College Dublin Press
Newman House
86 St Stephen's Green
Dublin 2
Ireland

www.ucdpress.ie


© the editor and contributors 2005


ISBN 1-904558-33-X

Cataloguing in Publication data
available from the British Library



Typeset in Ireland in Adobe Garamond and Trade Gothic
by Elaine Shiels, Bantry, Co. Cork
Text design by Lyn Davies
Printed in Great Britain on acid-free paper by CPD Wales, Ebbw Vale

# Contents

**Part 3** Issues

# Acknowledgements

Many of the contributors first presented drafts of their chapters at a two-day interdisciplinary conference on 'Sport and the Irish' which was hosted by the University of Ulster's Academy for Irish Cultural Heritages on 26 and 27 April 2002. This was only made possible as a result of the support given by the Academy's Director, Professor Brian Graham and the organisational skills of Neal Garnham. Although the editor was employed by the University of Ulster when the idea of this collection was first mooted, the editorial work has been completed at Loughborough University where the comradeship of new colleagues and the opportunities to get on with academic writing have been invaluable. Last but by no means least the editor owes a deep debt of gratitude to the contributors. Some are old friends. Others have become new friends. A few would be strangers were it not for the invention of electronic mail. What unites them all, however, is an attention to detail, a willingness to co-operate and a wealth of insights into Irish sport. Although only one name appears on the cover of this book, this has been a genuine collective effort. The editor is indebted to Barbara Mennell at UCD Press for reacting favourably to the initial idea for this collection and for her subsequent support and patience.

ALAN BAIRNER
*Loughborough*
*May 2004*

# Contributors to this volume

ALAN BAIRNER is Reader in the Sociology of Sport at Loughborough University having previously held the post of Professor in Sports Studies at the University of Ulster. He is a co-author (with John Sugden) of *Sport, Sectarianism and Society in a Divided Ireland* (1993) and author of *Sport, Nationalism and Globalisation: European and North American Perspectives* (2001). From 2000 to 2001 he was a member of the ministerial advisory committee which was charged with creating a strategy for the future of soccer in Northern Ireland.

THOMAS CARTER is Senior Lecturer in Leisure and Sociology in the Department of Sports Studies at the University of Wales, Newport. He has published in various international journals on the relationship between sport and globalisation in Cuba and Ireland. He is currently completing an ethnographic study of Cuban baseball.

MIKE CRONIN is Senior Research Fellow in History at the International Centre for Sports History and Culture at De Montfort University, Leicester. He has held visiting positions at Boston College and the National University of Ireland, Galway. His publications include *Sport and Nationalism in Ireland. Gaelic Games, Soccer and Irish Identity since 1884* (1999), and (with Daryl Adair) *The Wearing of the Green: A History of St Patrick's Day* (2002). He is currently working on a history of state spectacles in Ireland, 1922–66.

PAUL DARBY is Lecturer in the Sociology of Sport at the University of Ulster at Jordanstown. He is the author of *Africa, Football and FIFA: Politics, Colonialism and Resistance* (2002) and co-editor (with Martin Johnes and Gavin Mellor) of *Football and Disaster: An International Study* (2004). He is currently researching Gaelic games and the Irish diaspora in North America. He has played inter-county Gaelic football for Antrim at minor, under-21 and senior levels and has represented Ballyclare Comrades in Irish League soccer.

GARETH FULTON is a postgraduate student in the Department of Anthropology at the National University of Ireland, Maynooth. He is currently undertaking research into social and political aspects of soccer in South Africa, having previously written a Master's thesis on national and sectarian identities in Irish soccer. He has played Irish League soccer for the past eight years, most recently with Newry Town.

Neal Garnham is Senior Lecturer in History in the Academy for Irish Cultural Heritages at the University of Ulster. He is the author of *Association Football and Society in Pre-Partition Ireland* (2004) and he has published articles on sporting history in the *English Historical Review* and *Irish Historical Studies*.

David Hassan is Lecturer in Sports Studies at the University of Ulster at Jordanstown. His main research interest is the relationship between sport, politics and Irish identities and he has published on this theme in various international journals. He is a former inter-county Gaelic footballer and hurler with his native Derry and he has also played Irish League soccer for Cliftonville.

Tom Hunt is a teacher in Mullingar, County Westmeath. He is the author of *Portlaw, County Waterford: Portrait of an Industrial Village and its Cotton Industry* (2000). His research interests include Victorian sport in Ireland. He played inter-county hurling and Gaelic football for Waterford and was a member of the Munster inter-provincial football panel from 1982 to 1984, winning a Railway Cup medal in 1982. Unusually for a Waterford footballer he also won a Sigerson Cup medal, playing for University College Dublin. In 1998 he was the first winner of the RTÉ quiz *Know Your Sport*.

Katie Liston is Lecturer in the Sociology of Sport at University College Chester and Co-Director of the Chester Centre for Research into Sport and Society. She is currently completing her doctoral research for University College Dublin on the sociological analysis of the fields of sport and gender in Ireland. She holds national honours in Gaelic football, athletics and basketball and has represented Ireland at senior level in rugby union and soccer.

Jonathan Magee is Senior Lecturer in the Department of Tourism and Leisure Management at the University of Central Lancashire (UCLan). His research interests include soccer labour migration. He is Chair of the Operational Group of the International Football Institute, a research and consultancy partnership between UCLan and the National Football Museum. He played Irish League soccer for Linfield, Portadown and Bangor, winning an Irish Cup medal with the latter in 1993, and was capped at Under-21 level by Northern Ireland.

Paul Rouse is a reporter with *Prime Time*, the main current affairs programme on RTÉ television. He is a former Government of Ireland Post-Doctoral Fellow and has lectured in sports history at University College Dublin. He has won two Offaly county senior medals in Gaelic football with his club, Tullamore, and is desperately seeking a third.

LOUISE RYAN is a research fellow at Middlesex University, and has a PhD in sociology from University College Cork. She is the author of *Gender, Identity and the Irish Press, 1922–37: Embodying the Nation* (2002) and co-editor (with Ann Marie Gallagher and Cathy Lubelska) of *Re-Presenting the Past: Women and History* (2001) and (with Margaret Ward) of *Irish Women and Nationalism* (2004).

PETER SHIRLOW is Senior Lecturer in Geography at the University of Ulster at Coleraine. His main research interest is the analysis of identity formation and sectarianism in Northern Ireland and he has published articles on this topic in various international journals. He is currently involved in projects studying the development of politically motivated prisoner groups in Belfast and the problem of Protestant 'alienation' in Derry.

JOHN SUGDEN is Professor in the Sociology of Sport at the University of Brighton. He is the author of *Boxing and Society: An International Analysis* (1996) and of *Scum Airways: Inside Football's Underground Economy* (2002) and co-author (with Alan Bairner) of *Sport, Sectarianism and Society in a Divided Ireland* (1993) and (with Alan Tomlinson) of *FIFA and the Contest for World Football: Who Rules the Peoples' Game?* (1998). He played and coached soccer in Northern Ireland from 1982 to 1996.

JASON TUCK is Senior Lecturer in the Sociology of Sport at University College Winchester. His main research interest is the relationship between sport and national identity and he has published on this subject in various international journals and edited collections. He is currently writing a book (with Joseph Maguire) on Irish rugby union and national identity.

# Abbreviations

| | |
|---|---|
| BPP | British Parliamentary Papers |
| CCnG | Cumann Camogiochta na nGael (Camogie association) |
| CD | Command Papers |
| FCO | Foreign and Commonwealth Office |
| FAI | Football Association of Ireland |
| FIFA | Fédération Internationale de Football Association |
| GAA | Gaelic Athletic Association |
| IACB | Irish Athletic Club of Boston |
| ICA | Irish Cycling Association |
| IFA | Irish Football Association |
| IOC | International Olympic Committee |
| IRA | Irish Republican Army |
| IRB | Irish Republican Brotherhood |
| IRFU | Irish Rugby Football Union |
| LGAA | Ladies Gaelic Athletic Association |
| LVF | Loyalist Volunteer Force |
| NA | National Archives of Ireland |
| NACB | North American County Board |
| NLI | National Library of Ireland |
| PRONI | Public Record Office of Northern Ireland |
| PSNI | Police Service of Northern Ireland |
| RIC | Royal Irish Constabulary |
| SDLP | Social Democratic and Labour Party |
| UEFA | Union Européenne de Football Association |
| UVF | Ulster Volunteer Force |
| WSPP | World Sport Peace Project |

Introduction

# Sport and the Irish

Alan Bairner

## Introduction

Although the word 'sport' was used commonly in Ireland long before the period that is covered by any of the essays in this collection, it normally referred to hunting, fishing and other such activities enjoyed by the Irish gentleman. In addition were the games played by 'ordinary' people and rumoured to have their origins in Ireland's historic and mythic past. Sport, in the modern sense, arrived in Ireland shortly after it had first taken root in England. This did not mean an abandonment of the old rural pastimes: the people's games, such as hurling and football, were to be given new impetus in part because of the British sporting revolution. The result was to be a sporting culture arguably more varied than any other and certainly closely bound up with such perennially potent themes as the meaning of being Irish and the relationship of Irish people with each other and with the world beyond. There is no denying the fascination that sport exerts in the Irish – in particular the Irish male – psyche. Lansdowne Road, Croke Park and the Curragh are not places for the uninterested. Furthermore, sporting venues throughout the world have echoed to the sound of Irish voices as fans celebrate the achievements of their heroes and, on fewer but not less emotional occasions, their heroines.

In recent times, the Irish love affair with sport has also been celebrated in literature (Cunningham, 2001; O'Brien, 2000). George O'Brien (2000: 22) leaves us in no doubt as to why sport is fertile ground for the literary imagination and also a rich resource for intellectual inquiry.

> sport provides an introduction to aesthetics and a sidelight on politics. It's a vivid touchstone of memory and a blueprint of a home from home. It's a bright thread in the fabric of recent social history, and a clue to a generation's evolving cultural awareness.

Yet most academic writing on Ireland until relatively recently has tended to ignore sport along with a host of other forms of popular culture. The neglect of sport is of course by no means unique to Ireland. It has taken a considerable time for historians, sociologists, political scientists and the like to become convinced of the social significance of sport and its resultant worth as a subject for intellectual debate. This struggle goes on throughout the world. In Ireland it has resulted in a growing body of literature that has dealt with the history, sociology and politics of sport in Ireland per se and also within the British context (a development that is well documented in Rouse's bibliographical notes to the opening chapter of this volume, see pp. 252–3). Some of the main contributors to this process are represented in this book. The other authors are, in a sense, beneficiaries of the pioneering work of those who have gone before. It is now reputable to write seriously about Irish sport. Questions remain, however, as to how best this should be done.

It is apparent from the various chapters that are included in this book that the study of Irish sport is heavily influenced by some important dichotomies – history and social science, the Irish Republic and Northern Ireland, nationalism and unionism. Each element within all of these dichotomous relationships has already been well served by the academic study of Irish sport and is also prominent in this particular collection of essays. Other themes, such as gender, spatiality and comparative research, are profiled in this collection but remain relatively underdeveloped. Clearly much work remains to be done. But before indicating areas for future research, it is worth making some brief general observations based on work that has been done to date and more specifically the contributions that appear in this collection.

Virtually all of the contributors emphasise the role that sport plays in Irish life and in the construction of Irish identities. Moreover, the historical chapters (chapters 1–6) demonstrate that this is by no means a recent pheno-menon. They also reveal the importance of appreciating the subtlety of certain relationships that have often fallen foul of a tendency to oversimplify. Thus, contrary to much of the work that has been devoted to the Gaelic Athletic Association, Hunt comments on the non-political adoption of Gaelic games in Westmeath, on the links between Gaelic games and cricket and on the complex relationship between the early GAA and Irish nationalism. The need to approach the latter with caution is also highlighted in this volume by Cronin and Darby. Similarly, the problematic relationship between imper-ialism, Britishness and Ulster unionism is revealed and examined, historically by Garnham and in the modern era by Bairner and Magee.

Undeniably the chapters that make up this book reflect in their varying emphases the current state of play in relation to the academic study of sport in Ireland. Thus there is disproportionately more about sport in Northern Ireland than in the Irish Republic. This is bound up with the fact that the deeply divided nature of northern society has inspired a plethora of social scientific investigations of which sport, as well as other forms of popular culture, has been a major beneficiary. That said, the book contains a number of essays (Garnham, Tuck, Hassan, Fulton, Bairner) that explore the relationship between the two Irelands. Furthermore, there is sufficient evidence in the collection that, regardless of the current constitutional arrangements, there exist many more than two Irelands and a multiplicity of ways in which people might understand and articulate their Irishness in sporting and other contexts. In this regard, the chapters by Hassan and Fulton on the relationship between northern nationalists and the Republic of Ireland are particularly instructive. In general it might be argued that the types of questions that are addressed by all of the authors include: What is Ireland? and What does it mean to be Irish?

Clearly the answers to questions of this type can never be fixed any more than the nation or national identity can be presented as unchanging. Thus in chapters that are superficially very different, such as those by Ryan and Darby, similar questions concerning tradition, modernity and authenticity are addressed in an attempt to chart evolving understandings of Ireland, the Irish and Irish sport. As regards gender, however, evolution has been slow to say the least.

The focus of most of the chapters in this collection is on male sport. Even when this is not made explicit, the hegemonic dominance of men in the Irish sporting world is certainly implicit in all but two of the contributions. Once again, Ireland is not unique in this respect. Throughout the world, not only sport itself but also the main themes that are addressed by social scientists and historians of sport have always been governed by patriarchy. These tendencies have been challenged in recent years not least through a growing interest in female sporting experiences and the related but distinct emergence of a feminist perspective on sport. It is intended that the chapters by Ryan and Liston which are included in this collection make a contribution to these trends and provide solid foundations upon which future researchers may build. Gender, however, is not the only theme that has tended to be neglected in studies of Irish sport.

Although relatively copious, work on sport in Northern Ireland in the past has often been under theorised. It is to be hoped that all of the chapters in this collection that focus on the north have redressed the balance to some extent. Notable in this respect are the anthropological essays contributed by Fulton and Carter and Shirlow's application of the tools of his trade as a human geographer. Studies of Northern Irish sport have also been quite parochial in character. Perhaps reflecting a general trend within Northern Irish civic culture, there has been a tendency to become fixated on Northern Ireland's uniqueness instead of considering the issues raised by this problematic society in a more global context. It is refreshing, therefore, that both Darby and Carter have addressed the global issue of migration, albeit involving the movement of people in different directions. In addition, Sugden's very personal account which concludes the collection graphically demonstrates what can be learned in one conflict zone (Northern Ireland) and applied to another (Israel/Palestine).

What more then needs to be done? This collection, wide ranging as it is, is only a beginning. There is considerable scope for increased academic study of the social significance of sport in the Republic of Ireland. This means more people in the Irish Republic actually studying sport from historical and social scientific perspectives and also more people, wherever they are located, studying sport's role in the Republic. More studies of women's experiences of sport in Ireland are required as are more feminist accounts of Irish sport. With specific reference to the north, not only is it important for scholars to look beyond 'the narrow ground' but also to focus on the nuances and abandon sweeping generalisations that construct the two traditions as unchanging monoliths.

Finally, it is important for the study of sport, not only in Ireland but elsewhere, that more attention is paid to the athletes themselves. In this collection, there are hints of this in the contributions of Bairner, Carter, Liston and Tuck. Yet there remains enormous scope for manageable research projects that examine the attitudes of the men and women who actually play sport in and for Ireland. Moreover the focus should not be solely on the big team sports. So much has yet to be learned about the experiences of those countless people who do not play soccer, Gaelic games or rugby union. The motor sports enthusiasts, the golfers, the swimmers, the cricketers, the gymnasts and so on are all worthy of serious academic attention as indeed are the hunters and the anglers who were once the main exponents of sport in Ireland.

If it achieves nothing else, it is to be hoped that the collection encourages future generations to take up the challenge of explaining the relationship between sport and the Irish. In the meantime, however, it is also intended that the essays inform, provoke and entertain.

Part 1
# Histories

**Chapter 1**

# *Sport* and Ireland in 1881

Paul Rouse

## Introduction

On Christmas Eve in 1880, the newspaper, *Sport*, was launched in Dublin and for fifty years it offered a glorious, offbeat insight into Irish life. Its pages record the extraordinary range of sporting activity in Ireland in the 1880s and illuminate the society in which that activity took place. This chapter examines the first full year of the publication of *Sport* – 1881 – and considers how the paper managed to survive, and then thrive.

Profound social change in nineteenth-century England left more people with more money to spend, and with more leisure time in which to spend it. Industrialisation, urbanisation, technological advancement, shifting social norms and unprecedented population growth radically altered the lifestyles of large sections of the English population. The number of Britons grew from 10.7 million in 1801 to 40.1 million in 1911. Where they lived was crucial. In 1801 just one in three English people lived in towns, but, by 1911, this ratio had increased to four out of every five people. The urban masses passed their days in factories and offices, not in fields. Patterns of play were moulded to fit this new society. The traditional recreations of previous generations were recast on an urban stage as modern codified sports. Soccer steadily established itself as the game of the people, while rugby and cricket also enjoyed wide popular appeal. Not only were newly organised sports thriving, long-established ones such as horse racing remained popular among all classes. The growing commercialisation of sport reflected a society in which disposable income was now a central feature of the lives of the expanding middle and working classes. Regular sporting events involving amateur and professional competitors drew enormous crowds to purpose-built stadiums, while many more played games in the parks and pavilions of the growing suburbs. The power and prestige of the British Empire in the late nineteenth century facilitated the diffusion of Anglocentric sports across the world. The process was a complex one, but ultimately resulted in English rules of play dispersed to such an extent that the English could rightly claim to be the midwives of the modern sporting world.[1]

The relationship between two islands united in one kingdom ensured that Ireland was well represented through the formative years of modern sports. The geography and politics that bound together the two countries helped forge a cultural exchange, which was deepened by increasing travel and commerce. Some of the demographic and economic features crucial to the growth of English sports were not shared by its neighbouring island. Yet Ireland as a whole did not differ so profoundly from England as to leave it divorced from the English sporting world. Ireland did not industrialise as England had and its population was in decline, but some regions – notably the main urban centres of the east coast – experienced a change which drew them away from the rhythms of rural Ireland and closer to those of English cities. Only 15 per cent of Irish people had lived in towns and cities in 1841 and this figure had grown to 35 per cent in 1914. The industrialisation of Belfast saw the city rapidly expand its number of inhabitants from 100,000 in 1845 to 400,000 in 1914 as its heavy industry prospered in the docks and beyond. Dublin grew from 250,000 to 300,000 inhabitants in the same period and the slower rate of growth brought a different dynamic; change did come, but its arrival was less intense and, consequently, different in aspect. These growing cities of Empire adopted many of the characteristics of the English sporting world. Belfast most closely resembled the northern industrial cities of England with its professional soccer leagues and working-class sporting culture. The more sedate Dublin suburbs were home to tennis and golf clubs, while the wealthier schools – following the model of their counterparts in England – laid out pitches for rugby and cricket.

In the Irish countryside, as Hunt reveals in chapter 2, the fall in population and the relative failure to industrialise did not prove inimical to sporting development. Images of an agrarian backwater, a repository of racial purity, where peasants lovingly preserved an ancient and dignified way of life, were fundamentally at odds with the realities of rural life. In the latter half of the nineteenth century when modern sports organisations were reordering the sporting world, the Irish countryside was in the throes of immense change. The rural class structure was profoundly altered. The drift from the land was remorseless as the boats carried successive generations into exile in the cities of England and America. The marriage and birth rates declined, and the age of marriage rose. By the beginning of the twentieth century, 45 per cent of the population continued to be employed in agriculture in Ireland, but the nature of that employment had shifted. The number of agricultural labourers fell dramatically after the famine and that class eventually disappeared from the countryside. Farm sizes grew and this, together with the introduction of new crops and modern farming methods, increased income. Indeed, between 1850 and 1914 there were large gains in rural income as agricultural output grew and the numbers dependent on the land for their livelihood fell.[2] While many remained mired in poverty, others enjoyed a definite rise in income as the nineteenth century progressed. Tenant farmers became the largest social group in rural society and, benefiting most from increases in the prices of livestock and butter, came to enjoy a relatively comfortable existence. Further, the culture of rural Ireland was shaped by change in the wider world. This was not simply a place apart, unconnected to modernity and ignoring the sands of time. The obvious personal ties of contact with emigrant communities were supplemented by developments such as the spread of the railways. From a mere 65 miles in 1850, there were more than 3,500 miles of rail track across Ireland by the outbreak of the First World War. Not even the most remote parts of the country remain unmoved in a time of diminishing distance. Rural Ireland may not have danced to the same tune as industrial Britain, but it was increasingly familiar with the music played there.[3]

As part of the greater world of leisure in the later decades of the nineteenth century, newspapers began to draw a far wider readership. In Ireland, as in Britain, the abolition of stamp duty and enhanced printing technology facilitated the production of cheaper newspapers. Improved transport allowed for more efficient distribution, while improved rates of literacy – by 1911 88 per cent of the Irish population was literate – offered new sections of the population as potential readers. By 1880, in Britain, there were two daily papers dedicated entirely to sports reporting – the *Sportsman* and the *Sporting Chronicle* – and by 1884 they had been joined by a third, the *Sporting Life*. Each cost one penny and covered all manner of sports, with horse racing clearly the dominant feature. These papers sought to provide a complete and continuous record of an important and expanding social phenomenon (Mason, 1993). By the mid-1880s, these daily sports papers were complemented by sports or football 'specials', published in cities across Britain on Saturday evenings, carrying that day's results and, later, full reports, at the even cheaper price of one halfpenny.

In 1880, Ireland could not have supported a daily sporting paper, nor did it have the regularised sporting fixture list to warrant a 'Saturday special'. What emerged was a peculiarly Irish compromise: the 'weekly special'. The first dedicated sporting paper in Ireland was *The Irish Sportsman and Farmer* which was dominated by news of hunting and other horse-related activities, while also carrying reports on the corn and cattle markets of Britain and Ireland. Its 16 pages retailed at the cost of 4*d.* and cultivated an ethos of gentlemanly leisure. As the sporting world changed, it reduced its price and sought to reinvent itself in more populist terms. It failed. By the time of its demise in 1892, *The Irish Sportsman and Farmer* had never fully transcended the elitist aura of its origins and could not capture the mood of increasingly populist sporting times.

By contrast, the style, content and price see *Sport* fit easily into the story of the popular press in the Victorian world. It emerged as the Saturday publication of the *Freeman's Journal*, the best-selling Irish daily newspaper printed in Dublin.[4] Although its early numbers were printed on Wednesdays, *Sport* was soon completed late on Friday nights and distributed across Ireland on the early trains of Saturday morning. The self-styled 'New Weekly Sporting Organ for the Million', which also referred to itself as 'The Irish Pink 'Un', totalled 28 columns across four pages and was sold for what its editor called 'the people's price' of one penny (*Sport*, 24 Dec. 1880).

The first edition laid out the paper's aims with clarity: 'The want of a reliable and cheap organ of sport in this sport-loving country has for years been most keenly felt'. The priority would be racing coverage but 'no single branch of sport – hunting, yachting, shooting, cricketing, football or polo – will escape the constant vigilance of our staff' (*Sport*, 24 December 1880). That first edition, it was claimed, sold out its entire print run of 10,000. Impossible to prove, this claim is still more impossible to credit (*Sport*, 1 Jan. 1881). Even in an industry notorious for imagined circulation, this figure seems spectacularly creative and probably features at least one digit too many. Whatever the extent of the wider readership, fellow journalists had taken definite note. When the second number of *Sport* appeared on New Year's Day 1881, it carried with it letters of commendation from newspapers across Ireland and Britain. The *Cork Herald*, for example, predicted that the paper would usurp the 'cheap English sporting papers that now virtually monopolise Irish sporting custom'. Yet one of those supposed competitors, the Manchester-based *Sporting Chronicle*, saw not a rival but a soulmate, as it delighted in the arrival of a counterpart in Dublin, arguing it offered further proof that the day of the high-priced paper was now dead (*Sport*, 1 Jan. 1881). Cheapness alone was obviously no guarantee of success and apart from the obvious fact that it rightly identified an opening in the market – or, more properly, saw the potential to expand the market – the success of *Sport* was rooted in the quality of its content.

## Verbose journalists, quality drinking and a gentleman's corset

In keeping with the style of its era, journalists on *Sport* were verbose, self-regarding and always liable to slide off at a tangent to demonstrate their heavy burden of erudition and learning. These were educated men – and they were always men – who produced dense paragraphs of elongated sentences. A prime example was the stellar columnist, 'Lux', who wrote on horse racing. He was an outstanding crank who operated on the principle that everything modern was wrong. 'Lux' informed all and sundry that he could not have cared less if a whole host of the minor provincial meetings across the country collapsed once the old traditional racecourses such as Punchestown and the Curragh continued to prosper (*Sport*, 27 Aug. 1881). 'Lux' wrote,

There are some shortcomings associated with small gatherings which seem to be almost unavoidable. A good courseway may in some cases be difficult to procure; high class competitors would not run for small stakes, and their absence is therefore excusable; but that a dangerous course should be provided, and that the observance of punctuality be totally neglected, cannot even be palliated . . . I am convinced that something should be done to check the downward tendency of steeple-chasing – a pastime which is detrimentally affected by the frequent recurrence of badly-managed provincial meetings (*Sport*, 26 March 1881).

Many of those provincial meetings, he argued, 'are unfit to be classified under the heading of sport' and 'I would prefer, if guided by my own feelings, to allow those little meetings to pass unnoticed here'.

The demands of circulation and advertising, of course, forced 'Lux' to martyr himself by covering the minor meetings. His response was clinical; if he were forced to suffer, he would not do so alone. The provinces were slaughtered at every opportunity and it made for wonderful copy. A meeting in Frenchpark, County Roscommon was 'a complete failure . . . No matter how praiseworthy the intentions of the promoters of them be, I cannot encourage these gentlemen to persevere with such burlesques on sport, and it would be better for them to abandon the attempt if they cannot improve on today's exhibition' (*Sport*, 26 Mar. 1881). And when one reader complained of the severity of a particularly vitriolic attack from 'Lux', the paper's editor was unforgiving: 'We write of things as we see them and not as they ought to be' (*Sport*, 13 Aug. 1881).

It can only have galled those whom he criticised, but 'Lux' was able to match the arrogance of his reporting, with uncommon accuracy in his tipping. As yet another of his successful predictions was greeted with the unassuming headline 'Lux again triumphant', he noted that ten of his 14 tips had won at the Curragh on the previous weekend. He helpfully pointed out that on a £5 stake, a punter could have retired with a net profit of £61 6s. 8d. (*Sport*, 2 July 1881). Indeed, gambling opened a vital avenue for the paper's expansion. Frequent tipping successes brought the initiative that on the morning of every big race meeting in Ireland, the horses favoured by 'Lux' would be listed in *The Irish Times* and the *Freeman's Journal*. To decipher the tips, however, the reader would have had to purchase the previous Saturday's *Sport*, where a special coded number would have been placed beside each of the horses running.

If 'Lux' drew wide popular appeal through his tipping, the paper's intermittent editorials were also unashamedly populist. When magistrates in Cork banned from sale all alcoholic drink at the forthcoming Cork Park race meeting, the paper was apoplectic. It denied that there was any evidence of drunkenness or disorder at previous meetings, claiming that magistrates simply 'begrudged racing folk their glass of beer and sandwich between races' and were motivated by 'a strong desire to impart a lesson in temperance'. The editorial called on parliament to legislate on the right to drink at race meetings, but, clearly recognising that this would be impossible in time to avert the impending privations in Cork, it issued a rallying cry for all to attend with 'a heavy crop' of hip-flasks. Neatly, it disowned responsibility for any licentiousness which might flow from such flasks, by insisting that the responsibility for any misbehaviour would have to lie with the judiciary:

> Not in the least surprised will we be to see staggering men about a ring from which the vice of drunkenness has hitherto been most remarkable by its complete absence. Is it not a monstrous interference with the liberty of a subject to withhold from the respectable and temperate classes a glass of wine or a bottle of beer [so] needed on a racecourse during a long day? (*Sport*, 20 Aug. 1881 and 3 Sept. 1881).

The following week the paper lamented that the Cork Park meeting was host to only a small number of horses, which competed in front of a diminished attendance. The paper referred to the 'tameness' of the whole afternoon and its worry that the banning of drink at Cork Park was but the first in a series of such moves was borne out the following month when it reported that a similar appeal had been made to magistrates in Limerick. In that city's courts, Sub-Inspector Wilton applied to disallow the sale of alcohol at Limerick races 'in consequence of the riotous conduct carried on by the roughs at the last races' and 'the painful effects of men battering each other's heads from drink on racecourses'. Magistrates were divided on the issue, with some wanting to ban the sale of hard spirits but not of beer. No record of their ultimate decision is carried, but, for the newspaper, judicial reluctance in guaranteeing the availability of alcohol risked plunging an entire nation of horse enthusiasts into poor health. Deprived of the drink, good men could pass to their eternal reward against a fading soundtrack of galloping hooves: 'There are many whose health will not permit of their remaining a lengthened period without a glass of sherry or a glass of claret; and how many take [alcoholic] stimulants by the doctor's orders?' (*Sport*, 20 Aug. 1881 and 3 Sept. 1881).

It may be a matter of some dispute that alcoholic drink was crucial to the health of the average Irish racegoer, particularly in the phenomenal doses most reports suggest were the norm. Yet historians of public health find much to reward them in the pages of *Sport*. Its first issues covered the debate over the dangers of sporting involvement following the death of several players in rugby matches. The Honorary Secretary of the Irish Rugby Football Union, R. M. Peter, wrote to the paper and approvingly quoted from the medical journal, *The Lancet*, which had stated that while a sizeable number might be maimed or killed playing games, 'the undoubted value of athletic exercises to the individual and the nation more than counterbalances the occasional mishaps which must inevitably occur'. Indeed, the paper perceived that in an age of 'gentleman's corsets' and men writing 'maudlin poems in praise of each other', games were crucial in the ongoing battle to discourage effeminacy. It was asserted:

> Dancing night after night in crowded non-ventilated rooms is amongst the most unwelcome and dangerous practices of modern life and kills infinitely more persons than either the 'rugby' or the 'association' rules. The men who are killed by sitting in public houses or in club-houses, playing billiards or cards till the small hours, and drinking 'B and S', are not held up as warnings, while their fellows who happen to be killed while engaged in some sport which has in it a dash of nobility and pluck, are spoken of as 'frightful examples' of the evils of this or that amusement (*Sport*, 1 Jan. 1881).

Moreover, skills acquired on the football field were even more valuable off it – and in the most unique of ways – as a letter from 'an old football captain' asserted. Having almost been killed by a horse and carriage when crossing the road, he was saved only by 'an old football dodge'. He ended with a truism that has echoed through the generations: 'I am perfectly certain that football saved my life' (*Sport*, 8 Jan. 1881).

Games might not have saved all lives quite so melodramatically, but they could certainly improve the quality of living. *Sport* carried a report of a sports day held in Richmond Lunatic Asylum in Dublin, which included a 250 yards race, stating,

> A poor inmate, who for years past has imagined himself to be none other than the pope, caused some amusement by appearing on the mark with a pair of bright canary gloves of which, however, he divested himself before the signal was given. He finished a very puffed-out fourth and subsequently remarked to our representative that he was sure victory would have crowned his efforts had he not taken off his gloves. Another chimed in by observing that His Holiness was too fat, 'like all the popes' *(Sport*, 3 Sept. 1881).

And therein lay the reason for his poor form. But amidst the colour of the article lay a serious attempt to explain and de-stigmatise mental illness, as the paper offered the asylum the opportunity to show itself as operating a most progressive regime where few of the 1,014 inmates ever saw a barred window or a straitjacket.

There is clearly a strong measure of propaganda laced through this article, though it is unclear how exactly the paper could benefit from what was essentially an advertising feature for a mental institution. Other articles relating to stud farms, stables and various events were obviously framed with a view towards encouraging the sale of advertising. Such articles demonstrate the amount of money floating around the Irish sporting world. Reports are carried of money prizes in billiards, handball and rowing to mention but a few. The paper's advertising pages bear testimony to the growing commercialisation of sport. Hotels and train companies offered special deals. Horses were advertised for stud. Silversmiths competed to customise prizes for any sport in any county. Billiard halls and the sale of equipment to play the game were advertised, as were specially crested hunting gear ('The Ulster Overcoat') and special watches for timing all types of races. Elvery's sports shop announced its wholesale purchase of 1400 tennis racquets. Cantrell and Cochrane's deemed its super carbonated soda, 'supplied to the leading clubs throughout the world', as certain to appeal to the lovers of sport *(Sport,* 26 Mar. 1881, 2 Apr. 1881, 9 Apr. 1881 and 2 May 1881). The connection between product and personality was immediately made. In promoting itself, *Sport* proclaimed that the great English jockey, Fred Archer, had acquired a subscription and was endorsing the paper as 'a perfect gem' *(Sport,* 3 Sept. 1881).

Special editions were published to gather more advertising – notably for the Dublin Horse Show – and so great was the interest that the paper was forced to apologise to readers for the regular written features it had to drop to accommodate all those wishing to advertise *(Sport,* 27 Aug. 1881). In many respects, the sporting press was the great mediator in the union of games and commerce, but *Sport* was no mere advertising hoarding for businesses – nor did it simply hold up a mirror to Irish sporting life. It also policed the business of sport, and citing the example of Tramore in County Waterford, warned that excessive greed could also lose business. Here, it seems, the local meeting had fallen into decline because of 'the way people were mulcted by the hotels, livery stable-owners and lodging-house keepers' *(Sport,* 13 Aug. 1881).

The paper sought to act as a guardian of righteousness within the sporting world and made alliance with all whom it perceived as kindred spirits. It empathised with one Larry O'Connor, who travelled from Waterford in a boat to compete in a sports meeting in Belfast, only to find the whole athletics event dominated by a load of English visitors who were a 'rare bad lot' who had come over in an organised gang with their trainers, bookmakers, 'touts, et hoc genus omne', and 'if a spade must be so called, we simply say that they ran for their books, made money by it, and thus possess a very questionable claim to be considered amateurs; and the aforesaid bookmakers did have a day of it, [despite] proclaiming . . . their disinterested willingness to ruin themselves for the benefit of the community at large' *(Sport,* 23 Apr. 1881). The paper rarely missed an opportunity to criticise bookmakers. For example, in a tone that edged remarkably close to celebratory, it recorded that a bookmaker, Michael Costelloe, had been robbed of £500 while on a drinking spree *(Sport,* 7 May 1881).

*Sport* also immersed itself in a range of sporting activity. It offered advice to correspondents on the best means for the handicapping, starting and judging of athletics contests. It called for a campaign to encourage Cork businesses to subscribe £1,000 annually for the upkeep of a local racecourse, claiming that businessmen would recoup at least twice that amount from the commerce this would draw to the town. The paper also joined with the Great Southern and Western Railway to stage the country's first ever pigeon race. The winning bird travelled from Limerick Junction to the offices of *Sport* in three hours and 27 minutes, before being displayed for a week in the windows of the paper's offices.

In general, the paper involved itself in or supported many attempts to regularise sports across the country. What Tony Mason (1993) wrote about newspapers in Britain also seems entirely true for Ireland – and, in particular, for *Sport*. They provided free publicity, described the events and published the results. In the early days, they even offered prizes. The marriage of sport and the media has never been without rancour, not least in the disputes over who actually was in control. Yet it is hard to conceive of one without the other and, in many respects, it was the ideal union. It is difficult to deny the mutual benefits of a sporting world full of heroic men performing almost mythical feats which were spun by the media and sold to a public so in thrall to all manner of sports. In Ireland, from the 1880s, the press and sport enjoyed the easiest of courtships. But this was not merely an arrangement moved by commerce or convenience. Those who wrote in the paper were genuine lovers of sport. For this was the organ of the true believer, people who loved sport and loved writing about it.

## An intelligent horse, a snowball fight and some languid loving

Sport also reached beyond the confines of games and competition into the wider world of leisure. It recorded the arrivals and departures on the boats from England of those whom it termed 'notables', and it reported on the shows and musicals of Irish theatres. A lovely report of the circus at the Rotunda Gardens in Dublin noted the big crowds attending, despite the rival attraction of the English Opera Company, then playing at the Gaiety Theatre. Clearly, no aria could have competed with the lure of a big top whose stars were what *Sport* described as 'a pair of performing donkeys' engaged 'in a most amusing travesty'. The circus did not survive on cheap laughs alone for it also showcased a 'beautiful bay mare . . . [that] showed an amount of docile intelligence which would not discredit a human being' (*Sport*, 14 May 1881). The blossoming links between tourism and sporting events were also documented. The Miltown–Malbay race meeting committee in County Clare combined with local hoteliers and railway companies to offer discounted rates to prospective tourists and the paper noted, 'apart from the interest which is certain to be afforded by the races, visitors who attend will have much to repay them, as the course is within 200 yards of Spanishpoint, one of the most fascinating bathing places in the country, and scarcely 12 miles distant from Kilkee, Lisdoonvarna and the far-famed Cliffs of Moher' (*Sport*, 2 July 1881). The fishing correspondent, Greendrake, wrote of the arrival of English and continental tourists to fish on Irish lakes and rivers, hiring boats and native anglers for local knowledge, and buying tackle. He observed how the locals used 'the science of artificial fish-breeding' to improve the take on their rivers, while he recommended all anglers to visit Mrs Lawler's Inn in the Wicklow Mountains, commenting, 'she has built additional accommodation expressly for anglers. I know few inns in the country where a better cup of tea can be had' (*Sport*, 16 Apr. 1881). Greendrake later lamented how few Irish people were willing to follow his own example and holiday at home: 'Many an Irishman who could give minute instruction about the passes of the Alps and direct you as to the shortest route to the summit of Mount Blanc, could hardly tell where Lugnaquilla is situate, and probably never heard of the lovely valley of Glenmalure' (*Sport*, 13 Aug. 1881).

What Irish tourists ignored in the Wicklow hills, so have Irish historians aped in their neglect of Irish sport and in their unwillingness to visit the sporting traditions which so characterise the country. Obsessed by political and religious divides of unionist and nationalist, and of Catholic and Protestant, Irish historians have contrived gross generalisations to explain the country's sporting past. Insofar as they mention sport, Irish historians focus on the Gaelic Athletic Association (GAA) to the exclusion of every other sporting body. Further, even that organisation is assessed only through the prism of politics and invariably without research worthy of the name. A stellar example is Roy Foster's characterisation of the GAA as 'irredentist', 'chauvinistic', 'insular' and 'sectarian' (Rouse, 2003).[5] Presented as rounded judgement, such commentary on the political activities of a small section of GAA members is transposed on to the entire organisation as if it were a homogeneous entity, engaged only in a project of political and cultural liberation. Inevitably, every organisation or movement in Ireland was influenced to some extent by the political identity of the people who formed it, and by the environment in which it was formed. To suggest otherwise would be a nonsense and, to this end, there are some political asides in the reports featured in *Sport*. But by focusing entirely on the politics of sport and by reducing an understanding of Irish sports to mere associations of Fenians or of Saxons is absurdly simplistic.

The very first report of a football match that the paper carried offers a case in point. On New Year's Day, 1881, *Sport* reported that a team called Gitanos

had travelled west to Longford to play a team drawn from the counties of
Longford and Roscommon,

> The snow lay about half a foot deep on the field, which afforded the rustics
> excellent amusement, for they soon had the place studded with snowballs
> approaching the size of an ordinary sea buoy, while others of smaller dimensions
> were playfully used as missiles against the invaders. . . . [A]ll went well till the first
> Roscommon man was tackled and thrown. This, through some misconception by
> the rustics who had never seen the game before, was construed into an assault and
> they, determined not 'to see a Roscommon man beat', rushed in on the ground
> and knocked over a couple of Dublin men. The Roscommon players, of course,
> took the visitors part, and a free fight all round was prevented with difficulty. . . .
> Several more rows took place during the progress of play, and but for the ener-
> getic interference of Dr. Cochrane, JP, and Captain Jones, JP, who played for
> Roscommon, the consequences might have been serious. Messrs O'Kelly and
> McIntosh of the Visitors team, were so much hurt that they were unable to play
> to any effect. The match resulted, according to the umpire, in a victory for
> Roscommon by two goals to one goal. The visitors were most hospitably
> entertained by the Strokestown FC at dinner in the Longford Arms Hotel. After
> the usual loyal and other toasts had been duly honoured Mr McCarthy proposed
> the toast of 'The development of football in Connaught and the organisation at
> no distant date of a Connaught provincial fifteen to play in the annual inter-
> provincial matches'. . . . After several excellent speeches, songs, recitations, etc, the
> Dublin men returned to town by the 1am train (*Sport*, 1 Jan. 1881).

Of course it is tempting to focus on the politics of this reportage – the loyal
toasts and the presence of justices of the peace certainly suggest a political
context. But, what is far more instructive is the divide between urban and
rural Ireland and, crucially, the stark divide between various elements of rural
society. While the pitch was ringed by the type of illiterate peasant who was all
too obviously spoiling for a row, the Roscommon team sheet included a selection of landholders, doctors, an army captain and other like-minded chaps.

Clearly, in the Irish countryside, class was writ large across the landscape.
Within three years of that report, the green shoots of the GAA had emerged
and from the notions – both implicit and explicit – in that match report, it is
not difficult to see how the organisation drew such support from the Irish
countryside. By offering athletics and organised games to the assorted snowball
throwers and brawlers who were previously condemned to remain behind the
ropes of the Victorian sporting revolution, the GAA won immediate and
enduring popularity. Politics mattered, but, as Hunt demonstrates elsewhere
in this volume, so did so much more. The simplistic idea that the later divide
between 'foreign' games and 'Gaelic' games was the defensive creation of

nationalistic Catholic zealots denies a rounded understanding of the realities of daily living. Such zealots may indeed have sought to create a certain type of association built on exclusivity, but in this they were not alone. The building of the divide was enthusiastically sponsored by elements in several camps – and the reasons for building it were social and not merely political.

Beyond politics, and no more than any paper seeking popularity, *Sport* could not escape the meaning of its times, and this brought problems of consistency. On 16 July 1881 it bitterly condemned the manner in which L. E. Myers, an American, was prevented from winning a foot race in England because the local crowd had invaded the track when they saw the English men being beaten by Myers. *Sport* lamented this loutish behaviour, but pointed out that the gentlemanly people in the crowd had applauded Myers as he left the track, even if the majority of the rabble had booed him. Within a week, there was *Sport*, standing tall at the head of the rabble, almost hoarse from hurling abuse, as it recorded:

> [Myers's] complexion is very sallow, his lips rather thick and his moustache, the only hair worn on his face, small and black. His face is not at all suggestive either of intelligence or culture. He evidently belongs to a grade of society lower from that which the ranks of our amateur athletes are chiefly recruited.

The same report contrasted this with the 'utmost elegance' and 'humility' of the Irish athlete, Pat Davin, who won the long jump and the high jump at that same athletics meeting.

As a record of a people at play, the newspaper is a thing of some splendour. *Sport* shows Irish society ignoring its land wars and rebellions, and the sports grounds of city and country alike were fundamentally about social outings. While the Alpha males played for money or for fun, all around them the mating ritual of the wealthy Victorian was in high strut. Noting the attendance of women seemed *de rigueur* in every report of every sport. A cricket match in College Green against a visiting English team was looked forward to by the players, 'while our "fair sisters" anticipate three charming days promenading, arrayed in the choicest toilets after the latest fashions of Le Follet' (*Sport*, 14 May 1881). At a regatta in Ringsend, meanwhile, it was noted that 'there was an array of the fair sex that would have done honour to St. Patrick himself' (*Sport*, 18 Mar. 1881).

Even the non-appearance of women at a sporting occasion was a matter of great importance, especially when related to the flawed heroism of males seeking to impress. *Sport* reported a polo match from Ballyseedy, County Kerry,

> Capt. Ellice, 48th regiment, was to have played for Mr. Blennerhassett, but we regret to say that he met with a nasty accident when starting from Coralea – the

pony he was riding ran away, tried to jump a wire fence and threw the gallant captain, dislocating his shoulder. The pony got entangled in the wires, and was with difficulty extricated therefrom . . . In consequence of the accident, we regret that none of the fair sex honoured us with their presence, though several of them were ready in their carriages for the scene of action (*Sport*, 18 Mar. 1881).

It was in the scenery, rather than the action, of course, that women were expected to feature. The number of women appearing on the pages of the newspaper suggests a lack of conviction regarding their own suitability for athletic endeavour, as well as bearing testimony to the chauvinism of the sporting male and the social norms of the era. As in Britain, there were certain ideas about which games were suitable for women and which were not. The notion was still current that excessive sporting activity might diminish a woman's capacity to procreate. For all the emerging medical opposition, insti-tutionalised opinion continued to focus on a woman's physical limitations rather than her possibilities. The 'cult of athleticism' was avowedly masculine. And in the imagery of that cult, the body which the sporting male should aspire to – strong, vigorous, tough – was precisely that which the female was expected to avoid. The tendency to patronise and to parody the sporting female was widespread. *Sport* was not above swilling the occasional brandy with the boys and remarking censoriously, albeit in its in its own jocular way, on women's failings in matters sporting. This was unusual, however, as women were generally treated with reverence. The newspaper was inextricably bound up in the romance of what was being played out all around it. This was a world of lazy days, of louche escapism, of marching bands and minstrel shows. At the Irish tennis championships on Fitzwilliam Square, its reporter completely lost the run of himself.

Fashion and beauty strolled along the gravely [*sic*] walks or sat by the arena of peaceful strife; tuneful melody filled the pleasant air, and by four o'clock in the afternoon a bright sun shone down on an ampitheatre of loveliness in which the 'white-armed Nausicaa' would have loved to play. The play became more bril-liant – certainly more exciting – as the gentleman's singles drew towards the close; and when the lady competitors joined in their graceful movements on the soft green of the courts [it] gave a finished charm to the scene which only their presence was wanted to impart. Mothers, brothers and 'perhaps a nearer one yet and a dearer one', watched with anxious eyes the agile motion of the fairy form, now skilfully serving the ball, and, anon, returning it with the pretty twist of the supple wrist, . . . Cricket is confined to men, but in lawn tennis ladies can join, and the refinement of the drawing room is added to cheerful exercise in the open air (*Sport*, 28 May 1881).

This is but one part of a report that runs to many thousands of words. All five days of the championships were recorded in minute detail and the magisterial tone never faltered throughout. In parts it overwhelms, even smothers, but it is entirely devoid of cynicism and cliché. The breathless reportage of the attendance of the representatives of the crown in Ireland, the salutations to the military and the sheer relentless force of the language place the article most definitely into the old school of journalism. Newspapers were moving towards mass circulation but many of the people who wrote in them remained allied to a privileged elite. That elite did not wither and die as the middle classes grew in wealth and power, but it reached a new accommodation with the changing nature of sport and of newspapers. In parallel to developments in Britain, old order and new money united in the leadership of many sports. The alliance of blood, land and commerce was forged in rugby, tennis and golf clubs of the growing suburbs. Money found money as the middle classes bought into the legitimacy conferred by association with the old sporting gentry. That gentry was underwhelmed by some of the more *gauche arrivistes*, but even those who craved exclusivity could not deny the embrace of a new age. Ultimately, that embrace drew in many more than anyone could then have imagined.

## No apes, no angels, just athletes

In its first year, the balance of the paper favoured the established sports of the wealthy. It sought to shine a light on these sports, but the shadows it cast opened many other worlds for exploration. Over the decades, the shift of light and shade in the pages of *Sport* reflect the changes in Irish society. In 1881, in the half-lit hour before the full dawn of modern Irish sporting organisations, the paper is emblematic of the exploding interest in organised sport. Ireland was changing and the sporting landscape was reshaped by those changes. The proximity to Britain, and the ties of kinship and commerce, had further and obvious effects. The process of sporting evolution in England could not conceivably leave the Irish unmoved. The very establishment of the paper bears witness to this and its content, in the succeeding years, both charted and influenced the development of sport in Ireland.

Papers evolve over time. Before 1880, no Irish daily paper had consistently filled its pages with substantial sporting fare. Exceptional occasions – boxing matches, race meetings and other such happenings – enjoyed some coverage, but there were no regular features to which the reader could turn. Often, sporting events only made it into print in the event of the courts taking an interest. Dedicated sports newspapers changed that. That the public were interested in reading about sport was no longer in doubt. Through the latter decades of the nineteenth century and the first decades of the twentieth, daily newspapers greatly expanded their coverage of sport. Ultimately, this brought ruin to those papers that had thrived from the 1880s onwards. *Sport* managed to survive the 1924 demise of its founding paper, the *Freeman's Journal*, but it could not hold out indefinitely and in 1932 its presses rolled for the final time. By then, it was a pallid imitation of its former greatness. But *Sport* deserves to be remembered for the splendour and originality of its glory days. In the 1880s, when sports journalism had yet to fall into its dreary rehearsal of the formulaic set piece, the paper was most brilliantly defined by the freshness of all that it touched. It reported with a vigour and enthusiasm that was the hallmark of an era without precedent. That it did so at the time when the popular press in Britain was bewitched by notions of the stage Irishman and his simian *alter ego*, makes its presence all the more significant (Curtis, 1971). In the very best of its reporting, *Sport* offered a fascinating portrait of the Irish as neither apes nor angels, but athletes.

Chapter 2

# The early years of Gaelic football and the role of cricket in County Westmeath

Tom Hunt

## Introduction

The purpose of this chapter is to examine the development of the Gaelic Athletic Association within the county of Westmeath concentrating on the period 1888–94, when the movement was at its strongest in the area. The emphasis is on how the GAA worked at local level with a particular focus on the sporting dimension of the association as opposed to the political which has been adequately examined, at both the local and national levels, in several important studies (Mandle, 1987; Cronin, 1999). A number of issues will be examined including the initial growth and development of the association within the county. Club development and decline will be considered by using case studies of both rural and urban clubs. The nature of the games that were played and how they changed over the period of study will also be discussed and a socio-economic profile will be constructed of those who played and managed Gaelic games. The role of cricket as the game of popular choice for young men of all classes within the county in the 1890s will also be briefly examined. This in-depth study of games playing activity within Westmeath is based on an analysis of the four local newspapers published over the period of the study, the *Westmeath Guardian* (WN), the *Westmeath Independent* (WI), the *Westmeath Nationalist* (WN) and the *Westmeath Examiner* (WE). This has allowed a statistical analysis to be made of Gaelic football and cricket playing activity in County Westmeath. It is unfortunate that this type of evaluation has not been undertaken for other counties, thereby rendering impossible any meaningful comparisons with other areas.

## Chronology

The progress of the GAA in Westmeath followed a different pattern from the national one and that experienced in other midland counties. It developed later and survived the damage that was inflicted on other areas by the Irish Republican Brotherhood takeover and the fallout from the Parnell divorce case. The peak years of football activity in Westmeath extended through 1892, when 36 football games were reported in the local newspapers, and 1893, when 49 were played. Police reports provide quantitative evidence of the decline and fall of the GAA in the midland counties at the same time. In December 1892, the Royal Irish Constabulary reported the existence of only nine clubs in Kildare, a decline from 19 in December 1891 and 38 in December 1890 (CBS, S/2452).[1] In Cavan, where the influence of the IRB was particularly strong, 39 clubs existed at the end of 1891 but by the end of 1892 none existed (CBS, S/6216). A similar pattern existed in the other counties featuring in the midland crime branch special reports.

Space constraints prevent the outlining of a detailed chronology of GAA club development in the county. Nevertheless, by the end of 1890, football was played in Mullingar, Wooddown, Kinnegad, Athlone, Moate, Ballinahown, Killucan, Raharney, Rathowen and Kilbeggan. By 1894 young men in Ballinacargy, Ballinalack, Walshestown and Gaulstown Park had experienced the novelty of taking part in a football game. This flurry of activity in the county took place after a period of initial clerical opposition to the GAA. On 21 July 1889, Bishop Nulty and his clerics condemned the association from pulpits throughout the diocese. Nulty delivered his homily in Navan, the county town of Meath, where he condemned the playing of matches outside parish boundaries due to the increase in drunkenness and secret society activity (CBS, S21/1035). This clerical opposition was short lived in Westmeath, as within a few months, Fr Edward O'Reilly, a Mullingar based curate, was elected the first chairman of the Westmeath county committee. As will be explained in greater detail later in the chapter, O'Reilly's involvement in the GAA seems to have been brief as there is no report of his committee ever meeting but the GAA in Westmeath enjoyed, at a minimum, tacit Church support, as is clear from the social activities of many of the key personnel.

Based on the evidence contained within the police reports, Nulty and his clerics had very little cause for worry about secret society activity, as the IRB was weak in Westmeath. The most significant GAA-related IRB activity reported was at a football match held at Killucan in March 1890 where the presence of a 'good many local IRB men' was recorded; on two separate occasions at Moate in the same month the police had reported that nothing of importance was observed; in April in Mullingar 13 IRB men were reported to have attended a match (CBS, S21/159). Athlone presented a similar pattern in May whilst in Killucan only four IRB men were reported present in a crowd of over 400 people (CBS, S21/665). The early flourish of the GAA in Westmeath was an IRB-free activity.

Between 1886 and 1900, 90 different groupings are recorded in the newspapers as having played a football match. The word 'groupings' is deliberately chosen as in many of the games formally constituted clubs were not involved but instead *ad hoc* arrangements were likely to have been made by groups of people living in an area to challenge their peers in a neighbouring district to a football game. Of these combinations sixty played a maximum of three matches only. Of the combinations recorded, twelve of these represented the second or reserve teams of established clubs. Kinnegad Slashers on eight occasions, Mullingar FC on seven, Mullingar Shamrocks on five occasions and Thomastown Rangers on 14 occasions had sufficient players interested in the game to field reserve teams. This hierarchical development of football clubs was common to other football codes and in societies very different from that of Westmeath. This was the pattern discovered by Metcalf (1988) in his study of football in the mining communities of East Northumberland and by Tranter (1990) in his examination of football in central Scotland where at all levels soccer clubs came and went 'with the regularity of a yo-yo'. On the one hand, was a mass of ephemeral unaffiliated teams, and on the other a small number of semi-permanent formally constituted clubs. The latter were integrated into the practices of modern sport; the members of the former group still displayed many of the characteristics of pre-modern sport as defined by Adelman (1990). Their contests were arranged by individuals directly or indirectly involved in the teams and the rules were likely to vary from one game to the next and from one locale to another. The competition between the teams was only meaningful locally and public information on the contests was likely to have been limited, local and oral.

Four distinct forms of games were organised. Most common were intra-club games where the club members assembled each Sunday and selected sides to compete against each other. These sides took various forms. In Kinnegad, throughout 1899, teams of members calling themselves the Tories and Liberals played on a regular basis. In Athlone, the members of the T. P. O'Connor's club arranged games between 'the grocers' assistants and the rest' or between the natives and the outsiders. In Mullingar, the clubs tended to favour games played between selections made by the captain and the vice-captain. These games helped to train players in the basic skills and rules of the game and helped to maintain interest in the sport in the time lapse between properly constituted inter-club games.

Friendly games were normally organised between neighbouring clubs. Initiated through contact between club officers or club captains or occasionally by means of challenges issued through the local press, these were the most common type of event organised. Between 1888 and 1900 Westmeath clubs competed in 254 inter-club games (Figure 2.1). Games of the friendly or tournament variety formed 94 per cent of those played. The setting up of one game usually resulted in a second game as it was common practice for the participants to engage in a return match provided of course the first game was free of serious incident. Stronger clubs were also invited to travel outside the county to participate in the tournaments organised by some of the established clubs. Mullingar Football Club, for example, made its competitive debut in September 1891 by travelling to Ballinasloe to participate in a tournament organised by the local club.

*Figure 2.1* **Number of inter-club football games played involving Westmeath clubs, 1888–99**

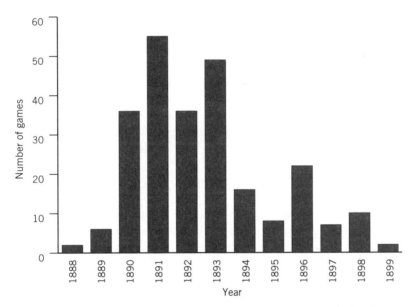

The establishment of a county committee in 1891 provided a short-term alternative to the *ad hoc* games arrangement. Clubs within the county were provided with a formalised competitive outlet but this structure did not survive beyond the early months of 1894. Three county championships were organised by this committee, attracting an entry of five clubs in 1892 and eight in 1893 but only two clubs affiliated in 1894.

The popularity of the game in the early 1890s attracted the attention of a conservative *Westmeath Guardian* reporter in November 1893, who wrote positively and optimistically, ironically at a time when the game was about to collapse within the county, on the future of the game in the district. Football provided one of the main topics of conversation in the town of Mullingar.

It is very interesting as well as amusing to listen to a conversation touching on the
relative merits of the different clubs, between men well advanced in years, and for
whom, you would imagine, such boyish sport would have but little interest.
Nevertheless arguments on the pastime are a nightly occurrence in this town.
Sometimes they assume a heated aspect. . . . It is undeniable that football takes the
lead of all other outdoor games, and to use a slang phrase 'you're not in it' unless
you are fully competent of taking part in discussions on 'full-backs,' 'half-backs,'
'forwards' etc (WG, 24 Nov. 1893).

The interest identified by the newspaper reporter was reflected in the
extraordinary attendances present at some of these games. The first match of
the 1892 championship between Mullingar Football Club and Thomastown
Rangers attracted an attendance of 'something like 4,000' spectators. The
semi-final between Mullingar Shamrocks and Raharney Rovers was played
before an estimated crowd of 2,000 people and according to the *Westmeath
Nationalist* 'there was certainly no less than 6,000 spectators present' at the final.
An 1888 tournament played in Athlone, between visiting teams, attracted an estimated crowd of between nine and ten thousand (WI, 12 May 1888). Attendance
at football matches was not an exclusively male preserve. Women were an
important part of football crowds at this time and their presence at games is
deemed worthy of inclusion in many of the reports of games of this period.

## The establishment of a county committee

Of the early Irish sporting bodies, the GAA was unique in that it organised
competitive games on a county basis with county committees established to
organise county championship competitions and manage the playing of the
games. Towards the end of 1890 unsuccessful moves spearheaded by the
Mullingar Commercials club were made in Westmeath for the formation of a
county committee (WE, 8 Nov. 1890). A county committee was eventually
formed at a meeting held in the Lecture Hall, Mullingar on 25 March 1891, a
committee distinguished by the selection of Fr Edward O'Reilly as the first
president of the committee. Nine months after the pulpit condemnation,
Fr O' Reilly was now at the helm of the county committee. There is no record
of this committee holding further meetings or engaging in any promotional
activities. In November 1891 a new committee was formed. The meeting
passed a number of important resolutions aimed at shaping and organising
the association in the county. Playing with more than one club was to result
in suspension for the player concerned. In an attempt to force clubs to affiliate
and exert control over the playing of games, a resolution was passed imposing
suspension on 'an affiliated team kicking against a non-affiliated team'. Most

importantly the committee decided to organise a county championship with clubs required to have affiliated by 1 January 1892 (WN, 3 Dec. 1891).

The composition of the county committee was geographically limited to officers representing clubs from the eastern half of the county with no representative from Athlone where there had been considerable football activity in 1890. By the time of the next meeting, held on 21 February 1892, nine clubs had affiliated. The desire of the Athlone members to become part of the Westmeath GAA community was essentially rejected at the meeting as the club was refused entry to the championship on the basis that their entry fee had not arrived in time.

The 1892 championship was a tame affair passing without major incident. However, the 1893 version was a tempestuous one, with the resulting fallout destroying the organisational structure of the Westmeath GAA for almost a decade. The championship had progressed smoothly to the semi-final stage but all this was to change with the local derby meeting of the two Mullingar teams. Violence and a controversial winning score that was followed by an assault on the referee characterised this game (WN, 13 Apr. 1893). The losing Mullingar Shamrocks team objected to the result and appealed against the decision of the referee to award the game to the Mullingar football club. In the course of the unsuccessful hearing, the county committee chairman, Martin McGreevey, was assaulted by the captain of the Shamrocks team (WN, 20 Apr. 1893).

The 1893 championship is significant in that it is the only occasion on which a Westmeath championship semi-final and final were played on the same day, 23 April 1893. The members of the Shamrocks club provided the stewards for the 1892 final to prevent the spectators from encroaching onto the pitch. A year later the RIC, under the command of Chief Constable Reddington, was present to prevent the members of the Shamrocks club from invading the pitch. In the semi-final Athlone T. P. O' Connor's beat the Wooddown Rackers 0–3 to 0–1 and after an interval of one hour lined up in the final against Mullingar Football Club. As they had threatened, the Shamrocks players also prepared to take the field but were prevented from doing so by the RIC. T. P. O'Connor's completed their double victory on a 2–3 to 1–6 score-line but one of the Athlone goals was bitterly disputed by the Mullingar side. Subsequent appeals to the county committee and to the Central Council failed to reverse the decision of the referee, Martin McGreevey, president of the Mullingar club and of the county committee, to award the game to the T. P. O'Connor's (WN, 27 July 1893).

Internal tensions associated with the breakdown of relationships between the Mullingar clubs and the fallout between the Mullingar FC and the Athlone club destroyed the newly created infrastructure of the Westmeath GAA and it was almost a decade later before a new and effective county committee was established. Martin McGreevey was unfortunate to have been the referee in the disputed final as well as club and county president. He severed his connections with the GAA in the county and continued his administrative career with organisations such as the Mullingar National Workingmen's Club and the Holy Faith Confraternity. Mullingar Shamrocks only played one more match following the events of 1892, and there is no record of the T. P. O'Connor's club again taking part in Gaelic football matches. Indeed, as we shall see later, most of the playing members of the club were to become key members of the Athlone soccer clubs.

## Social activities

The enjoyment of kicking a heavy ball around a makeshift football field was not the only attraction provided by the early clubs. The social activities organised around the actual match were also an important part of the culture of the game and undoubtedly constituted much of its appeal. Travelling to and from the games provided some of the entertainment. In January 1892 Mullingar FC travelled out to Kinnegad to play the locals using 'two brakes, six cars and two traps'. On the outward journey 'music and songs whiled away the time in enjoyable style' (WN, 28 Jan. 1892).

There was a strong emphasis on socialising after games and on occasion before matches also. In May 1893, the Dublin club C. J. Kickham's travelled to Mullingar to play a match with the Mullingar FC. At the railway station 'an enthusiastic crowd of local footballers and townspeople' met them. They were then escorted to the rooms of the Catholic National Young Men's Club 'where refreshments were lavishly provided and the best of good cheer was the order of the day for an hour or more'. Many of the Dubliners then took the opportunity to explore the attractions of Mullingar's hinterland and drove out to view Lough Owel and Lough Belvedere (WN, 22 June 1893). When the footballers of Mullingar arrived in Ballinasloe in September 1891 the reception party accompanied them to the Whelehan's Temperance Bar where they 'were provided with a sumptuous supper' (WE, 26 Sept. 1891). On the Sunday morning the members also made use of the available time to view the surrounding places of interest. After the games the festivities began. 'Hall and club were thrown open to the visitors, and singing and dancing kept up till the departure of the Mullingar men by the morning mail' (WE, 26 Sept. 1891). It was not unusual to have a team met at the railway station or on the outskirts of the town and accompanied to the football pitch or reception hall by one or more musical ensemble. This practice created a great sense of occasion glamorised, the participants and of course was also a great publicity-generating device drawing the attention of the public to the event. Teams marching in military formation presented the footballers of the day with an opportunity to publicly display their orderliness, organisation and sense of mission.

Social occasions were also organised by clubs. Annual balls were organised by some and the departure from the club of a prominent member was marked by the presentation of a testimonial usually centred on a social event. The Kinnegad Slashers had enough members in the early 1890s to hold an annual ball at the local national school building provided for the occasion by school patron, Fr Fitzsimons (WE, 4 Feb. 1893). This particular club was sufficiently organised to attract an attendance of an estimated one hundred couples to their events and 'the real old Irish jig, reel and hornpipe measures were indulged in to an advanced hour in the morning' (WN, 2 Feb. 1893). The departure from Mullingar of J. J. Bergin, a founding member of both the Catholic Commercial Club and the Commercial Football Club, was marked by a social event that included music provided by the dance band of May Brothers, 4 Stephen's Green, Dublin (WN, 24 Nov. 1892). The economic status of the individuals involved in these clubs is clearly suggested by the recruitment of a dance band from Dublin to supply the music for the occasion.

Surviving account material from a County Tipperary football (probably rugby football) team of the late 1870s provides evidence of the financial impact that the social dimension had on club finances.[2] The Kilruane football club in 1876 purchased two footballs, a set of caps, several yards of tape and a book on football. The expenditure on these items amounted to £2 5s. 9d. or 55 per cent of the total spent. The remaining expenditure was on the purchase of two half-barrels of porter and four gallons of ale. The expenditure on basic equipment would suggest that 1876 might have been the start-up year for the club as in 1877 the proportion spent on alcohol and lemonade had increased to 76 per cent. This was invested in the purchase of four barrels of porter, one gallon and one quart of whiskey, one gallon of malt and three-dozen bottles of lemonade. The final year of the accounts indicate a similar pattern of expenditure on alcohol with transport also an important item for the 1879 season.

Those who played football in Westmeath in the early 1890s were participating in a recreational activity that had become fashionable within the county in the short term, an activity that promoted adventure and excitement for the individual in an often-mundane society and that facilitated and encouraged social interaction between individuals of similar status. It is doubtful if the average member of a GAA club in Westmeath in the 1890s was conscious of participating in any great cultural nationalist crusade or was engaged in any political identity building process. The naming of the clubs in the county lends some support to this thesis. The choice of names suggests that cultivating a nationalist agenda was not a priority for the members of many of the Westmeath clubs. In the early 1890s it was traditional for clubs to proclaim their nationalism by choosing a name that honoured a

contemporary national political figure or one that commemorated a major
figure or major event from Ireland's nationalist past (Cronin, 1998a). The 31
County Meath clubs identified in the 1890 special branch report examined by
Cronin all carried political names and all were related to the IRB faction in the
county. A similar pattern is evident from an examination of the names of the
County Longford clubs. Twenty-five clubs were included in the special branch
report. The names of nineteen of these clubs had nationalist connotations
that embraced contemporary political figures and movements or nationalist
icons from the past (CBS, S/2452). Cronin (1998a) suggests that these clubs
were constructing an identity that stressed and publicised their links as
sportsmen to the nationalist mission that embraced all things Irish and
rejected West Britonism. Of the Westmeath clubs two were identified with
contemporary political figures (T. P. O'Connor and William O'Brien) and
one with a contemporary movement (Rathowen Leaguers). Other appendages
used included 'Shamrocks', 'Celtic', 'Emeralds', proclaiming an Irish identity
without any strong political or nationalist associations.

The contention that the men of Mullingar FC were essentially involved in
a sporting and social activity is reinforced by their participation in the
coalition of interests responsible for the organisation of the athletics sports in
Mullingar in 1893. The organisers of this initial athletic event included
representatives of the widest spectrum of socio-political opinion in the town.
The meet was held under GAA and ICA rules. The organising committee
was mainly composed of members of the Catholic Commercial Club and
associates of Mullingar FC. Military representative Captain Lewis (Adjutant,
9th Battalion Rifle Brigade) provided a liberal subscription as well as the ropes
for the enclosure and tenting facilities, while Colour-Sergeant Sparkes, from
the military garrison based in the town, was granted permission to assist the
committee in carrying out all field arrangements. Mrs Lewis presented the
prizes and the band of the Loyal North Lancashire regiment provided the
musical entertainment. The socio-cultural ecumenism was appropriately concluded when Sergeant Lipsett of the RIC won the 16 lb. hammer throw (WG,
22 and 29 Sept., 6 Oct. 1893).

## Club structure

This section explores the development of the club system in Westmeath by
examining case studies of the leading clubs in the county. Mullingar
Commercials was the first club established in Mullingar on a formal basis.
The name of this club gives a clear indication of the socio-economic background of its members. The occupations of the original committee elected by
the club are illustrated in table 2.1.

*Table 2.1* **Occupations of officers and committee of Mullingar Commercials GAA club 1890**

| Name | Position | Occupation |
|------|----------|------------|
| R.W. Moorwood | Captain | Retail trade |
| P. J. Shaw | Vice-captain | Grocer-Publican family member |
| J. J. Geoghegan | Treasurer | Supervisor at Doyne's drapery store |
| M. J. Geary | Secretary | Shop assistant |
| W. D.Clery | Committee | Publican |
| W. Fogarty | | |
| W. Weymes | Committee | Wool merchant family member |
| J. J. King | Committee | Shop assistant at Shaw's |
| C. Beirne | | |
| J. J. Bergin | Captain of football team. | Nooney's ironmongery employee |
| James Mulvey | Committee | Kellaghan's ironmongery assistant. |
| J. H. Smith | Committee | Publican |

The club had a relatively short existence and in the course of its two-year history played only six matches, winning only once (Hunt, 2002). This lack of success was instrumental in encouraging the movement to amalgamate the established Mullingar clubs. Civic pride motivated by the desire to form a strong competitive club capable of challenging for county championship honours was responsible for the establishment of Mullingar Football Club. Three clubs, Commercials, the Shamrocks and Newbrook Wanderers were active in the town in 1891. In September 1891, a committee that was representative of the three was established with a view to amalgamating the clubs. The idea was approved and the committee was empowered to decide on a name for the new club. A majority of one favoured the neutral name of Mullingar Football Club for the composite club and this decision caused the Shamrock members to reject the proposal as they refused to accept any name other than their own. The new club included all the members of the former Commercials, almost all the Newbrook Wanderers, and some members of the Shamrocks and claimed a membership of almost 100 by November (WN, 5 Nov. 1891).

The appointed officers of the club in 1891 and 1892 (WN, 15 Dec. 1892) were involved in the commercial life of the town and were generally employed as shop assistants. Many were also migrants to the town. The president of the club, Martin McGreevey, was a native of Carrick-on-Shannon, County Leitrim and was an employee of Messrs Shaw's, one of the leading hardware, wine and spirits store in the town. Both the captain and treasurer were employed at Peter Kelleghan's drapery store. Brett, the treasurer, was from Bansha, County Tipperary and Mulvey the captain was a Longford native. The secretary, Thomas Raftery, was from Loughrea, County Galway, and had distinguished himself as a rugby player in his native county (WN, 11 Aug.

1892). With the exception of McGreevey, these officers combined playing
with their administrative duties. Amongst the players the main employment
represented was that of assistant – in the drapery, ironmonger and pub trade.
The vice-captain, Joe Garry, was an exception as he farmed on the edge of the
town, at Clonmore. The popularity of Gaelic football with urban lower
middle-class white-collar workers was universal. One of the leading Dublin
clubs, Charles Kickham's, included in its ranks in 1898 13 drapers' assistants
(*Sport*, 18 Feb. 1898).

The socio-cultural world of the members of Mullingar FC may be partly
reconstructed by examining the contemporary newspapers. It was an era when
young men working in white-collar occupations were becoming increasingly
organised into social organisations that reflected the great Victorian desire for
self-improvement. The most popular club was the Mullingar Catholic
Commercial Club, which was established in October 1890 with the objective
of affording the members a means of 'social intercourse, mental and moral
improvement and rational recreation' (WG, 7 Nov. 1890). The ambitious,
professionally upwardly mobile young men could socialise at the club with
employer and fellow employee and develop useful business contacts in the
process. James Mulvey was the undoubted leader of this community serving
in a variety of administrative and authoritative offices that included captaincy
of the Mullingar FC and the Mullingar cricket club and secretary of the
county GAA committee. Much of their social life outside of sport was carried
out in associations and organisations that were clearly linked to the Catholic
Church. A core group were founding members of the Mullingar Catholic
National Young Men's Society, with two of the leading football club members
James Mulvey elected treasurer and Patrick Brett secretary of the organisation (WN, 12 Jan. 1893). Many were also members of the Holy Family
Confraternity, an organisation that mixed spirituality, Catholic triumphalism,
rational recreation. The rules of the confraternity required the members to
engage in daily prayer, attend bi-monthly meetings and receive monthly
communion on their specified Sunday. Fr Edward O'Reilly was spiritual
director between 1883 and 1901 and he inaugurated the public processions and
the excursions to the different parts of Ireland that normally concluded with
the athletic events that provided many young Mullingar men with their first
opportunity to compete in athletics.

The most important club in the western half of the county was the
T. P. O'Connor's club established in December 1889 with the election of
E. Doyle as captain, J. O'Flynn as secretary and R. Johnston as treasurer. The
secretary reported a membership of over forty, 'including some of the best
athletes of the town and neighbourhood' (WI, 4 Jan. 1890). The choice of
name is suggestive of a politically conscious club but it also celebrated a local
success story. T. P. O'Connor was a native of the Athlone district and a *Daily*

*Telegraph* journalist who was elected MP for Galway in 1880 and for the Scotland division of Liverpool in 1885, a parliamentary seat that he held until his death in 1929 (Sheehan, 1987). The police considered the club to be one that was 'kept up for the pastime and not as a political club' (CBS, 1893, S/6247). This club depended on the same economic constituency as the Mullingar FC for its membership with one notable difference. Many of the members of the club were the sons of important and successful Athlone businessmen. Doyle and O'Flynn were the sons of grocer and spirit dealers while Johnston was a member of one of Athlone's leading saddle and harness making families.

The competitive history of the T. P. O'Connor's club is important as the vicissitudes experienced by the club illustrate in stark reality many of the difficulties experienced by the early GAA clubs. A Westmeath football championship was played in 1890 in which four clubs competed and was eventually won by the Athlone club in unsatisfactory circumstances. Their opponents in the final, the William O'Brien club from Moate, walked off the pitch before the game concluded (WI, 10 Jan. 1890). The next important occasion for Athlone was in August 1890 when the club travelled to Dublin to play the Isles of the Sea in a tournament game. Having led by 0–1 to 0–0 at the interval, the club managed to lose the match by 6–11 to 0–2. Problems with the referee's interpretation of the rules it seems were responsible for this debacle. The Athlone men were so upset by the decision to allow the first goal scored by the Dublin team that 'they stood up and let goal after goal pass them'. The *Westmeath Independent* reported that the Athlone men were not prepared for the foul play indulged in by opponents (WI, 30 Aug. 1890). As we have already seen, Athlone's problems continued in 1892 when permission to affiliate to the Westmeath county committee was refused. Instead they represented Connacht in the All-Ireland championship semi-final match against Dublin. Midway through the second half an incident happened that resulted in the Athlone team walking off the field. Despite Athlone's objections Dublin were awarded the match and another perceived grievance was added to the Athlone list of injustices.

The final injustice experienced by the Athlone team was to happen within a matter of weeks when first the club were required to travel to Mullingar to compete against the Cullion Celtics in the county championship and return the following week to play in the championship semi-final and final. The final ended in controversy with the Mullingar FC disputing the final score despite the fact that the referee was Martin McGreevey, president of the Mullingar club and of the county committee. The Mullingar club contested the decision of the referee to award the game to the Athlone club at the highest level of the Association. The departure of the T. P. O'Connor's club from the GAA, 'owing to the unfair treatment to which they had been subjected' was formalised in December 1893. Under their new title of the Athlone Association

Football Club 'they bid fair to add many new triumphs to their record' (WN, 4 Jan. 1894). The extent of the changeover is illustrated by the composition of the Athlone association football team that played an exhibition match against Bohemians on St Stephen's Day, 1893. Ten of the eleven players were former prominent football players with the T. P. O'Connor's club.

The story of the T. P. O'Connor's club is important as it encapsulates many of the difficulties that bedevilled the early association. Of the four most important games played by the club, two were unfinished and two ended in controversy. The lack of a nationally accepted, clearly defined set of rules for the game, applied consistently by referees familiar with their content, caused difficulties on the occasions the club travelled to Dublin. Parochialism prevented their initial acceptance into the Mullingar-dominated county committee and it was the failure of that body to recognise the championship victory of 1893 that precipitated their change over to the association game.

Thomastown Rangers were one of the most active of the early clubs. Thomastown was a townland located within the civil parish of Killucan. The story of the club is important as it illustrates how the early rural football clubs conducted their business. The club was a composite one drawing its members and supporters from a number of townlands. The club relied on local sub-scriptions to fund its activities. At the annual meetings of the club, committee members were elected from surrounding townlands and these were the men charged with the responsibility of collecting subscriptions in their districts to fund the club for a season. The club was the most active of the early Westmeath clubs, taking part in at least 20 matches between March 1888 and December 1891. The club was also numerically strong enough on 14 occasions to field a reserve selection. After 1891 the club is recorded as having played only one additional match. This decline was related to tragic deaths suffered by key club members. The club secretary, Patrick Clinton, died suddenly in December 1890 (WE, 13 Dec. 1890), and the following October a railway employee and playing member Laurence Brock was killed in a railway accident (WE, 3 Oct. 1891). Club funds were invested and members subscribed to erect monuments in the graveyards to the memory of the deceased members and the remainder of the funds on hand was donated to the father of Laurence Brock (WE, 28 Jan. 1893). In January 1893 the Thomastown Rangers amalgamated with the neighbouring club Raharney Rovers (WE, 19 Jan. 1893). As a rural club it drew its main support from the farming community. It is possible to identify the occupations of 33 individuals who were playing members of the club from the enumerators' sheets in the 1901 census. Twenty were farmers or farmers' sons; eight were agricultural labourers; three had occupations that required an element of skill and there was a single railway labourer.

The pattern of GAA membership – dominated by farmers and farmers' sons in rural areas and shop assistants in urban areas, revealed from the above analysis of three of the leading Westmeath clubs – is supported by evidence from Longford, a county immediately to the north of Westmeath. The officers of 26 clubs were represented at the county committee meeting held at Longford on 15 October 1890 (CBS, 2452/S). Eighteen were farmers or farmers' sons and four from Longford town were shop assistants. The conclusion to be drawn from this analysis is that the first generation of football-playing members of the GAA was drawn chiefly from a narrow economic constituency confined mainly to shop assistants in urban areas and those with an interest in the land in rural areas. There were many reasons why this was the case. Shop assistants benefited from regulated labour hours, and were guaranteed work free Sundays. They were also relatively well paid and as single young men had disposable income which they were prepared to invest in leisure activities. Membership of a football club involved a financial commitment. Annual and weekly subscriptions had to be paid, transport to away games had to be funded and post-match entertainment financed. Football equipment also had to be purchased. This particular occupational group was also easily organised as in many cases the economic networks already existed and the transformation from an economic network to a social and sporting one was relatively straightforward. The urban labourer and farm labourer were the most disadvantaged economically in the Ireland of the 1890s and the evidence from this micro-study suggests that they were essentially excluded from the football network of the time. The farmer and his sons were independent enough to manage their own work schedules and as hirers of labour were in a position to organise their own free time. They were prepared to invest some of their leisure time and disposable income in football playing activities. Like the shop assistants, they were also prepared to risk the considerable chance of injury associated with the early football game.

## The nature of the game

Gaelic football was essentially a compromise game combining elements of traditional football with the association game and rugby. Maurice Davin probably codified the earliest rules. Davin's biographer, O'Riain (1998), has attested to the intensive study of the rules of field sports made by Davin over the years as revealed by the numerous entries made in his notebooks and his accumulation of cuttings from newspapers and magazines on the emerging rules of rugby and association football. Davin's background was in the world of organised athletics, where rules and regulations mattered and the codification system developed in Britain held sway. Unlike Cusack, he felt that abuses such as gambling and cheating were not problematic for Irish athletics but he was concerned at the decline of the traditional Irish events of weight throwing and jumping and of the need for games 'especially for the humble and the hard-working who seem now to be born into no other inheritance than an everlasting round of labour' (Mandle, 1987: 4). He also wished to see proper rules drawn up for both football and hurling declaring 'I would not like to see either game now as the rules stand at present' (Mandle, 1987: 4–5).

The game initially played regularly in Westmeath was in theory subject to the playing rules adopted by the association in 1889. These rules were notably short and imprecise in relation to the playing of the football game. Thirteen rules in total were introduced that dealt with pitch organisation, the number, the duties and the powers of match officials, the playing conventions of the game, methods of scoring and the type of playing gear to be used (Lennon, 1997). Despite the haphazard nature of the rules very few games in Westmeath remained unfinished. Unfortunately, with no comparable information from other areas, it is impossible to evaluate the typicality of the county. Problems developed when teams travelled outside their own districts to play in areas where a very different code of practice existed or when a referee, unfamiliar with local practices, took charge of a game as occurred when Cullion Celtics played the second team of Mullingar FC. The former disagreed with the interpretations of the Ballinasloe referee and walked off the pitch (WN, 26 Nov. 1891).

Such was the vague nature of the early rules that confusion was inevitable when games were organised. The 1893 championship match between Mullingar and Kinnegad Slashers, for instance, was reportedly played strictly in accordance to the Gaelic rules with one exception when, in the second half, a member of the Kinnegad team 'hugged the ball under his arm and in right true rugby style ran towards the Mullingar goal' (WN, 16 Mar. 1893). Problems with rule interpretation increased in scale when teams travelled outside the county for games. In July 1892, the Mullingar Football Club travelled to Clonturk Park in Dublin to compete in a festival of hurling and football. Following their match with Fontenoys, the members of the club passed a motion of condemnation 'at the transgression of the Gaelic rules' by the Dublin team and addressed their concerns in a letter to the editor of the *Freeman's Journal* and the national sports newspaper *Sport*. The principal objections were that the Fontenoys played in a style that was more like the rugby game than the Gaelic one, and used tactics that included lying on the ball on the ground, head-butting from behind and holding the ball rather than releasing it as the rules required (*Freeman's Journal*, 19, 21 July 1892; *Sport* 23 July 1892). Similarly, when the club travelled to Dublin to play the Dunleary Independents they found the Adelaide Road ground 'rather small for a Gaelic match', whilst the second half of the match was 'simply indescribable as the Dunleary men began to play under rugby rules and they pulled down the visitors whether playing the ball with the hands or the feet' (WE, 10 Mar. 1893).

The early version of Gaelic football played in Westmeath was essentially a winter-spring activity, the vast majority of games taking place between November and May. A monthly analysis of football matches played during the most active phase of the activity in Westmeath between 1890 and 1893 is illustrated in figure 2.2. Of the 155 matches reported, 28 per cent were played during the months of November, December and January and 44 per cent between February and April. This preference for a time of the year when weather conditions were likely to be least favourable had a practical and a theoretical basis. In a county where public recreational space was almost totally unavailable football clubs were dependent on the patronage of a co-operative farmer for the use of a suitable field for playing and spectators. These were the months when grass growth was essentially dormant so meadows were not damaged by the action of over forty footballers confined to a relatively small area, nor could the spectators that crowded to some of the venues cause irreparable damage. There was a belief within the GAA that the months of July, August and September were unsuitable for football (and hurling). This viewpoint was articulated at the Kerry GAA convention in January 1893 when attention was drawn to the increased popularity of summer football.

Delegates complained that the activity 'injuriously affects athletic sports and prevents numerous promising athletes from devoting their full attention to training'. An editorial in the journal *Sport* in March supported this belief. The editor believed that nothing was more 'likely to invite apathy and dislike for vigorous pastimes into the mind of a player than an hour's heavy play under the auspices of a scorching sun'. The player who has rested for the summer will return with 'fresh energy and enthusiasm' (*Sport*, 4 Mar. 1893). Westmeath people were equally suspicious of football playing in mid-summer. 'Sportsman' in his *Westmeath Nationalist* column considered football out of place in the 'very hot weather we have had recently' and proposed cricket 'ever so much a nobler game than the favourite lawn tennis' as the ideal summer game (WN, 14 Apr. 1892). In June 1893 Ballinahown and Cloghan played a game 'with the thermometer at ninety degrees'. In the reporter's consideration football in 'such conditions is far more toil than pleasure' making it 'very difficult if not morally impossible to maintain anything like regular play' (WN, 15 June 1893).

One of the reasons why young men played Gaelic football was that it presented them with an opportunity of extending their sporting and social activities over the winter months. Summer was the season for cricket playing. Mullingar FC was the winter version of the Mullingar Commercial Cricket Club. The Shamrocks football club was the winter extension of the Shamrocks cricket club. The latter was first reported as being active on the cricket grounds in 1887 and was involved in at least five matches each in 1888 and 1889. The interchange between the two games is clearly seen in the aftermath of the 1892 county football championship football final. Having won the title the members of the Mullingar Football Club announced that they would not be playing any more matches until the new season (WN, 12 May 1892). Instead they assembled at Michael Doherty's premises on 20 May 1892 'with the object of taking steps for the formation of a representative Mullingar cricket club' (WN, 26 May 1892). 'Representative', in this context, seems to have referred to the two main football clubs as the cricket eleven included members of the Shamrocks club and there are no reports of the football club featuring at the cricket crease. Of the 19 listed as having attended the inaugural meeting, nine had played in the football final. Charles Williams, one of the outstanding football players, was elected captain of the club. The earnestness of the desire for a representative team was confirmed when the Shamrocks football player and ubiquitous cricketer Percy Muldowney was elected vice-captain. James Mulvey, 'a man foremost in the promotion of every sport organised in town' and captain of Mullingar FC was elected president of the new cricket club. The Independent Wanderers also held a special meeting in May 1892 and decided to change the club to a cricket one for the summer (WN, 2 June 1892). A similar pattern existed in the Killucan district in the interchange between summer cricket and winter football in the early 1890s. Hugh Fulham who was captain of Raharney Rovers in the 1892 football final was a familiar figure on the cricket circuit also.

Gaelic football was played on Sundays, a decision considered by Neal Garnham (1999: 11) to be crucially important in popularising the sport as 'it ensured that rural workers and urban white-collar workers such as shop assistants, who could not be assured of a day of rest on Saturdays, were able to participate'. It is worth noting that the GAA was not responsible for the introduction of Sunday sporting activity in Westmeath. Sunday had by this time been well established as a day for sporting recreation with Sunday cricket-playing common in Westmeath by the mid-1880s as the game became increasingly democratised.

## Classless cricket

According to Marcus de Búrca (1980: 25) 'the rapid growth of the GAA also brought to a halt the spread of cricket in rural areas where the game had gained a foothold'. Sugden and Bairner (1993: 50) agree with de Búrca's analysis and suggest that the rapid growth of cricket experienced in the 1860s and 1870s was halted, especially outside Ulster, as an indirect consequence of Land League activities and as a direct result of the emergence of the GAA with 'its avowed policy to usurp such "foreign" games as cricket'. This generalisation

*Figure 2.2* **Monthly analysis of football matches played in Westmeath 1890–3**

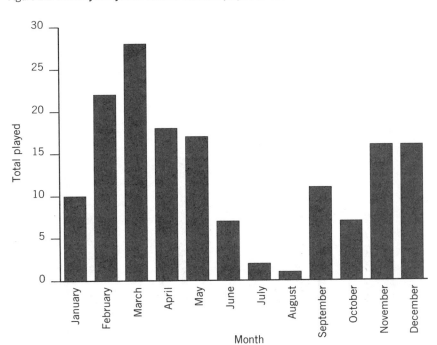

clearly does not apply to Westmeath where newspaper analysis reveals that cricket experienced a period of steady growth, both geographic and demographic, throughout the 1880s and 1890s. In the period 1885–1900, cricket was the most popular sport in Westmeath. It was played throughout the county and attracted support from all classes. This growth peaked in 1900 when 61 cricket matches, played by 30 different combinations, were reported in the local newspapers. The number of matches played and combinations active is illustrated in figure 2.3.

In the period between 1885 and 1900, a total of 632 cricket matches were reported for the county involving 135 different civilian combinations. Some of the teams that played in these matches were transient combinations that assembled for a single game and then disbanded. Many, though, were properly constituted clubs that held annual meetings at which officers for the season were elected, regular practice sessions held and annual balls organised at the end of the season. Seventeen per cent of the matches involved a team representing one of the military garrisons based in the urban centres of Athlone, Mullingar or Longford in inter-regimental matches or games against elite civilian teams. The popularity of the sport at local level is further emphasised by the fact that in the period 1898–1900 only one match featured a

military team. This was a result of the reduction in the numbers of military
personnel in both Mullingar and Athlone because of the war in South Africa.

*Figure 2.3* **Cricket 'clubs' active and matches played in Westmeath, 1885–1900**

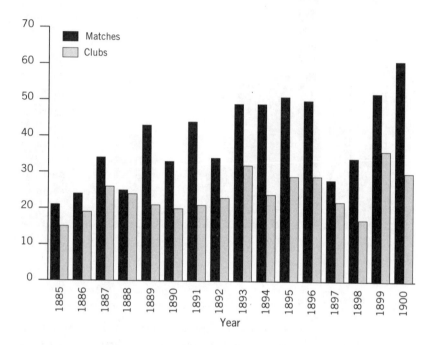

Non-military cricket teams in Westmeath in the period 1885–1900 can be
classified into a number of categories. One group, forming eight per cent of
the total, consisted of well-to-do individuals in the locality who assembled a
group of their friends to challenge a combination formed by individuals of
similar status in the area. This group chiefly included landed estate pro-
prietors but teams also included the selection of J. H. Locke, joint proprietor
of a Kilbeggan distillery, and the combination of the Church of Ireland rector
Rev. H. St George. The elite Westmeath County Cricket Club represented
the composite team of this particular group. A second group of teams was
directly associated with landed properties such as Lord Greville's Clonhugh
demesne, Charles B. Marley's Rochfort establishment and in particular the
Coolamber estates of the most sports obsessed of Westmeath's landed
families, the O'Reillys. This group formed about five per cent of the total. At
this level a cricket match was a good way of entertaining friends, neighbours,
tenants and villagers, and of bringing in eligible young men for daughters to
meet (Birley, 1999). At schools level the Athlone based Ranelagh School
Cricket Club featured in reports for ten of the years surveyed and the Farra

School located near Mullingar also participated. Fourthly, voluntary associations fielded cricket teams as a means of extending their social curriculum
and extending the range of activities available to members. Included in this
category are the Athlone Brass Band XI, the teams of Castlepollard, Killucan
and Mullingar working-men's clubs and the Catholic Commercial cricket
clubs of Mullingar and Castlepollard. Another small group of teams may be
categorised as works teams made up of employees of a particular work place
such as the Athlone Woollen Mills, the Mullingar Mental Asylum XI, and the
Killucan (Railway) Station XI. There were also several clubs that served the
sporting needs of particular employees in the urban and small town areas of
the counties such as Kilbeggan, Castlepollard, Delvin, Mullingar and Athlone.
These clubs made up 16 per cent of the total and were increasing in number
and activity by 1900. The Kilbeggan Cricket Club was reported to have played
14 games in 1900 for example and the Mount Street club in Mullingar played ten
games. Finally, the largest category of team represented the villages, parishes
and townlands scattered across the county. These teams formed 55 per cent of
the total that were active between 1885 and 1900.

Data on the popularity of cricket with the various economic groups is
illustrated in table 2.2. The information contained in the table was compiled
from a study of a sample of 170 players from 17 different teams that played the
game in 1900 and 1901. The enumerators' forms for the 1901 census were then
used to profile the players. The players came from a broad range of backgrounds, and from most sections of the Westmeath economy. The game
enjoyed its greatest popularity amongst the farm labourer and general
labourer classes, a finding that challenges the traditional perception of Irish
cricket as an elitist activity. Playing cricket presented members of this group
with an opportunity to earn respectability, display skill, and win prestige in
their own locality. It was a game that required minimal equipment and was
played in a relatively injury risk free environment.

*Table 2.2* **Occupations of cricket players in Westmeath in 1900–1**

| Occupation | Per cent represented |
|---|---|
| Farmer/son | 19 |
| Farm/general labourer | 41 |
| Un/semi-skilled | 10 |
| Skilled | 14 |
| Shop asst./clerk | 12 |
| Merchant/son | 1 |
| Professional | 1 |
| Student | 1 |
| Other | 1 |

Farmers and their sons provided the second most important core group support for the game. Moreover their importance was greater than simple numerical support for it was this group that made their land available for playing fields.

Cricket players were a youthful group. Sixty per cent of the sample group were less than 24 years of age in 1901; 23 per cent of this group were less than twenty years of age and 37 per cent were aged between 20 and 24 years. Another 30 per cent were aged between 25 and 29. The group of players was also overwhelmingly single. Only 12 per cent of the sample group were married in 1901. Towards the end of the nineteenth century, sport, at this class level, was the preserve of the single man. Marriage brought new responsibilities, commitments and expenses and the amount of disposable income available for investment in social and recreational activities dwindled.

In the period covered by this study, cricket provided working-class people with the main opportunity to participate in a sporting activity. In the years between 1888 and 1900, only in 1891 and 1892 did the number of football games played exceed the number of cricket matches. The relative popularity of football and cricket measured by the number of games played is illustrated in figure 2.4.

*Figure 2.4* **Number of football and cricket matches played in Westmeath 1885–1900**

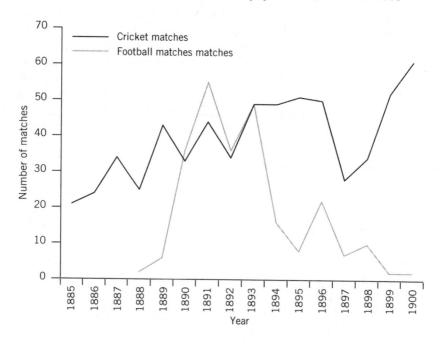

# Conclusion

National political issues had little impact on the development or decline of the early GAA in Westmeath. Part of the reason for the failure in the 1890s was mismanagement associated with the collapse of the county committee. The survival of a county committee required the achievement of consensus. Clubs had to sacrifice their individual interests for the overall benefit of the football game within the county. Despite the existence of rules and a hierarchy of officials to enforce them, ultimately this consensus was not maintained within the county. The two Mullingar clubs in particular refused to accept the committee's decisions and this resulted in the Athlone club abandoning football in favour of the association game and the disappearance of the Shamrocks club.

Codification was one of the characteristics of the transformation of sport from its pre-modern to modern manifestation. The process evolved slowly and the achievement of uniformity of rule interpretation and acceptance was protracted. In the interim, disputes on rules and regulations were common and retarded the development of the football game. Disputed scores and illegal tackles were important in damaging the development of the early GAA in Westmeath. In the absence of a football structure, cricket provided a recreational outlet that was more socially inclusive than the initial version of GAA in the country.

The average individual engaging with sport at the local level was motivated by the desire to socialise and expand their recreational and leisure activities. Political intrigue and struggles between the IRB and the constitutional nationalists for control at national level was of little concern to the ordinary member of the GAA in Westmeath.

An in-depth study such as this allows a detailed examination of the operation and management of sport and sports association at the local level and the conclusions reached form a small part of a jigsaw that may require a reassessment of commonly held assumptions. In particular the role of cricket in catering for the sporting needs of the Irish labouring classes in the 1890s requires further exploration.

44

## Chapter 3

# Rugby's imperial connections, domestic politics, and colonial tours to Ireland before 1914

Neal Garnham

## Introduction

Since the mid-1880s Ireland has been a country of competing sporting identities. The rise of the Gaelic Athletic Association from 1884 introduced a much clearer division into Irish sport than had been the case before. While upholding many of the contemporary values and ideals attached to sport in Victorian Britain, such as the primacy of amateurism and the inherent masculinity of athletic games, the GAA also imposed more distinctive and unique divisions into sport in Ireland (Cronin, 1998b; McDevitt, 1997). Through its choice of patrons, its administrative framework, and the involvement of committed republicans from the inception of the organisation, the GAA portrayed itself as Catholic, rural, and, most importantly, politically nationalist (Mandle, 1977). Eventually even a series of bans and exclusions were imposed, that effectively defined who was essentially 'Irish' enough to enjoy GAA membership, and the benefits of competition in Gaelic games (Rouse, 1993). As a direct result of these developments, almost by default, non-Gaelic sports, such as rugby, cricket and association football, became seen as the pastimes of the unionist minority. The situation became even clearer from the turn of the twentieth century, when supporters of Gaelic games launched uncompromising attacks on the adherents of such sports. Increasingly, sports and games that were outside the remit and control of the GAA were labelled as alien and unpatriotic.

Thus Ireland developed two distinct competing sporting identities that largely mirrored the country's political divisions. Gaelic games appealed predominantly to nationalists, while unionists overwhelmingly opted for their non-Gaelic counterparts. To a large extent these were antipathetic and exclusive cultures. However, even within some non-Gaelic sports similarly based divisions appeared. For example, in association football in Belfast, as both Fulton and Hassan note elsewhere in this collection, individual teams came to represent nationalist and unionist interests from an early date. This was primarily the result of the fact that this particular game drew support from both political traditions. Unionists and nationalists alike played and watched soccer (Sugden and Bairner, 1993).

Other non-Gaelic sports could also be used for political purposes by both sides and it is that phenomenon which this chapter examines. In particular it considers how colonial rugby tours to Ireland prior to 1914 were utilised by adherents of both the main political groups for their own purposes. It examines the extent to which these sporting events could be seen as part of a divided system of sporting and political identities; and it investigates the degree to which these events were seen as part of the wider imperial political and sporting context. Finally it offers some conclusions as to what these events and their perception in Ireland tell us of Irish politics in the years before 1914.

## Maoris, Springboks and All Blacks

Prior to the outbreak of the Great War, five touring rugby teams visited Ireland from the colonies. The first to arrive was the Maori team from New Zealand in late 1888. They played three games in Ireland: one in Belfast, and two in Dublin (Ryan, 1993). The series included a convincing victory over the Irish national side in the capital. However, the tour apparently generated little enthusiasm in Ireland, and the coverage these games received in the Irish press was minimal (*Belfast Newsletter*, 3 and 6 Dec. 1888). One English paper implied that this might have been due to the fact that the Maoris had beaten Ireland so comprehensively. The alleged Irish antipathy to their visitors was also later manifested in the suggestion that the tourists and the Irish Union had quarrelled over the division of gate monies (*Athletic News*, 4 Dec. 1888; *Ulster Cycling and Football News*, 15 Mar. 1889). In all events the visit was seen rather as a novelty than as a major sporting or imperial event.

In 1912, the last visit by a touring team in this period was the second made by a South African team. In this case too the press coverage was limited. This was probably primarily due to the extensive amount of column inches given over to the crucial political events of the time, and the apparently inexorable advance of Home Rule for Ireland. While the tour drew large crowds, including more than 10,000 for the game against Ireland in Dublin, there was little more than a passing interest shown by the press (*Freeman's Journal*, 2 and 5 Dec. 1912; *The Irish Times*, 2 and 5 Dec. 1912; *Belfast Newsletter*, 2 and 5 Dec. 1912).

In 1905, however, the visit of the all-conquering All Blacks caused a little more of a stir. Allegedly the triumphs of this team in 31 of their 32 matches against British and Irish opponents caused a wave of panic 'throughout the British Isles' (Nauright, 1991; 1996b). The failures of the British military during the Boer War, and the rejection on medical grounds of almost half of those who volunteered, had prompted the establishment of a Royal Commission on physical degeneration. Here now, with the success of the New Zealanders, was definitive proof of the failings of the British nation. The best men the mother country could offer were simply crushed by these colonial upstarts. In Ireland, however, reactions to the New Zealanders' victories were more muted and measured. Their triumphs over Ireland and Munster were put down rather to their 'superior system' of play (*Belfast Newsletter*, 27 Nov. 1905), and even 'sharp practices' (*The Irish Times*, 27 Nov. 1905). In fact the only comment on the idea of racial and physical deterioration in the Irish press referred to the idea as 'hysterical nonsense' (*Belfast Newsletter*, 27 Nov. 1905). Such considered assessments largely coincided with the Commission's own findings regarding the Irish. Amongst this race, it was suggested, physical deterioration was less of a problem than increasing idiocy and mental decay.[1] In effect the All Blacks had rather less of an impact in Ireland than elsewhere in the United Kingdom, and their relevance beyond the games field was seen as limited in the extreme.

Either side of the 1905 tour by the All Blacks, however, Ireland was visited by sides from Canada and South Africa. The Canadians visited Belfast and Dublin in 1902, and the South Africans the same two cities in 1906. On both occasions the opportunity was taken by journalists, sportsmen and administrators to use the game and its attendant activities for purposes far removed from the field of play.

## Canadians and South Africans

The Canadian visitors arrived in Ireland from Liverpool in mid-December 1902. The team stayed in the country for a week, and played three games before departing for Scotland. The initial match of the tour took place in Belfast against a team representing Ulster, and the last two were played against the Leinster provincial side and Trinity College, in Dublin. The Canadians' three-day stay in Ulster was rigorously planned by the Northern Branch of the IRFU, and included visits to the theatre and music hall in Belfast, as well as an excursion to the Giant's Causeway.[2] While the match against Ulster was eventually won by the Canadians, more interesting and important than the result were the rhetoric and ceremony that surrounded the match and its reporting in Belfast's unionist press. The game was seen by the conservative unionist *Belfast Newsletter* as 'a trial of strength between the representatives of the Dominions and their British friends', and extensively reported (*Belfast Newsletter*, 13 Dec. 1902). A pre-match luncheon was held for the two teams in the boardroom of the Dunville's distillery, at the invitation of James Barr, the company's managing director. The welcoming speech, by an official of the Northern Branch of the IRFU, stressed the common bonds the two teams shared, and the Canadians' role in 'extending their empire from the Atlantic to the Pacific.' The nature of the imperial connection was made even more explicit when Barr responded to the vote of thanks of the Canadian vice-captain. Barr noted 'how our Canadian brethren had come to the assistance of the mother country at the time of the Boer War' and pledged that 'their assistance would never be forgotten' (*Belfast Newsletter*, 15 Dec. 1902). This reference was to the role played in the war by volunteer troops from the Imperial Yeomanry who had been recruited across the United Kingdom and the white dominions for service against the Boers. The theme of imperial indebtedness was raised again later, at the post-match dinner. Charles Hardin, the President of the Northern Branch of the IRFU, insisted 'they were all proud of the part the Canadians had recently taken in the defence of the empire', and noted that three of the Canadian team had actually served in the war. Cheers and applause greeted his comments (*Belfast Newsletter*, 15 Dec. 1902; *Northern Whig*, 15 Dec. 1902). The *Ulster Echo*, which reported from a like-minded political standpoint, continued in a similar vein. Its rugby correspondent suggested that this game had added to the 'further cementing' of 'the bond of sympathy which exists between the British Isles and her colonies' (*Ulster Echo*, 13 Dec. 1902). The same paper's editorial column later went further, stressing again the Canadian contribution to the empire during the recent war. It was well known and extremely fortunate that 'the Canadians had shown their brotherhood so well in South Africa' (*Ulster Echo*, 15 Dec. 1902).

In short, political unionists in Ulster used the visit of the Canadians for a conspicuous display of imperialist rhetoric. Both the unionist press and certain individuals with unionist views used the opportunity provided by the Canadians' tour to stress the importance of empire, and the integral role of the white dominions in its maintenance. Their rhetoric centred primarily on the issue of contributions to the imperial war effort in South Africa. This was no chance happening, as the war was a live political issue in Ireland and not simply in the context of British foreign policy. For one leading historian of Ireland it was this war that 'focussed much moderate Irish opinion into an anti-imperial mould, and provided a mobilising "cause" against the government' (Foster, 1989: 433). For another it provided nationalists with 'a good grudge' and 'a strong sense of self-righteousness', while leading to a 'wave of almost hysterical anti-British feeling' (Boyce, 1990: 224). Essentially the Boer

War and its conduct had split Irish political opinion along already established lines. While unionists unanimously supported the British military intervention, nationalists drew parallels between themselves and the Boers, as subject nations struggling against British imperialism. For nationalists the war provided a force for rejuvenation in the later stages of the Parnell split. The Boer War, or rather opposition to it, became an issue around which all the various nationalist factions in Ireland could coalesce. For unionists the support offered by nationalists to the Boers was simply further proof of their disloyalty. These opposing allegiances were ultimately given force by the formation of Irish units within the Imperial Yeomanry, and two Transvaal Irish Brigades (Amery, 1908; McCracken, 1989). Rugby, and the presence of the Canadians in particular, provided an immediate imperial linkage in Ulster. The talk was not only of imperial expansion and the creation of common bonds, however. It was also of conflict and comradeship in the face of opposition. This demonstration of imperial solidarity had its wider supranational contexts of course, but it also clearly had its domestic political connotations. For some of Belfast's unionists the sports field had become a space for the reaffirmation of imperial bonds, and an arena for the demonstration of imperial vitality and masculinity.

The situation was prospectively very different, and certainly rather more complex, four years later. In November 1906 a South African team visited Belfast. Arriving from Scotland, having defeated all the English county sides, and being defeated only by the Scottish national team, the Springboks had two matches to play in Ireland. The first was against Ireland in Belfast, the second against Trinity College in Dublin. Although the latter game was widely reported in the Dublin papers, it was the initial match against the Irish national side that generated the most interest. Unionist rhetoric again centred on the theme of sport promoting imperial cohesion and sympathy. The *Newsletter* saw the game as a demonstration of the 'brotherhood' that existed 'now that Boer and Briton are under the one flag in South Africa.' Additionally it showed that amongst the Britons there was now a 'prevailing desire for the future of South Africa' that consisted 'of unalloyed good will'. In simple terms the game showed that 'nothing breaks down prejudice or removes misconceptions so much as the associations of the playing field'. All who saw the game were filled with 'Imperial pride' (*Belfast Newsletter*, 26 Nov. 1906).

The similarly conservative and unionist *Belfast Evening Telegraph* published an article a day before the match in the city, that likewise stressed the conciliatory role of sport within the Empire. It concluded that 'the visit of the South African footballers is certain to have consequences of the right kind', and that the tour would go a good way 'towards engendering good feeling between the British and the Dutch' (*Belfast Evening Telegraph*, 23 Nov. 1906). On the evening of the match itself the *Telegraph* reiterated the point, and added that 'there could be no better medium for the formation of reciprocal good feeling than the football ground' (*Belfast Evening Telegraph*, 26 Nov. 1906). The *Echo* also offered extensive match coverage (*Ulster Echo*, 24 Nov. 1906). The Liberal unionist *Northern Whig* largely echoed the established view that the game would 'foster goodwill towards the great colony'. It also suggested that the huge crowd was drawn to the game, at least in part, by the 'Imperial idea'. However the *Whig* was rather more explicit in the details it offered of the visiting team. Citing a conversation allegedly overheard in the crowd at Belfast, a report in the *Whig* revealed that several of the South African team had fought with the Boer forces during the recent war, and that at least two had been interned on St Helena. They were now no longer Boers, however, but 'colonials, and plucky gentlemanly athletic chaps who do South Africa credit'. The article concluded by stating that now 'no-one cared a straw' for the team's earlier allegiances, and that a 'most cordial feeling' was extended from the crowd to the visitors (*Northern Whig*, 26 Nov. 1906). In fact, of the 29 South African players profiled in another newspaper all but five had Boer names, and while one had 'assisted in the defence of Kimberley' at least two others had served with the Boer forces (*Ireland's Saturday Night*, 24 Nov. 1906).

The Dublin unionist press made no direct references to the game's imperial connections, but instead stressed the sporting side of the contest, and highlighted what the match proved about the state of Irish rugby. The match sparked an extended debate in *The Irish Times* over possible improvements that could be made in the Irish game. In general it was suggested that the Irish needed to develop greater co-ordination, and that the Irish game was too dependent upon powerful forward play (*The Irish Times*, 26, 28, 30 Nov., 1 and 4 Dec. 1906).

The nationalist press in Dublin also reported the match with little explicit mention of its imperial dimensions. The *Freeman's Journal* offered a long report of the game against Ireland, noting only that on their arrival in Dublin 'these representatives of the gallant Boer people' were loudly cheered by waiting crowds (*Freeman's Journal*, 27 and 28 Nov. 1906). Subsequent correspondence to the paper merely noted the inadequate arrangements that had been made for spectators at the Trinity College match (*Freeman's Journal*, 27 and 28 Nov. 1906). Thus there was perhaps a limited acknowledgement of the Boer connection and a guarded display of sympathy towards the Boers themselves. However, while ideas of imperial cohesion were not explicit in the coverage, there was also none of the violently pro-Boer rhetoric that had pervaded the same paper's columns a few years earlier. Back in Ulster though, matters were rather different.

The *Irish News*, the voice of Belfast's nationalist community, reported the Irish national side's game against South Africa at length. It also commented in detail on it in its editorial columns. The game was not actually between Ireland and South Africa the paper claimed, but 'between the representatives of the Boer and British nations'. The so-called Irish team included no one 'drawn from the classes who bred Irish athletes', that is the native Celts. Instead it was composed solely of British interlopers. Giving the match local resonance it went on to hope that the kind of welcome that had been accorded to men who had 'shot down a good many loyal men from Ulster' might one day be extended to nationalist politicians such as John Dillon and John Redmond, who had secured beneficial social reforms in Ireland. Direct reference was also made to a skirmish at Lindley during the War, when two companies of Belfast Imperial Yeomen were killed or captured by a small force of Boer commandos. In summarising the situation, Belfast's unionist establishment was seen as being hypocritical in the extreme (*Irish News*, 26 Nov. 1906).

The later crushing defeat of Trinity College by the Springboks prompted further analogies to be drawn. In this case the ongoing debate over the endowment of a Catholic university was brought to the fore. The demand for state provision of university education acceptable to both the Catholic clergy and that church's growing middle-class laity, had not been answered by various schemes in the preceding century. Non-denominational Queen's Colleges, the independent Catholic University, and the institution of the Royal University of Ireland had all failed to answer the perceived need. Latterly the argument for an acceptable provision began to centre on opposition to the privileged position of Trinity College, Dublin. This institution, which had only officially admitted Catholic students to its degrees from 1873, and which had not appointed a Catholic Fellow before 1880, enjoyed substantial endow-ments and a favoured position in the state (Paseta, 1998–9). Here, the *Irish News* now claimed, was the proof of the College's real value 'in the sustain-ment of Ireland's credit in the eyes of the world'. This was precisely nil (*Irish News*, 28 Nov. 1906; *Fermanagh Herald*, 1 Dec. 1906).

For northern nationalists, as for unionists, this tour assumed a relevancy beyond the rugby pitch. The explicitly imperial context was relevant for both communities, but while for unionists the emphasis was placed upon sport promoting imperial cohesion, for nationalists it was rather a case of sport demonstrating the divisions between nations, and the hypocrisy of an ideology. More importantly, the South Africans' visit was most relevant to nationalists not for what it told them of empire, but for what it revealed of the failings and duplicity of their British and unionist opponents. Whatever the medium, politics in Belfast became interpreted and understood most clearly in a purely domestic context.

# Conclusion

The events and the rhetoric that surrounded the visits of colonial rugby sides to Ireland, reveal something of the prevailing attitudes to empire in the country before 1914. On the whole these admittedly limited and very specific examples seem to support some of the suggestions of Alvin Jackson (1996) regarding Ulster Unionists' attitudes to empire. Unlike their mainstream British Conservative allies, the Ulster Unionists in the later nineteenth century invested little interest in matters of empire. The Maori visit of the 1880s was seen as no more than a novelty, with no reverberations beyond the sports pitch. With the passing of the Boer War, however, the empire took on a new role in unionist rhetoric, and possibly in their thinking (Jackson, 1996). If nothing else the visits of the Canadians, New Zealanders and the South Africans, all within a four-year period, gave the people of Ireland a new familiarity with empire and its products. The visits certainly generated a great deal of interest. Probably more than 20,000 people saw the South African team play in 1906, and many more saw them drive through the streets of Dublin wearing their distinctive slouch hats and carried in carriages provided specifically for the purpose by the leading men of Dublin. Others may have heard the South African captain preach at a Belfast Methodist church (*Belfast Newsletter*, 27 Nov. 1906). Many more probably purchased the picture postcard of the team that was published in the city (*Belfast Evening Telegraph*, 27 Nov. 1906). On their return in 1912 the Springboks were filmed for the local cinemas and commemorative badges were struck for sale by the Irish Rugby Football Union (*Northern Whig*, 3 Dec. 1912).

At the same time, the emphasis placed by the unionist press on sport as a means of fostering imperial cohesion was a more mainstream one. Across Britain, cricket and rugby tours were seen as useful mortar for cementing relations between Britain and the white dominions. Sporting exchanges solidified the links between the motherland and the colonies, by creating another common cultural bond (Holt, 1990). In one area at least, it seems Ulster's loyalists were displaying typically British attitudes.

With regard to nationalist sympathies, the coverage of the visits of the Canadians and the Springboks is also revealing. For the most part the matches were reported, but without the accompanying laudatory tales of empire. This is perhaps not surprising given the anti-imperialist sentiments of many in the nationalist community. When imperial considerations were in fact raised, it was only as long as they could be placed clearly in a domestic or local context. Nationalist sympathy for the Boers still existed by 1906, as the comments of the press show, but this had little to do with the imperial struggle that had been fought in a far off land. It had rather more to do with underlining the present failings of the British in Ireland, than with the past disasters of the British in Africa.

It has been argued that the 1906 visit of the Springboks to Britain 'was significant in helping to unite white South Africans' giving them 'a sense of achievement' (Black and Nauright, 1998: 25) and 'a collective national self-worth' (Black and Nauright, 1998: 33). For the white South African community, the Springboks, and the 1906 tour in particular, became a common focus around which both Boer and British South Africans could come together, and in which both groups could take a mutual pride. In Ireland the visit of the South Africans did exactly the opposite. The South African victories there simply served to further push apart an already divided nation.

Chapter 4

# The Irish Free State and Aonach Tailteann

Mike Cronin

## Introduction

In August 1928 Dr Pat O'Callaghan travelled to Kanturk, County Cork, to attend a civic reception in honour of his victory at the Olympic Games of that year in Amsterdam. O'Callaghan, the first Irishman from the independent state ever to win an Olympic title, told the gathered crowd:

> I am glad of my victory, not of the victory itself, but for the fact that the world has been shown that Ireland has a flag, that Ireland has a national anthem, and in fact that we have a nationality (Healy, 1997: xi).

O'Callaghan's speech offers an excellent example of how national prestige and identity can be achieved through success at a major international sporting event. Such a victory was as important to a new nation such as Ireland in the 1920s as it was for the post-1989 ex-Soviet bloc countries. The Olympic games and the football World Cup have consistently functioned as markers of national identity and measurements of success, yet they are not the only means through which sport can be embraced to project the nation.

In addition to competing at, and even winning international events, it is the staging of major sporting competitions that has commonly been understood by most governments as a means of securing national and international prestige. In 1929, the Irish Free State hosted the International Motor Race or Grand Prix in Dublin's Phoenix Park. Over 100,000 people gathered in the park to watch the Russian driver, Boris Ivanowski, win and collect his cash prize and the 20-inch solid silver Phoenix trophy (Tsigdinos, 2003). The event was attended by all the major government ministers, and the prizes were presented to Ivanowski by W. T. Cosgrave, the Irish Free State President. While the event could be dismissed as a simple motor race, albeit attractive in light of the glamorous connotations of speed and danger that were prevalent in the 1920s, *The Irish Times* well understood the significance of the event for the new Irish nation. It argued that

> When, as during the last few days the government displays an economic energy and a generous spirit that exalts the Free State in the world's eye, then Irishmen rejoice not merely for themselves, but for Ireland (cited in Tsigdinos, 2003: 64).

Hosting events such as the International Motor Race would have given any nation, let alone a new one trying to find its way in the world, an exposure in the media, and allowed it to display itself and its success. In essence, the motivations of staging such an event and the anticipated rewards, although different in scale, were no different in the 1920s from 2004 for Athens or in 2008 for Beijing hosting the Olympic games. That sporting events brought prestige and allowed the nation to display itself was well understood in Ireland in the 1920s. Even provincial newspapers such as the *Offaly Independent* could argue, in relation to the 1929 International Motor Race, that

> the Saorstat has been the venue of an increasing number of events in recent years of sufficient importance in the international character to be worthy of countries whose opportunities are far greater than ours, is certainly a matter in which Irish people cannot help entertaining a feeling of pride . . . [the International Motor Race] must certainly be regarded as further fruit gained under the Treaty. Other instances of the fruits of that liberty are to be found in the increased interest taken in making old established events in the country more attractive and the founding of new ones (*Offaly Independent*, 20 July 1929: 4).

While O'Callaghan was correct in his reading of the meaning of his 1928 victory, and the commentators of the late 1920s understood the relevance of a major motor race as a marker of the successes of independent Ireland, it was actually four years earlier, in Dublin, that the Irish Free State first cut its teeth in hosting a major sporting event. Although few remember Aonach Tailteann,[1] the Irish olympiad, of 1924, 1928 and 1932, they were a major sporting attempt at state building, and were used as a method of showing the world that the flag, anthem and nationality that O'Callaghan would so warmly embrace in Amsterdam in 1928 existed in fact and were no longer the dreamings of advanced Irish nationalists.

This chapter aims to explore the history of Aonach Tailteann, and to demonstrate that the newly independent Irish state fully understood the potential political and identity forming benefits of staging a major sporting spectacle. It will argue that while the conception of the nation was necessarily narrow, the use of new media and sporting technologies enabled the Irish Free

State to demonstrate to its own people, and to many commentators from overseas, that independent Ireland was a functioning reality. In this, however, the Irish were not unique. The inter-war period witnessed many major sporting and cultural festivals across the western world. Whether the Empire Exhibition at Wembley in 1923 or the New York World's Fair in 1939, the concept of national spectacle, or what one author has termed the 'mega event' (Roche, 2000), was not unusual. What tied these events together, and Aonach Tailteann was no different, was the need to display, in a public and mass-consumed fashion, the cohesion, wealth and success of the nation. Essentially, whether for a new nation such as the Irish Free State, or an established imperial power such as Britain, major public sporting and cultural spectacles were an necessary part of state formation and reinforcement in the inter-war years. While Aonach Tailteann was a sporting and cultural festival, embracing Gaelic games, athletics, literature, dance and art, the main concern of this chapter will be the ensuing embodiment of the new nation through the sporting part of the games.

## The ancient origins of Aonach Tailteann

As with many features of the nation-building process in the Irish Free State, the idea of Aonach Tailteann was not a new one. Along with the designs for the new national coinage or the imagery that was included on the first series of independent postage stamps, much that emerged as defining the Irish in the 1920s was a recasting of ancient legend. It is clear that the Gaelic revival of the later decades of the nineteenth century had a profound effect on those charged with imaging, designing and delivering the livery and liturgy of the new state. Aonach Tailteann was no different. Its origins stretched back into the mists of time, and the concerted push for the recreation of the games emerged during the high point of the Gaelic revival.

The original Aonach Tailteann had been staged in County Meath in 1896 BC as funeral games or *Cuiteach Fuait*, to celebrate the life of Queen Tailte. Aonach Tailteann was reputedly celebrated on the same fields in Meath every year until the time of St. Patrick. Subsequently the games were held at infrequent intervals. In 1169 the last traditional Aonach Tailteann was staged. A writer of the time noted that

> On this occasion the Aonach Tailteann was celebrated by the King of Ireland and the people of Leath-chuinn; and their horses and cavalry were spread out on the space extending from Mullach Aidi to Mullach Tailteann [it is estimated that this is a stretch of land that covers nearly seven miles] (Nally, 1924: 34).

The celebration of Aonach Tailteann in 1169 was symbolically and historically significant as the reigning King of Ireland at that time was Rory O'Connor: the last High King of Ireland, and the final independent domestic ruler of Ireland until the twentieth century. In the autumn of 1169, not long after Aonach Tailteann had closed, the first Norman invasion took place, and the long and troubled history of British involvement with Ireland began.

The traditional Aonach Tailteann, had been staged at the burial ground of Queen Tailte at Caill Cuain in County Meath. The games began on 1 August and continued for approximately a week. They were called together by the High King, and attended by all minor kings, chiefs and nobles from across Ireland. The games of the early period fulfilled three basic purposes: to honour the illustrious dead, to promulgate new laws and to provide entertainment for the people. Aonach Tailteann was conducted in three phases. The festival was opened by a solemn religious ceremony that was led by the Chief Druid. The aim of the ceremony was to recount the family history and personal exploits of Queen Tailte and to lament her loss. The next component was a proclamation by the High King of a truce in all disputes and wars that would last for the duration of the festival. The truce was strictly enforced and underpinned another legal function of the festival: the High King took the opportunity of gathering those subservient to him to announce all new laws that were to be enacted and enforced in the future (Egan, 1980). With the legal and religious functions of the festival completed came 'the Cuiteach Fuait, or third great function consisting of the Funeral Games in honour of the dead' (Nally, 1922: 34). The games consisted of athletic, gymnastic and equestrian contests of various kinds. In addition to what we would understand as sporting events, was a whole series of cultural contests based around literature, poetry, music, dancing and story telling. A central feature of Aonach Tailteann, and a tradition continued to this day at events such as the Rose of Tralee, was a matchmaking festival where single women could find a suitable partner. In its entirety Aonach Tailteann was one of the most central events in the calendar of pre-Christian Ireland. It encompassed many themes that would subsequently feature in the Olympic games, and served to mark the cultural, geographical and military independence of Ireland during the period.

In the late nineteenth century, as Irish nationalism emerged as a steadily coherent and organised ideological force, the concept of bringing Aonach Tailteann back to life gathered support. But why should an ancient festival, that had its origins centuries earlier, have any resonance for late nineteenth-century nationalists? The resurgence of organised nationalist party politics had acrimoniously stalled in 1889 in the wake of the Parnell scandal. It took another decade before party politics based at Westminster reclaimed its primary role within nationalism under the leadership of John Redmond. In the intervening years it was cultural nationalism, particularly that which revolved around the Gaelic League, the literary revival and the Gaelic Athletic Association (GAA), which took centre stage. These different bodies all promoted, amongst other ideas, an historical and traditional embrace of Ireland's ancient culture. They argued that Ireland had been stunted intellectually and artistically by centuries of British rule, and that a semblance of what could be considered a true, or at least undiluted Irish culture, was to be found in the years preceding 1169. From such thinking emerged a language movement that looked back to the High Kings of Ireland, its ancient heroes and legends. The literary work of writers such as Yeats and Lady Gregory was inspired by modern readings of pre-modern tales, and formed symbolic representations of the imagined nation. In a climate where individuals were encouraged to embrace Ireland's long history and tradition of Celtic culture, the ideal of reinventing Aonach Tailteann was appealing.

## The rediscovery of Aonach Tailteann

The Gaelic revival affected many different thinkers and activists in the late nineteenth century, and although it is primarily remembered as a movement that promoted literature and the arts, the revival also had sporting adherents. The GAA was central in producing a physical embodiment of the Gaelic revival, and Archbishop Croke's letter accepting the position of patron of the organisation can be read as a manifesto for sporting revivalism and separatism. At the same time as the GAA was emerging, the first sustained calls for the staging of a modern Aonach Tailteann began to circulate publicly. Initially the calls for a restaging of Ireland's ancient games came from the land agitator and nationalist politician Michael Davitt. He was accompanied in his calls for a revival by Ireland's leading sportsman of the time, and founding patron of the GAA, Maurice Davin (Mandle, 1987). Indeed, Davin envisaged the Association's 'Invasion of America', which Darby explains in chapter 6 below, as a means of raising the necessary funds to stage Aonach Tailteann in the early 1890s. The 'Invasion' was not, however, a financial success, and the plans came to nothing. By the turn of the century, the idea of a revived Aonach Tailteann had been widely discussed in nationalist circles, and was seen by many activists, both political or sporting, as a goal worthy of pursuit. During the Irish revolutionary period, the leading nationalist party in Ireland, Sinn Féin, embraced the Tailteann ideal. The outlawed Dáil Éireann, established in 1919, began arguing for the renewal of the games, and leading figures such as Eamon de Valera threw their weight behind the campaign.

## Restaging Aonach Tailteann

With the resolution of the War of Independence and the signing of the Anglo-Irish Treaty, the first government of the Irish Free State began planning a modern Aonach Tailteann in earnest under the guidance of its most vociferous supporter J. J. Walsh. Why, though, would a government charged with forming a newly independent state, especially one saddled with the legacy of a bitter civil war, want to embark on the organisation and staging of a costly sporting and cultural event? John Turpin (2000: 194) has argued that Aonach Tailteann was

> a direct expression of the cultural revival by the newly installed government of the Irish Free State. It was a public manifestation of Cultural Revival ideology, which was now state-sponsored, and which sought to restore what it believed was a lost Gaelic society. In reality, it was attempting to create a modern political entity, distinct from Britain, with its own cultural events and emblems.

This is a key to understanding the enthusiasm of men such as Walsh and their belief in the Tailteann enterprise. It was not simply a sporting event to be staged in Dublin, but a festival for the new Irish nation that would revive old traditions and thereby implicitly reject the centuries of British rule over Ireland.

A plan to stage the revived Aonach Tailteann was mooted in 1922, and Walsh was put in charge of the organising committee. Despite the impending political crisis of 1922, the Provisional Government granted Walsh £6,000 to begin work on the extensive planning and putting the necessary infrastructure in place.[2] A further grant, of £10,000 was given to the Tailteann committee specifically for the updating of Croke Park in Dublin, the stadium that was to be used for the majority of the sporting events. The grant was paid on the understanding that the owners of the stadium, the GAA, would allow the venue to be used free of charge during the period of the Aonach.[3] Later, in July 1922 the Department of Finance made clear that the grant was in fact a loan.[4] Despite Walsh's best laid plans, and the recognition by the Provisional Government that Aonach Tailteann was a venture worthy of investment, the Civil War intervened and Walsh's planning was put on hold.[5]

The Civil War created an understandable financial drain on the government of the state. The damage incurred across the country by military action and the cost of maintaining a large army wreaked havoc with the finances of the government. In this context grandiose schemes such as Aonach Tailteann, irrespective of how much Ministers such as Walsh believed in the value of the event, meant that funding for a major spectacle was not available. This dichotomy would hamper Aonach Tailteann throughout its existence. The government of the newly independent state understood that events such as Aonach

Tailteann were invaluable in projecting a new image for the Irish Free State. However, in a period when the Department of Finance was keen to tightly control the nation's purse strings, displays of extravagance, no matter how valuable, were difficult to justify and fund. Blank cheques, it had been made clear to Walsh in July 1922, would not be written. If Aonach Tailteann was ever to be staged, the Government should not be left out of pocket. The Irish Free State then, while more than willing to take the kudos offered by such a major event, and eager to project an image of an Ireland on to the wider stage, was hesitant to fund Aonach Tailteann, at any level considered excessive.

## Aonach Tailteann 1924

The first modern Aonach Tailteann was eventually staged in August 1924. Despite the passage of time, the ethos of the original games and the political context of 1924 bore similarities. The original games were held under the terms of a national truce, and aimed to celebrate the illustrious dead. The modern games came a year after the ending of a bloody civil war that had resulted in thousands of deaths and the destruction of the Irish infrastructure. The games, while a celebration of Celtic culture and a newly independent Ireland, were also a time of reflection, remembrance and a signal to move beyond old hostilities. These themes were common in speeches made at the various Tailteann ceremonies, in the official programme and in much accompanying press comment. The *Irish Statesman* offered the opinion that the Irish 'badly want a clash of colour and gaiety after the long gloom in which we have been submerged' (*Irish Statesman*, 19 June 1924: 687), and that the *Aonach* offered a chance for the nation to stop 'feeding and sickening itself with these sinister [Civil War] sensations' (*Irish Statesman*, 26 July 1924: 611).

W. B. Yeats, who was Chair of the Aonach's Distinguished Visitors Committee, spoke at the opening banquet. He stated that the Aonach was a symbolic coming of age for the Free State:

> The nation is, as it were, a young man just entering upon its prosperity, of whom it impossible to say whether he is a wise man or a fool, whether he will enlarge his estate or be a mere spendthrift. He is celebrating his coming of age, and asks the goodwill of his neighbours . . . out of a period of terror of strained hearts and tragic incident we are reverting to normality (*Irish Statesman*, 9 Aug. 1924).

The first modern Aonach Tailteann was staged shortly after the 1924 Olympic Games in Paris (the first to be attended by a team from the Irish Free State), and was scheduled to follow the Dublin Horse Show, one of the city's largest social events, which regularly drew large crowds. The games were held, as the traditional games had been, in August. As Ryan reveals in detail in the chapter that follows, the actual Tailteann festival was a fascinating mix of traditional Celtic or Gaelic culture and elements of modernity. Throughout the whole festival there ran a strand of triumphant nationalism and a celebration of Irishness. In the sporting arena, the events included those that were traditionally, or even specifically Irish, such as hurling, Gaelic football and camogie. There was a long list of athletic contests based primarily around the Olympic model, and other sports such as swimming, tennis, golf, boxing, horse racing and billiards were also evident. The 1920s fascination with speed and danger was demonstrated by the inclusion in the programme of motor cycle racing, speed boat racing and aeroplane races – events that could hardly be considered to possess any traditional Celtic virtues or heritage.

Apart from the specific sporting events, the Tailteann festival programme included competitions in all forms of literature, Irish dancing, theatre, art and music. Concerns were expressed in some quarters that the sporting programme overshadowed the cultural aspect of the Aonach. The *Irish Statesman* claimed that the Aonach, 'whatever its sporting merits may be, is not to be a confession of Irish artistic bankruptcy' (*Irish Statesman*, 28 June 1924: 485). One of the most popular events was the industrial pageant through the streets of Dublin, which allowed Irish firms to demonstrate their traditionalism and nationalism, as well as their adherence to modern industrial methods by displaying their wares on the back of floats paraded through the centre of the city. For the shops of Dublin, which were non-manufacturers, and thus excluded from the pageant, there was a window-dressing competition. All stores were encouraged to enter, but the displays were limited, as were the floats in the industrial pageant, strictly to those displaying only Irish goods. During the period of the Aonach, Dublin welcomed distinguished guests from around the world. The responsibility for invitations lay with W. B. Yeats. In the spring of 1924 he sent invited a host of distinguished men, requesting that 'this great traditional celebration be attended by representative men in Science, Literature and Arts'.[6] Although some of Yeats's more colourful invitees, such as the Italian poet D'Annunzio, declined to attend, an eclectic list of guests, including the cricketers Jam Sahib of Nawanagar [7] and C. B. Fry, Sir John and Lady Lavery, G. K. Chesterton, Sir Edwin and Lady Lutyens, and Francis Hackett were in attendance.

The programme of Aonach Tailteann ran daily from Saturday 2 August 1924, until the closing ceremony on Sunday 17 August. The Dublin sporting newspaper, *Sport*, an enthusiastic and vociferous supporter of the project, opened its Tailteann coverage by proclaiming:

> This afternoon there will be inaugurated in Croke Park the greatest sporting carnival ever organised in Ireland and surpassing in its extent and scope even the

modern Olympic Games . . . the hosting of our kin from across the seas must prove a stimulus to our racial spirit in every way . . . the new Aonach Tailteann may well be like the Aonach of old, a rallying and unifying event, instinct with the best characteristics of days of national glory and athletic renown (*Sport*, 2 Aug. 1924: 1).

The opening ceremony took place at the headquarters of the GAA, Croke Park in Dublin. The ceremony, attended by a crowd estimated to number 20,000, began with the triumphal and symbolic entry into the stadium of Queen Tailte and her court. Such an entrance was choreographed in an attempt to link the modern revival of Aonach Tailteann directly with its traditional forerunner, and to imbue the whole festival with a sense of traditional cultural display. As Ryan points out in the next chapter, Queen Tailte's role was also part of a gendered narrative that surrounded the event as whole. Following Tailte, in the style of the opening ceremony of the modern Olympics, were the athletes from all the competing nations. Competitive entrants to the games were restricted to those individuals of Irish birth and those who could lay claim to an Irish heritage. Therefore, although Aonach Tailteann built on many of the traditions of the modern Olympics, its exclusion of all non-Irish peoples, while understandable in the context of recently achieved national freedom, produced a sporting festival that was essentially a celebration of a single ethnic group. The emphasis on those of Irish birth and heritage understandably restricted those nations that could take part in the Tailteann games to traditional areas of Irish immigration. In 1924 the teams that took part were drawn from Ireland, Scotland, England, Wales, the United States, Australia, Canada, South Africa and New Zealand. The competing countries remained unaltered for the two further games, and were, despite Irish independence, effectively dominated, with the exception of the United States, by the nations of the white British Empire.

Reporting the opening day's events *The Irish Times* stated that it:

> had seemed almost impossible that so much ruin could be got out of the way, so many discouraged and apathetic people stimulated into action, so large and complex an organisation completed in a time of political anxiety and industrial distress (*The Irish Times*, 4 Aug. 1924: 4).

Like so many other aspects of political and social life in the newly independent Ireland, Aonach Tailteann was not solely a focus for sporting endeavour, but offered a symbolic victory over the bitterness, division and destruction of a Civil War that had drawn to a close only 13 months earlier. The paper concluded that the opening of the games gave the people of the Irish Free State, 'a success which gives us a new confidence in ourselves. Last Saturday well may prove to have been, in the strictest sense, the most important psychological moment in the history of the Free State' (*The Irish Times*, 4 Aug. 1924: 4). The *Irish Independent*, in its coverage of the opening night banquet at the Metropole Hotel, noted that 'throughout all the speeches ran a note of the confidence as to the future greatness of the country' (*Irish Independent*, 4 Aug. 1924: 4). The paper concluded, in its coverage of the Aonach Tailteann concert which was held at Dublin's Theatre Royal on Sunday 3 August, and closed the opening weekend's events, that

> into a few brief hours were crowded scenes that might fittingly be described as the drama of a nation, the historic pageant of a scattered race, the symbol of its unity and the revival of tradition whose origin is lost in the midst of time (*Irish Independent*, 4 Aug. 1924: 4).

Once opened, the games progressed smoothly, and proved popular amongst the Dublin population. There were criticisms made of local employers who would not allow people to finish work early to attend the games. Criticism was particularly vociferous during the week of athletic competition when events at Croke Park began at 5 p.m., and the period of the swimming tournament at the Dublin Zoological Gardens which began at 4 p.m. Attendances were kept down, commentators felt, as employers did not understand the attraction for working-class men and women of the spectacle of top-class athletes in competition. For those living outside Dublin the different rail excursion packages that were offered also brought many thousands into the city during the Tailteann period.

It is clear, however, that some events failed to ignite the enthusiasm of the populace. The only camogie match played for a Tailteann medal in 1924 was held at the University Parks in Terenure. An Irish team easily defeated an English team by eight points to nil, but only 100 spectators were in attendance. From the newspaper reports, it seems that while the billiards tournament at the Catholic Club on O'Connell Street was keenly contested (the average match lasting 14 hours), spectators rarely numbered more than a dozen. Another problem was the lack of a genuinely competitive field in many of the events. While events such as boxing, staged at the gymnasium at Portobello Barracks attracted fighters from all the competing nations, the rowing attracted entries from only three countries, while the men's golf tournaments at Dollymount saw only one non-Irish entrant. The women's competition at the Hermitage course had no competitors from outside Ireland. In the entire athletics programme, while there were six gold medallists from the recent Paris Olympics, and thus quality, there was not a large competitive field. The Irish had the biggest team with 39 athletes, the US 20, England 18, Australia 9, Canada 6, Scotland 3, while Wales, New Zealand and South

Africa had only a single entrant each. These competitors were supposed to fill a five-day athletic programme between them.

## Reactions

At the close of the 1924 Aonach the press reaction was generally positive. While not making a profit, the Tailteann festival had not apparently collapsed into the financial chaos and debt that some had feared. The festival had brought many tourists to Dublin, and had provided a much-needed boost to the general economy. On the actual fields of play the Irish had performed well, and finished second overall in the final medal tables, although the failure to finish first did provoke some criticism from the Dublin press. The USA led the way with 14.5 first places, 7 runners-up and 6 third-place finishes. Ireland was second with 6.5 first places, 12 seconds and 11 thirds. Australia was placed third in the medal table, well ahead of fourth-placed England. The press reaction, while accepting that total attendance 'may not have come up to the expectations of the promoters' (*Irish Field and Gentleman's Gazette*, 16 Aug. 1924: 9) was favourable. One of Ireland's leading papers concluded in its editorial, 'it has been, from every viewpoint, a triumph beyond expectation' (*Irish Independent*, 16 Aug. 1924: 9).

## Aonach Tailteann and *Dublin Opinion*

While most newspapers and commentators were supportive of Aonach Tailteann, and understood its significance as an event that boosted the prestige of the new state, it was left to the satirical *Dublin Opinion* to make some of the most pertinent criticism of the games. What *Dublin Opinion* concentrated on was a reading of Aonach Tailteann as a spectacle to be consumed by the general public, and did not concern itself with the overall meaning of the event for the country. While this may seem churlish given the evident success of the Tailteann games in boosting national self-esteem, the criticism from *Dublin Opinion* is central to an understanding of why the event eventually folded. As a sporting and cultural event the problem for Aonach Tailteann was that there were too many events that did not necessarily have a cohesive rationale. The field of competitors for most of the events was not of international standard, and the line up of athletes in many was simply too small to attract serious attention. Given the sheer number of events that the organising committee had undertaken to stage, what talent that there was became thinly stretched. It seemed that there was a medal or trophy for everything, and to win a title did not necessitate a world beating performance.

*Dublin Opinion* was a monthly publication, and the August and September issues in 1924 were dominated by attacks on the games. In one cartoon an American lynch mob is depicted as having captured a criminal who is standing on a wagon, a noose around his neck awaiting execution. The 'Master of Ceremonies' asks the condemned man if he has 'anything to say before ye'r lynched?' He replies that he was counting on visiting Ireland for the Tailteann games. In response the Master of Ceremonies tells the gathered crowd, 'release him boys, fate's taken the job out of our hands' (*Dublin Opinion*, Aug. 1924: 181). The reader is asked to understand attendance at the games as an empty and dispiriting act that will do nothing for the spectator. It seemed that death, through boredom and unsated expectation, awaited the Tailteann spectator. The mix of culture and sport also caused the magazine much cause for criticism and merriment. In listing a set of rules for the better governance of Dublin during the period of the games, the magazine suggested that in the unlikely event that any park or enclosure for the games became overcrowded, the Police Force shall be 'empowered to cause one, or more, of the prize winners in the Open Poets' Competition to recite their wares. This should clear the ground, and is preferable to machine gun fire as an expedient for the purpose' (*Dublin Opinion*, Aug. 1924: 182). The eclectic list of competitors, and the fact that the rules defining Irish birth and nationality were loosely applied to get as many athletes to attend as possible, was also a target for the magazine. A cartoon based on the swimming event depicts a steward in conversation with a stereotypical (and racist) image of a black African. The steward quizzes the African on his heritage and is incredulous that the man could be Irish born. The African replies that 'Ah sure am boss. Ah hab Irish blood in me. Ah done ate de las two Free State Consuls' (*Dublin Opinion*, Aug. 1924: 185). While the humour is based around a mythical African, one concludes that it is in fact a sideways swipe at the successful American competitor in the swimming events (and later star of the Tarzan films), John Weissmuller. It seems that he and many American and Australian stars from the recent Olympics were attracted by the promise of a holiday in Ireland en route to home, and that they had little, if any, family connection with Ireland.

The magazine was also clear in its belief that the Tailteann games were a second-class attraction. The Irish press generally was fascinated by the Empire Exhibition at Wembley and was impressed by the cost and scale of the event. Regular adverts appeared in the newspapers selling trips to London so that the Irish could witness the spectacle for themselves. Encapsulating the preference for the attractions of London above those on offer at Croke Park and elsewhere, one cartoon depicted two well-dressed men walking along the seafront of Dublin. They are both civil servants and one expresses the hope that the government will give them a holiday for Tailteann week. The other replies, 'Yes, I'd like to go to Wembley, too' (*Dublin Opinion*, Aug. 1924: 191).

For those who did attend the games, a large number travelled on special train excursions from around Ireland. These were cheap, and were marketed as an opportunity to visit the capital as much as to see the games. It is clear from the spectator figures that not all of those who took part in the excursions necessarily got to the competitive events. A cheap day out in Dublin was perhaps more attractive than attendance at sporting events. Depicting a traditionally dressed and historic Lugh of the Long Arm greeting Queen Tailte, the question is asked what her majesty thought of the games. She replies, 'to tell you the truth, Lugh, I couldn't get to see them all. I was too busy going round the shops' (*Dublin Opinion*, Sept. 1924: 241). The two most damning cartoons in *Dublin Opinion*, were also the most truthful and demonstrate effectively how the sheer size and scale of the sporting programme at the games had led to an event that was in many ways artificial, watered down and unimpressive as a spectacle. The first is a double-spread cartoon that depicts a packed Tailteann crowd watching two athletes in the middle of a huge arena. The athletes in question are two young boys crouched on the floor competing in the 'final of the Tailteann Marbles Competition' (*Dublin Opinion*, Aug. 1924: 198–9). The second cartoon, published the month after the games, was entitled 'Aftermath. A post-Tailteann study'. It depicts a pawnbroker's shop, whose window is crammed full of Tailteann trophies, statues and medals. A large sign in the window of the shop reads 'No more prizes accepted' (*Dublin Opinion*, Sept. 1924: 249). Although harsh, the criticism from *Dublin Opinion* was in fact fair. It is clear that while the event as a whole performed an important state-building function, as a sporting spectacle it fell short of being a successful venture. There were too few quality athletes competing in too many events. Essentially the games did not provide the spectators with a genuinely international sporting event with which they could connect. Too many medals were on offer for, in most sports, a limited amount of effort in small competitive fields. What *Dublin Opinion* understood only too well was that major sporting events had to attract the best athletes on a scale that was manageable and focused. Trying to do everything without competitive spectacle was a recipe for failure and derision.

## Aftermath

Despite such criticism there was a generally warm welcome for the Aonach, and it was viewed as a success by most commentators. However there was, after the closing of the games, real friction between the organising committee and the government. The central problem was one that had dogged the whole Aonach enterprise from the beginning – money. Shortly after the Aonach had finished, the Organising Committee requested the payment of a £7,500 grant that the Government had agreed to in the 1924/5 estimates. The view of the Department of Finance was that as the Aonach had finished, and the Committee should have been in possession of profitable gate receipts, the grant was no longer needed. Walsh was beside himself at such a decision. He wrote to the Minister of Finance, Ernest Blythe, in August 1924, arguing that

> even the most ordinary observer must see that what we are doing is of immense value to the State, not only financially, but also from the point of view of stability and advertisement abroad, and instead of trying to bleed us in this way, the Government of any other country would have given us a free grant of tens of thousands of pounds to run these Games, if not perhaps a million and a quarter, as the French Government freely voted to the Olympic Games. To say the least, the whole thing is petty and unworthy of the occasion.[8]

In response, the Department of Finance, following the Cumann na nGaedheal policy of frugality, argued against Walsh's plea for the funding. In a Department of Finance memo, Minister Blythe was advised that,

> as the receipts from the Aonach may now be presumed to have come into the hands of the Council, it may well be contended that the occasion for the advance has passed and it should now not be made. The only conceivable advantage which the Council could derive from the advance [would be] to by reason of a shortage in the receipts.[9]

The advice received by Blythe was well founded. The Council of Aonach Tailteann owed the Revenue Commissioners £3,000 in unpaid Entertainment Tax, and Blythe was advised that any Government grant to the Council, without the settling of the Revenue Commissioner debts, would lead to a liability for the Government itself.[10] By late November 1924 the Department of Finance had decided to settle the Aonach Council's Revenue Commission bill, and to advance the remainder of the grant so that the whole enterprise was not left owing money. Effectively, the Free State Government, no matter what their feelings towards the whole enterprise and its value, had to underwrite the Aonach so that any negative press comment regarding what was seen as a Government initiative, was deflected. In the eyes of many of his colleagues, however, Walsh's reputation was tainted, and they sought to distance themselves financially and politically, from the running of the event four years later. A report by the Chairman of the Finance Committee in 1925 offered Walsh and his supporters hope. The report noted that, despite the losses that were incurred, 'that, being successful, the holding of the Games had a steadying effect on the National outlook, thereby helping the State'.[11]

## Later games

The second Aonach Tailteann was staged four years later in 1928, and the final event in 1932. The format of the games in later years was little changed from that of 1924, and there were constant arguments between the organising committee and the Department of Finance over the issue of money. With the change of government in 1932, the long-term future of Aonach Tailteann was thrown into doubt. The whole project was firmly linked with Cumann na nGaedheal, and was not something that Fianna Fáil wished to continue with. Although the new government honoured the decision to stage the event in 1932, they did not pursue it beyond that. For Fianna Fáil, new exercises in state building and moves to deconstruct the terms of the 1921 Treaty took centre stage.

In 1932 the last ever Aonach Tailteann was staged to coincide with the Eucharistic Congress that was being held in Ireland in July that year. The decision was by no means popular. It was clear that no top class athletes would attend, and even the Irish Olympians had set sail for Los Angeles before Aonach Tailteann began. The GAA's enthusiasm for taking part in a festival that was departing from its original traditional and Gaelic roots, was waning rapidly. Most centrally, the newly installed Fianna Fáil government led by Eamon de Valera, which would enter a two-decade long policy of careful economic housekeeping in 1932, was not prepared to continue funding a festival whilst government loans remained unpaid. Also, the government viewed the whole event as one that had been set up by their political opponents and which represented the Irish state as imagined by the leadership of Cumann na nGaedheal. The decision to end Aonach Tailteann after 1932 was as much an act of political rejection, as it was a statement of financial frugality.

The 1932 Aonach Tailteann was staged for only a week's duration, rather than the usual fortnight. Compared to the estimated crowd of one million people that packed Phoenix Park to attend the Eucharistic Congress mass, and hear a live broadcast message to the Irish people from the Pope, Aonach Tailteann seemed rather pedestrian. Although encouraging of the whole Tailteann enterprise, the press began asking questions prior to the opening ceremony such as 'Do we believe in the Tailteann games?' (*Irish Field and Gentleman's Gazette*, 2 July 1932: 2) and arguing that the games lacked glamour (*Dublin Evening Mail*, 19 June 1932: 4). By their close, the 1932 games, although following the model set by the 1924 and 1928 festivals, were criticised for being excessively parochial, weakly publicised, poorly attended and lacking in foreign stars. The Fianna Fáil government, which clearly viewed the Aonach as something that it had inherited from the previous government, invested only £1,000 into the event. At the close of the Aonach the games had recorded a loss of £12.[12] In light of the unpaid loans from the first two events, the Aonach had effectively shown itself as financially untenable. Although there was an attempt to organise a fresh event in 1939, support from the Government was not forthcoming. Walsh held de Valera responsible for the decision, and argued that a quadrennial investment by Government of £10,000 into an event that brought the nation such prestige was not unreasonable. De Valera and the Fianna Fáil government were unmoved, and the Aonach was never again staged.

## Conclusion

In conclusion we have to recognise that the decision to stage the Tailteann games in 1924 was a successful exercise in state building as it gave the new Irish nation a platform to display itself and its achievements to both a domestic and international audience. It also importantly delivered, on a grand scale, many of the ideas and concepts of the Gaelic revival that had underpinned the revolution. Despite this success, we also have to recognise that as a sporting spectacle the Tailteann games fell well short of being a successful venture. They were financially draining on a government that was strapped for cash and which had many other more pressing calls for expenditure. Equally they were the preserve of one vision of post-independence Ireland, that of Cumann na nGaedheal. In light of the change of government in 1932 the Tailteann games were bound to disappear as they did not match the ideological concerns of de Valera or Fianna Fáil's view of what Ireland should be. In their entirety the Tailteann games demonstrate how sporting events could be, and remain, an important part of state building and projection. At the same time they also demonstrate that central government has to be fully committed financially to the delivery of sporting excellence and organisation. These events cannot be entered into half-heartedly. The very success of the Olympic games and the World Cup finals is that they provide focused and world-class sporting performance to an expectant audience. The Tailteann games, as with many other events that nations have tried to harness for state-building purposes, did not have a central sporting rationale, and failed to provide, as *Dublin Opinion* so successfully parodied, a focused and competitive spectacle to its audience.

Chapter 5

# Aonach Tailteann, the Irish press and gendered symbols of national identity in the 1920s and 1930s

Louise Ryan

## Introduction

According to legend, Aonach Tailteann – or Tailteann festival – was initiated by Lugh Lamh Fhada (Lugh of the Long Hand) in honour of his stepmother Queen Tailte. It was claimed that the festival of games, music and dance began in the ancient period and continued until the Norman invasion of the twelfth century. Their revival in 1924 marked the return to independence after centuries of occupation (see also chapter 4 above). The games represented continuity with Ireland's ancient and glorious past. Modelled in part on the Olympics, the festival was timed to coincide with those games in 1924, 1928 and 1932. For the newly established state this was an opportunity to host a large, modern, international event which celebrated Irish heritage and its cultural, as well as its sporting traditions. Thus the games embraced both the ancient and the modern in an attempt to define the identity of the nation and, perhaps more significantly, the 'race'. This chapter analyses the reimagining and reconstruction of ancient traditions in the modern Irish Free State through a case study of the 'revival' of the Tailteann Games and the newspaper representations of the central female icon of Queen Tailte. The 'rediscovery' of this ancient motherly figure, and the many conflicting legends which surrounded her, illustrate the processes through which Irishness, Gaelic masculinity and the idealised Irish woman were being negotiated and defined in the 1920s–1930s.

Following the Anglo-Irish War of Independence (1919–21), the establishment of the Free State in 1922 created a need to define not only political boundaries but social and cultural ones as well. According to Maurice Goldring (1993), this new state faced a crisis of legitimacy. In the wake of the bloody Civil War, the new middle-class leaders of the state 'had to justify their power to their own people, to the world and maybe first of all to themselves' (Goldring, 1993: 18). In actively pursuing a programme of nation building, the state was ably supported by the Catholic Church. As Terence Brown has argued, 'crucial to the institutional and popular achievements of the Church . . . was the role played by Catholicism in confirming a sense of national identity' (Brown, 1987: 28). Religion helped to distinguish Irish cultural identity and lifestyle from Englishness and thus had formed part of the impetus for Irish political independence. However, following independence, the Catholic hierarchy expressed concerns about declining morality in Ireland. Foreign cultural influences and years of war and political unrest were blamed for the corruption of Irish virtues (Ryan, 1998).

To counter the corrupting effects of foreign, modern influences, cultural nationalists drew upon a repertoire of traditional images, myths and legends. But it would be simplistic to assume that such cultural symbols were simply accepted and shared by all the peoples of the nation. The case study of Aonach Tailteann illustrates the many complexities and tensions involved in the 'revival' or reinvention of national traditions. It is especially interesting to examine the gendering of symbols and imagery and the processes of inclusion and exclusion that operated to define the limits and boundaries of national identity.

## The symbolic woman

newly independent Ireland was endowed with a repository of myths, images and motifs, literary modes and conventions cultivated to a degree that might indeed have been the envy of most emerging states in this century of infant, fragile nationalisms. The antiquarian literary and cultural activity of the preceding one hundred years had offered Irishmen and women a range of modes of thought and feeling that could confirm national identity and unity (Brown, 1987: 79).

According to Terence Brown, the 'imaginative assets' generated by the late nineteenth-century Literary Revival were particularly important in affirming 'the heroic traditions of the Irish people, directing their attention to the mythological tales of their past, to the heroes and noble deeds of a vanished age' (Brown, 1987: 80). Writers including Lady Gregory, W. B. Yeats and John Millington Synge revived or reinvented the ancient Celtic folklore of brave warriors such as Cuchulain and beautiful, iconographic figures such as Deirdre (Innes, 1993).

Brown argues that this 'literary antiquarianism' could be used as a powerful propagandist weapon because it helped to suggest 'a continuity of experience' between contemporary Ireland and an ancient and noble past (Brown, 1987: 80). Such images and mythologies of the past could be used not only to legitimise but also to define the identity of the newly emerging nation state. The impact of these mythological figures and symbols can be seen throughout the early years of the twentieth century, not just in the plays and poetry of the literary set but in militant nationalist rhetoric and visual representations. For example, the 'cult of Cuchulain', who heroically sacrificed himself in battle, bravely fighting to the end despite his fatal injuries, had a particular resonance for many in the nationalist military movement (Innes, 1993). The connection between the Celtic hero and the Republican uprising of 1916 is visibly represented by the statue of the dying Cuchulain which has been erected in the General Post Office on O'Connell Street, Dublin, the military headquarters of the uprising.

While there were a number of male heroes who represented the warrior spirit of the past, the majority of images, motifs and symbols in Irish nationalist iconography were female (Sharkey, 1994). These female figures represented Ireland as a nation as well as simultaneously embodying national characteristics. Female allegories embodied national sacrifice and suffering (Shan Van Bocht), national purity and integrity (Roisin Dubh) and national vulnerability (Erin or Hibernia). These female icons were evoked by poets, playwrights, politicians and revolutionaries (Gray and Ryan, 1998). Womanly symbols were portrayed as passive, silent, suffering, in opposition to the active strength, courage, heroism and martyrdom of the men they inspired. Of course, the use of female symbols is certainly not unique to Irish nationalism. A range of studies from nationalist campaigns in many different countries indicate the extent to which nationalism is underpinned by a gendered ideology (Mosse, 1985; Parker et al., 1992).

'Gender relations are crucial in understanding and analysing the phenomena of nations and nationalism' (Yuval-Davis, 1993: 621). Writing in the early 1990s, Yuval-Davis stated that little work had been done on systematically analysing the interrelations between gender relations and different dimensions of the nationalist project (1993: 621). Similarly, McClintock (1997: 90) argues that 'feminist analyses of nationalism have been lamentably few and far between'. Over the last decade, Nira Yuval-Davis (1997) alone and also with Floya Anthias (1993) has made a major contribution towards a systematic conceptualisation of gender and nation. In addition, the work of McClintock (1995; 1997), the edited collection by Parker et al. (1992), and the collection of essays edited by Mayer (1999) all go some way towards analysing the complexities of gender relations within nationalisms:

> All nationalisms are gendered, all are invented and all are dangerous ... Nationalism becomes ... radically constitutive of people's identities, through social contests that are frequently violent and always gendered. But if the invented nature of nationalism has found wide theoretical currency, explorations of the

gendering of the national imaginary have been conspicuously paltry (McClintock, 1997: 89).

Both Yuval-Davis (1993) and McClintock (1997) point out that it is necessary to go beyond narrow models of nationalism. McClintock (1997: 93) states that 'there is no single narrative of the nation . . . nationalisms are invented, performed and consumed in ways that do not follow a universal blueprint'. Nevertheless, she claims that all nationalisms are gendered and employ a family iconography that contains women in subordinate and domestic roles.

In analysing the impact of gendered nationalist discourses in India, Shakuntala Rao (1999) argues that the use of female iconography to represent a nation marginalises and simplifies the complexities of real women's experiences. Nationalist rhetoric privileges the imaginary woman over real women.[1] As Hobsbawm (1992) has argued, nationalist legitimacy relies heavily upon 'an invention of tradition'. Or, to borrow Rao's phrase, national identity draws its validity from reimagining, reconstructing and rewriting the pre-colonial and pre-modern. This is particularly apparent in the representations of Queen Tailte.

In analysing gendered symbols of national identity this chapter draws upon both national and provincial newspapers. Newspapers present the most commonplace and widely accessible of all gendered images and symbols of nation and nationhood. They are particularly important for analysing the process of nation building because, as Benedict Anderson (1983) has argued, the print media have facilitated the emergence of national consciousness and the dissemination of national symbols and meanings. In fact, the printed media provided a means through which the national community could be imagined (Anderson, 1983: 44).

## Newspapers representing the nation

> Historians are adept at using media sources as evidence or as primary data, but rarely examine the ways in which newspapers and the broadcast media orchestrate and construct their messages (Gibbons, 1996: 10).

Newspapers played a key role not only in reporting the project of nation building but also actively participating in that project. In addition to being widely available to the general public, newspapers, unlike, for example, novels, plays and poetry, claimed to be impartial and objective in their representations of Irish people and society. In the early decades of independence, newspapers were the dominant form of media communication and played a key role in supporting, defining and explaining the newly created Irish Free State to their readers (Ryan, 2002). The press was additionally important in the Irish case because of the very high rate of literacy. Newspapers disseminated messages from politicians, regularly reprinting political speeches, usually reinforced through editorial comment. Newspapers also helped to disseminate the teachings of the Catholic Church: sermons, Lenten pastorals and various speeches were regularly reprinted in great detail in both national and provincial papers. As a result newspapers are useful for analysing the powerful gender ideologies underpinning the political and religious structures of the state. Goldring (1993) indicates that the press formed part of a series of relays and transmissions that actively sought to contribute to the formation of Irish national community and identity.

In many ways, the newspapers were clearly aware of this role. For example, in January 1925, the *Irish Independent* editorial stated the policy of that paper as being 'to foster a strong spirit of sane nationalism, to help in guiding the people's thoughts towards the problems of practical politics and . . . to serve the nation by honest and fearless criticism' (*Irish Independent*, 2 Jan. 1925). However, the study of newspapers in this chapter also attempts to illustrate the other discourses that existed alongside and in opposition to the dominant voices. An examination of the national and provincial press uncovers a variety of conflicting and competing discourses. In fact, newspapers provide an insight into the complex and multifaceted nature of attitudes and opinions in the Irish Free State and offer a fascinating and under-researched insight into the many-layered constructions of Irishness in the early years of the Free State.

## Gendered symbols and the 'revival' of Aonach Tailteann

On 20 August 1927, *The Kerryman* newspaper reprinted an article from the Irish-American paper *National Hibernian*:

> The Tailteann games are to Ireland what the Olympic games were to ancient Greece. Nothing that the Irish people could do in a political way has rivalled what the Tailteann games will do eventually to knit the nation into unity. Only among such a people as the Irish could there have existed through more than two thousand years the games and sports which are a symbol of a race (*The Kerryman*, 20 Aug. 1927).

The article claimed in addition that the games would help to unite the scattered Irish peoples from across the world so that, in time, they would look to 'Ireland as the Motherland'. The games provided an opportunity for 'Irishmen' throughout the world to come together in celebration of Ireland. The Tailteann games had 'risen from the past to be a beacon for the future'.

In this sense the games simultaneously represented continuity with past traditions and a bright hope for the future of the country. Newspaper articles such as this provide a valuable insight into constructions of Irish national/ cultural identity and the celebration of traditions as well as looking forward to the bright prospects for the future. But, as Cronin has demonstrated in the previous chapter, in this case as in so many others, newspapers offer diverse accounts which provide a range of possible interpretations of national events such as Aonach Tailteann. For instance, while some papers celebrated the success of the games, others condemned them as badly organised and a waste of money (*Wicklow People*, 21 Jan. 1928).

Of all the papers, it was the Dublin-based, national dailies – the *Irish Independent* and *The Irish Times*, and later the *Irish Press* – which devoted most coverage to the festival. For example, the games of 1928 received widespread coverage. Between 11 and 26 August 1928, the Tailteann games were held in Dublin (although some events were staged outside the city, such as the rowing events held on the River Lee in Cork). On 4 August 1928, the *Independent* gave lengthy coverage to the Aonach Tailteann which was heralded as the return of the Gael. This 'return' had a double significance. On the one hand, it represented the return to Ireland of Gaels from all over the world, emigrants and the children of emigrants. On the other hand, the notion of 'return' also represented the re-establishment of Gaelic pride, identity, tradition after centuries of suppression, a return to past glories and self-confidence. *The Irish Times* cited the director of the games, Mr J. J. Walsh speaking at the Tailteann banquet in Dublin on the eve of the opening ceremony: 'Aonach Tailteann was nothing new. Rather did it go right to the root of Celtic history . . . Tailteann of Tara was the beacon of light of a distinct and vigorous civilisation'. He added that the revival 'was proof of the tenacity with which their race had clung to the ideal of a distinctive place in the family of ancient peoples' (*The Irish Times*, 13 Aug. 1928).

The national dailies highlighted and celebrated the symbolism of the festival. The festival was named after the ancient Celtic Queen Tailte and her image was strongly associated with the revived games. The papers carried photographs of the actress, Nancy Rock, who played the part of Queen Tailte in the pageant that marked the opening of the festivals in 1924, 1928 and 1932. On 12 August 1924, *The Irish Times* carried a photograph of Miss Rock as she was about to portray Queen Tailte for the first time in a play at the Theatre Royal in Dublin. On the following day, 13 August, *The Irish Times* published a review of the production under the heading 'Queen Tailte: A Vision Play'. Written by Major Lawlor of the National Army, the play was based on a reconstruction of the life of Tailte shown through a series of tableaux. Between each tableau, a *seanachi* (storyteller) narrated the story of Tailte, her husband Eochaidh, last of the Firbolg kings of Ireland, and her stepson Lugh

Lamh Fhada. 'Miss Rock looked every inch the Queen'. The play was directed by her mother, Mrs Rock, and most of the participants were members of the Rock School of Dance and Drama.

On 4 August 1928, the *Independent* carried a photograph of Nancy Rock dressed in 'traditional' Celtic clothing. Wearing a long dress and cloak tied with a large Celtic brooch, her hair plaited into two long braids reaching her waist, she was adorned in bangles and other jewellery rich in Celtic design and symbolism. On 13 August 1928, *The Irish Times* and the *Independent* carried a whole series of photographs from the opening ceremony of the games. The *Irish Times* described the event under the headline 'Tailteann Games: Opening Ceremony at Croke Park, 20,000 Present'.

> The most appealing note was struck by the tableau of Queen Tailte, attended by Chieftains and maids, presented by the players who are to take part in the production of *The Vision of Queen Tailte* at the Theatre Royal on Sunday night. Miss Nancy Rock was an impressive figure in the part of the Queen (*The Irish Times*, 13 Aug. 1928).

There was a close-up picture of Miss Rock/Queen Tailte in profile pose. She was wearing a head-dress and enormous earrings in a Celtic design which obscured her face. Yet again she was draped in a cloak fastened by a large brooch.

The *Independent* carried similar photographs of the procession and pageant. Included amongst the photographs was a large picture of a procession of men and women 'wearing ancient Irish costume'. In the foreground were two rows of women walking across the packed arena. All dressed like Queen Tailte, with long braided hair, they carried very tall spears which towered over their heads. The men were in the background wearing short tunics and carrying shields and spears. There was a separate picture of Queen Tailte (Nancy Rock), 'after whom the games are called'. This time she was standing, again dressed in 'traditional' Celtic clothes, with an Irish wolfhound by her side, but it is noteworthy that she also wore rather modern, 1920s-style high-heeled shoes (*Irish Independent*, 13 Aug. 1928).

From her first appearance as Tailte in 1924, Nancy Rock seems to have become a central figure of the festival. This striking young woman came to embody the ancient Queen but in so doing she both shaped and was shaped by notions of the glorious past.

As discussed at the start of this chapter, the deliberate reimagining and reconstructing of a pure and ancient indigenousness, free from all colonial/ foreign influences, is a central part of nationalism. The figure of Queen Tailte embodied ancient Ireland. Her hair, clothing, jewellery and even the wolf-hound, locate her in the distant past, or at least a particular representation of the past. Unlike the short skirt-wearing, bobbed-haired, cigarette-smoking flapper of the 1920s, who embraced modern decadence and foreign fashions, Queen Tailte embodied all that was good and pure in Irish society (Ryan, 2002). However, the photograph of Miss Rock wearing modern high-heeled shoes represents a jarring note although in so doing it also symbolises the many inherent contradictions in this image of Ireland, Irishness and Tailte herself.

## Reconfiguring Tailte: from Celtic goddess to Gaelic mother

On closer examination it seems that the Celtic queen was a very ambiguous character. On 2 June 1928, the *Sligo Champion* provided additional back-ground history to the origins of Aonach Tailteann:

> Aonach Tailteann was instituted by Lugh Lamh Fhada, a prince of the Tuatha de Danaan. The festival was in commemoration of Queen Tailte, a Spanish lady wife of Eochaidh, king of the Firbolg (*Sligo Champion*, 2 June 1928).

This history locates the festival deep in the mists of ancient Celtic legend, in the time of noble warriors and warring tribes when Ireland was ruled by scores of rival kings and armies. However, what is most noteworthy about this short paragraph is the fact that it describes the famous queen as 'a Spanish lady' – not Irish at all. The identity of Tailte remained a matter of speculation. Interestingly, it was in the *Irish Press*, founded by de Valera's political party *Fianna Fáil* in the early 1930s and arguably the most Catholic and nationalist of all three main dailies, that an alternative reading of Tailte was provided in 1932. In a special feature article, Seamus MacCall explores the possible origins of Tailte and offers a more analytical and critical perspective than most other sources at that time.

> Aonach Tailteann is the oldest of several great festivals which were periodically celebrated in Ireland. It is also the newest. It began in some period too remote to define with certainty (*Irish Press*, 20 June 1932).

In this opening paragraph, MacCall expresses his awareness of the extent to which Aonach Tailteann is 'new' and hence reconstructed in the modern period. He is wary of asserting any precise starting date for the festival. However, he agrees that the festival shares many similar characteristics with ancient Greek festivals. Indeed, he pushes this comparison further than other commentators had done.

The 'rationalised' tradition tells us that the first Aonach Tailteann was an 'assembly of lamentation' ordained by Lugh in honour of his foster mother Tailte (*Irish Press*, 20 June 1932).

MacCall repeats the story that she was the daughter of a Spanish king. But then he begins to cast serious doubt on this 'rationalised' version of events. He suggests that the notion that Tailte was from abroad, across the sea, a foreigner, is really an indication that she was otherworldly, that she was not from this world:

> Tailte or Tailtiu was no mortal but a goddess whose known attributes clearly indicate that she was patroness of agriculture, or in other words a goddess of fertility. . . . Lugh, her supposed foster son, was even more certainly the old Irish sun god, whose 'long arms' were to be seen in the sun's rays (*Irish Press*, 20 June 1932).

MacCall goes on to make the argument that the festival, which traditionally took place in August, was also known as *Lughnasadh*. It may well have had its origins in a kind of harvest festival 'in which the first ripening was symbolised as a meeting of the sun god and the goddess of fertility'. As is the case with similar Greek festivals, the gods were honoured by displays of games, dances and contests. MacCall draws on a number of classical texts and, although he is strongly influenced by interpretations of Greek mythology, his analysis of Celtic symbols and myths is convincing. Clearly Tailte was a highly complex and ambiguous figure. On the one hand, her previous incarnation as a sexualised goddess of fertility might well suggest that she was an unsuitable icon for a Catholic nation. But, on the other hand, the success with which she was reconstructed as a safe, motherly symbol suggests a very deliberate, self-conscious process of nationalist reappropriation and reinvention of the past.

This reinvention was framed by the ambiguity of Celticism versus the Gaelicisation of Irish society. Catherine Nash (1993) has written about the contrasts between different schools of thought on national identity in Ireland at the beginning of the twentieth century. She refers to the 'Celtic' symbols associated with the Literary Revival of Yeats and Lady Gregory. These drew on pagan mythology and represented a sexualised image of Irish womanhood perhaps best symbolised by Cathleen Ni Houlihan. On the other hand, there was a 'Gaelic' notion of Irishness associated with the Irish-Ireland movement of D. P. Moran and Daniel Corkery. This proposed a more sanitised, de-sexualised representation of Irish women symbolised by the Sean Bhan Bhocht. The Celtic/Gaelic dichotomy represented a conflict not only in terms of language and religion but also in terms of the particular reading of Ireland's past and its implications for Ireland's future (Nash, 1993). Nash argues that the constructions of femininity by cultural nationalists in the early 1900s, and later by the church and the new state:

denied women an autonomous sexuality in their idealization of asexual motherhood. The young woman was replaced by the depiction of the old peasant woman
who could represent the successful outcome of a life lived in accordance with the
demands of motherhood . . . and way of life extolled in the state (Nash 1993: 47).

Nash's work is important because she indicates the existence of, and indeed
opposition between, two contrasting symbolic representations of Ireland and
Irish women. The analysis of Tailte in this chapter suggests that this particular
female symbol visibly embodied the tensions and contradictions between the
Celtic and Gaelic discourses of Irish national identity. It is apparent that
Aonach Tailteann was predominantly represented as Catholic/Gaelic although
the myths and symbolism upon which it was based could equally be termed
pagan/Celtic.

Some of these tensions are hinted at in an *Irish Times* editorial in August
1924:

> Persons who lay stress on the Gaelic element in the racial origins of the Irish
> people take the old Aonach Tailteann as standing for a tradition of Gaelic cul-
> ture . . . there are, of course, large numbers of Irish people to whom the Gaelic
> tradition has never made very strong appeal. They, however, with their share of
> Irish imagination and idealism, have appreciated the purpose of the promoters of
> a revived Aonach Tailteann, and the festival now enjoys the sympathy . . . of
> *Irishmen* of every class [emphasis added] (The *Irish Times*, 4 Aug. 1924).

This quotation demonstrates simultaneously the inclusiveness and exclusive-
ness of the ideology underpinning the festival. The ambiguity of the Celtic
versus Gaelic symbolism allows for the inclusion of all of those who share an
interest in Irish history and culture even if they disagree about the precise
origins of its traditions. However, this quotation also underlines the masculinity of the festival and in so doing highlights the ways in which women were
both excluded and celebrated within the revival of Aonach Tailteann. As has
been argued above, the process of nation building and defining national
identity was highly gendered. The masculine strengths of national manhood
were constructed in opposition to the dependency, fragility and purity of
national womanhood (Gray and Ryan, 1998). Particularly in Gaelic-Catholic
iconography, the Gael was an exclusively male figure who represented the best
aspects of Ireland's past glory and future aspirations. The corresponding
female role was that of the idealised mother, devoted, selfless and desexualised
(Nash, 1993: 47). It is surely no coincidence that while the Gaelic man was to
test his manhood on the sports field, woman as depicted by Queen Tailte was
constructed as loyal wife and mother – or in the case of Tailte stepmother to
Lugh Lamh Fhada.

This imagery of motherhood was used repeatedly by the press in describing the significance of the festival. It is apparent that the entire festival of games, Irish songs and dance took on a cultural and national importance far beyond the particular event itself. On 11 August, the *Independent* carried an article entitled 'In the Name of an Irish Queen'. The sub-heading read: 'Tailte takes her children to her bosom. Old Glories Revived.'

> The sons of the scattered Gael have come home again. They have crossed the seven seas at the bidding of the land from which their sires have sprung. They have come in the name of an Irish Queen, and today mid the regal splendour of far-off days, and the pristine glory of a Golden age, she will clasp them to her bosom in joyful, loving welcome (*Irish Independent*, 11 Aug. 1928).

This quotation is rich in gendered symbolism. Queen Tailte represents Ireland, a motherland from whom 'sires' had 'sprung', now clasping her long lost sons to her welcoming bosom. Thus the Gaels are all represented as men, while the land/nation is female. This motherly symbol embodies continuity with past glories, heritage and tradition. If the legend of Tailte originated in the fertility goddess Tailtiu, as MacCall suggested, then her reappropriation as mother Ireland seems oddly appropriate. But that process of her reinvention also indicates the extent to which she was sanitised and transformed from powerful Celtic goddess to the weaker and more passive mother of the Gael.

## The manly Gael

The gendered symbolism of the festival was reinforced in an editorial in the *Independent* a few days later:

> Few races have a stronger sense of historic continuity than the Irish, and through long centuries not least of the aims of the national struggle was to restore contacts that had been ruthlessly severed by the laws, as well as by the sword of the invader. There have been few happier inspirations than the decision that the emergence of a new Ireland should be followed by the revival of Aonach Tailteann. The festival dates back almost to the dawn of history . . . the tradition embodied in the games is expressive of emotions and ideals that make as strong an appeal to the Irishman of today as they did to his ancestors (*Irish Independent*, 13 Aug. 1928).

Although the British invaders had tried to undermine traditional Irish language and culture, the revival of the festival ensured the continuity of a distinctive Irish national identity. However, this symbolism continues to be gendered in the sense that the spirit of the games appeals to Irish man. The

Irish race is thus not only constructed as distinct, unique and ancient but also as masculine. The festival aimed to include Irish competitors from around the world and was especially keen to attract Irish-American athletes. Indeed, participants were reported from Canada, New Zealand, Australia and parts of Britain as well as the USA. But there was concern that perhaps not all of these were of Irish descent. Later in the month, when the games were completed, the *Independent* editorial returned to the topic:

> The revival of Aonach Tailteann after a lapse of seven and a half centuries was a bold and ambitious undertaking . . . The changes wrought by time could not be undone; and so the promoters had the delicate task of devising a scheme that would fit into the modern order of things without doing violence to the essential character of the ancient festival, and to preserve the racial solidarity of which Aonach Tailteann was once a living proof . . . If the games are to fulfil their purpose the organisers must see that only those of Irish descent participate (*Irish Independent*, 27 Aug. 1928).

It is not clear if this editorial referred to one particular athlete or group of athletes who had participated in the games. It is apparent that some competitors were not Irish at all. For example, the swimmer Johnny Weissmuller, who later became famous in the Tarzan films, was invited to participate in the 1924 games despite having no Irish connections.[2] It is very clear, however, that the *Independent* viewed the games as a showcase for Irish talent and an opportunity to assert racial solidarity free from any foreign, i.e. non-Irish, interference. Nevertheless, it would appear that not everyone agreed on the game's racial exclusivity. In 1932 when the third revival was held, *The Irish Times* devoted an editorial to the question of who should be allowed to compete:

> The games of 1932 promise to surpass in all respects the festivals of 1924 and 1928 . . . in the present games – it was not possible to observe the rules strictly in the two preceding festivals – every competitor is Irish or of Irish descent. The surprise is that, under such a limitation, the entry has been so large and has come from so many quarters of the earth (*The Irish Times*, 30 June 1932).

However, the editorial adds a note of caution. While generally supporting the rule, the article speculates on the possibility of embracing 'a selected few of the great foreign athletes whom Ireland sees all too seldom'. Their inclusion would make the games no less Irish in character. Thus for *The Irish Times* at least, foreign athletes, especially very great ones, should be invited to attend the games, although few foreign athletes attended the games in 1932. This was not merely as a result of the Irish descent rule but also because, unlike in 1924 and 1928, the Olympic games were not being held in Europe and thus most international athletes were not available to travel to Europe in the summer of 1932. However, the games did coincide with another event in Ireland that may have helped to boost the attendance. In 1932 Ireland played host to the Eucharistic congress which saw bishops and cardinals from around the world attending numerous religious ceremonies across the country. Many of these turned out to watch the opening ceremony on 29 June.

Once again, the *Irish Independent* and *The Irish Times*, now joined by the newly established *Irish Press*, included vivid descriptions of the elaborate opening ceremony and parade of athletes. As in previous games, the image of Queen Tailte (portrayed once again by Nancy Rock) continued to be very much in evidence:

> Something of the historic glory of the court of Tailte, Queen of Ireland, was revived in Croke Park, Dublin, yesterday afternoon, at the opening ceremony of the third revival within recent years of the games, first organised in 632 BC by Lugh Lamh Fhada, in honour of his foster mother, Queen Tailte (*The Irish Times*, 30 June 1932).

The comments are interesting, firstly because they reiterate the notion of 'historic glory' so often mentioned in the previous reports of Aonach Tailteann. Nearly a decade after their initial revival the games were being repeatedly described as a symbol of continuity with the ancient past. Secondly, that past was now being linked very specifically to the date 632 BC. Considering that *The Irish Times* had earlier described the central characters as 'fabled' (*The Irish Times*, 13 Aug. 1928), it is curious that an exact historical date was being accorded to the commencement of the games. Thirdly, although Tailte was here described as foster mother rather than stepmother, she was nonetheless being contained within her mothering relationship to Lugh, who remained the active founder of the games, whereas she is merely the muse, the passive source of inspiration.

In anticipation of 'Ireland's Great Sport Festival', the *Irish Press* published a special feature article on 28 June 1932. Across the top of the page were the photographs of 11 sporting heroes, all male, who were expected to participate in the games. These included boxers and hurlers, both Irish born and of Irish descent. Beneath them was a picture of a bronze statuette of Queen Tailte, holding a laurel wreath in each of her outstretched hands. She wore a long flowing gown and a cloak fastened over one shoulder. The lengthy article which accompanied these photographs reinforced the gendered imagery. The games were described as important in strengthening 'moral fibre' and so enhancing 'chivalry' and 'manhood'. The games were not only a display of national distinctiveness but celebrated the traditions of 'a virile race'. The fact that scores of women competed in events such as swimming and the vigorous game of camogie (a female version of hurling), as well as in the cultural events of dancing and singing, was not represented at all either in the images or the words of this article.

The opening ceremony of 1932 was presided over by Eamon de Valera (who had boycotted the original revival in 1924), having recently been elected president of the Free State. De Valera was accompanied on the viewing stand by his eminence Cardinal MacRory, leader of the Catholic Church in Ireland. This led to a rather interesting and unspoken anomaly:

> The crowd beheld a young man clad in skin garments leading a large Irish wolfhound . . . massed bands of Irish pipers, with the Black raven standard at their head, led the members of Tailte's court into the arena. The glory that was Ireland, a young giant with sun tanned limbs, Lugh Lamh Fhada, preceded them. All the splendour of their court robes was revealed as Queen Tailte, her hand-maidens, druids and warriors extended their right arm in salute to Cardinal MacRory (*The Irish Times*, 30 June 1932).

The image of 'Celtic' royalty extending a salute to the head of the Catholic Church reveals many of the underlying tensions and contradictions in the revival of such ancient pagan myths in a modern, Catholic democratic state.

During each of the three festivals, the national press devoted a great deal of daily coverage to the wide range of sporting and cultural events. There were regular reports on the traditional Irish singing and dancing competitions as well as more unusual events like the pipe band competition. Traditional Irish games such as handball, Gaelic football, hurling and camogie shared the programme with athletics, swimming, gymnastics, boxing, rowing, cycling, chess and the marathon. The press reiterated the games' great importance to the nation. As has been discussed by other researchers, including contributors to this collection of essays, sport has played a particularly significant role in constructions of Irish national identity (Bairner, 2001a; Cronin, 1999; McDevitt, 1997). Revived games such as hurling and Gaelic football produced an image of Irish masculinity based on order, strength and virtue (McDevitt, 1997). These games, organised by the nationalist Gaelic Athletic Association, served the dual purpose of giving Irish men a form of self-expression which was perceived as entirely distinct from British sporting activities. In addition, these healthy, energetic and skilful pursuits helped to counter British stereotypes of the Irish as lazy, disorderly and unskilled.

The Catholic Church's views on sport were clearly stated in an article that appeared in the *Cork Examiner* in July 1928 in the regular weekly section, 'Catholic News of the Week'. The article emphasised that sport taught discipline, teamwork and the importance of rules. 'The youth learns to curb his character and passions'. Physical training brought the body under control and this led to the 'greater honour and glory of God'. At a time when the Church was obsessed with the sexual immorality of young people, the value of sport in regulating behaviour was important for both sexes:

> The hockey fields, tennis grounds and gymnasiums have brought out the better development of young girls, so important to her in afterlife for the bringing up of healthy children (*Cork Examiner*, 14 July 1928).

Thus sport was also a healthy pursuit for young women as it took their minds off clothes, dancing and cinema. In addition, sport prepared women for their true role in life – motherhood. While women did participate in Aonach Tailteann, most of the focus of attention in the press was on male competitors with the masculine Gaels representing the spirit of the games. The most prevalent female image was Queen Tailte herself, who passively embodied Ireland and Irish traditional culture rather than actively representing female participation in the games. Thus, as argued at the beginning of this chapter, women are usually not well served by womanly symbols. Instead, female icons frequently silence and exclude women from public nationalist discourses. In this particular case, the imaginary woman (Tailte) is privileged over real women (the female competitors).

## Conclusion

Brown (1987) argues that within the harsh economic climate of the 1920s and 1930s events such as Aonach Tailteann failed to inspire widespread public enthusiasm. Attempts to stage the festival in 1936 were abandoned largely because of financial problems. Nevertheless, as this chapter has shown, events like Aonach Tailteann provide a fascinating insight into the symbolic repertoire of nationalism. The process of nation building is a highly gendered project. Nationalist symbolism, iconography and rhetoric are all underpinned by representations of the idealised national male and female. Like many other anti-colonial nationalist projects, Irish nationalism defined the process of national reconstruction through a moral discourse that was inherently gendered (Thapar-Bjorkert and Ryan, 2002). Newspapers offer a valuable and under-researched insight into these gendered nationalist symbols (Ryan, 2002). This analysis of press reporting on Aonach Tailteann 1924, 1928 and 1932 reveals many aspects of the ways in which the Irish press engaged with and reinforced particular representations of Ireland and Irishness in the early decades of the Irish Free State.

It is important not to underestimate the complexity and multifaceted nature of nationalist myths and symbols. As Nash (1993) has argued, ancient legends and iconography provided a site for a range of competing discourses. Gendered symbols of national culture, tradition and identity reveal the processes through which the nation was imagined and depicted. Images of virtuous masculinity and motherly femininity overlapped with Catholic and nationalist iconography of Irish identity. Continuity with the 'glorious past' and a stable, successful future were embodied especially in female allegories of Ireland and Irish womanhood. However, the discussion of Aonach Tailteann also suggests that representations of the nation and nationalist programmes of nation building were by no means straightforward and unproblematic. As Cronin has already demonstrated in the previous chapter, the press did not speak with one monolithic voice. Newspaper reports indicate the tensions that existed between various interest groups. Perhaps these tensions suggest why ambiguous symbols like Queen Tailte were so useful as they helped to smooth over the tensions and divisions, by representing a very general notion of past glories and future possibilities.

Chapter 6

# Gaelic games and the Irish immigrant experience in Boston

Paul Darby

## Introduction

On the first Sunday of September 2000, two evenly matched Gaelic football teams took to the field of play to contest an eagerly awaited championship final. The game took place amid rituals, emblems and symbols quintessential to Ireland and Irish identity. For example, the players were led by on to the field by a traditional Irish pipe band and were paraded around the pitch perimeter behind a flag bearer carrying the Irish tricolour. Following the singing of *Amhrán na bhFiann*, the Irish national anthem, the gathered ranks settled in their seats to await the conclusion of a season which had begun the previous March. On completion of the game, the victorious captain made part of his acceptance speech in Irish. At around the same time, similar events had taken place or were about to take place in every county in Ireland. However, the events described above occurred almost 3,000 miles from Ireland in the Boston suburb of Canton which had just played host to the North American Gaelic Athletic Association play-offs and had witnessed a team from Chicago (St Brendan's) overcome one from Boston (Cork).[1]

Although Gaelic sports have been played in an organised fashion for over a century in the United States, academic research on the development and functions of these sports amongst the Irish diaspora has been extremely limited. That this is the case is hardly surprising given the more general disregard for the significance of sport in the burgeoning literature examining the Irish experience in America. In its most general guise, this study seeks to redress this neglect. More specifically, the chapter explores the transfer of Gaelic sports from Ireland to one of the most significant focal points of Irish immigration, Boston. This analysis identifies and examines the key agencies and individuals responsible for the early growth and subsequent development of Irish sports in Boston and assesses the extent to which they eased the transition from the 'old country' to the New World. Central to this study is a consideration of the role that these sports played in allowing the Irish émigré in Boston to preserve and promote a distinctively Irish ethnic identity and to give vent to Irish nationalist sentiment.

## Sport and the Irish immigrant in late nineteenth-century Boston

For those who arrived in Boston from Ireland during the great waves of immigration between 1815 and 1860, life was generally inhospitable and harsh. They were confronted with a city dominated by an establishment that was Anglo-Protestant and puritan and which harboured deep suspicions of and distaste for Catholicism. Social, economic and racist discrimination and prejudice by established Bostonians and nativists contributed to a sense of alienation and persecution within the Irish enclaves that sprang up predominantly around the dock areas, in the slums of the city's north end and in South Boston. Despite the difficulties encountered by Boston's Irish community in this period, they were sustained, in many ways, by a range of institutions, not least of which was the Catholic Church and newspapers such as the *Boston Pilot*, which allowed them to preserve a sense of communal identity. Irish ethnic neighbourhoods were particularly important in this respect. Although they had functioned in many senses as 'ghettoes of mind and place' (McCaffrey, 1992; McCaffrey, 1997), they gradually came to represent 'psychological havens . . . focused around the Catholic parish . . . preserving faith, tradition, and values, perpetuating a sense of community' (McCaffrey, 1997: 71).

The decline of the American Nativist Party in the late 1850s, distinguished service in preserving the Union during the Civil War and a rapid advance within local ward politics in Boston in the post 1860 period did much to facilitate a degree of acceptance and social mobility for sections of the Irish immigrant population. The abilities and electoral successes of a range of Irish politicians increasingly provided the Irish community with a voice with which to challenge the established Protestant hegemony and gradually redress the discrimination that emanated from it. Thus, with improving opportunities, prospects and standards of living, the Boston that welcomed Irish immigrants in the second half of the nineteenth and early years of the twentieth centuries was considerably more hospitable than that encountered by those who had arrived in the city earlier.

It has been widely recognised that the successes of their politicians, the efforts of their Church and the solace, identity and friendships offered by a whole range of their social, cultural and political organisations did much to help the Irish adapt to life in urban Boston. Less has been said about the role of sport in helping them deal with the rigours of adjusting to what was, in the 1880s, an improving but still difficult environment. Only the work of Ralph

Wilcox (1992), Steven Reiss (1992) and, to a lesser extent, Lawrence McCaffrey (1992) has examined the significance of sport in this respect. They have demonstrated the ways in which the Boston Irish drew on American sports, particularly baseball and later basketball, to provide much needed self-esteem, ease their assimilation into their new environment and protect and preserve Irish ethnic pride and identity. Although these authors have all touched on the significance of Gaelic games in the lives of the Irish émigré in late nineteenth-century Boston, there has yet to be the type of sustained analysis of the functions of these games for the Boston Irish that now follows.

## The origins and early years of Gaelic sport in Boston

The roots of Gaelic games in Boston can be found in the inception of the Irish Athletic Club of Boston (IACB) in September 1879 which was founded by and composed of first generation Irishmen (*Boston Pilot*, 4 Oct. 1879: 5). In view of the club's composition, it is unsurprising that its central remit was to promote 'the preservation of the national games, sports, and pastimes of Ireland' amongst Boston's Irish community (*Boston Pilot*, 12 June 1886: 8). On 29 September in its inaugural year, the club organised its first annual field sports meet or 'picnic' as it was referred to at the time. The meet took place at the Centennial Grounds in Wandem, Massachusetts, north of Boston, and consisted of a varied sporting programme which included activities such as high and long jumping, a form of football and a number of games that were specifically Irish in their intonation. For example, the ancient game of *baire* or *goaling*, which involved the striking of a hard ball with a hurling stick, was one of the focal points of the day's proceedings. In the press reports of the afternoon's activities much was made of the Irish roots of the game: 'It [*baire*] is specially an Irish game, and the etymology of its Irish name takes us back into remotest antiquity' (*Boston Pilot*, 4 Oct. 1879: 5). The fact that the event closed with a 'great hurling match' involving 32 players from each county in Ireland further reinforced the specifically Irish complexion of the afternoon's sporting activities.

During the 1880s, the IACB repeated its midsummer festivals and on each occasion the promotion of specifically Irish sporting pastimes and culture was very much to the fore. For example, the meet held at Oak Island, north of Boston, on 17 June 1886, was celebrated as an *Aonach*, or festival, of Ancient Ireland, whilst two years later the event was reorganised in order for it to encompass 'a full representation of peculiarly Irish [games]' (*Boston Pilot*, 12 June 1886: 8, see also *Irish Echo*, July 1888: 4). From the mid-1880s onwards, these festivals and participation in Gaelic games more generally were portrayed in the Irish American press as being integral parts of Irish culture and quintessential to what it meant to be Irish. For example, in May 1887, *The Gael*, a monthly New York journal devoted to the 'cultivation and preservation of the Irish language and the autonomy of the Irish nation' (*The Gael*, January 1882: 1), published a poem which carried a romanticised, but nonetheless evocative, account of the place of the sport of hurling in the Irish national consciousness and its significance for the Irish Diaspora. 'An Irish Hurling-Green: A Ballad for the Gael' opened with the following lines:

> Full many years, 'neath foreign skies,
> A stranger have I strayed,
> I've mingled in their sportive joys,
> And heard their music played;
> But still the dearest spot on earth –
> Which links me to its scene –
> For cheerful, hearty, guileless mirth,
> Is an Irish hurling-green (*The Gael*, May 1887: 705).

The tone of newspaper reports of the formation, in 1884, and early activities of the Gaelic Athletic Association (GAA), was very much in keeping with this idealised but rousing interpretation of the centrality of Gaelic games in the construction of Irish identity. For example, in an article in the *Irish Echo* on the 1888 annual field sports meet at Oak Island, the GAA's activities were reported in the following manner:

> recently the spirit of patriotism and freedom by which the Irish at home are being animated, has suggested to them that their national games and pastimes should be revived, and the result is a national association called the Gaelic Athletic Association. . . . and the movement is encouraged by no less a personage than Archbishop Croke of Cashel, who is the patron of the national association (*Irish Echo*, July 1888: 4).

The significance of narratives like this and the more general portrayal of Irish sporting pastimes as emblematic of Irish identity and aspirations for independence was that they reinforced the resolve of organisations like the IACB to persevere with its endeavours to spread and promote Gaelic games throughout Boston. In addition, by conveying the philosophy and ideals of Gaelic sport in this manner, such press coverage also bolstered the desire of nationalist-minded Irish immigrants to support the games of the 'old country' either through participation or financial investment.

The programme of activities during those meets held in the second half of the 1880s continued to be made up of games that were, at least according to modern standards, uncodified. However, in 1886 Boston witnessed the first game of Gaelic football played outside Ireland under the new rules laid down by the GAA. The game took place on Boston Common in June when Galway and Kerry, two of the strongest and most successful Gaelic football clubs in Boston today, contested a keenly fought match (Hehir, 2000; Irish Cultural Centre, 1999). In a similar fashion to the IACB's annual field sport meets, this game served to heighten interest and increase awareness of opportunities to engage in sports which offered the émigré a sense of the familiar in strange surroundings. The growing profile of Gaelic sport was augmented two years later by an initiative aimed at reviving the ancient Tailteann Games.

As Cronin noted earlier in chapter 4, Michael Cusack, the founding father of the GAA, envisaged that the first edition of the revived games would take place in Dublin in the summer of 1889 and optimistically anticipated that the event would attract participants and spectators from all over Ireland and from the Irish Diaspora in America and Britain (De Búrca, 1999). In a move intended to raise the £5,000 required to implement Cusack's ambitious vision, Maurice Davin, the first President of the GAA, approached the Association's Central Council in April 1888 and proposed a fundraising tour by Irish athletes to America.

The touring party's arrival in New York in late September was heralded in the Irish American press at the time as the 'Gaelic Invasion of America' (*Irish Echo*, Oct. 1888, 4). During their six-week visit they played exhibition hurling games and participated in athletic contests in New York and in a number of other centres of Irish immigration including Boston, Philadelphia, Trenton, Newark, Patterson, Providence and Lowell (*Donahoe's Magazine*, Nov. 1888: 474). Although the 'invasion' was viewed as a failure in Ireland because it did not generate sufficient funds for a Tailteann Games in 1889, it is difficult to classify the tour as anything other than a resounding success when considering its impact on the development of Gaelic sport in the United States. This is certainly the way *The Gael* interpreted the impact of the venture, arguing that it had made 'the Irish national pastime extremely popular with the exiled Gaels of Greater New York' (Sutton, 1900: 258). However, it was the status of Gaelic sport in Boston that benefited most from the exercise. Attendances at those exhibitions hosted in the city were the highest of the tour and in the aftermath of the Irish athletes' departure, Boston's Gaelic sport fraternity comprising four hurling clubs (including Wolfe Tones, Emmets and Redmonds) and two Gaelic football clubs (Kerry and Galway) flourished. This healthy complement of clubs was added to with the inauguration of the Young Ireland Hurling Club in 1897.[2]

## John Boyle O'Reilly: patron of Gaelic games in Boston

The key figure in the promotion of Gaelic games in Boston in the 1880s was undoubtedly John Boyle O'Reilly. O'Reilly was closely involved in the organisation of the first field sports meet in 1879 at which he acted as chief judge and referee and this was a role he repeated on a yearly basis up until his death in 1890 (Roche, 1891). He had a particular interest in hurling and his desire to see the game develop was such that in 1880 he presented the IACB with the John Boyle O'Reilly Hurling Cup, 'a magnificent silver cup, superbly ornamented, unique in design, and of great value' that was to be competed for by Boston's hurling clubs on an annual basis (Dineen, 1901: 292). The early practical development of Gaelic games in Boston was clearly aided by his patronage and organisational abilities. However, the ethos and philosophy underpinning the promotion of these specifically Irish pastimes were also shaped by O'Reilly's political beliefs and broader social outlook.

John Boyle O'Reilly has been described by the eminent historian of the Irish in America, Andrew Greeley, as first and foremost a leader of the Irish immigrant population in Boston but also one of Irish America's leading Irish nationalists (Greeley, 1981). O'Reilly's nationalist credentials are borne out by his remarkable early life story which saw him arrive in Boston as an escapee from a penal colony in West Australia where he had been incarcerated by the British authorities for membership of the Irish Republican Brotherhood and recruiting British soldiers to Fenianism. On arrival in Boston in 1869 he quickly gained renown as editor of the *Boston Pilot*, the influential weekly Catholic newspaper. However, it was his 'crusading zeal and a humanitarian sympathy for the underdog' (Shannon, 1966: 197) and his undoubted status as an advocate, albeit a moderate one, of the Irish nationalist cause which marked him out as one of the most popular and respected Irish-American figures of this era.

O'Reilly's patronage of Gaelic games during the late 1870s and 1880s must be viewed in the context of his life history and, more specifically, as an extension of his nationalist beliefs. As well as seeking to provide recreational opportunities for working-class Irish immigrants, O'Reilly was clearly advocating participation in sports that were part of the broader cultural revival aimed at providing a rallying point for Irish nationalism and separatist demands. This assertion is made on the basis that he was widely known as an enthusiastic proponent of 'any movement which promised the enfranchisement and liberty of his native land' (*Donahoe's Magazine*, Oct. 1890: 396–60). Paradoxically, O'Reilly's promotion of Gaelic games was very much couched in a sporting ethos which drew heavily on the philosophies of rational recreation and muscular Christianity, both of which were fostered on the playing fields of the English public school. However, in much the same way as GAA officials in Ireland had done, O'Reilly was able to repackage and present Gaelic games in Boston in specifically Irish terms and hence ensure their continued popularity amongst the Irish immigrant population.

## Gaelic games and Irish nationalism in Boston in the late nineteenth century

From the preceding narrative it is clear that as well as keeping Irish Catholics in touch with Ireland, culturally and psychologically, Gaelic games in Boston in the late nineteenth century served as an arena in which Irish nationalism was fostered and promoted. The relative ease with which these sports became linked in the city to the broader Irish nationalist mission was augmented by the fact that the first ten years of their development coincided with a period of revival for Irish-American nationalism. The activities of Clan na Gael, a secret organisation committed to the physical force tradition which had been formed in 1867, and a resurfacing of nativist sentiment did much to sustain Irish nationalism as an expression of Irish Catholic identity in America. Charles Stewart Parnell's tour of America in 1880 to meet the leaders of Irish America and solicit funds for the Land League also endeared the cause of Irish freedom to the hearts and minds of Irish Americans. Consequently, from the early 1880s support for constitutional and physical force nationalism was provided by Irish Americans in abundance and it was they who effectively bankrolled Parnell's parliamentary nationalism whilst others provided funds for republicanism (McCaffrey, 1997).

The promotion of Gaelic games in Boston in the 1880s can be clearly interpreted as part of this broader groundswell of support for Irish nationalism. As has been demonstrated, the coverage that these sports and the formation of the GAA in Ireland received in Irish-American newspapers and journals in Boston was couched in nationalistic terms. The cause of Irish nationalism was also uppermost in the minds of those who were more directly involved in the promotion of these activities in the city. As highlighted earlier, the IACB was clearly comprised of Irish nationalists who sought to bolster support for the broader struggle for Irish emancipation by encouraging and promoting a vibrant Gaelic culture in America. Likewise, pioneering figures such as John Boyle O'Reilly viewed the promotion of Irish cultural forms in Boston and beyond as crucial to the development of sustained support for the nationalist cause in Ireland. The early picnics at which traditional Irish sports and culture featured so prominently were also linked to Irish nationalist aspirations and identity formation and in some cases also made a practical contribution to the advancement of Irish nationalism in Ireland. For example, at a number of these events from the mid-1880s onwards, funds were collected from both spectators and participants for the Irish Parliamentary Fund, a scheme inaugurated by 'friends of Ireland in Boston' to enable Parnell 'to carry on the work of the redemption of Ireland to final success' (*Donahoe's Magazine*, April 1886: 7).

The founders and patrons of Boston's earliest clubs also articulated and celebrated their nationalism by naming their clubs after historical and popular nationalist personalities and organisations. This trend is widespread amongst GAA clubs in Ireland (Cronin, 1998a) and the practice and the meaning associated with it was, and still is, replicated in Gaelic sport in Boston. Whilst some clubs were named after those counties of Ireland from where the majority of members originated, the appropriation of names such as Emmets (after Robert Emmet, leader of the failed 1803 United Irishmen Rising), Redmonds (after John Redmond, leader of Irish parliamentary nationalism in the early twentieth century), Wolfe Tones (after the popular Irish nationalist figure) and Young Ireland Hurling Club (after the organisation of that name), reveals that these clubs were embracing Irish nationalism and giving their support to the struggle for Irish independence from Britain.

The value of Gaelic sports as a medium for the promotion of Irish nationalism was also recognised by a range of Irish societies and political organisations including the Ancient Order of Hibernians and Clan na Gael. The latter group in particular recognised the mobilising power of Gaelic sport and used it to attract new recruits to a brand of nationalism rooted in the physical force tradition. As Steven Reiss (1992: 192) has noted, 'Irish sport was also promoted by overtly political organisations, most notably the Clan na Gael (United Brotherhood), a secret revolutionary society that arranged athletic meets to gain favourable publicity, attract new adherents, and promote Irish nationalism'. At the same time Gaelic sports clubs benefited from the patronage of such influential organisations in terms of access to finances, equipment and facilities within Irish neighbourhoods.

## Fluctuating fortunes: Gaelic games in Boston 1900–37

By the late 1890s, Gaelic sports had thrown down deep roots amongst Boston's Irish community. The connections between the GAA and Irish nationalism were clearly significant in their early development and did much to encourage politically conscious immigrants to get involved as players, spectators or administrators. In his brief assessment of the birth of traditional Irish sports in Boston, Reiss (1992: 192) correctly asserts that 'Irishmen living in the United States quickly adopted these sports to show solidarity with revolutionaries'. Between 1900 and 1914 the infrastructure that had been built in the latter stages of the previous century was strengthened with the addition of new clubs, such as Boston Galway Hurling Club, founded in 1908 and the development of formally constituted competitions. The fact that these clubs were supported and promoted by various County Associations and Irish societies like Clan na Gael and the Ancient Order of Hibernians maintained the link between Gaelic games and Irish nationalism. Equally important was the fact that the patronage of influential political and cultural organisations meant that access to finances, equipment and facilities within Irish neighbourhoods in Boston proved relatively unproblematic.

The disruption of the Great War of 1914–18 brought a temporary halt to the development of Gaelic football and hurling in Boston. However, during the 1920s, Gaelic sports clubs once again began to cater for the sporting, recreational and cultural needs of Boston's Irish community. In this period, the growth and popularity of Gaelic sports was facilitated in no small measure by the fact that they were increasingly incorporated into the programmes of Irish dancing festivals or *feiseannas* in Boston (Cullinane, 1997). The key development in this decade though was the inception of the Massachusetts Gaelic Athletic Association in 1923. As a consequence of this initiative and visits to Boston by the Tipperary hurlers in 1926 and the Kerry Gaelic footballers a year later, Gaelic games became a more central aspect of the lives of increasing numbers of Irish immigrants. Indeed, between 1927 and 1929 nine hurling and 15 football teams had affiliated to the Massachusetts GAA (North East GAA, 2000).

Although some of the most high profile county football and hurling teams continued to play exhibition matches in Boston and Massachusetts, including the All-Ireland football champions Galway in 1935 and their hurling counterparts Kilkenny in the following year, the popularity of Gaelic games in the second half of the 1930s began to wane. There were a number of reasons for this. The depression of the late 1920s and 1930s, precipitated by the Wall Street crash, was keenly felt in areas of heavy industrialisation and Boston's Irish community, most of whom depended for their livelihood on unskilled labour, were victims of the worst economic ravages of the era. In such an environment identifying ways of alleviating socio-economic hardship as opposed to seeking to preserve the sports and games of the 'old country' became the priority for the Boston Irish. With such economic conditions restricting the flow of new members and players into the Massachusetts GAA, the association suspended its activities in 1937. With the outbreak of the Second World War and a sharp slump in Irish emigration to the United States, the playing of Gaelic games, in an organised fashion, ceased to form a significant part of the lives of the Irish diaspora in Boston.

Whilst socio-economic factors undoubtedly constituted the main reason for the demise of Gaelic games in Boston during the 1930s, the more general decline in Irish nationalism in America in this period also contributed to a loss of interest in sports forms which had been used to promote sympathies for the Irish nationalist cause. The US government's decision to enter the war in 1917 and the response of Irish Americans revealed that loyalty to their new home was gradually supplanting patriotism to Ireland (McCaffrey, 1997). Although sections of Irish America continued to fund Sinn Féin and the IRA, the establishment of the Irish Free State led to a gradual decline in interest in Irish affairs amongst the Irish diaspora throughout America. As a corollary of this it is possible that organisations that were linked to the promotion of Irish nationalism in Boston and amongst the broader Irish diaspora throughout America also suffered a decline in interest, adherents and investment.

## Post-war growth: Gaelic games in Boston 1947–90

The falling level of interest in Gaelic sport in the major Irish-American communities led to the development of a lobby within GAA circles in Ireland, championed by the influential Clare-born Central Council delegate Canon Michael Hamilton, aimed at arresting the marginalisation of Gaelic games in the USA. Sections of the GAA's Central Council were relatively unmoved by this lobby and felt little inclination to cater for the sporting needs of the émigré (De Búrca, 1999). This antipathy can be explained as part of a broader mistrust between GAA headquarters and the Association's American wing that stretched back to the 1920s. On a number of occasions in this decade the Dublin and American units of the GAA had come into conflict resulting in 'an unwillingness [on the part of the Dublin-based GAA] to accept the Gaels in America as totally sincere about the promotion of the games' (Hanna, 1999: 353).[3] Despite such sentiments Canon Hamilton persisted with his exploration of ways in which the GAA in Ireland could reignite interest in the national games amongst the Irish diaspora in the USA. At the GAA's Congress in 1947, he tabled a motion, which was eventually accepted, to hold the All-Ireland football final at the New York Polo Grounds. Although the game attracted a disappointing crowd of 35,000, the playing of the All-Ireland Final on American soil did much to revive interest in Gaelic games and within three years the National Council GAA of the United States was established. This body ran into difficulties following the New York region's withdrawal in 1956 and it was replaced, in 1959, by the North American County Board.

At around the same time that the foundations for the current organi-sational infrastructure for the GAA in the US were being laid, Gaelic sport was also becoming re-established in Boston. By the late 1950s six football and three hurling clubs were competing at senior level whilst four football clubs were fielding teams for junior competition. Interest was also growing in the women's game of camogie and as early as 1950 exhibition matches were occurring in South Boston involving the Shamrock and Celtic camogie clubs (*Boston Pilot*, 1950a; *Boston Pilot*, 1950b). Steady growth continued to characterise the development of Gaelic games in Boston during the 1960s and 1970s with an increased number of clubs affiliating to the NACB. Visits from representative teams from Kerry and Roscommon as well as exhibition matches involving the Connaught Railway Cup footballers and the All-Star select team helped maintain the profile of Gaelic football and hurling throughout the New England region. Another development, the first live broadcast of the All-Ireland football final from Croke Park in Dublin, further cemented the status of Gaelic sport in Boston in this era. The effect was such that between 1974 and 1985 ten new clubs catering for Gaelic games were established. Significantly for the level of sporting provision for Boston's female Irish community, three of those clubs were devoted solely to the playing of camogie.[4]

## Gaelic sport, socio-economic networking and county-based loyalties in Boston

The fact that Gaelic games in Boston grew and developed in the post-war period, despite a decline in support amongst Irish Americans for aspects of political nationalism, illustrates that there were reasons, other than identity politics, why Boston's Irish community promoted and took part in these sports. For those of a sporting disposition, the significance of the Gaelic football or hurling club in smoothing the transition from rural areas of Ireland to a rapidly expanding, industrial city was immense. The GAA afforded Irish Catholics with opportunities simply to associate with like-minded individuals and engage in social and sporting activities resonant of 'home'. For some, immersion in Gaelic games undoubtedly helped alleviate the feelings of dislocation and alienation that the Boston Irish often felt. It is also likely that involvement in a GAA club or attendance at a match in Boston provided entrance into the social networks that enabled newly arrived immigrants to find work and accommodation. Whilst those responsible for promoting Gaelic games in the city around the turn of the century were aware of the significance of these sports as markers of Irish ethnic identity, the extent to which the GAA in Boston attempted to link their activities to politicised expressions of Irish nationalism began to decline. With the establishment of the NACB in 1959 and the inauguration of a number of regional competitions, the focus shifted to sporting concerns and expressions of identity that were linked more to benign county-based rivalries.

Since the inception of Gaelic games in Boston, clubs had often been formed and appropriated by individuals with the same county affiliation and matches between such clubs allowed players, administrators and benefactors an opportunity to renew the intense county rivalry upon which elite level Gaelic sport in Ireland was based. Although clubs such as Cork, Kerry, Mayo, Donegal and the many others that were formed with county loyalties in mind have not always been comprised solely of players and officials from one county, they still allowed sections of the Irish diaspora to identify themselves not only as Irish but also as belonging to a particular county in Ireland. One member of the Kerry club put into words the significance of membership of GAA clubs in allowing individuals the opportunity to express a sense of allegiance and belonging to 'their' county:

> I find it very hard if a person comes over from Kerry and he plays for another county. I actually feel offended . . . At our banquets we would have 400 people attend and 90 percent of them would be from Kerry. So people from the same county do support each other. Most of the other clubs would be the same. For example, Cork are very clannish and they support each other 100 per cent (Interview with author, Belmont, Massachusetts, 30 July, 2000).[5]

Thus, in the post-war period, Gaelic sport in Boston continued to serve a number of more practical but no less important social and economic functions both for those who have made Boston their long-term home and those whose stay has been of a more temporary nature. Furthermore, the capacity of Gaelic games to provide new Irish arrivals in Boston with a sense of the familiar in an otherwise alien environment and allow them to maintain an important psychological link with 'home' continues to the present day. John Hehir, a highly respected figure in Boston GAA circles and former president of the NACB, eloquently describes the extent to which immersion in the GAA can help alleviate the feelings of dislocation often felt by Irish immigrants in the city:

> The GAA is very important especially for newcomers because on the day you arrive here you may have left home for the first time. So you meet some friends and they take you down to Dilboy (former home of the GAA in Boston). Well, you are immediately in an environment that you recognise quickly as being a friendly one. It took some of the edge and roughness of being 3,000 miles from home (Interview with author, Brighton, MA, 15 August 2000).

This view was reinforced by Connie Kelly, Public Relations Officer for the North-Eastern GAA Board, who described the GAA in Boston as 'an extended family' which 'helps people settle into life over here straight away' (Interview with author, Belmont, MA, 30 July 2000). Furthermore, the solace and support provided by the GAA for the city's Irish population has not just been of a psychological nature. Involvement in a GAA club or attendance at a match in Boston were often the first steps in securing employment and somewhere to live. Such opportunities were particularly important for the longer term Irish émigré, legal or otherwise. More recently, those arriving for shorter durations such as students with J1 visas which allow them to live and work in the US during their summer vacation and those who have gone through the GAA's sanction system to play Gaelic football in America in the summer months have also availed themselves of the opportunities provided by the GAA to obtain work and accommodation. Indeed, the incentive package offered to higher profile Gaelic footballers and hurlers to sign for clubs in Boston during the summer Championship period often includes opportunities for work, usually unskilled labour, along with free accommodation.[6] In addition, elite-level players, that is, those who play or who have played at senior county level, also receive financial inducements to sign for particular clubs for the summer.[7] This is a practice which has been roundly condemned by the GAA in Ireland because it clearly contravenes the amateur ethos of the Association. However, in their quest for divisional and national honours, clubs throughout North America are prepared to overlook this supposed cornerstone of GAA activities and pay top-level players for their services.

## Gaelic sport in Boston since 1990

The final decade of the twentieth century was a hugely significant era in the development of Gaelic games in Boston. The addition of three new clubs, Boston Mayo, Notre Dame and Aidan McAnespie's, brought the total number of clubs in the greater Boston area to 24. As a reflection of the rapid popularisation of ladies' Gaelic football in Ireland during the 1990s, four of these clubs, Boston Shamrocks, Tir na nOg, Roscommon and Waterford were established in order to provide sporting opportunities for Boston's female Irish community (Gaughran, 1999). In addition, provision for under-age football in Boston received a boost with the formation of the New England Minor Football Board in 1996. The response to the activities organised by the Board was such that in 1998 it was renamed the Irish Sports Youth League of New England to reflect the broadening of its target age range (*The Boston Irish Reporter*, 1999b: 35). The fact that these developments occurred at a time when fewer Irish men and women were emigrating to the US and more were returning home as a consequence of Ireland's economic boom is testament to the buoyancy of Gaelic sport and Irish culture in Boston.

The century ended with one of the most influential developments in the evolution of Gaelic sports in Boston. In terms of playing facilities, participants and spectators had enjoyed their national games in a variety of rented venues throughout Boston and New England.[8] However, the construction of purpose-built facilities in New York and Chicago led to a movement, in the late 1980s, for a permanent home for Gaelic sports in Boston. After deciding that such a venture should encompass other elements of Irish culture such as music, dance and language, the Irish Cultural Centre, a non-profit corporation, was established in 1990. After a series of annual festivals and other fund raising initiatives, the Centre was able to purchase 47 acres of land in 1996 in the Boston suburb of Canton. Three years later Phase I of the project was complete and as part of an agreement which guaranteed GAA clubs exclusive use of the playing fields, the north eastern division of the NACB made a $200,000 contribution to the Irish Cultural Centre (*Boston Irish Reporter*, 1999a). As a sign of the Canton facility's status as the new focal point for Irish sporting and cultural pastimes in Boston and its neighbouring suburbs and towns the opening was attended by Dermot Ahern, the then Irish Minister for Social, Community and Family Affairs and GAA President at the time, Joe McDonagh.[9] In his dedication of the new facility, McDonagh commended the vibrancy of the North Eastern GAA board and referred to Boston as 'a bright jewel in the crown of the GAA's growth outside Ireland' (*Boston Irish Reporter*, 1999c: 20).

The 1990s were clearly significant for the GAA in Boston in a sporting sense. However, the decade also saw an increase in the extent to which Gaelic games were drawn upon specifically to mobilise Irish nationalist sentiment. Since the 1920s the Irish had begun to feel more secure and comfortable in America and this had led to a declining preoccupation with demonstrating their affinity and ties to the 'old country'. However, the emergence of the 'troubles' in Northern Ireland in the late 1960s had been greeted with anger and frustration by much of Irish America and this led to a concomitant upsurge in the numbers of those who identified themselves as Irish nationalists. In much the same way that Irish nationalism in Ireland was characterised by deep ideological and political fissures, predominantly over the way the country's relationship with Britain was managed, so too were Irish nationalists in America divided over how best to express their sympathies for and commitment to the Irish nationalist cause. There were those, encouraged by Irish Americans holding prominent political and religious positions, who championed a constitutional nationalist agenda which sought to support the broader political, territorial and social aspirations of Irish nationalists. However, there were others who articulated a nationalism that was revolutionary and supportive of the physical force tradition. The clearest manifestation of this support for a revolutionary approach to the constitutional status of Ireland's six most north-eastern counties can be seen in the fundraising activities for the Provisional IRA and the republican political party, Sinn Féin, which have occurred on a regular basis since the 1970s.

The GAA in the Boston area has always contained members who were quite clearly republican in political orientation. Although some members of the Association have been involved in organising fundraising for groups such as NORAID, or have at least contributed from their own pockets,[10] the GAA in the region did not directly align itself to overtly political expressions of Irish nationalism in the first two decades of the 'troubles'. However, at various stages during the 1990s, Gaelic games became inextricably linked to an Irish nationalism that, whilst not uniformly supportive of physical force, was more belligerent and hostile towards the continued presence of the British in the north of Ireland and the difficulties, perceived or otherwise, which this presented for the minority Catholic, nationalist community.

One of the clearest examples of this came in 1993 with the formation of Aidan McAnespie's Gaelic Football Club in Boston. The club was inaugurated in memory of Aidan McAnespie, a member of the Tyrone GAA club Aghaloo, who was shot dead by a British soldier in February 1988 as he crossed the border on his way to a Gaelic football match. McAnespie's death was viewed by many within the Association, on both sides of the Atlantic, as a clear manifestation of what they believed to be an organised and concerted campaign of violence, intimidation and harassment, perpetrated by the British Crown forces and loyalist paramilitary groups against GAA members in the north of Ireland (Bairner and Darby, 1999). The fact that the case of the soldier who had fired the shot did not go to trial owing to 'lack of evidence' (Fahy, 2001)[11] served to intensify this belief and hardened the attitudes of sections of the GAA towards the British authorities.

The depth of resentment at McAnespie's murder was most keenly felt in the GAA's northern counties and served to solidify the links between the Association and the broader political agenda of northern nationalism. The waves of sorrow and revulsion at McAnespie's death were also felt across the Atlantic. Driven by a desire to express solidarity with the McAnespie family, a number of individuals involved in Gaelic games in Boston decided that a new club would be a fitting and lasting tribute. Although their motives may have been first and foremost a gesture of sympathy and remembrance, membership of and support for the club also provided Irish Catholics living in the Boston area with a vehicle for expressing a more politicised and belligerent Irish nationalism. This point is made explicit by John Hehir, former President of the NACB, who commented that 'the formation of the McAnespie's club was about the promotion of Irish nationalism' (Interview with author, Brighton, MA, 15 August 2000). The fact that the founders also intended using the profile of the club to 'highlight political injustice in Northern Ireland' (North American County Board, 1998) reinforced the extent to which sections of the Boston GAA could draw on their games to demonstrate their solidarity with the aspirations of northern nationalists in Ireland.

Further attacks on GAA members in Northern Ireland in the second half of the 1990s strengthened the politicised Irish nationalist character of Gaelic games in Boston. The murder of Fergal McCusker by the Loyalist Volunteer Force on 18 January 1998 was particularly significant in this regard. McCusker had played junior football for McAnespie's the previous summer and intended to travel back out to Boston that spring to look for work and resume his association with the club. In the aftermath of his murder, the body responsible for overseeing the development of Gaelic games in the greater Boston area took the decision to change its name from the 'New England' to the 'North Eastern' GAA Board, thereby removing what was a superficial but no less symbolic connection between the Boston GAA and England. As Connie Kelly, public relations officer of the North Eastern Board explains, McCusker's murder was central to the name change:

> We used to be known as the New England Board. Now we are the North Eastern Board because a number of our players recently got killed in Northern Ireland. The Board decided that we should eliminate 'England' from our name. This happened almost three years ago when Fergal McCusker was killed (Interview with author, Belmont MA, 30 July 2000).

The murders of Aidan McAnespie, Fergal McCusker and other prominent GAA figures in Northern Ireland such as Sean Brown, Chairman of Bellaghy Wolfe Tones GAA club and Gerry Devlin, manager of St Enda's senior Gaelic football team, by loyalist paramilitaries served to further harden the political outlook and attitude of the GAA's northern counties. This was particularly manifest in relation to Rule 21 of the GAA's constitution, which prohibited members of the British Crown security forces and the Royal Ulster Constabulary (now the Police Service of Northern Ireland) from participating in GAA activities (Sugden and Bairner, 1993; Bairner and Darby, 1999; Cronin, 1999). These attitudes were apparent at the GAA's Congress in 1998 when the former President Joe McDonagh attempted to introduce a motion to have Rule 21 removed from the Association's rule-book. McDonagh was clearly acting in the spirit of compromise that the peace process had engendered. However, he misjudged the resolve of sections of the GAA, particularly those members most directly affected by the 'troubles', to maintain a measure that they believed was a legitimate response to the increasing attacks on their members and it came as no surprise that the motion was rejected. Given the responses that attacks on GAA members in Northern Ireland had elicited from the GAA in Boston, it should also come as no surprise to learn that had the motion to remove Rule 21 gone to the floor of the Congress the North Eastern Board would have voted for the maintenance of the clause. The difficulties which the Board had in responding more positively to this issue were compounded by the fact that sections of the GAA community in Boston are staunchly republican in political orientation. As one anonymous source revealed, 'there are IRA sympathisers in the GAA over here and they are going to resist removing Rule 21' (Interview with author, Brighton, MA, 2 August 2000).[12] This continued support for preserving Rule 21, despite the ongoing peace process in Northern Ireland, was perhaps the clearest example of the extent to which Gaelic games in Boston had become linked to an articulation of Irish nationalism that is intensely political, hostile to Britain and Ulster loyalism and arguably sympathetic to a physical force solution to the constitutional status of Northern Ireland.

## Conclusion

According to Kieran Conway, a GAA aficionado and journalist with the Boston newspaper, the *Irish Emigrant*, the profile and development of Gaelic sports in the United States has been dependent on 'the pendulum of migration' (Interview with author, South Boston, 25 July 2000). Although the Celtic Tiger has slowed the pace of emigration from Ireland and has led to an increase in the numbers of those returning home from the USA, Gaelic games in Boston continue to go from strength to strength. With more than 3,000 members, the North Eastern Board is undoubtedly the strongest of the NACB's ten divisions and is currently the largest unit of the GAA outside Ireland. This is clearly a consequence of the fact that since the 1820s the city has been one of the primary focal points for Irish immigration. Gaelic games have also prospered under the stewardship of influential leaders of the Boston Irish as well as the tireless efforts of administrators and benefactors who have invested much in terms of vision, energy and finances.

However, as this chapter demonstrated, it would be wrong to quantify the significance of GAA activities in Boston purely in terms of numerical strength or organisational efficiency. Since their formal inception in 1879, Gaelic games have played a crucial role in the lives of many Irish immigrants. Their social and economic impact and the extent to which they have helped alleviate the sense of dislocation and alienation often felt by new arrivals have been immense. Involvement in Gaelic football, hurling or camogie, be it as a player, administrator or spectator, has clearly done much to provide a sense of continuity between their lived experiences in counties, cities and parishes throughout Ireland and their lives in Boston. Crucially, consumption of these distinctively Irish pastimes has also allowed for the preservation and articulation of the broader ethnic and national identities of this most significant of immigrant groups in Boston.

Part 2
# Identities

## Chapter 7

# Rugby union and national identity politics

Jason Tuck

## Introduction

The aim of this chapter is to contribute to the growing body of knowledge that seeks to investigate the complex and dynamic relationship between sport, national culture and identity in the Irish context. More specifically, the focus here is on the 'place' of rugby union and international rugby union players in this relationship. This research complements the work on sport in Ireland carried out by, amongst others, Bairner (1996; 2001a), Cronin (1997; 1999), Sugden and Bairner (1993) and Sugden and Harvie (1995) and also work on rugby union and national identity carried out by historians such as Nauright (1990; 1996a; 1997) and Williams (1985; 1988; 1991).

If one considers a fusion of existing theories on nationalism (incorporating the primordialists, the modernists, the statists, and the political mythologists) it is possible to appreciate the complexities of national identity.[1] A commonly held view is that identifications with the nation are harboured in the 'national narrative' (or national history – both ancient and modern) that, immersed in mythology, is continually communicated through stories, memories and images. The symbolic historical ritual of this narrative is consequently loaded with connotations which constitute the shared experiences (the recollection of both triumphant and disastrous common occurrences) of a people which, by reference to an 'imagined community' (Anderson, 1983), imparts meaning and social unity onto the nation.

It has been widely acknowledged that sport and national identity have been closely associated over the past century and a half (Maguire, 1994). Sporting competition arguably provides the primary expression of imagined communities with the nation appearing more 'real' in the domain of sport. Bale (1986: 18) states that 'Whether at local, regional or national level, sport is, after war, probably the principal means of collective identification in modern life'.

The specific focus here is on a 'player-centric' approach to researching sport and national identity. By positioning Irish international rugby players at the centre of the inter-relationships between sport and national identity one can gain a different perspective on the sport-national identity 'union' in the Irish context. The players who were interviewed represent the most visible link between rugby union and the nation and their 'stories' clearly merit some attention. The contention here is that an appreciation of the contemporary position, role and perceptions of international rugby union players can help shed further light on the interdependencies that have developed between rugby union and national identity.[2]

Some of the key themes which arise are the centrality of rugby union to Ireland and notions of Irishness, the significance of national anthems and national symbols, the multi-layered nature of personal identity (especially those players with dual nationality), and the stereotyping of Irishness and the Irish style of play. In addition to these elements there seems to be a growing awareness amongst the players regarding the impending (and subsequently increasing) professionalisation of the game and the growth of a club/province based European cup. These latter developments could well have significant implications for issues related to national identity.[3]

One only has to observe the way in which players clutch the national symbol (and are thus seen to be holding the nation in their hand) on their jerseys and sing 'their' national anthem vociferously before the match to understand that these players are an embodiment of their various nations. Their role in the relationship between rugby union and national identity should not be taken lightly; in playing for the shamrock we see them representing a single Ireland writ large.

Thinking through these 'intersections' between the individual and the nation, and between rugby and national identity, it is possible to see that these relationships are contoured by a series of interlocking processes. By thinking processually, one can bring a figurational framework to bear on these intersections and begin to reveal the complex social (and historical) bonds that can bind together the individual and the nation in a sporting context. In contrast to other schools of thought, the figurational position on national identity advocates that the cultural representations of the nation can become part of a person's habitus (the deeply embodied emotions which are socially learned and become 'second nature' to the individual) and thus appear more 'real' (for example, through sporting affiliations) rather than simply 'imagined'.

Norbert Elias's introduction to *The Established and the Outsiders* contains a significant passage that is a valuable aid for conceptualising 'the nation'. He writes:

A striking example in our time is that of the we-image and we-ideal of once-powerful nations whose superiority in relation to others has declined. . . . The radiance of their collective life as a nation has gone; their power superiority in relation to their groups . . . is irretrievably lost. Yet the dream of their special charisma is kept alive in a variety of ways – through the teaching of history, the old buildings, masterpieces of the nation in the time of its glory, or through new achievements that seemingly confirm the greatness of the past. For a time, the fantasy shield of their imagined charisma as a leading established group may give a declining nation the strength to carry on. In that sense it can have a survival value. But the discrepancy between the actual and the imagined position of one's group among others can also entail a mistaken assessment of one's resources and, as a consequence, suggest a group strategy in pursuit of a fantasy image of one's own greatness that may lead to self-destruction. . . . The dreams of nations . . . are dangerous (Elias, 1994: xliii–xliv).

Clearly these thoughts have some resonance for the Irish context. One can begin to consider the 'special charisma' of Irish nationalism as a 'fantasy image' or 'dream' for some (and this may differ between groups, for example the nationalists and unionists in Northern Ireland). In contrast, the established group in the British Isles, the English/British, clearly have some hegemonic role to play in the Irish context, most notably in the '(self-)destruction' and reincarnation of Ireland.

International sports are, in essence, forms of tribal gatherings and 'patriot games.' The individuals representing 'their' countries therein become highly visible embodiments of these nations – they are 'patriots at play'. These sporting patriots are significant actors who both define and reflect the 'special charisma' of nations writ large and, through their practices, sport becomes one of the 'fantasy shields' whereby 'imagined (and 'real') charisma' is both fuelled and protected (Maguire and Poulton, 1999). International sport, imbued with national symbols, therefore provides an environment rich in collective identifications and identity politics.

In this respect, rugby union in the 'British' Isles represents a unique arena for the construction, reproduction and contestation of national identities and produces a series of national cultural paradoxes. These include the juxtaposition of the Anglo-Saxon English against the Celtic nations in the annual Six Nations Championship, whilst additionally uniting the best players from the 'Home Unions' as British and Irish Lions every four years, and also appearing to unite the people of a politically divided nation – Ireland.

## The British and Irish 'national' sporting context

The British Isles has a complex sporting identity. Blain et al. (1993: 12–13) comment that:

> While politically the United Kingdom is a single state, at many international sporting events, and within the domestic sports arena, it has four 'national iden-tities' (though arguably, given the periodic Northern Ireland/Republic distinction in team formation this is sometimes yet more complicated).

For example, at the Olympic games, athletes from the British Isles either compete for Great Britain or Ireland; on the soccer pitch there are teams representing England, Scotland, Wales, Northern Ireland and the Republic of Ireland. In rugby union, it is significant that the Irish (essentially a consti-tutionally divided nation) compete as a united nation against the English, Scottish and Welsh. As a consequence of this, the 'southern Irish' also become eligible to represent Great Britain (of which they are not politically part) if selected to play in what is more usually referred to as the 'British Lions' touring team. It is appropriate to note, however, that this team should be known as the 'Great British and Irish Lions' (Thomas, 1996).

With particular reference to Ireland one must consider that this seemingly 'imaginary' Celtic nation is in fact composed of two separate political entities: Northern Ireland (part of the United Kingdom) and the Republic of Ireland. Whilst it is not possible to review all the arguments and counter-arguments about the island of Ireland here, it is necessary to briefly contextualise the nation(s) that are being explored in this chapter and endorse Cronin's (1999) view that there are several dynamic Irish national identities in existence on the island (and within the Irish diaspora) at any one moment in time, many of which are discussed elsewhere in this collection. According to Cronin (1999: 23) 'sport and nationalism are inextricably linked and play a key role in defining Irish nationalism and nations of Irish national identity. This role, as with the very nature of Irishness, is constantly in a state of flux as sport is an ever changing vehicle for the transmission of both ideology and identity'.

## A brief history of rugby union, national identity and Ireland

The 'story' of Irish rugby, and how it allegedly developed from a Celtic ball-carrying game called *cad*, has already been extensively documented, most notably by Diffley (1973) and Van Esbeck (1974, 1986, 1999). In considering the more specific relationship between rugby union, the players, (invented) traditions and national identity in Ireland, it is useful to revisit Van Esbeck's

(1974: 2) prefatory statement that 'the essential physical character of the game is certainly compatible with the essential character of the Irish temperament'. In seeking to explain this, it is necessary to return to Diffley's (1973: 11) account, where he aims to capture the essence of Irish rugby:

> The players may . . . play as intensely as teams from any other country but always bubbling close to the surface is the saving grace of gaiety which makes sure that matters seldom become too dour. Even in the hottest and most serious matches one can expect the odd shaft of Celtic wit to keep matters in their proper perspective. . . . And a dashing, devil-may-care manner of play ensures that the world-wide popularity remains . . .

Here, rugby is intertwined with a sense of Irishness and further parallels are drawn with a wider Celtic consciousness to demonstrate how an Irish rugby habitus can begin to be characterised.

It is interesting to note that the formal organisation of Irish rugby began with a division between Belfast and Dublin. After the Irish Football Union had been formed by Dubliners in 1874, overlooking those from Belfast, the Northern Football Union was formed in Belfast in response (Diffley, 1973). Although these were separate organisations, an agreement was made to support the Irish nation in the first international match (against England) the following year. These bodies eventually amalgamated in 1879 to form the single governing body for Irish rugby, the IRFU. This organisation continues to the present day to promote rugby throughout Ireland. Commenting on the relationship between rugby and politics in Ireland, Diffley (1973: 14) states that 'what rugby football has done for Ireland is to provide a different definition of Irishmen from the acrimonious political one. Politics, too often, have tended to divide the Irish. Rugby football has worked to widen friendships and unite'. Such playing down of the politics of division in rugby union appears as a constant theme in the various historical studies of Irish rugby and as Bairner reveals in chapter 10, is also part of the discourse offered by certain Irish rugby players themselves. However, this overt dilution of the sport–politics relationship could, in itself, be identified as part of the dynamic of national identity politics.

Rugby percolated throughout the provinces of Ireland from the second half of the nineteenth century, in spite of strong competition from Gaelic sports (football and hurling) and association football. However, according to Diffley (1973), it was rugby that was then perceived to be tied more closely to the Irish identity. This connection between Irish politics and national habitus was also evident in the IRFU's involvement in a series of debates over national flags (and whether the Irish tricolour or the Union Jack should be flown at international matches at Lansdowne Road) after the formation of the Irish Free State.

However, arguably the most significant debate over national flags in Irish rugby occurred in 1954. Diffley (1973: 49) refers to the players' strike in 1954 before the match against Scotland to be played at Ravenhill in Belfast as 'perhaps the most closely guarded secret of all in Irish rugby' and goes on to explain that

> it was a time of rather simplistic attitudes in Irish politics and some of the Southern players held a meeting on the morning of the match and decided that they were not prepared to stand to attention before the game for the British national anthem unless the Irish anthem was also played and the Irish tricolour flown, both of which were illegal north of the border.

The compromise by the IRFU was to state that all further internationals would be played in Dublin at Lansdowne Road (a decision also coloured by the financial consideration that this was a larger stadium in a more populous location). According to Diffley (1973), the largely covert actions of the IRFU successfully minimised the risk of (political) disruption to Irish rugby.

The 'Golden Years' of Irish rugby (between 1948 and 1951), when only four matches were lost, were characterised by the evolution of a new style of play and the development of two world-class players, Jack Kyle (outside-half) and Karl Mullen (hooker and captain). Borrowing from the South African tactic of forwards working in close support of each other, the Irish employed hard, fast, tough, 'devil-may-care' forwards as attacking spearheads (Diffley, 1973: 97). Of course, the 'hustling and harrying' qualities of Irish forward play are also connected with other tactical developments in the game, such as 'the Garryowen' (named after the Irish club), where the ball is kicked high and deep giving the forwards time to charge up to the catcher at full tilt.

Since this period the Irish have been characterised by their 'swashbuckling', 'rollicking', 'whirlwind' style of play (Diffley, 1973: 94). However, the over-exuberance and lack of control that this style breeds has been a long-standing concern for national coaches. These styles of play contribute to the Irish rugby habitus and habitus codes appear with some regularity throughout the official histories and in media reports. In turn it is pertinent to consider here that the Irish rugby habitus (and its historical construction and reconstruction) co-exists with and feeds into a broader Irish habitus to colour the we-image of the Irish and the they-image of the Irish as held by outsiders.

## Irish players, Irish rugby habitus and national identity politics

By considering the perceptions of current/recent Irish international rugby players and reflecting on the context of Irish rugby habitus and national identity politics, it is possible to identify four emerging themes. These are the importance of rugby union to Ireland and Irishness, national anthems and symbols in the Irish rugby context, the complex and multiple identities of Irish dual national rugby players, and the stereotyping of Irishness and the Irish style of play.

## The importance of rugby union to Ireland, the Irish and Irishness

All the Irish players who were interviewed regarded rugby union as a central part of their particular national culture. Rugby union clearly occupies a very special place within Irish national identity – the sport is perceived to have a unique ability in Ireland to transcend political, religious and social class divisions. The centrality of rugby to Irish politics was displayed in the 1996 'Peace International', played between Ireland and the Barbarians at Lansdowne Road and designed to contribute to an ending of the Troubles in Northern Ireland.[4] Rugby union is one of the few sports in which a united (albeit invented) 'All-Ireland' can compete relatively successfully on the world stage. One player, Samuel, stated that:

> Everybody looks to national teams. . . . One of the few team sports [in which] you can compete at the world level is rugby football and we are competing in a World Cup as a national team in an international arena. It's very important to do well . . . – it helps to keep Ireland in world focus . . . [and] any successful sporting team gives the nation . . . a sense of pride.

Indeed it was notable that pre-World Cup training camps have taken place in towns such as Kilkenny, part of Ireland more associated with Gaelic games (especially hurling). Whilst there the players went on various engagements to promote the 'special charisma' of the sport in the local schools and many commented that they were overwhelmed by the receptions they were given and the interest the children seemed to have in rugby.

Stephen made reference to the tremendous support for the Irish at Lansdowne Road 'through two different nations' and remarked on the fact that perhaps rugby does not mirror the divisions in Irish society. Liam noted:

> rugby's one of the only sports in Ireland where you have guys from the North and South playing under the same title with the same colour jersey. . . . So having a successful rugby team is important, not only for rugby, but for the country as a whole.

When victorious the Irish team was seen by the players to generate a sense of national pride in both Northern Ireland and the Republic. Additionally even during the darkest moments in North–South relations, the players could not recall the Troubles ever materialising in a rugby context. Samuel, from Northern Ireland, commented:

I'm playing with my friends here, guys that I've played with for years. I don't know how they feel towards us but there's never been any problem – even in the worst times during the political situation. There's never been any problem in a rugby arena that I can ever remember.

At the end of the interview, when probed about the effect of the political situation on rugby in Ireland, he remarked:

I don't want to get too controversial about the Northern Ireland–Republic of Ireland thing. It's a funny situation . . . for someone outside Ireland . . . [who] don't really understand it. We have just got to accept that there are two different countries - but in rugby terms we are one country . . . Nobody has ever made a political issue out of it and they never will because rugby is bigger than that. In terms of the way rugby was set up, it was always . . . on a provincial basis; i.e. Ulster, Munster, Leinster, Connacht . . . So . . . with the provincial set up there could be a division but it didn't have the same effect because we played for Ulster, even though Ulster is Northern Ireland. But it is not, never has, and never will be an issue – not in sport.

These observations suggest that rugby does indeed serve at one level to bring the two Irelands together but the players did not make too many references to a truly united Ireland. Moreover, Samuel was wrong to reproduce the common but erroneous assumption that Ulster is Northern Ireland since it is in fact made up of nine counties, six of which form Northern Ireland, three of Ulster's predominantly Catholic counties (Cavan, Donegal and Monaghan) having been ceded to the Irish Free State in 1922 to create an artificial Protestant majority in Northern Ireland.

On closer inspection it is also evident that there is still a feeling of 'them and us' between the Northern Irish (or Ulstermen) and those from the Republic. This is perhaps most apparent in terms of language (the southern Irish having access to a Gaelic language which the vast majority of northern Protestants cannot and would not wish to speak). In rugby union, this manifests itself in issues surrounding the choice of anthem played at Ireland's international matches.

Rugby union's ability to apparently rise above the various divisions in Ireland was acknowledged by the Irish players. The main benefit was not perceived in political terms but, rather, as allowing the Irish to join forces in order to compete more effectively at the international level. That Ireland was being invented as a nation in a rugby context did not seem to be an issue for the players and several commented that political and religious differences had no effect on how rugby is played throughout the island. However, national 'inventions', which are located in the discourse of national habitus, can clearly become very 'real' through the medium of rugby (Maguire and Poulton, 1999). Thus, the Irish players, visibly acting as embodied representatives of the nation, are central figures in activating 'Ireland' from the imaginary to the, at least temporarily, real.[5]

**National anthems and symbols in the Irish rugby context**
The majority of the players commented that the principal moment that tended to raise their awareness of national identity was when they lined up for the national anthems as the final part of the pre-match build-up to internationals. However, the existence of two Irelands (and two different linguistic traditions) outside rugby union has also created some problems in both the selection and rendition of the 'Irish' national anthem. Until the 1995 World Cup the official anthem sung by the Irish rugby team was, in most instances, *Amhrán na bhFiann*, the anthem of the Republic of Ireland (which recounts the fighting heritage of the Irish in the face of the English invader and is imbued with anti-English sentiment, making references to 'the Saxon foe' and 'the Tyrant'). This was adopted as it was the anthem of the nation in which the international rugby matches were played. However, the national anthem for those players from Northern Ireland, being part of the United Kingdom, is 'God Save The Queen'. Samuel observed:

> I can't sing the Anthem because I don't know the words . . . Me being from the North, it's not my Anthem so I don't sing it. I respect it, I stand still for it . . . but it's in Gaelic . . . so I don't know it.

As a sort of 'in' joke, some of the Ulster players spoke of the coaching they had received in the past from the Southern players who had attempted to teach them suitable replacement lyrics in English so that they could sing along (albeit in meaningless terms) and keep their mouths in time with the others. Although the Ulstermen did not understand the meaning of the anthem they all admitted that it did move them and put them 'in the mood' (John). Peter, another Ulsterman, declared that:

> The Anthem is officially played because the game is played in Dublin, not because it's the team anthem . . . But they've brought the new song ['Ireland's Call'] out . . . to give the team a sense of identity so that all the members of the team could associate themselves with this song, with Ireland, with Irish pride . . .

Indeed, one of the Ulster players, Stephen, stated that he was playing for 'his country' and that he had always supported Ireland as a 'whole nation'. However, an Ulsterman who plays for 'his country' should technically be representing either Northern Ireland or the United Kingdom whereas clearly Stephen perceives that he is playing for his country when representing

Ireland. Such contradictions were manifest in the language of many of the Irish players and these provide a valuable illustration of the complex duality of Irishness, a theme that is examined in more detail by Bairner later in this collection with specific reference to Ulster unionism.

The potential conflicts and contradictions surrounding the playing of anthems at international rugby matches prompted the IRFU to select a new 'sporting' anthem in the 1990s – 'Ireland's Call'. Sung in English (and heard for the first time in the 1995 Rugby World Cup), this has a particularly relevant chorus – 'Ireland, Ireland, Together standing tall, Shoulder to shoulder, We'll answer Ireland's call'. The 'anthem' seeks to promote a unified Irish group charisma with members from both Irish political nations rallying as one, 'shoulder to shoulder', on the rugby field 'for the four proud provinces of Ireland'. These lyrics mirror the ways in which rugby union is perceived as an 'All-Ireland' game. In effect, 'Ireland's Call' explicitly generates an Irish we-image around rugby by employing a series of collective cultural references to make a unified Ireland appear, temporarily, a reality.

In addition, as a response to the continuingly delicate political situation in Ireland, an agreement was reached between the rugby football unions of Ireland and England not to play *Amhrán na bhFiann* when Ireland play England at Twickenham. The official response illustrates how contemporary Irish identity politics can be demonstrated in a sporting context. It also highlights the complexities of 'Irishness' and the problem of national symbolism, which has been an issue in Irish rugby since the founding of the Irish Free State in 1922 (Sugden and Bairner, 1993). This also provides further evidence for the unifying nature of a 'national' anthem as a 'symbol of particularity' and its relevance to sport (Billig, 1995).

As an addendum to the agreement between England and Ireland regarding the playing of anthems, a significant change occurred on 15 February 1997 in the fixture between the two countries played in Dublin. The pre-match events, which took place against the backdrop of ongoing efforts to negotiate an IRA ceasefire in Northern Ireland and mainland United Kingdom (and also the professionalisation of rugby union in Britain), were reported by David Walsh of *The Sunday Times*:

> Before the professionalism came the politics. Fifteen minutes before the game a light aircraft circled the stadium – 'Stop. Cease Fire Now' blazed a trailing banner. It expressed a hope for peace which no one disagreed with. The arguments would come later. The man on the public address solemnly asked us to respect the national anthems. This was the first time in the modern era that 'God Save The Queen' had been played at Lansdowne Road and there was more than a touch of curiosity about how it would be received. It passed off swimmingly (*The Sunday Times* [Internet Edition], 16 Feb. 1997).

These developments demonstrate that, whilst perhaps more is changing in rugby union than in the complex political situation in Northern Ireland, one cannot divorce Irish sport from Irish politics. In addition these changes further illustrate the significance of the linkages between identity politics, national anthems and international sport.

**The complex identities of Irish national and dual national rugby players**
The complex and shifting structure of personal identity provided some interesting, contradictory statements from the players. Some of the players likened representing their country to creating an additional layer of identity 'icing' (see also Maguire and Stead, 1996) which, put simply, was seen to increase their responsibilities as they were now playing for the nation.

When asked whether he felt he was playing for himself, the team or the nation, Mick remarked that it was:

> A little bit of everything really. You are representing not just yourself but your family. You have a huge bond with the other fourteen guys and . . . you're obviously proud of representing your country.

When asked the same question, Liam replied:

> Wearing the [Irish] jersey's a great honour for me. It's a kind of dream for any rugby player to represent his country . . . you . . . feel very proud to wear it. You're sort of representing everyone else who plays in your position in the country. . . . [In addition] you're representing your family, your friends, everyone who knows you, as well as representing your country.

This multi-layered and flexible nature of identity suggests that the first 'level' of identity is your self and your own performance, then the team, followed by your friends and family and the Irish public. These findings are in keeping with observations made by Elias (1991) and Mennell (1994) regarding the characteristics of social habitus. Amongst the players, there were found to be essentially four competing elements or 'identity markers' at play which are self, team, family and friends, and nation. These markers can be viewed as points along a diachronically varying continuum that ranges from the particular (the self) on one axis to the general (the nation) on the other.

This also suggests that different levels of national identification existed both between and within the personal identities of the players interviewed. Some seemed to deny an overt national identity, some revelled more openly in the perceived honour of being a representative of their nation whereas others seemed to fall into both of these categories. As previously discussed, a person's habitus is complex and some players, whilst being aware that they were representing their nation, tended to restrain or subdue these feelings when playing. This trend towards the subjugation of players' national identity can be seen as a deliberate 'professional' response to the extra pressure of representing the nation. Indeed this practice is probably a significant part of players' conscious and subconscious pre-match preparations (and is likely to be especially important for those with less experience of international matches). This subverting of potentially distracting emotions may considerably help players remain focused on the match at hand and stay in 'the now'.

Within the Irish squads the blend of players from Northern Ireland (who also considered themselves British) and the Irish Republic, along with some dual nationals, made for an intriguing melting pot of national identities. Samuel typifies this cosmopolitan nature of the Irish team:

> I consider myself an Irishman, but I also consider myself a Northern Irishman . . . [and] a British citizen . . . – it complicates things but in terms of sporting iden-
> tity I want to play for Ireland, that's my country . . . I'm Irish but I am a British
> citizen – I can therefore have dual nationality if I want (I can have a British and an
> Irish passport). In terms of everyday life I'm British, in terms of rugby I'm Irish
> and there'd be none more Irish than me on the rugby field.

This statement illustrates the multiple layers of personal identity, how an individual can possess more than one national identity and how these layers are both temporally and spatially specific (Mennell, 1994; Maguire, 1994).

It was interesting that the majority of the Irish players viewed the British and Irish Lions as a higher achievement than representing Ireland. Indeed, Ireland has a long history in contributing significantly to Lions tours (Coughlan, 1983). The Irish players also recognised the tradition behind the Lions and the impor-tance of bringing the four Home Unions together and, as Stephen stated:

> [the Lions] . . . brings different nations together and creates a bit more of a
> bind. . . . Every different country has their own style of play and every country has
> their own players with their different attributes. If you've got a British Lions side
> with Scottish, Irish, Welsh and English in it . . . The English are very good at
> control and technically they're superb. The Scottish are superb at rucking . . . The
> Welsh have got . . . drive and flair, they bring a little bit of adventure into the side.
> The Irish have got strong tacklers and they hustle and bustle and cause a bit of
> chaos . . . I think if you combine them together and get the best coach to organise
> it . . . [then you] get the best you can out of a mixture of them all. It gives you
> different options of play as a British side.

Such statements further illustrate the complex (sporting) relationship between the constituent nations of the so-called British Isles. As Lions, and

Celtic cousins, who traditionally view the English as 'the enemy', but are asked to bond with Anglo-Saxons and 'play' as a unit, the Scots and the Welsh have historically and constitutionally co-existed with the English. However, few players who had represented the Lions felt that they had ever taken on a British identity when they donned the famous red shirt. These feelings were endorsed by Gerald Davies (a British Lion in 1968 and 1971):

> Even the sense of Britishness is inaccurate, and therefore it, too, is confining . . . It is the jersey, uniquely, that creates the fusion. It is also in knowing that the honour is a pinnacle of achievement; the pride in individual performance insists that it must be one for all and all for one . . . The four nations, rich in their cultural diversity and character, accepted each other's weaknesses and strengths as Lions, and were made to feel better and more rounded personalities for the empathy. As separate nations at Lansdowne Road and Murrayfield, Twickenham and the Arms Park, different emotions are aroused (*The Times*, 'Lions Tour Special Report', 19 May 1997: 1).

The residual nature of British identity ensures that the nation remains a more primary source of identity. The players feel English, Irish, Scottish and Welsh either instead of or as well as British. 'Britishness' then becomes a far less tangible construct manifesting itself at a deeper level within the habitus making it even harder to demarcate.

Within the Irish World Cup squads of 1995 and 1999 there were two notable dual nationals who presented extremely intriguing biographies. Both Mick and Liam could have played for England but made conscious decisions to play for Ireland. Their experiences further complicated their 'identity maps'. Mick never wanted to play for England despite being born and bred there. He did not like what English rugby represented and he laid his cards on the table by joining London Irish at a young age. When asked how Irish he felt he replied:

> Well it's a difficult question for me because I was born in London and [have] lived there all my life. It's very easy for people to knock (especially with this accent) and . . . ask how Irish can he be? And you have to ask the question yourself. I would be a totally different person if I had been born in Cork or Dublin . . . It's just that when Ireland are in competition, no matter what sport, . . . you want Ireland to do well . . . to be successful. How Irish you feel and how Irish you are probably two different things. In many ways I'm . . . very Irish . . . . My father was English, . . . my mother's Irish and [yet] I've lived all my life in England.

When this point was probed further he argued that it was hard to define what 'Irishness' is. Mick then shared the following experience, which he described in some detail:

decisions [regarding which country you can play for] have to be made when you're very young. I was playing for London Irish and I was picked on the same night to play for London Irish and the London Division. The London Irish game was a friendly but [they] . . . were short. Mike Gibson was captain at the time and was fairly insistent that I play . . . [he] asked the question '. . . who do you want to play for, England or Ireland? What are you doing playing for London if you want to play for Ireland?'. So I went away and played for London Irish at Moseley and we lost by forty points. It was the end of my England career - but I didn't want an England career . . . Basically you nail your colours to the mast on that day . . . I don't even say [that] when I joined London Irish I wanted to play for Ireland because it didn't really cross my mind that I would. But I did want to play for London Irish and after that [decision had been made] I could [represent Ireland].

This could be seen to demonstrate either a strong desire to be true to his Irish roots, or a degree of 'sport-specific reasoning' in order to compete at international level by opting to be eligible for a weaker team. This type of sporting 'mercenary' (Maguire, 1996) is becoming increasingly prevalent in rugby union and these particular individuals will seemingly play for anyone in order to experience international rugby. Liam admitted that he chose Ireland partly because of the strength in depth of the competition in his position in England at the time (at the age of 21) when he had to make a decision between the two, but mainly because of his family. Talking initially about how Irish he felt he commented:

I consider myself very Irish really. The only thing is that I was born in England . . . But I consider myself Irish seeing that my whole family is Irish . . . the fact that I was born in England, I don't think, has any sort of consequence as [to] whether I am English or Irish . . . If you go up to an Irish person . . . [having been] born in England, having an English accent and having been educated in England . . . and say I'm Irish, they'd probably laugh at me . . . but deep down I feel Irish and I feel proud to say to anyone 'I'm Irish'.

He then continued:

I think one of the reasons why I chose Ireland was the fact that in Five Nations rugby . . . England were very successful. They had two very established [players in my position] and at that time I was struggling a bit. [So with] my family being Irish and always . . . [having] that Irish connection playing for London Irish there was that sort of pull towards Ireland and I suppose when you come to the age of twenty-one/twenty-two you have to choose – and I chose Ireland, the main reasons being my family.

Liam also implied that playing rugby for Ireland had made him more Irish as people could identify him as such because he wore the coveted green jersey. He had represented England at school, student, under-19 and under-21 levels, yet, ironically, he made his full international debut against England. This may indicate that he did not really consider his national identity until he graduated from student/youth rugby and indeed the process of 'choosing' the country to represent could be seen as part of his graduation to adulthood.

These responses from dual nationals provide extreme examples of the complex tensions that can exist both between and within national identities. They also illustrate some of the varying criteria that are required for players to officially 'belong' to a nation. Some players subjugate their 'home' nation through their sport in order to become more assimilated to their 'adopted' nation. These developments can lead individuals to seek to convince others that they belong to 'their' nation as part of the process of convincing themselves. None of the 'Irish' dual nationals claimed to have divorced themselves totally from their 'home' nation – nor was there evidence of disinheritance from their birthplace. Indeed there were many instances when the players provided contradictory interpretations of their we-image, illustrating that an individual can possess multiple national identities and that these might be of equal or different strengths depending on the moment and the location.

### 'Irishness' and the Irish style of play: we- and they-images

In defining the we-image built on an Irish rugby habitus, the Irish players characterised their style as fast, aggressive hustle and bustle with the players, as described by Stephen, being 'chasers and scavengers'. The Irish game was described by Peter as 'purposeful chaos' and the situation was neatly condensed by Liam who spoke of the indefatigable Irish fighting spirit:

> we may not have tremendous flair but the team has great spirit and when you put on an Irish jersey you'd die for each other on the pitch. You realise when you come up against the likes of England and France that you can't outplay them, the only way you can really take it to them is to test them out, see if they have the same sort of spirit you have.

The Irish viewed the Scottish as a rucking team that adopted a similar very fast wrecking and spoiling game. The English were seen to be organised, technically good and play a predictable, slow, controlled, mauling game using heavy forwards to wear down the opposition and force errors. The Irish players thought that the Welsh tried to play with flair and adventure but were in a quandary themselves over which style to play.

By considering the views of players from other nations, one can also piece together an outsider's view of Irish rugby. Justin, an England international, perceived the Irish to play more 'off the cuff' thriving on chaos – 'they fly everywhere, they just generate mayhem . . . it's just hit everything and anything'. Generally, Irish rugby teams were seen by the English as groups of extremely fervent individuals who, although unlikely to make it into an England team, always upped their game once they donned their national jerseys and played as a unit. Tim, another England international, referring to the Irish team's ability to be stronger than the sum of its parts, stated that:

> They're fifteen individuals who, while wishing them well, would probably not get into the England side . . . The difference is . . . as soon as they put on their national shirt . . . they become a different player.

Three of the Scottish players (Craig, Hamish and Rob) saw similarities between all of the Celtic nations' styles of play – all being seen to be prepared to 'die for the cause' (Craig). The Irish style of play in particular was seen as being not dissimilar to the Scottish style. However, the Irish style was characterised as more frantic, 'up and at 'em' (Hamish) and Rob stated that 'Ireland usually stop opponents playing their game and live off scraps'. The majority of the Scottish players also expressed an affinity with the Irish. This was encapsulated by Gordon who commented, 'they are a good-natured people, the country is lovely and I know a few players and get on with them well'. Craig added to this by revealing an 'affinity to the Irish because they have a similar style of rugby to the Scots and are very similar in nature. Both also have similar resources and constraints in playing terms'.

All the Irish players, reciprocating Scottish views, expressed an affinity to, and saw some similarities with, the Scots (in terms of playing styles, approach to life and national identification). The matches between the Irish and the Scots were seen as fierce but the after-match celebrations were seen as the wildest and the most enjoyable. In contrast, England was perceived as the 'old enemy' (Peter) and the chief 'target'. With reference to this aversion, Samuel stated:

> Everybody hates the English – it's tradition . . . I think it's because of their personalities. We tend, as Irish people, to . . . like to be underdogs – I think it's because we always have been . . . Whereas the English . . . [are] confident, it comes from their history. They're used to ruling the world . . . so they walk about with this . . . attitude and everyone dislikes them for it. They have supreme confidence in their own ability, which is fine, you can be arrogant but you don't have to be impolite with it.

The common denominator from the evidence gathered appears to be the existence of some similarities (and affinity) between the playing styles of the

Celtic nations (especially Ireland and Scotland) in contrast to those of England. The members of the Celtic teams appear to have formed a 'we'-identity, or Celtic fantasy image, which is juxtaposed against the dominant Anglo-Saxon English ('them'). These shared national (sporting) characteristics can act as strong identity markers in the development of a shared group charisma between 'Celtic cousins' reflecting a type of ethnic defensiveness.

## Conclusion

This chapter has provided an insight into the complex relationship between rugby union, identity politics and national habitus construction in Ireland. The sport is clearly seen by the players as a prominent fantasy shield in the Irish context and as being deeply interconnected with the special charisma of Ireland. The players, representing 'their' Ireland, appeared to be able to lift the consciousness of the nation from behind its fantasy shield into the hearts and minds of the populace. This transformation of group charisma from the 'imaginary' to the 'real' provides evidence of a united Ireland becoming, at least temporarily, more than an imagined or notional community.

Considering the specifics of rugby in the Irish context, the following themes emerge. Firstly, rugby union appears to be significantly connected to the national habitus of Ireland. In Ireland, rugby has created a unique arena for the testing of 'Irish' and 'British' identities. Secondly, the players are, in many ways, embodied symbols of 'Irish' national pride and patriotism. Thirdly, the experiences of dual national 'Irish' rugby players reinforce the complex and multiple character of national habitus. Fourthly, the players, the media and officials use styles of play (on the rugby pitch) and national stereotypes (off the pitch) as habitus codes to differentiate between nations. Finally, rugby in the context of the British Isles appears to foster a complex of I/we and us/them relations, exemplified in the juxtaposition between the Celtic fringe and the Anglo-Saxon English.

Rugby is seen by the players as an important source of national pride and as a central part of Irish national culture. The dominant theme is that rugby transcends political and religious divisions as well as providing a unique opportunity for the Irish nation to unite and compete as 'Ireland' on a world stage. The principal moment that tends to raise the national 'consciousness' of the players is the evoking of national habitus codes when the Irish anthems are played immediately prior to the kick-off of international matches. All agree that, whatever the anthem, this moment acts as a psychological tool for both focusing the mind on the task at hand and for remembering whom (and what) the players are representing. In this context, the anthems provide the most significant generation of I/we identity and group charisma.

An Irish rugby habitus forms one of the primary signifiers of the multi-layered personal identity of these elite sportsmen. The comments of the players, especially those made by dual nationals, indicate that identity politics and feelings of national charisma are 'at play' on the rugby field. Their observations as international rugby players, and the varied habitus codes they reveal, appear to lend credence to the notion that they are, indeed, highly visible embodied representatives of 'their' nation. As 'eighty minute patriots' these representatives of the nation awaken various embodiments of a united Ireland.

It is also interesting to note that the players' we- and they-images of the 'style' of Irish rugby are quite similar. The 'outsider' they-image of the Irish is centred on the perception that they are generally less talented individuals who, when playing for Ireland, can 'up' their game and produce displays full of aggression amidst a fog of chaos. This complements the Irish players' we-image of themselves as chaotic scavengers with a great team spirit. These descriptors are also readily found in the media and 'endorsed' in the official documentation of the IRFU.

Looking at Irish rugby as part of a wider figuration of rugby in the 'British Isles', there is a clear divide between Anglo-Saxon English players and those from the Celtic nations. This divide is even more apparent when one considers how the players perceive the playing styles and characteristics of their (and other) nations, and their construction of us/them identities. The players from the Celtic nations have a clearly defined they-image of the English and for a whole variety of reasons 'they' were the team to beat. The players from the Celtic nations perceived a special (rugby-inspired) Celtic charisma and we-identity. The Scots and Irish players, in particular, frequently described each other as Celtic cousins and seemed to share some playing characteristics and have similar outlooks on life.

To put all this in perspective, it is poignant to consider the words of Dan:

> Rugby for the island of Ireland is important, perhaps more so than other places as it brings even closer the different communities that put together the nation . . . I am very proud to be both British and Irish and don't feel the need to assert my national identity on others by marching or bombing. I'm just proud to be Irish.

In summary, it appears that the interdependencies binding rugby with national identity in the Irish context are complex, dynamic and particularly relevant in the late-modern era. Whilst sporting national habituses are sometimes symbolic and temporary, through the actions of certain people, especially the players, they can become very 'real' indeed. What is certain is that rugby union appears to be a significant part of Irish national culture and identity, where the Irish can be 'together standing tall'. However, making sense of the sport's role in the Irish context, to use Elias's words, is indeed a habitus problem par excellence.

Chapter 8

# Sport, identity and Irish nationalism in Northern Ireland

David Hassan

## Introduction

Northern Ireland contains a population of approximately 1.5 million people of whom around 600,000 are members of the Catholic faith (Elliott, 2000). Whilst the majority of the Catholic population is also politically nationalist and would support moves towards Irish unification, or at least greater involvement in the governance of Northern Ireland by the Irish Republic, other members of this community accept that Northern Ireland remains constitutionally British. In so doing some Catholics in the Province implicitly subscribe to a form of quasi-unionism with the remainder of Great Britain. What emerges is a less than uniform picture of either the present or future aspirations of the nationalist minority in Northern Ireland (northern nationalists). This chapter demonstrates how sport helps to provide a clearer picture of the ambitions of northern nationalists in the wider society and reveals a more heterogeneous approach to the study of sport and Irish national identity than has previously been offered.

The chapter begins with a detailed analysis of the theoretical framework underpinning this research by examining the construction and ideological significance of northern nationalism. There follows a specific focus on the different ways in which three major sporting activities in Ireland, Gaelic games, soccer and rugby union, are engaged with and utilised by northern nationalists to reveal wider socio-political ambitions, specifically with regard to the constitutional position of Northern Ireland. The analysis concludes by examining some of the emerging themes of the study, including how participation in certain sports can reflect a preferred future for different sections of the nationalist people within the Province. As the first part of this chapter makes clear, for many northern nationalists this is a future defined by an often turbulent past.

## Northern nationalism

Historically the study of Irish nationalism in Northern Ireland has been the subject of comparatively little academic investigation. In truth only the work of Todd (1999, 2001) and Phoenix (1994) has sought to address a clear imbalance between the sophisticated analysis of Ulster unionism (for example, Aughey, 1995 and Cochrane, 1997) and the relative dearth of any equivalent work on northern nationalism. What makes the scarcity of research into this community all the more significant are the numerous complexities and paradoxes associated with its actions and beliefs. Some Catholics in Northern Ireland are what Porter (1996: 66) refers to as 'liberal unionists', supporters of what NicCraith (2001: 3) describes as an 'Ulster British ideology'. This grouping, composed of both Catholics and Protestants, 'may consider themselves Irish, Northern Irish, British or whatever. The point is that Unionism as a political identity is *culture-blind*' (NicCraith, 2001: 3). The growing Catholic middle class includes an increasing number of citizens who advocate such a civic interpretation of life within Northern Ireland. A further difficulty associated with any analysis of northern nationalism is that it has traditionally lacked ideological consistency and has been fluid, conditional and dependent upon evolving circumstances. Todd (1990: 32) defines northern nationalism as 'a complex, internally differentiated ideology, based on an interrelated core of concepts which cut across and qualify each other. It has a rich and flexible conceptual structure which allows it to express divergent interests and accommodate very different political tendencies.' Nationalism for northern nationalists is about more than the achievement of Irish unification. In fact more localised issues, such as the pursuit of equality, justice and a sense of shared grievance endured by this community retain equal importance. Nevertheless, as the discussion thus far suggests, northern nationalism should not be viewed as an all-encompassing doctrine, one that avoids the discord typical of even the most resolute ethnies. Rather, there are those nationalists for whom the pursuit of justice and equality within Northern Ireland and an acceptance of the legitimacy of a nationalist presence in the country by the majority Ulster unionist population are sufficient, at least in the interim, to meet their needs. There are other groups for whom this is merely a necessary prerequisite ahead of Irish unity. 'Purer still is the nationalist vision that, in the short term at least, places the cause of Irish freedom above all other considerations' (Bairner 2001a: 80).

As if to illustrate the often paradoxical position adopted by northern nationalists on this issue, one need only examine the philosophy adopted by large numbers of this community during the late 1960s and early 1970s. Throughout these years the northern nationalist population was subjected to one of the most violent and oppressive periods of the recent ethno-sectarian conflict in Northern Ireland. During this era, characterised by the emergence of the Northern Ireland Civil Rights Association (NICRA), which had as its principal aim equal treatment for the Catholic/nationalist minority, nationalists in Northern Ireland were forced to decide between justice and nationalist ideology and they overwhelmingly chose the former (Todd, 2001). Nevertheless, it was perhaps inevitable that in seeking equality, justice and recognition of their right to express a distinctly Irish identity, previously dwindling support for Irish unification would be reignited. However, for many, the goal of a united Ireland was sought as much as a solution to ongoing social, economic and cultural discrimination at the hands of unionists as the fulfilment of traditional nationalist goals. This suggests that some degree of identification with Northern Ireland was present amongst the nationalist people but their continued subjugation in the province prevented this view from being couched in more positive terms.

Indeed, one of the most significant developments following the signing of the Good Friday Agreement on 10 April 1998 was a heightened degree of civic nationalism, born out of a new sense of political republicanism and founded on issues of equality and justice promoted throughout Northern Ireland. Yet arguably a consequence of this was the creation of a convenient 'escape route' out of the Northern Ireland problem for some in the Irish Republic. Despite stronger North–South links being integral to the peace accord, in reality a context was created in which many in the south could simply absolve themselves from any emotional unease they may have experienced over their attitude towards the plight of northern nationalists. The latter had historically viewed the Republic of Ireland as a loyal confidant, a solace in the face of what they considered an often-hostile northern state. Nationalists had actively sought the intervention of the southern government on issues of perceived injustices against their community and fought for its role as unofficial co-implementer of the peace deal itself.

However, there was a sense that the southern administration was a reluctant participant in the entire process, motivated in no small measure by a desire to finally extricate itself from the affairs of Northern Ireland. Writing in 1983, Padraig O'Malley (1983: 97) had claimed, '(Irish) Unification is no longer an article of faith in the south. The ability to pay for it absent, the willingness questionable. Increasingly there is a fear that a united Ireland would be an unstable Ireland. Having gained a little, she is loath to lose all on behalf of northern Catholics with whom she shares little other than a common religious denomination.' Since then, other commentators on the Republic of Ireland have considered localised disputes increasingly irrelevant amid the growing influence of Europe upon Irish life and have expressed concerns about the potential opportunities spurned as a result of the Republic's continued association with the conflict in Northern Ireland (O'Leary and McGarry,

1993; O'Connor 1985). Commenting on this development, Desmond O'Malley, TD (2001: 2), a former Fianna Fáil member (until his expulsion in 1985) and subsequently leader of the Progressive Democrats, states:

> For 30 years the Provisional I.R.A. would wage a cruel and dirty war in pursuit of an atavistic 'Brits Out' strategy. For 30 years they would so besmirch the name of nationalism that many Irish people no longer felt comfortable calling themselves nationalists. It is ironic that the ultimate effect of the Provo's long war has been to undermine totally the political philosophy upon which the campaign was based.

On occasion, nationalists in Northern Ireland, the overwhelming majority of whom advocate a constitutional resolution to the issue of Irish sovereignty, have been crudely portrayed as providing at least tacit support to the actions of militant republicanism. At the same time, there has been a sense of isolation, abandonment even, amongst northern nationalists. Thus, O'Connor (1993: 223–4) states:

> Many [northern nationalists] detect less southern sympathy for northern nationalists than for unionists. This strikes them as fundamentally improper, yet predictable. They had inherited a powerful sense of betrayal and rejection by the southern state.

It was against this growing sense of alienation that a new found sense of independence was born. According to Bairner (2001a: 80), 'the attitudes of northern nationalists toward the Irish Republic are ambivalent to say the least. In the main, there remains some sense that it is a kind of metaphorical home whereas the north, which is truly home, is tainted by unionism and is, therefore, at some level a hostile environment'. However, confronted with an increasingly liberal and pluralist Republic, sections of the northern nationalist population have acquired a degree of realism regarding their future options. Few within this community are prepared to admit openly that Irish unification may not be as important or even desirable as previously thought. Indeed, as this chapter and also Fulton's argument in chapter 9 below illustrate, it is often left to the realms of popular culture to reveal the true socio-political aspirations of many northern nationalists. Admittedly there is a danger in drawing too many assumptions about the relationship between sporting participation and issues of identity and constitutionality. However, the link between cultural and political nationalism in Ireland is such that it is possible to extract fairly sound conclusions regarding the wider ambitions of sporting nationalists. Of these the most controversial remains the belief that sport may act to reinforce ideas of separation from the rest of Ireland amongst northern nationalists. This issue would seem particularly relevant to the Gaelic Athletic

Association (GAA), a body concerned with the promotion of a comparatively monolithic view of Irish nationalism that seeks to regard all parts of Ireland as broadly similar. In fact, as the next part of this chapter makes clear, recent debates surrounding the future direction of the GAA, specifically its attitude towards police personnel becoming members of the organisation, reveal a quite discernible north–south divide.

## The Gaelic Athletic Association (GAA), Northern nationalism and the repeal of Rule 21

Since the controversial abolition on 17 November 2001 of the GAA's Rule 21 which had prevented members of the British security forces and police personnel in Northern Ireland from joining the association, the reaction amongst rank and file members in Northern Ireland has been remarkably calm. It was unlikely that large numbers of British Army personnel or their counterparts in the Police Service of Northern Ireland (PSNI) would seek immediate membership of the GAA. Nevertheless northern Gaels have demonstrated a fair degree of pragmatism about events in light of their almost unanimous opposition to the ban's removal. However, in the short period since its eradication, two separate developments have brought into sharp focus the reality of life for GAA members in Northern Ireland post-Rule 21.

Firstly, on Wednesday 30 October 2002, at Westmanstown GAA club in County Dublin, the PSNI played its first ever Gaelic football match against the Gárda Síochána, the police force of the Irish Republic. The game was shrouded in secrecy and the identities of the PSNI players remained confidential. High-ranking members of both police forces, including the Chief Constable of the PSNI Hugh Orde, attended the game. PSNI Chief Superintendent Brian McCargo, a former Antrim county Gaelic footballer, claimed prior to the match, 'We are going to have to test our skills now but winning isn't everything. What is important is taking the field to do something that has been prohibited for the entire history of the police force' (*Irish Independent*, 19 Nov. 2001: 34). Images of police personnel playing Gaelic football, a medium often used by northern nationalists to demonstrate disassociation from the Northern Ireland state, provided a stark reminder of how times had changed since the signing of the Good Friday Agreement barely three years previously.

PSNI members playing Gaelic football in their own company is one thing; seeking integration into established structures for the sport is an entirely different matter. There have been reports of violence at a small number of club games, particularly in the mid-Ulster area, between suspected members of the new police service and supporters of certain rival teams. Such violence is at its worst dispersed, irrational and founded upon a historical aversion towards agents of the state. Nevertheless the revelation that a playing member of the Michael Dwyer's club in Keady in south Armagh had joined the new police service and wished to continue playing for the club's Gaelic football team drew widespread media attention. Officially his decision has been met with considerable good faith in an area traditionally viewed as a stronghold for Irish republicanism. However, at ground level, the club has been affected by internal rancour, threats to remove funding by individual sponsors and a decision on behalf of some club members to refuse to travel with the side to certain parts of south Armagh for fear of reprisals against the club.

Both of these examples underline the importance of the GAA for many northern nationalists and the extent to which it has been affected by a climate of change within Northern Ireland. Yet each also highlights an untrusting, suspicious approach on the part of many northern Gaels towards the motives of those beyond the boundaries of their own communities. There exists an enduring sense of isolation amongst GAA personnel in Northern Ireland, mainly due to the high numbers of attacks individual members and clubs have experienced during the course of the recent 'Troubles'. Inevitably the role the GAA has performed throughout this period, acting as a significant meeting point for nationalists and functioning as an important counter hegemonic association, has seen it implicated in the affairs of the body politic. For many northern Gaels the organisation of the GAA, as an all-Ireland entity, represents a sporting manifestation of their political utopia. As a result, throughout the 1980s in particular, the GAA experienced difficulty distancing itself from identity politics in Northern Ireland. It was often crudely portrayed as one part of a republican machine embroiled in a violent dispute with loyalist paramilitary groupings and renegade State forces. Throughout these difficult times the solidarity of the organisation's membership in the Republic of Ireland remained steadfast, even if there was little the central administration of the GAA could offer its northern bloc other than occasional expressions of sympathy. It could not properly empathise with the experiences of people like Sean Bradley, Chairman of Wolfhounds GAA club, Limavady, situated 15 miles east of Derry city, in an area where nationalists constitute a minority and there exists a total rejection of Gaelic games activity by sections of the unionist population. Bradley recalls some of the problems his club encountered over a number of years at the hands of loyalist paramilitaries:

> The goalposts were cut down, so we put them up again. They were actually cut down five times. The pitch was strewn with broken glass. They [loyalists] sprayed the pitch with chemicals to make a large Union Jack in the middle of the pitch. There were various threats against individuals. I would have received telephone

calls saying that I would be shot dead. On adjoining land a new [Catholic] chapel was being built and on one November night it was blown up. The Ulster Defence Association [the largest loyalist paramilitary organisation] placed statements in the newspapers at the time claiming the reason why the chapel had been blown up was because the Catholic authorities had given the GAA a pitch to play on (Interview with the author, 5 Aug. 1999).

These and similar events helped to galvanise a sense of northern unity 'but they also fuelled the demand among many nationalists, GAA members included, for a united Ireland in a period when that aspiration was weakened considerably in the Irish Republic' (Bairner, 2001a: 81). In contrast to the situation in Northern Ireland, the Irish Republic now displays a more liberal view of nationalism than at perhaps any time in its history. According to Cronin (1999: 45), 'within the Irish Republic there currently exists a very positive and self-believing nationalism which accepts the forces of change that have impinged on nationalism in recent years. To be Irish in the 1990s and to proclaim such nationalism is unproblematic'. Herein lies the essential difficulty the GAA encounters in preserving its cultural homogeneity in Ireland. Ironically this ideological discrepancy has become more pronounced during the most rapid period of evolution and modernisation in recent GAA history. The removal of Rule 21, in particular, was initially met with some dismay by GAA members north of the border. Its existence remained important for many GAA members in Northern Ireland as it demonstrated, in their view, the continued unacceptability of the policing in Northern Ireland. This was a belief that evidently was not shared by their southern counterparts. What resulted, therefore, was further evidence of northern nationalists' isolation in Irish society, their continued interdependence upon each other and the discrepancy between ideological tokenism and the reality of life in Ireland at the turn of the twenty first century.

It is worth briefly exploring the context in which initial discussions regarding the deletion of Rule 21 took place in the latter part of the 1990s. On the whole it was one of an evolving and largely improving political climate in Northern Ireland. Paramilitary ceasefires on the part of all the major terrorist groupings, discussions between most of the political parties in the north, the arrival at a form of political agreement and the establishment of a representative and devolved assembly in Northern Ireland were developments welcomed by an overwhelming majority of citizens on the island of Ireland. Unquestionably it created problems for nationalists, and particularly republicans, in that it confirmed the legitimacy of Northern Ireland as a political entity. Yet, for all this, northern nationalism did reasonably well out of the Good Friday Agreement which proposed a range of measures, including anti-discriminatory legislation and the ultimate reform of the RUC.

However, as with any agreement of this nature, pressure came to bear on institutions and associations aligned with nationalism and the GAA felt the need to demonstrate its commitment to the changing climate by debating the removal of Rule 21. Following previous discussions on this issue in 1995 and 1998, the GAA again found itself having to debate old dogmas which, whilst of little direct relevance in the Republic of Ireland, continued to have profound resonance in Northern Ireland. Arising out of a combination of political brinkmanship, skilful leadership on the part of the then GAA President, Sean McCague, and an overriding sense that removing the rule was 'the right thing to do', every delegate from the Republic of Ireland amongst the 301 strong gathering at the City West Hotel, County Dublin, voted to abolish the rule. This was a significant departure from previous displays of solidarity by southern counties with their northern counterparts and marked a new beginning to relationships within the organisation as a whole.

The role played by southern delegates was made somewhat more palatable following the decision made by club representatives from County Down, two days in advance of the special congress, also to vote in favour of deleting the controversial clause in the GAA's rulebook. The other five counties based in Northern Ireland – Derry, Antrim, Armagh, Fermanagh and Tyrone – each decreed that the rule should be retained, essentially because they felt there was insufficient evidence that proposals designed to reform policing in Northern Ireland had fully taken effect. The issue was made more complex by the internal divisions evident within some of the aforementioned counties, which were linked in some instances to ongoing disputes between supporters of Sinn Féin, SDLP and dissident republicans who objected to elements of the Good Friday Agreement and the peace process more generally. Such disagreements gave rise to disputes and ill feeling within certain northern counties as some GAA members felt that the proper democratic procedures for arriving at agreement on such contested issues had been subverted. Certainly the assertion by President McCague, a native of County Monaghan in the northern province of Ulster and therefore someone with a degree of empathy for the plight of northern delegates, that 'the overwhelming nature of the vote showed I had my finger on the pulse. As far as I'm concerned it's just another day. It will be forgotten about next week' (Official GAA Website, 22 November 2001) was somewhat premature and only added to an already growing sense of alienation amongst the wider GAA constituency in Northern Ireland.

However, ultimately the removal of Rule 21, and similar discussions surrounding the possible deletion of Rule 42 which prevents the playing of sports such as soccer and rugby at GAA grounds, highlight the sizeable contrast in views between northern Gaels and their southern counterparts (Doyle, 2002). These are opinions that are likely to be replicated across a range of social, economic and political forums in the years ahead as the division between nationalists on both sides of the Irish border becomes more pronounced. That such views are already evident within the GAA, one of the largest all-Ireland bodies, is perhaps the most noteworthy development within Irish sport for many decades. In contrast, the deep divisions that have existed within the game of soccer in Ireland for at least the last eighty years have demonstrated the isolation and, at times desperation, of many northern nationalists with a love for 'the beautiful game'.

## Still the garrison game? Soccer, identity and Northern nationalism

It is ironic that a sport with strong historical links to England, a country often viewed by nationalists as an oppressive and unwelcome presence in Ireland, has become so popular with the nationalist people of Northern Ireland. Scornfully referred to by some northern nationalists as 'the garrison game' because of its celebrated links with the British army in Ireland, especially throughout the early part of the twentieth century, soccer carries an undoubted appeal for large numbers of the nationalist community. However, work by Finn (1994) suggests an ambiguous role for soccer in the lives of this community. Citing the example of Belfast Celtic, *the* nationalist soccer team of the twentieth century, Finn outlines how soccer allowed some northern nationalists to display an affinity with Northern Ireland by creating a sense of northern 'place'. Yet he concludes that the game also presents ample opportunity for other nationalists to reject ties with Britain through their fervent support of certain clubs, and in latter times, the Republic of Ireland international side, a relationship that is discussed at greater length by Fulton in chapter 9.

Through their support of 'nationalist' teams in the Irish League, the domestic league of Northern Ireland, northern nationalists are arguably legitimising the existence of such a construct and, by implication, perpetuating their own subordination. This analysis is strengthened by the fact that the history of nationalist involvement in soccer in Northern Ireland has been one of discrimination, injustice and ultimate withdrawal from the game, arguably attributable to the activities of unionist and loyalist factions associated with rival clubs and to unequal treatment at the hands of the game's administrators, the Irish Football Association (IFA) (Cronin, 1999; Sugden and Bairner, 1993; Hassan, 2001). Although clubs such as Belfast Celtic, Derry City and Cliftonville have served as focal points for counter hegemonic activity by northern nationalists, the fact that only Cliftonville remains an active member of the Irish League is of greatest significance. Belfast Celtic and Derry City resigned from the league in 1949 and 1972 respectively following sustained periods of discrimination from other clubs as well as clear instances of prejudicial arbitration on the part of the IFA (Coyle, 1999; Cronin 1999).

In the case of Belfast Celtic, such a development had added significance as it represented a change of policy on behalf of the club. Finn (1994: 39) claims that 'Belfast Celtic, as its decision to remain within Northern based Irish football in 1924 demonstrated, was certainly associated with Irish nationalism, but it also reflected a Northern Irish sense of place and identity'. Indeed, the club withdrew from local soccer in 1949 precisely because this sense of Irish nationalism and local identity, which had sustained its participation throughout difficult periods in its history, had become the object of resentment on the part of other, predominantly unionist, clubs in the Irish League. Until its resignation, in part as a result of events surrounding an infamous clash with Linfield on 27 December 1948 that ended in widespread rioting and an attack on Celtic's Jimmy Jones, the club had been determined to retain its membership of the Irish League. This derived from an understanding that, regardless of their political and religious differences, clubs like Belfast Celtic and Linfield, with its predominantly Protestant support base, had sporting, social and geographical links that could not be easily dismissed. Moreover, the location of Belfast Celtic in west Belfast, a socially and economically deprived region, underlined the importance of the club's survival beyond the realms of sport.

The importance of localised geographical and social identity is reaffirmed when examining the case of Derry City and the circumstances of its withdrawal from the domestic game in Northern Ireland. As Eamonn McCann recalls:

> They (Derry City F.C.) resigned from the Irish League in 1972 after several years of what they regarded as discriminatory behaviour by the football authorities in Belfast and they were right, absolutely right. And some of it was sheer religious bigotry. They didn't want to come to the Bogside to play their football (Interview with author, 20 July 1999).

Although violence was commonplace across the whole of Northern Ireland in the early part of the 1970s, the trouble involving Derry City, whose home ground, Brandywell, is located in the republican Bogside area of the city, was always constructed as politically motivated. Derry was portrayed as a rebellious club, alien to the unionist ethos of other Irish League teams and their followers (Duke and Crolley, 1996). This served to accentuate an already firmly held regional identity, the result of the unique circumstances that Derry nationalists had endured during the late 1960s and early 1970s. According to John Clifford:

> It's a very closed community in Derry. It all goes back to the 'Troubles' when they had to stand shoulder to shoulder at the bottom of the Rossville Street to take on the police and the [British] Army and the 'B' Specials and whoever else was

coming at them. At one stage you were defending your area for three days and you had to do your bit (Interview with author, 8 Jan. 2000).

In the light of this ongoing, factional and apparently institutionalised repression within soccer in Northern Ireland it was inevitable that, over time, northern nationalists would look beyond the confines of the state for a suitable outlet to express their soccer fandom. This community, with some notable exceptions, now supports the Republic of Ireland soccer team in international competition (Cronin 1999; Hassan 2001). Thus the popularity of the game amongst Irish nationalists in Northern Ireland, far from questioning their sense of national identity, appears to provide many with an opportunity to express their support for the idea of Irish unification. In this respect, as Fulton reveals in the following chapter, soccer acts as a vehicle by which Irish unity can be constructed in its imagined form, with the Republic of Ireland team, representing 26 of the 32 counties on the island, being reconstructed as a *de facto* all-Ireland team.

Their support for the Republic also implies a rejection of the legitimacy of the Northern Ireland state and its international soccer team. In recent times, northern nationalists have justified this stance by highlighting the maltreatment of prominent Catholic players, including Celtic's Neil Lennon, who have been selected to represent Northern Ireland. Lennon announced his retirement from international soccer on 23 August 2002, two days after he was due to captain Northern Ireland in a friendly international against Cyprus at Windsor Park, Belfast. On the afternoon of the game the player had received a death threat, purporting to come from loyalist paramilitaries. He subsequently withdrew from the game and, in so doing, highlighted the difficulties talented players from the Catholic community encounter when playing international soccer for Northern Ireland.

From a socio-political standpoint, therefore, soccer fulfils three main functions for northern nationalists. Initially, it provides a sense of northern 'place' and localised identity for followers of certain 'nationalist' teams. This is most pronounced when the very existence of such clubs is at stake, as the examples of Belfast Celtic and Derry City both confirm. Secondly, for some nationalists the game creates a forum for counter hegemonic activity and opposition to their continued subjugation within Northern Ireland. Moreover, few pastimes, apart from soccer, allow for regular and direct interaction between the two main ethnic groupings in the country. Clashes between clubs representing the two communities often take on a symbolic significance beyond the confines of a mere football match. Finally, the third main reason for nationalists attaching added significance to the game is their support for the Republic of Ireland soccer team. In this case nationalists locate themselves within an 'imagined' Irish nation, reconstructing the side as one representing the entire island of Ireland. None of these three positions remains mutually exclusive and in fact they often co-exist, even if the attraction of Irish League soccer for northern nationalists remains minimal. Indeed, soccer's ability to fulfil several contrasting roles underlines its added importance when studying the relationship between sport and identity in Northern Ireland. It should of course be added that the game is also utilised by Ulster Protestants in a variety of different ways as Magee amply demonstrates in chapter 11.

Compared with Gaelic games and soccer, rugby union has been given little scholarly attention by those seeking to unravel the complex strands of sporting nationalisms evident within the Province. This lacuna has been addressed earlier in this volume by both Garnham and Tuck (chapters 3 and 7) and the precise relationship between rugby and identity formation in Northern Ireland will be examined in depth by Bairner in chapter 10. Previous neglect can be partially attributed to the particular appeal rugby holds for the country's Protestant population. Traditionally Catholics have not played rugby in any sizeable numbers in Northern Ireland. The reasons are many and varied and will be examined in more detail in the ensuing analysis. Nevertheless the growing trend amongst Catholics to become involved in the sport and socialised into rugby's cultural *mores* is interesting and worthy of closer examination. How can such a shift be explained and what indications, if any, does this drift towards rugby provide regarding northern nationalists' social, cultural and political ambitions?

## Northern nationalists, rugby and the rise of the Catholic middle class in Northern Ireland

Recent research into the impact of social class in Northern Ireland concludes that there is 'considerable evidence to suggest that in terms of social interaction the middle classes are more integrated than the working classes' (Bryan, 2000:14). This is important in relation to developments within rugby because, as Bairner (1996) suggests, certain factors, such as class, appear to dilute the ability of sport to act as a coherent focal point for the projection of national sentiments. Bairner (1996: 331) claims that 'sport's capacity to help forge national identities is weakened by the fact that sport is also intimately bound up with those divisions that are a feature of even the most homogenous nation-state'. This assertion also reveals the possibility that identities projected through the medium of sport may not equate to political or constitutional views. This explains why, as Bairner demonstrates in chapter 10, Ulster unionists are able to reconcile their wish for Northern Ireland to remain part of the United Kingdom, and for them to remain British, with a willingness to represent an all-Ireland rugby team, which at the very least alludes to the existence of a sovereign and independent Irish nation state. Conversely it may permit some northern nationalists to play rugby in Northern Ireland, a context in which the sport remains primarily the preserve of those who wish to retain links with Britain, and yet still aspire towards the achievement of a united Ireland in broader political terms. However, in reality, the latter's willingness to become involved with rugby appears to reveal a wider form of quasi unionism, a passive acceptance of the status quo in Northern Ireland.

Catholics involved with the sport of rugby union in Northern Ireland have either played it at school, been socialised into the sport as a result of business or social contacts or have been actively recruited by individual clubs keen to exploit a previously untapped pool of talent. Whatever the exact reasons for their participation in rugby, 'in certain cases once Catholics join a club they almost immediately shed any sense of an exclusively nationalist identity' (Hassan, 2001: 264). Some are even reluctant to describe themselves as Irish, as if to do so would be to endorse a very narrow definition of this term. As Graham (1997: 7) states, 'national identity is created in particular social, historical and political contexts and, as such, cannot be interpreted as a fixed entity; rather it is a situated, socially constructed narrative capable of being read in conflicting ways at any one time and of being transformed through time'. Recognising their minority status in the sport, the fact that some of these nationalists are reluctant to highlight particular expressions of Irishness and prefer to abide by the established conventions of the majority unionist membership, is perhaps not totally surprising. By exercising an overwhelmingly unionist ethos alongside a largely Protestant officialdom, the Ulster Branch of the IRFU promotes a form of unionist hegemony that belies its involvement with an all-Ireland association. There are some exceptions, such as City of Derry Rugby Football Club which has a disproportionate number of Catholics involved in the club and a more nationalist habitus. This is, in part, a reflection of the context in which the club operates, as Catholics constitute a large majority of those who live in Northern Ireland's second city. City of Derry also has an extremely progressive cross-community strategy, one that has received the unlikely support of Mitchel McLaughlin, Sinn Féin Assembly member for the area. In congratulating the club on the occasion of its Ulster Senior Cup success in 1999, Mr McLaughlin spoke of the excellent work the club had done in attracting cross-community support and personnel (*Irish News*, 25 Oct. 1999: 5).

On the face of it rugby appears to be a sport that offers solace for those who abhor the divisive nature of association football and GAA in Northern Ireland. Yet it remains so, in this context, only to the extent that nationalists must be prepared to compromise on their perceived political ambitions and in turn are rewarded by unionist willingness to countenance an all-Ireland team. In practice this has resulted in a policy tantamount to the cultural and political assimilation of Catholics playing and administering rugby in Northern Ireland (Hassan, 2001). Mark McFeeley, a middle-class Catholic lawyer practising in Derry, typifies the approach of many nationalists who, like him, have become socialised into rugby:

> I have a big house and a earn a good living. To be perfectly honest, I don't think a united Ireland is going to give me anything I don't already have (Interview with the author, 2 September 1999).

McFeeley personifies those middle-class Catholics who have found a new confidence and affluence in Northern Ireland, things that most nationalists were denied for the greater part of the twentieth century. They are keen to promote this but are wary of being reviled by their own community, many of whom ironically appear more comfortable cast in the role of a member of the oppressed minority. In such cases nationalist participation in rugby symbolises a kind of staged withdrawal from the underclass and is often endorsed by educated young men who have experienced the benefits of inclusion in wider society. Unquestionably they are viewed with suspicion by many in the nationalist community, on the one level because of their involvement with a foreign sport but equally because they see themselves as middle class and therefore 'above' their fellow Catholics. O'Connor (1993: 41) cites the feelings of a number of nationalists who deeply resent the new-found status of their co-religionists quoting one interviewee as saying, 'some accuse this new class of being hedonistic, not fired with any strong ethos, much more materialistic than anything else. They are very much participators in the good life – and that doesn't make for radicals'.

In the main the same could be said of rugby playing Catholics. They do not aspire towards immediate Irish unification nor do they seek the reconstitution of Northern Ireland. Their Irishness is adequately expressed through the apparently ecumenical, apolitical Irish international rugby team. On the face of it, such a construct sits neatly with an idealised vision of Irish sporting nationalism. A team that draws its players from Northern Ireland and the Irish Republic, one that contains both Catholics and Protestants, with its base in Dublin and the popular support of the Irish nation, north and south, has much to commend it. Indeed ahead of the Ireland *versus* England international on 30 March 2003 which was to decide the destination of that season's Six Nations' Championship, there appeared genuine cross-community, cross-border support for the Irish side. Yet this was tempered by a broad apathy towards the activites of the team on the part of many working-class nationalists and a marked reluctance by Ulster loyalists to lend their support to an all-Ireland team. Some loyalists wore the Ulster rugby shirt whilst watching the game at Lansdowne Road, presumably to illustrate their conditional support of the Irish side, which contained only two players, David Humphreys and Gary Longwell, from the northern Province. Yet amongst the middle classes in Northern Ireland, Protestant and Catholic alike, support for the team remained resolute. It is at this level that the most significant developments in the relationship between sport and identity in Northern Ireland over recent years are to be found.

## Conclusion

The aim of this chapter has been to highlight how sport, perhaps more than any other medium, reveals the nature of internal division within northern nationalism/Catholicism and provides some indication of likely trends that may emerge in the years ahead. It has been demonstrated how Gaelic games, quintessential Irish cultural pastimes, perform a multitude of functions for northern nationalists. Initially, because of the manner in which they are organised, they provide a forum for the projection of local, parish-based identities. Yet, simultaneously, they sustain a bond between Irish nationalists due to a mutual investment in the games and a unique interpretation of Irishness. However, it is now also appropriate to highlight the division that exists, along state borders, between the GAA fraternity in Northern Ireland and that of the Irish Republic. The unique conditions endured by northern Gaels have galvanised that community in a most resolute manner. Alongside a growing sense of alienation from the Irish Republic has developed a sense of independence amongst northern nationalists that questions the claim of the GAA to be a monolithic, all Ireland sporting body. The extent of this divide was starkly portrayed in the events surrounding the eventual repeal of Rule 21. The unanimous decision by GAA representatives in the Republic of Ireland to ignore the genuine and overwhelming desire of the GAA fraternity in Northern Ireland to retain the rule has implications for the long-term future of the GAA in its present form. This seemingly partitionist approach is equally manifest within discourse on the proposed removal of Rule 42, as if the presence of all controversial rulings within the GAA statutes, exist solely to pacify the association's northern bloc. In spite of this, it is much too early to refer to the existence of an unofficial 'Northern Ireland Gaelic Athletic Association'. Nevertheless the degree of cohesion amongst the organisation's membership, specifically between its followers in Northern Ireland and the Irish Republic, has unquestionably been damaged as a result of recent events.

Soccer, on the other hand, has been organised on a partitionist basis in Ireland for more than 80 years. Initially it found favour amongst urban, working-class nationalists because, like Gaelic sports in rural areas, the game expressed a sense of belonging – to a district, a community, or a place. In time it also created a focal point for the display of counter hegemonic sentiment as a highly visible platform for disobedience was seized upon by sections of the nationalist people to highlight their opposition to a range of discriminatory practices implemented by the Unionist-led government. That said, Catholics did support the Northern Ireland international team, particularly during the 1970s and 1980s. As a consequence, soccer provided an opportunity for some in this community to express tacit allegiance to the state. However, as opposition to Catholic involvement with the Northern Ireland side grew over subsequent years, widespread northern nationalist disaffection towards the team took hold. As a result an overwhelming sense of apathy and occasional delight at Northern Ireland's lack of success became evident within nationalist areas. The rise to prominence of the Republic of Ireland side in the early 1990s, combined with moves in the political domain which appeared to make the prospect of Irish unification more likely, allowed northern nationalists to 'imagine' themselves supporting an all-Ireland, essentially Catholic and nationalist, soccer side. Even many ordinary Catholics in Northern Ireland, with little or no interest in the game, now refer to the Republic of Ireland team as 'their' team.

Whilst this situation is likely to continue for some time, there remains the possibility that northern nationalists will seek greater integration into soccer within Northern Ireland in the years ahead. In recent times both Donegal Celtic and Lurgan Celtic Bhoys, two Intermediate sides with nationalist followings, have resorted to legal recourse to guarantee their participation in senior soccer (Fenton, 2000). Moreover, after witnessing nearly two decades of sustained verbal and, at times, physical attacks upon players from the nationalist tradition, Windsor Park is now a much-improved venue on international match days. It is regrettable that in the midst of this period of change, Neil Lennon, the country's most high profile Catholic player of the last 15 years, felt obliged to retire from international football because of threats on his life. Nevertheless, there is a reformed atmosphere at the ground when Northern Ireland play, a development for which the IFA deserves some credit. That said, a decision by the football authorities in Belfast to replace the playing of 'God Save the Queen', with an anthem more acceptable to all sections of the Northern Ireland community, would be a welcome and magnanimous gesture appreciated, in particular, by the nationalist community. It would unquestionably do much to convince Catholics about the degree of change that has taken place within the country's soccer administration in recent years. A commitment to making this change, coupled with an improvement in the team's fortunes on the pitch, could well persuade Catholics in Northern Ireland to assume a greater interest in the affairs of the country's international side.

In contrast to soccer, Catholic involvement with the game of rugby union is limited. Nevertheless, the involvement of the small, yet growing, number of this community who do partake in the sport provides a fascinating insight into their preferred socio-political and constitutional futures. This is because rugby in Northern Ireland remains a largely middle-class, Unionist pastime, although on the international stage the sport is represented by a united Irish side. As Bairner argues in chapter 10, the distinction between sporting and official nationalisms allows political unionists to endorse rugby's structural arrangements on the island. Despite this, there remains some uneasiness within the wider northern nationalist community regarding Catholic involvement in rugby. There is a sense that rugby playing Catholics are essentially liberal unionists and have no immediate desire to question the constitutional legitimacy of Northern Ireland. Their Irish identity is simply different from those nationalists involved with Gaelic sports and contrasts still further with nationalists who follow certain club sides in the Irish League. It is this fundamental disparity that is at the root of this analysis, which suggests that rather than cling endlessly to the assumption that all nationalists are somehow the same, those studying the relationship between sport, national identity and constitutionality should accept, and indeed celebrate, the extent of diversity that exists within this community.

This chapter has examined the role sport plays in the lives of nationalists living in Northern Ireland. Specifically it has sought to provide insights into the supposed political and constitutional aspirations of members of this community. No claims are made that such analysis somehow equates to an exact science or that other forums for the projection of such views do not exist. Instead because of the manner in which sport is organised in Northern Ireland, essentially to reflect separate social and political standpoints, participation in certain sports, or expressing allegiance to certain teams, implies a range of wider goals and aspirations. Yet this relationship is by no means a straightforward one. If this chapter has achieved anything it is to highlight the different, and at times contrasting, roles certain sports perform for members of the nationalist community in Northern Ireland.

Chapter 9

# Northern Catholic fans of the Republic of Ireland soccer team

Gareth Fulton

## Introduction: 'playing' the same game

A significant body of writing dealing with the social, political, and cultural aspects of football in Ireland has emerged in recent years. However, as David Hassan noted in the previous chapter, within the existing literature there have been fleeting references to, but little sustained analysis of, northern Catholic support for the Republic of Ireland football team, an omission that can be explained with reference to two factors. Firstly, the thinking of most socio-logical writing on football in Ireland, with some justification bearing in mind the institutional organisation of the sport on the island, has tended to mirror the geo-political border, with authors focusing on either the north or the south. Most analyses of football in the north have focused on the ways in which the Northern Irish international team and local clubs have been appro-priated as symbols of, and vehicles for, various Protestant identities, with reference being made to the alienation from the sport felt by many northern Catholics (Bairner, 1997; Bairner and Shirlow, 1998a; Sugden and Bairner, 1993). Indeed, this point is further emphasised by Jonathan Magee in chapter 11 below. Recent writing concerned with football in the south has emphasised the Republic of Ireland football team's role as a vehicle for the expression of a specifically southern brand of nationalism, the attitudes and experiences of supporters from Northern Ireland either being ignored or subsumed within broader discussions of the nature of the Republic's fan-base as a whole (Cronin, 1999; Giulianotti 1996; Holmes, 1994). Secondly, most studies of the links between sport and nationalism in Ireland, of which northern Catholic support for the Republic of Ireland team is but one manifestation, have focused on the GAA, the repository of 'national' games in the south and an important focal point for many Catholics and nationalists in the north (Bairner, 1999a).

This chapter examines northern Catholic support for the Republic of Ireland football team both as a reflection of, and as a particular mode of expressing, a northern nationalist sentiment. On the one hand it points to the importance of football as a means through which northern Catholic fans can construct their nationalist identities. In this sense the analysis has resonance in the work of Buckley and Kenney (1995) who account for the persistence of sectarian division, not in terms of assumed cultural differences between Catholics and Protestants that are said to be negligble, but with reference to the ways in which shared cultural ideas and practices are *used* in specific, con-crete situations. In suggesting that the two ethnic groups in effect construct or 'negotiate' their identities using the same cultural materials, they remark: 'As with two sides in a soccer match the two ethnic groups attack and defend different goals and they wear different colours. Nevertheless they play the same game' (Buckley and Kenney 1995: 195).

Football is certainly an apt metaphor for describing how identities are constructed in Northern Ireland, but it is also much more than that. Football, for supporters, players, and officials, is a lived reality, an arena wherein par-ticular identities are produced and reproduced, and a symbol of and vehicle for these identities. The particular effectiveness of football in this regard resides in the fact that unlike other sports in Northern Ireland it is not a cultural activity that is peculiar to either of the two ethnic groups. It is a game that is 'played' by both sides, literally as well as metaphorically, and, as such, it does not necessarily indicate a political preference or national affiliation (Sugden and Bairner, 1993; Bairner and Darby, 1999). Ironically, perhaps, it is precisely for this reason that the sport has become particularly vulnerable to political exploitation facilitating rivalry between the two ethnic groups.

Although support for the Republic of Ireland team is one particular way in which northern Catholic fans can construct and express their nationalist identities, the analysis of this body of fans may, on the other hand, be used to reflect upon broader characterisations of northern nationalism. In other words, this study, like that of Hassan, provides a suitable 'lens' (Klein, 1997) through which to view broader concerns with the nature of the Catholic com-munity, whose attitudes and experiences are said to be increasingly nuanced, heterogeneous and changing (McGarry and O'Leary, 1995; O'Connor, 1993; Ruane and Todd, 1996).

Unlike previous work on football culture(s) that have taken either the north or the south as their political, social and cultural contexts, an investi-gation into the attitudes and experiences of northern Catholic fans of the Republic of Ireland team necessitates a consideration of 'fandom' that does not, and cannot, simply reflect the geopolitical border. Rather, these supporters constitute and construct an important aspect of northern Catholic football culture that transcends the border and, furthermore, may serve to symbolically deconstruct it. The chapter is therefore organised according to three main strands of analysis. First, northern Catholic support for the Republic's international team is set in historical context by examining the nature of northern nationalism, and the development of football in Ireland against the prevailing political backdrop, in the period up to the early years of the 'troubles'. The argument then proceeds to consider these fans in relation to what is generally seen as the reconstruction of northern nationalism from the 1960s, and in the context of the links that have been drawn between football and politics in the north and south during this period. Thus, the second strand of the analysis is concerned with Catholic alienation from the sport in the north, focusing on the ways in which supporters negotiate definitions of themselves through constructing definitions of the Protestant, unionist or loyalist 'other'. Finally, the chapter addresses the nature of the identification and affiliation that northern Catholic fans have with the Republic's team, highlighting the need to discern how the southern side helps supporters construct their Irish, or northern Irish nationalist, identities.

## Football, politics and history

A growing amount is now being written about Irish, and northern Irish, nationalism (Boyce, 1995; Phoenix, 1994), and about the early development of football in Ireland (Brodie, 1980; Sugden and Bairner, 1993). However, the links between them, specifically the extent to which football in Northern Ireland in the first half of the last century was appropriated as a symbol of, and a vehicle for, northern nationalist sentiment, has received rather less attention. The history of sportive nationalism in Ireland, on the contrary, has been dominated by the GAA, an organisation that for many years successfully construed football as a foreign game that only served to bolster British cultural imperialism. The image of football that the rhetoric of the GAA helped to create was encouraged, furthermore, by the nature of the support for the game in both the northern and southern parts of the country. In the north, particularly in Belfast, football attracted most support from members of the Protestant working class, whilst, in the south, the game remained closely associated with the Anglo-Irish community, garrison towns, and a British sporting culture.

That said, although the GAA played a central role in the construction of Irish national identity in the early decades of the last century, it is equally apparent that for many northern Catholics, especially in urban areas, football provided a platform on which national affiliation could be expressed. The GAA did not articulate the views of all Irish nationalists and the organisation's stated position *vis à vis* foreign sports was certainly not heeded by those Catholics who followed the fortunes of the Belfast Celtic football club in the early twentieth century (Coyle, 1999). Formed in 1891 and modelled on its

Glasgow namesake which had been established three years earlier, the club drew the vast majority of its support from the Catholic working class, members of which, in electoral terms, overwhelmingly voted for Home Rule or nationalist candidates before and after partition respectively. For these supporters, not only did following a particular football team not compromise their national identity, it actually provided them with a vehicle through which they could express it.

The case of Belfast Celtic is significant in a number of respects. It illustrates that the links between football and nationalism in Northern Ireland, of which northern Catholic support for the Republic of Ireland is but one contemporary manifestation, is not a new phenomenon. It also reinforces the historic links between the north-east of Ireland and Scotland that have been drawn in much of the literature (Sugden and Bairner, 1994) and demonstrates that football quickly established a place in the affections of working-class Catholics, as well as working-class Protestants in this corner of the island. It shows that even in the formative years of the last century when nationalist opposition to 'foreign' games was strong, football, at club level at least, could be appropriated as a symbol of Irish national identity. Finally, it illustrates how class, north–south, or rural–urban differences, manifest in nationalist attitudes, could be reflected in sporting terms.

Belfast Celtic remained an important focal point for northern Catholics and a significant symbol of Irish nationalism up until the club withdrew from the north's Irish league in 1949. Furthermore, its emotional appeal is apparent in the recollections of surviving fans. As Bairner and Shirlow (2001) have persuasively argued, even as an imagined team Belfast Celtic is still one of the most feared and hated teams in Irish league football. The authors suggest that this fear and hatred is shared by many Protestant football fans and supporters of the GAA alike, the attitudes of the former rooted in sectarianism and the potential threat of Belfast Celtic's success on the field of play, the views of the latter reflecting an internal struggle within the northern Catholic community for the sporting soul of Irish nationalism. However, although Belfast Celtic and more recently Derry City (see Duke and Crolley, 1996) provide striking examples of the links between football and nationalism at club level, it is evident that a northern nationalist sentiment failed to find expression at international fixtures. Towards setting northern Catholic support for the Republic of Ireland team in historical context it is also necessary, therefore, to explain why there continued to be broad-based Catholic support for the north's national team during the years of the Stormont regime and throughout the first decade of the recent 'troubles'.

If we were to relate Catholic support for the Northern Ireland 'national' side directly to how northern nationalists have been characterised in the years preceding the recent conflict, notably as a population caught between following a strategy of abstention from and participation in the state (Phoenix, 1994), it might be tempting to deduce that the position of these fans was ambiguous and that the nature of their support was essentially confused. On the contrary, it is apparent that Catholic fans were neither ambivalent nor half-hearted in their support but rather tended to be as enthusiastic and passionate as football fans throughout the world are in following 'their' team. The success that the northern side enjoyed until the 1980s relative to its southern counterpart no doubt served to encourage Catholic support. The Northern Irish team qualified for the 1958 World Cup in Sweden and more recently competed in the same tournament in Spain 1982, and Mexico 1986. It was only following the Republic's qualification for the European Championships of 1988, and their participation in three of the last four World Cups, that the fortunes of the north and south have been reversed.

Instead of relating Catholic support for the north's national team directly to how northern nationalism has been characterised in the years between Partition and the troubles, it is perhaps more appropriate to situate this body of fans within the wider social and political context of the period. In this way we can note that the recent conflict, and its consequences in terms of increased division, segregation and polarisation between the two ethnic groups in the north, was yet to have a significant impact upon football, and sport generally. It is certainly evident that the conflict of the last thirty years has had a divisive impact on football, as on many other aspects of social life, and clearly this wider social and political context is crucial in explaining why many Catholics in recent years have expressed an affiliation with the south. However, to account for the presence at Windsor Park of large numbers of Catholic fans of the north's national team in the period up to the early years of the troubles solely with reference to the absence of the recent conflict is inadequate and is to indulge in an exercise in 'reading history backwards'. Although divisions between the two largest ethnic groups in the six counties have been greatly exacerbated as a result of the events of the last thirty years it is equally evident that Northern Ireland in the preceding fifty years also constituted what many commentators are prone to label a 'divided society'. Football at club level, most notably in matches between Belfast Celtic and Linfield, the biggest Protestant club in the north, for many years provided a platform on which the divisions between northern nationalists and unionists could be 'played out'. In order to understand why these divisions, currently expressed in terms of Catholic support for the south and Protestant support for the north, were not manifest to the same extent at international level in the earlier period, I would argue that it is also necessary to examine the nature of the relationship between Northern Ireland and the Republic, in football terms, during this period.

Following Partition, the relationship between the Irish Football Association (IFA) and Football Association of Ireland (FAI), the game's governing bodies in Northern Ireland and the newly constituted Irish Free State respectively, and during the middle decades of the last century, can most suitably be characterised in terms of points of divergence and convergence. It would appear that where their interests diverged the two associations tended to lead quite separate existences and thus tensions between them were negated. Where their interests converged, the divisions between the two governing bodies were exacerbated. The relationships cultivated by the two associations with FIFA, and the fact that their respective international teams were not drawn to play each other until the 1970s, mark important points of divergence. Following its formation in 1921, the first priority of the FAI was to gain international recognition. This was vital not only in terms of having its representative team entered in international competitions, but also in relation to bolstering the organisation's nationalist credentials. The IFA, on the other hand, as one of the world's oldest associations that continued to administer the game in the north, did not need such international recognition. In fact, the north's governing body was so sure of its position as a significant national association that following disputes with FIFA it forfeited its membership, along with its British counterparts, between 1928 and 1946.

The different courses pursued by the two associations, along with the cool relations between the Irish Free State and Britain during this period, help explain why the southern side did not play any of the United Kingdom's associations until 1946, when England visited Dublin. More significantly, the legacy of the strained relations that existed between Northern Ireland and the Republic, along with the fact that their respective national sides were not drawn to play one another in international competition until the 1970s, conspired to dictate that the rivalry between the north and south was played out, not on the football pitch, but in the offices of administrators. Thus the wider social and political context, as well as a lack of international fixtures, meant that football itself was incapable of inspiring the same rivalry between the northern and southern states that it has done in more recent years.

However, although the FAI and the IFA had different priorities in respect of their status within international football, their interests did converge on two important issues that served to exacerbate existing tensions. Firstly, until the late 1940s the northern association continued to select representative sides from players born throughout the island. The international fixtures of the two associations rarely clashed and so the situation arose where players could represent both jurisdictions. Consequently, even if there were officially two national teams in the period after Partition, the overlap of players meant that in practice there were all-Ireland teams in so far as players from both the north and south competed alongside each other. The policy of selecting players from outside the six counties was based on the second issue around which the interests of the two associations converged, namely the right to use the term

'Ireland' in describing their national teams. In the period before the Irish Free State became a republic, the IFA recognised its southern counterpart only as an association with dominion status. In so doing they declared their right to remain the 'national' association on the island and to be the only association entitled to be called 'Ireland'.

These two issues, in which both associations had a vested interest, constituted a struggle over both players and symbols and clearly served to exacerbate divisions between the north and south. In footballing terms, the period between Partition and the first decade of the recent conflict thus emerges as one that anthropologists are inclined to label as 'liminal' (Turner, 1974), a term used to denote a transitional or interstitial condition during which time symbols and the meanings attached to them are usually said to be ambiguous. The ambiguous status of international players and to a lesser extent the two associations, and the symbolic struggle over the title 'Ireland' and the meanings with which it was to be imbued, reflect the liminal state of Irish football at this time. It was only in the late 1970s that the official practice of describing the northern side as 'Ireland' was dropped in favour of the more commonly acknowledged 'Northern Ireland' and the reassertion of cultural and political order in footballing terms was confirmed.

It is important to note, however, that in addressing concerns relating to how the term 'liminality' can carry connotations of someone or some-thing not being one thing or another (i.e. nothing), anthropologists have consistently shown how people in liminal conditions are often not passive, but rather are usually exceptionally creative. The policies of the two asso-ciations to select players from outside their jurisdictions to represent them, and the ways in which they both sought to appropriate the term 'Ireland', demonstrate the creativity of the participants in the liminal conditions which characterised Irish football at this time. It seems reasonable to suggest that within this liminal context, participants, whether as players, fans or admini-strators, were not so much *playing for* (or supporting) an essentialised Northern Irish or Irish identity but rather were *playing with* various Irish identities.

The wider social and political context, and the 'liminal' nature of Irish football up to the first decade of the recent conflict, determined that the Northern Ireland team attracted a broader range of support amongst both Catholics and Protestants. However, it is worthwhile cautioning against constructing a simplistic 'then and now' narrative that traces sectarianism and division, and their manifestation in sport, to the start of the troubles. Although the Northern Ireland team was not yet the symbol of the various Protestant identities that it was to become during the 1980s, football at club level, as has already been noted, had long been a vehicle for the dramatisation of northern nationalist and unionist identities.

## Narrating alienation: becoming Republic of Ireland fans

It is evident, therefore, that throughout most of the twentieth century Catholic football fans did not experience the expression of a northern nationalist sentiment and support for the north's international team as mutually exclusive practices. Although football was appropriated by many supporters as a symbol of northern nationalism and a means of resisting the northern state, the sport simultaneously served to integrate the Catholic population within broader Northern Irish society, an argument pursued elsewhere by Bradley (1998) in his consideration of the role of Glasgow Celtic as a symbol of Irish immigrant identity in Scotland. Belfast Celtic's involvement in the sport and the widespread appeal of the game for northern nationalists, especially in urban areas, allowed for participation in a popular facet of the larger society. The role of football as an integrating force is reflected, furthermore, in broad-based Catholic support for the Northern Irish team. Northern Catholic support for the Republic's football team thus emerges as a relatively recent phenomenon, the product of the last twenty years or so. The recent conflict, and its impact on football in Northern Ireland, provides the more immediate context within which the attitudes and experiences of this body of supporters must be understood.

Although football continues to be embraced by both Catholics and Protestants, the north's international team, in recent times, has become synonymous with the expression of an exclusively Protestant identity, a development Sugden and Bairner (1993) persuasively argue must be related to the 'siege mentality' which is so central to unionist ideology. The collapse of the Stormont regime and the introduction of Direct Rule, as well as the subsequent political developments of the last thirty years which have been viewed as largely consisting of concessions to nationalists and republicans, has heightened many Protestant fears of being abandoned by Britain. The authors suggest that in the perceived absence of British support, and confronted with the fear of being subsumed within a united Ireland, many Protestants and unionists have readily clung to organisations and emblems, such as the north's international football team, which are exclusive to Northern Ireland. In particular, the northern side has provided loyalist working-class males with a vehicle through which they can express their masculinity, sense of identity, and unwavering loyalty to the province (Bairner, 1997). The appropriation of the team has been most visibly manifest in the emblems, symbols, and paraphernalia displayed and worn by fans, and has been audible in the instances of highly emotive anti-Catholic chants, songs and rhetoric which have consistently characterised support at international matches in the relatively recent past.

Despite their support for the Republic of Ireland, many northern Catholic fans have attended matches involving the Northern Ireland side. Some older fans have been to more Northern Ireland than Republic of Ireland games owing to their support for the northern side over a number of years. Others recall going to a series of games during the 1980s when the north's national team enjoyed a period of unprecedented success. A few have attended fixtures in recent years, though as 'neutral' spectators more concerned with admiring the skill and talent of opposing teams and players than with supporting the northern team. Virtually all fans, however, express an affinity with the Republic's football team, the origins, maturity, and strength of which can be related to their experiences of following football in Northern Ireland, for different lengths of time and to different degrees, during the course of the troubles. It is within the context of the Protestant atmosphere that came to surround the north's national team during the last two decades that we must seek to understand what I would argue is the *process* whereby northern Catholic football fans have come to narrate a sense of alienation from the northern side and have readily come to support its southern counterpart.

In examining the *process of becoming* Republic of Ireland fans it is evident that two factors, namely age and class background, are important in structuring the experiences of northern Catholic supporters. For those fans old enough to recall their experiences of following the north's national team in the middle decades of the last century, current support for the Republic constitutes, at most, a conscious change or switch of allegiance, and, at the very least, an increased interest in the southern side. Both, or either, must be related to the wider political climate in the north during the troubles. The experiences of those fans who came to maturity only during the course of the recent conflict, however, whilst they must also be related to this wider context, need to be considered in terms of the socialisation process itself. Unlike those supporters whose decision to withhold their support from the Northern Ireland team was taken many years after they came to maturity, the process whereby younger supporters have come to narrate a sense of alienation from the northern side is intimately bound up with their experiences of growing up during the last 30 years or so. The affinity these fans have with the southern side must be related, in particular, to the increased political awareness that accompanies maturity. To those older fans who previously followed the fortunes of the northern side, and to those who grew up in the early years of the recent conflict, we can add those individuals who have only come to maturity, and thus have only become fans in recent years. For many of these fans, who would seemingly guarantee continued northern Catholic support for the southern side in the foreseeable future, support for the Republic of Ireland is all that they have ever known.

Although northern Catholic support for the Republic is constituted of fans from various socio-economic backgrounds, it is clear that class also remains an important factor in analysing the differing experiences of this group of supporters. Many commentators, including O'Connor (1993) and Coulter (1994), have considered the widening class divisions within the Catholic community since the introduction of Direct Rule. Whilst improved employment opportunities have helped create an enlarged, as well as a socially and spatially mobile, Catholic middle class, it has been noted that poverty and unemployment have continued and indeed worsened for many working-class Catholics and Protestants. As a result the experiences and attitudes, the 'world views', of middle- and working-class Catholics are often markedly different, the former having increasingly come to participate, however provisionally, in Northern Irish society, the latter often being further alienated from it. Importantly, as a game that continues to attract most support amongst male members of the working classes, football in Northern Ireland has served as a significant arena in which Catholic working-class males have experienced, at first hand, alienation from the wider society. Equally, the alienation from the Northern Ireland team felt by the Catholic middle classes and reflected in broad-based nationalist support for the Republic perhaps illustrates the limits to which this section of the population actively participates in Northern Irish society. Ultimately, broader changes in the Catholic class profile in the last three decades, which are often reflected in the experiences of fans, are significant when analysing the process whereby supporters have come to follow the Republic of Ireland team.

The sense of alienation felt by many northern Catholic supporters certainly must be seen in the context of the broader resonance of the Protestant symbolism that came to surround the Northern Ireland team during the course of the recent conflict. However, it is apparent that fans do not usually articulate their attitudes in broad, abstract, terms, but rather tend to relate their experiences in relation to specific instances of, and in terms of particular issues concerned with, sectarian rivalry. The sectarian abuse directed at Catholic players, the sectarian rivalry inspired by fixtures between the northern and southern teams, and the sectarian atmosphere that many fans appear to view as being inherently associated with Windsor Park, are those issues that are most regularly commented upon by supporters. The views of many fans, furthermore, are influenced by their experiences of following local club football in the north. It is worth briefly elaborating on each of these four themes, for although the nature of Catholic alienation is anticipated in existing literature dealing with football in Northern Ireland, these issues have only been addressed in so far as they serve to illustrate Protestant appropriation of the sport.

The sectarian taunts directed at some Catholic players have undermined attempts by administrators and officials, who have been quick to point out that the composition of the Northern Ireland team has always been representative of both ethnic groups, to present the northern side as some form of cross-community initiative. Rather, it is clear that for many football fans in the north, both Catholic and Protestant, an interest in individual players coexists with or has been prioritised over an interest in the team. Some Protestant supporters have singled out, and have directed sectarian abuse at, certain Catholic players who have been conceptualised as 'the enemy within' (Sugden and Bairner, 1993) and have been accused of not being fully committed to the Northern Ireland 'cause'. Similarly, for many Catholic football fans, the extent of their interest in the northern side is often limited to following the fortunes of individual players who often play for the clubs they support and who are seen to be representative of their ethnic group. In both cases individual players in the one team are appropriated as 'proxy warriors' (Hoberman, 1986) for each of the two largest ethnic groups in the north. Far from fostering cross-community co-operation, the northern side can actually be seen to embody the wider divisions in Northern Irish society.

Although Catholic players, the 'enemy within', have intermittently been targeted for sectarian abuse, the rivalry with the Republic of Ireland, the 'enemy without', has also served to heighten sectarian tensions and to foster a sense of alienation amongst supporters. Since the late 1970s, when the two Irelands, north and south, were drawn to play one another, there have been a number of fixtures involving the two sides. In the absence of an established rivalry, and played in the period before specific political developments such as the Anglo-Irish Agreement and the current 'peace process' served to further fuel unionist fears of being 'under siege', the earliest matches between the two teams did not arouse the same tension as have more recent fixtures. However, in the wake of such political developments, matches against the Republic of Ireland, a team which represents a state that for many years claimed the north for itself, assumed increased significance for many Protestant fans of the northern side (Sugden and Bairner, 1994). An exaggerated sense of Protestant opposition to the Republic's team, manifested in the heightened tension that surrounded matches between the two teams in the early 1990s, served further to alienate northern Catholic football fans, most of whom were already declaring their allegiance for the south.

To focus on the taunts directed at Catholic players on the Northern Ireland team, as well as at fans and players of its southern counterpart, is to emphasise how identities are dramatised, and relationships constituted, through sectarian discourse. However, in considering how most football grounds in the province are situated in predominantly Protestant areas, Bairner and Shirlow (1998a) show that identities are not just expressed through chants, songs and symbols, and demonstrate the ways in which relationships are spatialised, a theme which Shirlow takes up once again in chapter 14. Linking their argument to the 'siege mentality' thesis, Bairner and Shirlow suggest that football clubs, and their grounds, provide for continuity with a Protestant past in the face of political developments that are seen to be concessions to northern nationalists. One particular place, namely Windsor Park, the home ground of both Linfield and the north's national team, is an especially important space in and through which Protestant fans can construct their identities. It is also a place in and through which Catholic supporters narrate their sense of alienation from the Northern Ireland team. In articulating their sense of alienation most fans make reference not just to the sectarian atmosphere *per se*, but to the sectarian atmosphere at Windsor Park. The atmosphere is often conceived as being inherently associated with the ground, and the stadium is usually seen to be conducive to a sectarian atmosphere. The overriding sense that emerges, however, is not necessarily that the ground is unsuitable and unattractive to Catholic supporters because it is where Northern Ireland play, but rather because it is the home ground of Linfield. Of course, for many fans the fortunes of and the nature of support for the north's national team and Linfield are inextricably linked. Nevertheless, the views of fans towards Windsor Park reflect that their alienation from the northern side, and their support for its southern counterpart, cannot be divorced from their experiences of following local club football.

The problems encountered by a number of Catholic clubs in Northern Ireland have certainly contributed to the process whereby fans have come to reject the north's national team and identify with the south. Although there have been many incidents involving different clubs, which have varied in time and space, and which have differed in their degree of seriousness, in virtually all cases the fate of the club involved is described by supporters in terms of injustice at the hands of the IFA. This is a significant point; many supporters relate their lack of affiliation to the northern side, not just to the fact that the team is representative of the northern state as a political entity, but to the fact that it is representative of the IFA which is perceived to be a particularly unjust institution operating within that state. Although the attitudes of fans are derived from their experiences as supporters of particular clubs, they are also influenced by a belief that the IFA has not done enough to tackle sectarianism at international fixtures.

It must be pointed out, however, that in the same way that many football clubs have been appropriated by Protestant supporters as vehicles for the expression of loyalist or unionist identities, so Catholic fans have also used clubs, such as Belfast Celtic, Derry City, or Cliftonville, to dramatise their nationalist or republican identities. Although Catholic alienation from the north's national team is reflected in the fact that many fans refuse to attend games, local club football has continued to provide some supporters, albeit in increasingly diminished numbers, with a platform on which they can assert their own identities. Thus it is inadequate to perceive these fans as passive agents who, confronted with broader structural constraints, such as the wider social, political, and historical context and its relationship with football, have simply acquiesced in their sense of alienation. Catholic fans have been able to communicate their nationalist or republican identities through sectarian chants and emblems, and in particular their appropriation of football spaces.

The way in which the IFA tends to be characterised by northern Catholic football fans, along with their experiences of and views on sectarian chanting and Windsor Park, are recurrent features of their *narratives of becoming* Republic of Ireland supporters. Their stories both reflect and describe how football in the province continues to provide an important platform on which the conflicting identities of the two ethnic groups can be 'played out'. From this perspective northern Catholic support for, and identification with, the Republic's football team emerges, not as the outcome of some northern nationalist essence, but as a result of the lived experiences of fans. The sport can be seen to have provided northern Catholic and Protestant supporters with an arena in which they have been able to construct their identities in opposition to the ethnic 'other'.

## 'Negotiating' (Northern) Irish nationalist identities

Although much has been made of the alienation of Catholics from the Northern Ireland football team, it is evident that the sport remains for many a significant aspect of social life. This is witnessed in support for local, as well as English and Scottish, clubs and is reflected in support for the Republic of Ireland. With this in mind it is restrictive simply to consider Catholic support for the southern side with reference to alienation from the game in the six counties, for such an analysis falls short of explaining the nature of northern Catholic support for, and identification with, the Republic's team. National identity, as Jenkins (1997) points out, is constructed through social interaction across boundaries between groups *and is also* concerned with creating a sense of shared meaning amongst members of the 'nation'. Support for the Republic of Ireland football team is one way in which northern Catholic fans can 'negotiate' their (northern) Irish nationalist identities and, in the process, construct a sense of shared nationalist meaning amongst the broader Catholic community.

In commenting on the nature of his support for the Republic of Ireland team one supporter noted: 'There is a political element. As Father Denis Faul says, "everything in the north is political" and people need not say otherwise. Support for the Republic of Ireland team has a strong political element and what else would it have really.' The remark perceptively alludes to the diffuse nature of politics in Northern Irish social life and rightly encourages us to question those analytical models that initially conceptualise sport and politics as two distinct spheres, even if these same models then proceed to show how the two spheres are related. Politics 'lives', and political subjectivities are reproduced, in and through football; politics does not have to be connected to it. It is possible to examine how northern Catholic fans 'negotiate' definitions of themselves, and others, through their support for the Republic of Ireland team, by considering their attitudes and experiences in relation to existing literature which has sought to describe what is generally seen as the 'reconstruction' of northern nationalism during the course of the troubles (McGarry and O'Leary, 1995; O'Connor, 1993; Ruane and Todd, 1996; Whyte, 1990). It is suggested that this process of reconstruction has involved the redefinition of the Irish nation in terms of people not territory, has been characterised by a political pragmatism that has focused, not on Irish national issues *per se*, but on the redress of Catholic grievances within the north, and has attracted nationalists to the possibility of being 'Irish in Northern Ireland'. However, to examine the ways in which a northern nationalist sensibility is expressed through support for the Republic of Ireland is to focus on how identities are embedded in, and reproduced through, social practice. Such an analysis differs from many macro-scale interpretations of the conflict, including, for example, that offered by Ruane and Todd (1996). In seeking to account for the persistence of division the authors emphasise that ideological continuity is simply the result of the 'structure' of the conflict, a disembodied and abstract concept that neglects to consider how conflicting identities are continually produced and reproduced in specific social contexts.

The nature of northern Catholic identification with the Republic's football team is often explained with reference to two factors that, although relevant, alone do not stand up to analytical scrutiny. Firstly, the affiliation of this body of fans with the southern side is simply dismissed as a consequence of the team's recent success. In fact, the persistence of northern Catholic support for the Republic, despite that team's failure to qualify for the 1996 European Championships in England or the 1998 World Cup in France, illustrates that support is not simply premised on qualification for major tournaments. Secondly, it is often suggested that Catholic fans withhold their support from the northern side because they refuse to recognise the northern state and by association its football team. Although a view expressed by some, that the vast majority of fans do not articulate their support for the southern side in these terms is perhaps partly reflective of the political pragmatism of northern nationalists whose representatives work fairly comfortably within the existing political framework.

This is not to say that most northern Catholic fans are supportive of the geopolitical status quo. Evidently, the vast majority of fans aspire, at whatever time in the future, to a united Ireland, and indeed support for the southern team is one means, and a particularly enjoyable medium, through which they are able to symbolically deconstruct the border. What is crucial, however, is that their deconstruction of the border through their support for the Republic's team is based on a recognition, not non-recognition, of its existence. Paradoxically, their affinity with the Republic of Ireland is both premised on the existence of the border, and is a means through which it can be deconstructed. Significantly, in deconstructing the border supporters are able to negotiate definitions of themselves as 'Irish' as opposed to 'northern Irish' (whether as northern Catholics, northern nationalists, northern republicans, or a combination of these). In other words, they are able to construct an Irish identity that, although not necessarily confined to the 32 counties, certainly transcends the border and, in part, is defined in terms of the territorial integration of the island. That territorial unity remains important to the negotiation of northern nationalist identities is reflected in the views of supporters, most of whom stop short of conceptualising the Republic as the 'true' or 'authentic' Irish team, and many of whom express the desire to support a 'real' all-Ireland side.

In emphasising a cultural affinity with, rather than a political allegiance to, the south, many northern fans attempt to draw a rigid distinction between culture and politics, a distinction which support for the Republic of Ireland demonstrates cannot easily be maintained. Rather, the views of those who suggest that their support for the southern side is not politically inspired tend to be based on a realistic appraisal of the wider political context and a recognition that their romantic aspiration for a united Ireland is unlikely to be accomplished in the foreseeable future. The retention of the aspiration, nevertheless, would appear to persist amongst the vast majority of fans. That the aspiration to Irish unity retains significance at a time when northern nationalists are driven, more so than ever before, by a sense of political pragmatism, suggests that it is necessary to temper the rigid theoretical dichotomy which is often drawn between 'traditional' and 'reconstructed' northern nationalism(s). Northern Catholic support for the Republic of Ireland football team, which incorporates elements of both, allows for a glimpse of the complexity of northern nationalism. In fact, support for the southern side is one particularly effective means through which fans can reconcile the divergent strands within so-called 'traditional' and 'reconstructed' perspectives. Northern-based fans can both appropriate the Republic's national team to help construct their Irish identities within the six counties, and at the same time they can use the southern side as a vehicle through which their aspiration for a united Ireland can be symbolically realised.

Although support for the Republic of Ireland enables northern Catholic fans to construct an Irish identity that transcends the border, it also serves to reproduce their northern nationalist identities. In other words, whilst their support for the southern side can potentially serve as an integrative force, bringing fans together in a common cause, it also serves to reproduce and maintain social, political, and cultural boundaries between supporters. The heterogeneous character of the Republic's fan-base, and the fact that the team is often imbued with different meanings by different groups of supporters, has been noted elsewhere by Bairner (1996) and Free (1998). Significantly, fans themselves readily acknowledge, either explicitly or implicitly, that they form a particular sub-group within the broader Republic of Ireland fan-base. Northern supporters often congregate in the same sections of football grounds, or in the same pubs, in order to watch games. In commenting on the surprise with which their presence at Republic of Ireland matches was greeted by many southern-based fans, especially in the early 1990s, many northern fans are also often drawn to remark on southern supporters' 'ignorance' of Northern Ireland politics. Thus, both in particular spaces, and through discourse that points to the divergent political cultures and betrays a sense of the 'cultural stereotyping' that serves to maintain cultural separation between the north and south of Ireland (Wilson 1993), fans negotiate their northern nationalist identities in relation to *the* national identity of which they are considered to be a part.

It is important, however, not to exaggerate internal ambiguities, contradictions, and tensions within the Republic of Ireland fan-base. Whilst northern Catholic fans are aware of their position as a particular sub-group, and whilst they appreciate the multi-vocal nature of the southern side, their continued enthusiastic support reflects a feeling that the team, in some sense, 'belongs' to them. This sense of belonging must be related, first and foremost, to northern Catholic fans' appropriation of the Republic's team as their 'national' side. However, in order to explain the persistence of their support, particularly the continuing attraction of travelling to attend matches, it is also useful to consider the 'culture of carnivalesque' (Giulianotti 1996) which has come to characterise the support that surrounds the Republic of Ireland team.

Although northern Catholic fans acknowledge that their support for the Republic is one manifestation of a northern nationalist sensibility, many are also keen to stress, somewhat ironically, that their support for the southern team is also motivated by a desire to 'escape' the political connotations associated with the sport in the six counties. Their narratives, in this respect, support the argument that that we should consider how politics 'lives' in sport. After all, for those fans who talk of escaping the political connotations associated with football in Northern Ireland, often with references to the 'carnival' atmosphere at Republic of Ireland matches, the distinction between politics and sport is not predetermined but is an achieved reality. This is not, of course, to disavow any link between national identity and football but is rather an acceptance that northern Catholic fans, unlike in Northern Ireland, can support a national football team in an environment where their national identity is not a contested social construct. Within this context most fans, as they embrace and contribute to a football culture that can be seen to transcend the geopolitical border, rarely feel the need to make ostentatious statements dramatising their northern nationalist identities. In fact, to do so would be to mark northern nationalist supporters out as 'not the same Irish' as the rest of the Republic's fan-base. Thus, supporting the Republic of Ireland team provides fans with the opportunity to express their Irishness, to 'play' with their Irish and northern Irish nationalist identities, and, paradoxically, to support a team that is often said to have 'no political baggage'.

## Conclusion: Where does politics 'live'?

The idea that politics and sport constitute two distinct spheres within society is one that continues to underpin much of the non-academic literature that is concerned to examine what is regarded as 'the relationship between politics and sport'. This chapter has argued that this conceptual dichotomy, even if only an initial analytical opposition, is restrictive and misconceived. Politics does not initially exist outside the sporting arena before coming to be reflected or symbolised within it. Rather, politics is more appropriately conceived as 'living' within sport. Sport is a specific, concrete context within which groups and individuals can construct their identities, national and otherwise. It is a 'field', in Bourdieu's (1977) sense, wherein embodied sentiments and political subjectivities are reproduced. In other words, far from divorcing politics from sport – the 'political' from the 'cultural' – from this perspective politics is actually seen to be a form of cultural work.

Thus, the popular belief that northern Catholic football fans support the Republic of Ireland simply *because* they are nationalists, and *because*, therefore, they want a united Ireland or greater justice and equality in Northern Ireland, is clearly insufficient as an explanatory tool. Such a view misrepresents the nature of nationalism, a socially constructed as well as a historically and con- textually contingent phenomenon (Jenkins 1997), and makes the mistake of conceptualising politics as existing prior to, and outside, football. From this perspective the meanings attached to the latter are merely reflective of the former. Rather, northern nationalist identities, as this chapter has sought to demonstrate, are continually produced and reproduced in and through football 'fandom'. Support for Catholic clubs throughout the last century, as well as the more recent emergence of broad-based support for the Republic of Ireland football team, has enabled fans to forge a shared (northern) Irish nation- alist identity. In so doing, northern Catholic supporters, and their Protestant counterparts, have continually constructed their conflicting identities and the boundaries between the two ethnic groups, in and through football.

**Chapter 10**

# Sport, Irishness and Ulster unionism

Alan Bairner

## Introduction

When the relationship between sport and nationalism in Ireland is discussed, attention turns almost inevitably to the role of the Gaelic Athletic Association (GAA). Indeed, even in this book, the governing body that presides over the 'national' pastimes has already been considered either directly or indirectly in chapters 2, 4, 5 and 8 by Hunt, Cronin, Ryan and Hassan and in Paul Darby's account of the place of Gaelic games within Boston's diaspora community. The link between sport and Irish nationalism (or nationalisms) is widely acknowledged. But what about the Ulster unionists? To what extent, if any, does sport play a part in the construction of their identity (or identities)? Moreover, if sport does impact on their lives in this way, how far can the resultant identity formation be conceptualised in relation to such concepts as the nation, nationality, national identity and nationalism?

The relevance of these concepts to the situation in which Ulster unionists find themselves has been outlined in detail elsewhere (Bairner, 2001a; Bairner, 2003). The main purpose of this chapter is simply to explore, within the context of both association football and rugby union, the degree to which sport reflects and contributes to certain politically significant ambiguities within unionism in relation to the idea of national identity – the sense of belonging to a nation as opposed to nationality which can be conferred upon us officially by others. Some of the arguments advanced in relation to football have been rehearsed elsewhere (Bairner, 2001a; Bairner, 2003). However, some new insights will be offered on the basis of what Northern Ireland's most famous player, George Best, tells us in his own words and by his deeds about his Irishness. The analysis of rugby will be sharpened by the use of interview material, most of which has not previously appeared in print.

## Questions of identity

Nationality is essentially a formal business, the way in which we are legally identified in relation to particular nation states. National identity is an altogether different matter. The concept refers to how we feel about ourselves with respect to the idea of the nation. This comparison is of particular relevance to identity politics within what were once known as the British Isles and now go under a variety of headings such as 'the north Atlantic archipelago' or, more simply, 'The Isles' (Davies, 2000). The overwhelming majority of the inhabitants of the United Kingdom of Great Britain and Northern Ireland possess British nationality. This was also true of the people who lived in the 26 Irish counties that became known as the Irish Free State as a consequence of partition. Most of them, however, like many of the current citizens of the United Kingdom, possessed a dual national identity or, in many cases, a single national identity that was at variance with their official nationality. In contemporary Scotland, for example, most people think of themselves as Scottish first and British second if at all. But this has not always been the case. Thus, as Graham (1997: 7) notes, 'national identity is created in particular social, historical and political contexts and, as such, cannot be interpreted as a fixed entity; rather, it is a situated, socially constructed narrative capable of being read in conflicting ways at any given time and of being transformed through time'. It is for this reason that, for centuries, Scots have wrestled with identity questions – a consequence of a more general collective fascination with contrasts and dualities.

One of the most celebrated attempts to conceptualise the importance of dualism in Scottish political and cultural life is Gregory Smith's idea of 'the Caledonian antisyzygy'. According to Smith (1919),

> perhaps in the very combination of opposites – what either of the two St Thomases, of Norwich and Cromarty, might have been willing to call 'the Caledonian antisyzygy' – we have a reflection of the contrasts which the Scot shows at every turn, in his political and ecclesiastical history, in his polemical restlessness, in his adaptability, which is another way of saying that he has made allowance for new conditions, in his practical judgement, which is his admission that two sides of the matter have been considered.

The principle was encapsulated in the life and work of the poet Hugh MacDiarmid (1987) whose personal ambition was to inhabit 'nae hauf-way hoose, but aye be whaur extremes meet', 'a most Scottish of conditions' according to David McCrone (2002). But contradiction surrounding identity issues is by no means exclusive to the Scots. Commenting on Gregory Smith's 'antisyzygy as a device for Scottish literary criticism', Carl MacDougall (2001:

25) remarks, 'this twinning of opposites is not solely a literary phenomenon; it is an equally important feature of our other major art forms. Nor is it especially Scottish'. At certain times, however, and by certain groups of people, identity questions are answered in relatively straightforward ways. Thus, at present very few Catholics in Northern Ireland would think of themselves as anything other than Irish even though they are British citizens. How they understand their Irishness, not least in relation to that of the citizens of the Irish Republic as well as their fellow northern nationalists, remains a contentious issue as both Fulton and Hassan reveal in chapters 9 and 8 respectively. Furthermore, there are some in their number who would almost certainly vote for the retention of partition whilst simultaneously reaffirming their cultural Irishness. In general, however, Catholics in Northern Ireland possess an Irish national identity and express dissatisfaction to varying degrees about a set of constitutional arrangements that could lead the outside world to believe that their nationality is British.

At one level, the identity of the Protestant population of Northern Ireland might appear even less contested. The consistent political defence of the union of Britain and Northern Ireland appears to confirm an unquestioned British identity that complements an official British nationality. On the other hand, it has been argued, for different reasons, that Ulster unionism and national identity are uneasy bedfellows. In his attempt to establish the theoretical principles of a 'civic unionism', Aughey (1989: 202) argues that 'the idea of the Union is properly one which transcends such outdated concepts as nationalism'. Writing from a very different political perspective, Tom Nairn supports the contention that there is a disjuncture between Ulster unionism and nationalism but suggests that, in relation to 'normal' politics, this is a weakness rather than a strength. According to Nairn (1981: 236), 'trapped in this extraordinary way between past and future, Ulster Protestantism was unable to formulate the normal political response of threatened societies: nationalism'. Neither account is wholly accurate. In fact, Ulster Protestants have consistently played around with notions of nationalism and national identity. In the past, Irishness and Britishness were conjoined – the yoking of opposites – just as Scottishness and Britishness co-existed in another part of the United Kingdom. With a changing political context, however, this particular version of the Celtic antisyzygy became increasingly difficult to sustain. As Coulter (1999: 22) reveals:

> The nationalist enterprise insisted that 'Irishness' and 'Britishness' represented ways of being in the world that were essentially incompatible. As the demand for national autonomy gathered pace, unionists came increasingly to accept this particular reading. Throughout the present [i.e. twentieth] century the unionist community has gradually demoted feelings of 'Irishness' in favour of a sense of Britishness.

In broad terms, Coulter is correct in his claim that Britishness has tended to replace Irishness as the national identity of the Ulster Protestant population. It is important to recognise, however, that Britishness is itself a contested concept within this context. Thus, according to Todd (1987: 1), 'together, the Ulster loyalist and Ulster British traditions constitute the two main strands in Unionism'. The former is defined by a primary imagined community of Northern Irish Protestants and a secondary, conditional loyalty to the British state. Ulster British ideology, on the other hand, is defined by a primary loyalty to the imagined community of Greater Britain and a secondary, regional patriotism for Northern Ireland. Social class, together with varying degrees and forms of religiosity, also impact on the construction of these alternative modes of seeing the union. What they share, however, is a rejection of Irishness as a way of 'being in the world' to use Coulter's phrase. As this chapter seeks to show, however, this rejection of Irishness in all its manifestation is by no means universal within Ulster unionism. Indeed, a sense of being Irish is able to co-exist with both of the traditions that Todd identifies although to a much greater extent, ironically perhaps, with the Ulster British tradition. It is this claim for the existence of an ongoing Celtic antisyzygy within Ulster unionism that will now be tested in relation to sport.

## 'Up to our knees' – again

As has been indicated elsewhere in this volume and many times before, sport in Ireland has been intimately bound up with the politics of division. Early analyses of this relationship were arguably somewhat crudely mechanical (Sugden and Bairner, 1993). Catholics played and watched Gaelic games. Protestants, specifically in Northern Ireland, played British games. In addition, many Irish people played games that could be termed universal and which were therefore of less interest to the social scientist concerned with identity politics. The exception of course was association football or soccer, which despite its universality reflected the divisions that existed within Ireland and, at least in the north, made a major contribution to the reproduction and consolidation of sectarian identities. It can be argued that more recent contributions to the debate about sport and identity in Ireland, this collection included, have been more nuanced, less inclined to speak in terms of monolithic communities and more willing to get beneath the stereotypical surface. In relation to soccer, however, certain 'truths', it would appear, remain self-evident.[1]

As Fulton showed in the previous chapter, northern nationalists are largely convinced that association football in Northern Ireland is run by Protestants in the interests of Protestants. This is not to deny the widespread support for the game within the Catholic community. One could argue indeed that nationalist involvement in association football represents a degree of assimilation into the dominant culture, not least when compared with the GAA's attempts to provide distinctively nationalist games for the nationalist people. The willingness of northern Catholics to play for Irish League clubs with predominantly unionist support and also for the Northern Ireland 'national' team might be taken as further evidence of tacit acceptance of the post-partition and certainly the post-Good Friday Agreement political context. Yet there is more to nationalist involvement in football than simple acquiescence in the face of cultural hegemony.

As both Hassan and Fulton have shown, nationalists also use football for counter hegemonic purposes. It is a vehicle for resistance not only to cultural hegemony but also by extension to the political status quo. Support for 'nationalist' clubs – such as Belfast Celtic, Derry City, Cliftonville and Donegal Celtic – and for the Irish Republic's national team allows nationalists to engage with the world's most popular game whilst simultaneously challenging the right of unionists to control the game and, by extension, their cultural and political lives.

Overall, however, domestic senior soccer in Northern Ireland is essentially a Protestant affair (Bairner, 1997; Bairner, 1999b; Bairner, 2004). The major rivalry involves two clubs with predominantly Protestant support – Glentoran and Linfield, and not, as an outsider might imagine, between a nationalist and a unionist club along lines established by the Old Firm in Scotland (Bairner and Shirlow, 2001a). Furthermore, as Magee reveals in the next chapter, many of the teams that seek to challenge the supremacy of Belfast's 'Big Two' are perceived by some of their fans as being involved in a struggle for success not only on the field of play but also in the realm of intra-Protestant rivalry.

The 'national' team is also largely a Protestant concern. Most of the fans are Protestants. Indeed, given the demise of many of the institutions that were once inextricably linked with the Northern Ireland state – a Unionist-controlled parliament, the Royal Ulster Constabulary, the Ulster Defence Regiment - the 'national' team has become one of the few major signifiers of Northern Ireland's status as a separate entity. Catholics play for Northern Ireland but not, it should be added, without some difficulty. Even at times when the team was relatively successful or prior to the advent of the troubles, Catholic players have at best had to perform whilst substantial sections of the Northern Ireland support have engaged in a range of anti-Catholic rhetoric. In more testing times, either politically or on the field of play, Catholic players have been subjected to personal abuse by their 'own' fans. The most notable case was that of Neil Lennon, whose Catholicism had tended to be ignored by the fans until he signed for Celtic Football Club. It is almost

certain that Lennon regards himself as unreservedly Irish although he had
proved himself willing to play at international level for his 'football country'
– Northern Ireland. By signing for Celtic, however, he provided at least some
of the Northern Irish support with incontrovertible evidence that he was one
of 'them'. All of this would appear to suggest that the identity that is most
clearly endorsed in the world of Northern Irish soccer is that described by
Todd as 'Ulster loyalist'. However, it is not only northern Catholics whose
identity is therefore problematised as a direct result of involvement in
Northern Irish soccer.

## Simply the best

George Best played his first game for Northern Ireland alongside Pat Jennings
who was also making his debut for the 'national' team. But the songs that
were sung by the home fans were far more familiar to him than they were to
the Catholic from Newry. As Best (1991: 5) records in his first autobiography,
written in collaboration with Ross Benson, he was born in Belfast on 22 May
1946 'into a solid, working-class family, Protestant by religion, decent and
honest in its beliefs'. Lovejoy (1999: 15) describes the Bests as a religious family
'in an entirely non-political way' and as Free Presbyterian without 'any of the
bigotry associated with Ulster sectarianism'. Best himself, however, under-
stands the political implications of these labels rather better than his biographer.
In his later autobiography, Best (2002: 32) asserts, 'religion has never bothered
me and there is no way you could ever call my family bigots'. He adds,
however, 'if you were a Protestant, you joined the Orange Order, as I did, and
my dad and grandad both had spells as master of our local lodge'. There are of
course strong cultural factors that lead working-class Protestants to identify
with Orangeism or, more recently, with loyalist paramilitarism. The fact
remains, however, that individual choice plays a part. Not all working-class
Protestants join the Orange Order. To do so is to become sectarian, at least in
the proper sense of that word. Indeed Best (2002: 33) admits, even in his
childhood years before the advent of the troubles, the Orange Order's
Twelfth of July demonstrations constituted 'a sectarian festival'.

It was in that sectarian environment that Best grew up. This is not to
suggest that he or his family were overtly anti-Catholic or anti-Irish. At the
same time they could not escape those elements of Ulster unionist ideology
that were unashamedly pro-British. Ironically, however, when Best moved as
a young man to so-called 'mainland' Britain, he did so at the behest of a
football club that had always had strong Irish connections.

In the words of John Scally (1998: 11), 'Manchester United have excited
Irish soccer fans like no other team'. Celtic supporters would no doubt dispute

that claim. On should bear in mind, however, that Celtic is one of only two Scottish based clubs that have ever had the potential to command the support of Irish Catholics.[2] Amongst English clubs, on the other hand, the range of choice would appear, at least superficially, to be much greater and Irish Catholics do indeed give their support to numerous English clubs, not least Liverpool, Everton and Arsenal. Manchester United, however, reigns supreme.

Scally (1998) seeks to explain the Irish obsession with Manchester United by reference to the history of the Irish diaspora in the city of Manchester itself. He notes that by 1841, one tenth of the city's population was Irish. Furthermore, 'whilst most Irish immigrants were anxious to protect their national identity in foreign fields, they were also anxious to blend into their new environment' (Scally, 1998: 42). By the 1870s, one important way of doing this was to play and watch association football. As a result, football became 'a badge of identity which enabled Irish immigrants to consider themselves as Mancunians' (Scally, 1998: 46). The game was 'the battery that drove Irish immigrants' imaginative lives and dared them to see themselves in a very different light – as pillars of the Manchester community' (Scally, 1998: 48). The particular club to which most of them turned was Manchester United whose ground was owned by a prominent Catholic family, the De Traffords. In addition, according to Scally (1998: 45), 'from the very beginning, Irish players were at the heart of United'.

Scally (1998: 98) exaggerates when he claims that 'anyone who is Irish Catholic in Manchester is expected to support Manchester United, who have always being [*sic*] seen as the Catholic team'. United's Irish connection are nevertheless secure, not least as a consequence of the club's numerous Irish-born players, both before and after the Best era. Until the 1950s, most of these had been Irish Catholics. In addition, there had also been a succession of Catholic managers, including, most famously, Sir Matt Busby whom Scally (1998) transforms into an honorary Irishman as well. Based on the fact that the legendary manager's maternal grandfather had emigrated from Ireland to Scotland, Scally (1998: 12) claims, 'of course, Busby was an Irishman – at least more so than many who have lined out for the boys in green [the Republic of Ireland] in recent years'. Undeniably Busby was a devout Catholic who became particularly close to some of his Catholic players, most notably Pat Crerand (Lovejoy, 1999), another Scot of Irish ancestry, and his assistant Jimmy Murphy, Welsh born but with an Irish immigrant father.

Despite Manchester United's Catholic image, much is made of its integrative capacity by both Scally (1998) and also by Chris Moore (1999) who has written on Manchester United's links to Northern Ireland. With reference to support for the club from throughout Ireland, Scally (1998: 12) writes, 'what is particularly remarkable about this obsession is that in a country where ecumenism has been so absent, this passion is shared by northern Protestants and southern Catholics alike'. Moore (1999: 12) adds, 'speaking of my Irish friends who also follow United brings me around to the fundamental purpose of writing this book, United Irishmen. When it comes to the Red Devils, Ireland *is* United' (Moore's emphasis).

The fact remains that over the years, many Ulster Protestants have consciously rejected Manchester United as their English club of choice. Noting that snooker player Alex Higgins is a United fan, his biographer comments that this is unusual 'for a Belfast Protestant' (Borrows, 2002: 123). This is a gross exaggeration. But it is certainly the case that some northern Protestants dislike Manchester United because of the club's Irish Catholic connections.[3] It is within this context that the significance of George Best's arrival at Old Trafford and his subsequent impact at the club must be understood.


## The wearing of the green

Best played for Northern Ireland on 37 occasions. Nevertheless, his continuing links with his parental culture are far weaker than they might have been. According to Lovejoy (1999: 163), 'Northern Ireland rarely saw the jewel in their crown in its best light'. In part this was a direct result of the rival demands of club and country and Best was by no means the first player to represent his country less often than he might have done because of his obligations to his principal employer. It is also significant, however, that the Northern Ireland team was in one of its troughs during the heyday of Best's career. Thus, as Lovejoy (1999: 157) reflects, 'by accident of birth, a player on the same plane as Pele and Cruyff was condemned to scratch around with the no-hopers of Northern Ireland, and missed out on all the major tournaments'. Best himself has contributed to this verdict, claiming that 'playing for Northern Ireland was recreational soccer – there was hardly any pressure on you because you were not really expected to get a result unlike the Brazilian or Italian or even the English teams are – and the way Manchester United is'. Lovejoy (1999) quotes with apparent approval the view expressed by former Northern Ireland player, Derek Dougan, and also from time to time by Best himself, that the latter's career might have lasted longer had he been in a position to play for a more successful international side. The fact is though that by the time Best's career was coming to an end Northern Ireland was on the verge of qualifying for the 1982 World Cup finals, a feat that was emulated four years later. Cynics, and certainly some cynical Ulster unionist observers, might be inclined to argue that as self-confessed advocates of an all-Ireland national soccer side, neither Dougan nor Best were sufficiently committed to the Northern Irish team. Best (2002: 302) writes, 'I have always believed that the two associations should have got together and form one national team'.

He argues that politics and money have stood in the way of such a development, adding that 'the hangers on and the officials of the two Associations are too frightened of losing their freebies and their status' (ibid.). Dougan was also an Ulster Protestant with strong views on the need for Irish unity at least at the level of sport (Dougan, 1972).

It is conceivable that Dougan and Best's opinions and feelings were shaped by the experiences that they shared with so many people who grew in Northern Ireland's pro-British tradition but, having moved to England, became largely indistinguishable from other Irish people in the eyes of the outside world. Best's first wife, Angie (Best: 2001), constantly refers to his Irishness – 'this little Irishman' (p. 6), 'this drunken little Irishman' (p. 19), 'the Irish charm' (p. 19), 'the wild Irish charms' (p. 19) and 'the charming little Irishman' (p. 56). As Best (2002: 302) recalls, a similar view, at least with reference to his national identity, was expressed by the Metropolitan Police officer who arrested him in 1984 on a drink driving charge and addressed him as 'You little Irish wanker. You Irish scum. Another piece of Irish dirt' (Best, 2001: 326).

Playing for a team with such strong Irish connections in a country where all Irishmen, whether Ulster Protestant or southern Catholic, are simply 'Paddies', Best has inevitably been confronted by his own personal antisyzygy. Moreover he has contributed to this particular reading of his identity, describing himself in Michael Parkinson's (1975: 61) biography as 'a mad Irish sod'. Julie Burchill (2002: 8) confirms this assessment, comparing Tom Jones with Best and commenting that 'above all, these Celtic princes drank for Wales and Ireland respectively'. In addition, other commentators have sought deeper meaning in Best's Irish and, by extension his supposed Celtic, ancestry. For example, Parkinson (1975: 57) quotes the celebrated sports journalist, Hugh McIlvanney, who wrote of Best:

> I suspect that deep in his nature there is a strong self-destructive impulse. The Celts whether Irish, or Welsh, or Scots, whether sportsmen or artists or politicians, have always been pretty strong in the self-destructive department. If hell did not exist the Celts would have invented it. Sometimes I think they did. With George Best I have frequently had the impression that he felt uncomfortable when things were going too well.

Such an analysis might help us to understand why, having received a successful liver transplant, Best was reported during the summer of 2003 to be drinking alcohol again. As an explanation of the man's cultural identity, however, McIlvanney's comments leave a lot to be desired. Yet, Parkinson himself (1975: 7) pursued a similar line of inquiry when he claimed that 'people who like theories about genes will be interested to know that Anne

Best [Best's late mother] is of pure Irish stock but Dick Best's [his father's] family were immigrants from Scotland'.

In fact neither Best's Irish nor his Scottish ancestry make him Celtic in any meaningful sense except perhaps inasmuch as he would be perceived by many people outside Northern Ireland as simply another Irishman. Risking a descent into racial stereotyping, it might be suggested that Best's lifestyle, particularly his fondness for alcohol, has helped to confirm his Irishness. But strong drinking accompanied by periods of introspection are at least as common within the Scottish Presbyterian tradition to which Best is more directly connected. Nevertheless, the theories put forward by McIlvanney and Parkinson do point up the problems that are inherent in the relationship between an Ulster Protestant and an Irish identity – the Celtic antisyzygy.

The manner in which George Best has lived his life epitomises the split mind or antisyzygy that has so often been explored in Scottish letters. In addition, this phenomenon has been closely linked to a Calvinist theology shared by Best's family. His playing career involved a three-way dislocation – from his working-class origins, from Northern Ireland and, not least because his most successful years were spent with Manchester United, from his Protestant background. In England and specifically at Old Trafford, he was simply another Irishman. This was not something that he sought to deny but nor could it have been entirely unproblematic for an Ulster Protestant.

Even those Protestants who want to celebrate their Irishness recognise the difficulties. As Belfast librarian John Gray comments, 'my imagined identity is Irish, and my desired identity is Irish, but I am very specifically Northern Irish' (McKay, 2000: 71–2). Caught betwixt and between, in matters of identity as in so many other respects, the Ulster Protestant community has come to regard itself as what broadcaster David Dunseith calls 'an embattled minority' (McKay, 2000: 26). This helps to explain the significance of a national soccer team, the very existence of which testifies to a Northern Irish identity – neither British nor Irish – and thus offers some kind of solution to the antisyzygy. Best played for this team and in so doing confirmed his Northern Irish identity no matter how else he may have been interpreted. For most Ulster Protestant sportspeople, however, this option simply does not exist. To play their chosen sport at the highest possible level, it is necessary for them to represent Ireland. Although few of them have represented the Jekyll and Hyde syndrome in such a dramatic fashion as Best, the Celtic antisyzygy has also been a significant feature of their sporting lives.

## Red hands, green shirts

Association football is something of an exception in terms of the organisation of sport in Ireland. The overwhelming majority of sports that are played in Ireland are organised on an island wide basis. This is particularly under-standable in the case of Gaelic games, with the GAA acting as a national cultural and sporting organisation. The all-Ireland character of other governing bodies is, however, slightly more surprising given the British origins of so many of the sports involved combined with the constitutional separation of Northern Ireland and the Irish Republic. The fact is, though, that most of these governing bodies came into existence long before the political division of Ireland – the Irish Lawn Tennis Association (1877), the Irish Rugby Football Union (1879), the Golfing Union of Ireland (1891) and the Irish Hockey Union (1893). They did so, it should be added, as part of a global, or to be precise, an imperial process whereby British pastimes were imported to the various corners of the world. As Stoddart (1988: 651) claims, 'through sport were transformed dominant British beliefs as to social behaviour, standards, relations, and conformity, all of which persisted beyond the end of formal empire, and with considerable consequences for the post-colonial order'. In the case of Ireland, the popularity of 'British' sports was part of a more general relationship between the two countries, which leads to Ireland becoming both post-colonial and post-imperial (Bairner, 2003). One consequence, however, is identical to that which emerges in more unequivocally post-colonial societies. The Irish, including avowed Irish nationalists, embraced those sports that were dismissed by the GAA as 'foreign'. That they did so, however, was in large part because such activities, unlike Gaelic games, allowed the Irish to take on their former oppressor and beat the English at their own games. For one community in Ireland, however, the adoption of British games had a rather different meaning.

Arguably the major sporting achievement for Northern Ireland in 1999 was the victory of the Ulster rugby team in the European Cup Final played at Lansdowne Road in Dublin on 31 January. Not only was the victory cele-brated by local rugby enthusiasts, the Ulster players were also identified as having brought the people of the north of Ireland closer together. Writing in the *Guardian* on the eve of the final against the French club side, Colomiers, Frank Keating (1999) suggested that the occasion would give 'a unifying shot in the arm to the Good Friday peace agreement'. According to Keating, 'rugby, unlike football [soccer] and other sports, cuts across the political and sectarian divide'. In fact, although a considerable number of Catholics did go to Dublin to support the Ulster team and many more did so from the comfort of their own homes, the overwhelming majority of the 'home' crowd at Lansdowne Road and of the rugby fraternity in Ulster as a whole belong to the unionist tradition. Catholic involvement in rugby has undoubtedly increased in recent years. There are two main reasons for this. First, as professionalism has impacted on the game in Ireland as elsewhere, leading Ulster clubs such as Dungannon and Ballymena have recognised the need to recruit players from as wide a range of sources as possible. Inevitably this has meant recruiting Catholics, many of them with a previous sporting background in Gaelic football. Second, one of the most discernible developments in the course of the troubles and one which some might regard as the result of a socio-political response to the conflict has been the growth of a Catholic middle class in the north of Ireland. Given that rugby union has tended to be associated with a middle-class lifestyle and provides key element in the social network of the middle classes in Ireland, as in many other places, it is scarcely surprising that sections of the emergent Catholic middle class in Ulster have been attracted to the game. It was they who showed most interest in the fortunes of the Ulster rugby team and created the impression of a people united by a shared sporting enterprise. Many working-class nationalists in the north, however, found little cause to cheer on 'the Ulster boys' and, for that reason, it is safe to say that Frank Keating's remarks were considerably wide of the mark. What does need to be recognised, however, is not just the extent of northern nationalist interest in the game, which has in any case been relatively minimal to date, but rather the fact that the north's predominantly unionist rugby fraternity has always been conscious of its Irishness.

Despite recent developments in the world of Ulster rugby, the principal nurseries in Northern Ireland for games such as rugby, cricket and men's field hockey are the state (predominantly Protestant) schools. Although these do not formally bar Catholics from entry, in practice some have been virtually exclusive to the unionist community, in part because of the existence of an alternative grant-maintained Catholic education sector. In addition, the institutions which nurture the British games players of the future are mainly the grammar schools, in a system which divides children at the age of 12 on the basis of perceived academic ability. The result is that not only are the overwhelming majority of players of British games Protestant, they are also middle class and, as such, more likely to have grown up in areas less directly affected by political violence and the more extreme ideologies which have flourished in such areas and have helped to sustain the conflict. This is not to suggest that the people involved are apolitical or that they successfully eschew sectarian attitudes in their entirety. It is arguable, however, that in most cases they are more able than working class soccer fans to keep their sporting and political interests separate. The sports that they play, administer and watch are organised on an all-Ireland basis and 'national' teams represent the whole of Ireland. This explains why northern unionists finish up representing an entity (a 32-county Ireland) which they would not wish to see being given constitutional legitimacy. Their background and upbringing explain why this is not a problem for most of them and also why their unionism remains unaffected by their sporting allegiance, just as the latter is largely unaffected by their political views. If the only way to play international rugby or cricket is to play for an all-Ireland team, then so be it. Thus former Irish international rugby player, Willie John McBride, asserts,

> I stand for anyone's national anthem and when I pulled on the green shirt I was playing for Ireland. It was about the performance on the field. I want nothing to do with politics. I am not a flag waver and never will be. (Interview with Simon Mason, 6 Feb. 2000).

In this comment, there are clear traces of sporting pragmatism. Indeed in that respect there are even higher ambitions than merely playing for Ireland. As Nigel Carr commented, 'The greatest honour I had in the game was to play for the Lions because less people get picked for the Lions than for Ireland and similarly Ulster' (Interview with Andrew Gibson, 18 February 2002). Furthermore, sporting expediency need not be taken as evidence of political uncertainty. For example, Davy Tweed, the former Irish player, now a highly visible member of the Democratic Unionist Party (DUP), certainly did not become any less of a unionist as a result of his time with the Irish rugby squad.

> Well I think everyone wants to play as high a standard as they can. I always was an Ulsterman and got a huge sense of pride playing for Ulster. The pride I got playing in my Ulster jersey and I would have died in it. Not taking anything away from the Ireland jersey that meant a terrible lot, but to answer your question I would say that the Ulster jersey meant more to me. (Interview with Andrew Gibson, 18 Dec. 2001).

Willie Anderson similarly sought to minimise the political significance of certain symbols by emphasising the sporting context when he commented:

> For me coming from a Unionist, Orange background I didn't have any problems at all. When I hear the Soldier's Song it reminds me of my first cap, one of the greatest days of my life. (Interview with Simon Mason, 29 Jan. 2000)

Players know that at such moments they are wrestling with matters of identity. As Nigel Carr expressed it, 'In playing for Ireland I never felt that I compromised my British citizenship' (Interview with Andrew Gibson, 18 Feb. 2002). Yet there is nothing inappropriate about playing for Ireland. As Gary Longwell, another Ulster Protestant who has represented 'his' country, remarked:

> I have played for Ireland at schools, under 21, universities and senior levels. Rugby
> is played nationally. It gets support both north and south. I have grown up
> supporting Ireland. It's just natural (Interview with Andrew Gibson, 18 Feb. 2002).

This reflects the unionism of those who are British in political terms but are
willing to admit to an Irish dimension to their lives – the 'Ulster British' to
use Todd's phrase. This joint identity makes it perfectly consistent to play
rugby, and other sports, for Ireland whilst defending the union between
Great Britain and Northern Ireland. Another former international player,
Jeremy Davidson, eloquently expressed the various issues involved:

> Even though most rugby players in Ulster come from a Protestant background it's
> your main goal to play for Ireland because of the tradition. It's the only sport to
> unify the whole country. I am British. I have a British passport but at the same
> time I am Irish. It's a strange situation I am British but I live on the island of
> Ireland so I am Irish as well. (Interview with Andrew Gibson, 20 Dec. 2001).

Indeed some have claimed that rugby demonstrates the extent to which the
Irish, however their Irishness is interpreted and expressed, can live alongside
each other in harmony. As Trevor Ringland suggested:

> My view is that rugby has been a tremendous influence in this island and has kept
> bonds of friendship which otherwise might have been destroyed. In rugby circles
> we have always respected the differences that we may have and tolerated it and
> looked at the greater good of us working together for a common goal. We never
> had any threat and treated each other as equals. It has kept a real bond of friend-
> ship between large groups of people on this island. (Interview with Simon Mason,
> 26 Jan. 2000).

It would be easy to discount the utopian vision that Ringland conjures up.
What is undeniable, however, is that rugby union, and other sports which are
played on an all-Ireland basis, have helped certain Ulster Protestants to come
to terms with the Celtic antisyzygy. It is ironic that most of these sports are
identifiably British in origin whereas Gaelic games together with the universal
game of association football have been demonstrably unsuccessful, give or
take a few exceptions, in encouraging Ulster unionists to recognise their
Irishness.

## Conclusion

In their very different ways, George Best and the Ulster players who have represented Ireland at rugby have struggled with the same issues that were so central to the social thought of the poet John Hewitt. As Hewitt put it:

> I'm an Ulsterman of Planter stock. I was born on the island of Ireland, so Secondly I am an Irishman. I was born in the British archipelago and English is my native tongue so I am British (Hewitt, 1974: 4).

In 1993, John Sugden and I argued that 'as regards political attitudes, the rugby men of Northern Ireland for the most part endorse the views of the social and cultural community from which nearly all of them originate' (Sugden and Bairner, 1993: 62). This remains the case. However, I have subsequently offered a somewhat more nuanced analysis:

> there is a kind of unionism that takes on board the Irishness of Ulster Protestants but which nevertheless stops short of supporting moves towards the establishment of a thirty-two county Irish Republic. This is the unionism of those who are British in political terms but are willing to admit to an Irish dimension to their lives. This joint identity is perfectly consistent with playing rugby for Ireland and defending the union between Great Britain and Northern Ireland. It is ironic that British sports are part of the process through which a limited degree of dual identity has been maintained within the unionist population' (Bairner, 2001: 36).

Not only does this chapter underline that later analysis, it does so by listening to the voices of the players themselves or, in the case of Best, by examining the life and times of Northern Ireland's most famous sporting product. There is no denying the Irishness of the sportsmen discussed in this chapter. But theirs is a qualified sense of being Irish. Their Irishness is combined with a deep and persistent sense of being British and of belonging to that part of Ireland which is constitutionally linked to the United Kingdom. This is their particular antisyzygy, their yoking of opposites. However, as Magee reveals in the next chapter, for other Ulster Protestants, Britishness necessarily implies anti-Irishness. For them the bringing together of opposites is linked to a rather different set of identity issues.

Chapter 11

# Football supporters, rivalry and Protestant fragmentation in Northern Ireland

Jonathan Magee

## Introduction

The study of soccer in Northern Ireland has been dominated by three important issues – cross-community tension and sectarian rivalry, the national team as a Protestant symbol, and the politics that surround the governance of the game by the Irish Football Association (IFA), with particular reference to its relationship with Linfield Football Club and the territorial politics regarding Linfield's and Northern Ireland's Windsor Park ground (Sugden and Bairner, 1993, 1994; Bairner and Darby, 1999; Bairner and Shirlow, 1998, 1999). These themes all reappear in the chapters in this collection in which Hassan and Fulton discuss the relationship between soccer and northern nationalism. In addition, the all-Protestant rivalry between the largest Belfast teams, Linfield and Glentoran, is commented on by Sugden and Bairner (1993) and Bairner (2001a, 2002) However, intra-community analysis has not been extended beyond these clubs.

Whilst it is not in dispute that Protestants have historically attached themselves to senior soccer in Northern Ireland in such ways as to make it 'symbolically Protestant, unionist, loyalist' (Bairner, 2001a: 33), the depth and variety of Protestant meaning, on both urban and rural landscapes, need to be considered to further develop knowledge regarding sport, soccer and Northern Irish nuances. This chapter takes up the challenge by focusing on a number of linked themes.

The first aim of the chapter is to comment on the historic rivalry between Linfield and Belfast Celtic[1] as an important cultural identifier for both the unionist and nationalist communities from which their supporters respectively came. Not surprisingly, given the political and religious difficulties located within Belfast and Northern Ireland as a whole, the fierce rivalry that developed between these clubs became a significant focal point for sectarian contention that helped to politicise the early days of Irish League soccer.

The second part of the chapter focuses on how the withdrawal of Belfast Celtic became a critical moment in the realignment of Irish League rivalries and the increased importance of intra-Protestant contests. Glentoran, another Belfast Protestant club, filled the void left by Belfast Celtic as Linfield's main rivals, allowing the 'Big Two' to develop into 'the most bitter rivalry in the Irish League' (Bairner and Walker, 2001: 82). Intra-community issues fuelled the rivalry between the two clubs, increasing the importance of soccer as a contested symbol of ethnic identity within the Protestant community.

The third theme of the chapter is Linfield's iconic status as 'the Protestant symbol' (Sugden and Bairner, 1994: 131) and how it is that their Windsor Park ground has come to be regarded as 'a Protestant place for Protestant people . . . [where] Catholics must require special dispensation to be there' (Bairner and Shirlow, 1998: 160). Against this conventional wisdom, however, the chapter's fourth section explains that Linfield are not as universally popular within the Protestant community as previous literature has indicated. Overall, this chapter uses the example of Protestant supporters of Irish League clubs Glenavon and Portadown[2] to examine how and why supporters of other 'Protestant' teams contest Linfield's status in ways that do not fit in with the typical ethno-sectarian differences that are characteristic of Irish League soccer (Bairner and Shirlow, 2001). The final aim of the chapter is to examine the extent to which the relationship between Belfast clubs Linfield and Glentoran on the one hand and mid-Ulster clubs Glenavon and Portadown on the other are essentially rural–urban conflicts in soccer that reflect the changing socio-political context of 'the new loyalism'. Fratricidal disputes within the Protestant / loyalist community, particularly involving paramilitary groups, have become commonplace and such internecine disagreements have impacted on, and been given a public forum by, soccer matches between Belfast's 'Big Two' and the mid-Ulster clubs.

## Early history and the original 'Big Two'

The first element of the chapter is a contextual reminder of why it is that in Northern Ireland soccer 'has been a significant focus for sectarian rivalry' (Sugden and Bairner, 1993: 81). It is clear that soccer and the Northern Ireland Protestant tradition are inextricably linked and that, at Irish League level, the game has traditionally been 'essentially a Protestant affair' (Bairner, 2001a: 34). A key factor in this Protestant hegemony is that clubs were formed in industrial areas that were predominantly Protestant. This helps to explain why it can be argued that 'most Irish League grounds are situated in what could be described as Protestant spaces and the atmosphere surrounding the majority of games is unionist and loyalist in terms of imagery, symbolism and rhetoric' (Bairner, 2001a: 31).

Because the game prospered in industrial areas of Northern Ireland and Scotland at the end of the nineteenth century, however, 'Catholics in Northern Ireland were attracted immediately to the game' (Sugden and Bairner, 1993: 81).[3] Bairner (2001a: 33) notes that 'given soccer's almost universal appeal it would have been curious had it made no impact on an emerging Catholic working class'. As the most industrialised city in Ireland, Belfast was a natural home for the game and witnessed the emergence of a number of clubs that drew support from both communities. However, the establishment of soccer clubs in Belfast and the development of Irish League soccer in general were immediately affected by ethno-sectarian rivalries.

The Protestant workers of the Linfield mill of the Ulster Spinning Company in south Belfast were instrumental in the formation of Linfield Athletic in 1886, adopting the Meadow ground at the back of the mill as the club's head-quarters. Not long after dropping Athletic from the name, Linfield won their first trophies with the league championship and Irish Cup double in 1891. More triumphs intensified pressure to relocate to a ground capable of accommodating the club's burgeoning support and land close to Lower Windsor Avenue in south Belfast was purchased in 1904 'to give Linfield a home on a permanent basis, a home which everyone associated with the club wanted so passionately' (Brodie, 1985: 11). Windsor Park, as the ground was named, has since played a significant role not only in the history of Linfield and of Northern Irish soccer but also in that of Northern Ireland itself.

In the same era, workers for another Protestant-dominated employer, the Harland & Wolff shipyard, founded Glentoran in the east of the city in 1882, drawing heavily on support from the immediate vicinity. Visitors to Glentoran's ground, The Oval, are still left in no doubt as to the shipyard's role in the club's history as Harland & Wolff's famous David and Goliath cranes, instantly recognisable features of the Belfast landscape, tower over the ground as notable guardians. Glentoran registered their first major triumph in 1894 by winning the Irish League championship but it was not until 1914 that the club won the Irish Cup.

Across the city, soccer enthusiasts could also be found in the largely Catholic Falls Road area of west Belfast. Following discussions between local residents regarding the maximisation of sporting opportunity, Belfast Celtic was founded in 1891 (Coyle, 1999). As its name suggests, the club was modelled on Glasgow Celtic and green and white hooped shirts, along with the naming of the ground as Celtic Park, were shared features of the clubs.[4] The first trophy won by the club was the County Antrim Shield in 1895 but it was not until 1896–7 that Celtic entered the Irish League, becoming champions for the first time in 1899/1900.

The changing membership of the early Irish League, before it settled into a period of relative stability during the inter-war years, also helped to establish the rivalry between the three Belfast clubs. Some established and influential Protestant teams of the late nineteenth and early twentieth century either became extinct (Ulster and Oldpark), reverted to junior football (Milford and Moyola Park) or simply returned to military duties (Lancashire Fusiliers and Gordon Highlanders). As a consequence, from the inaugural Irish League membership of 1890, only Linfield, Glentoran, Distillery and Cliftonville remained beyond 1914, with Linfield, Belfast Celtic and Glentoran dominating from the turn of century.

Despite some of Celtic's successes being dependent on attracting players from the Protestant community to play for them, their image as a nationalist side was something that the club never lost:

> In the eyes of Protestants, Belfast Celtic was guilty by association: it was a nationalist side for nationalist players and supporters. Contrary to the Protestant view, Belfast Celtic officials never regarded the club as an exclusively Catholic preserve . . . the popular image of Celtic was kept alive by friend and foe (Sugden and Bairner, 1993: 81).

From the very start of Celtic's Irish league venture, crowd violence with 'sinister political overtones' (Sugden and Bairner, 1993: 82) was common at matches with Linfield and Glentoran.[5] Thus the pattern of ethno-sectarian violence at Irish League soccer grounds was established early on as member clubs, particularly in Belfast, became important symbols within their respective communities.

The Linfield / Belfast Celtic / Glentoran axis was strengthened by the dominance of three clubs on the field of play as well as through their embodiment of broader ethno-sectarian rivalries. However, it is worth noting that the rivalry also possessed an intra-Belfast character as each club was based in a particular quadrant of Belfast: Linfield in the south, Celtic in the west, and Glentoran in the east.[6] Following Linfield's move to Windsor Park in 1904, the rivalry between them and Celtic was sharpened because of the now close physical proximity of the two grounds on either side of the boundary that separates west and south Belfast. Matches between Belfast Celtic and Linfield / Glentoran thus involved supporters from one community entering a rival locality, creating an obvious opportunity for ethno-sectarian conflict bound up with the defence of space and the intrusion of the 'other', an issue discussed at greater length in chapter 14 by Shirlow.

Bitter sectarian rivalry dominated the relationship between Linfield and Belfast Celtic, often leading to outbreaks of violence among rival supporters (Coyle, 1999; Kennedy, 1989). The violence that had become a regular feature was to have a dramatic effect on the future of Northern Irish football when, following a violent 1948 Boxing Day confrontation between Belfast Celtic and Linfield,[7] the former withdrew from Irish League football at the end of that season.[8] Whilst the match in question produced some of the most violent scenes ever witnessed at Irish League grounds, it was the product of long-standing ethno-sectarian rivalry that had become familiar at matches between the two clubs. With Celtic's demise, the absence of a senior club in west Belfast denied the local Catholic population a recognised opportunity to engage with local soccer for most of the rest of the twentieth century,[9] leaving Linfield and Glentoran to turn their attention to each other and their 'Big Two' contests.

Sectarian rivalry was reduced but not eradicated at Irish League grounds following Belfast Celtic's withdrawal. Indeed, with the advent of the troubles, further problems were perhaps inevitable and in 1972 Derry City suffered a similar fate to Celtic. By the late 1960s the club became caught up in ethno-sectarian conflict, the proximity of the Bogside nationalist estate to the club's Brandywell ground helping to precipitate violence between locals and visiting supporters of Protestant dominated clubs which ultimately forced Derry City to withdraw from the Irish League in 1972.[10] Subsequently, in the absence of a sustained challenge from a club which drew heavily from the nationalist population for its support, intra-community rivalry became an increasingly prominent issue as Protestant-dominated clubs, mainly Linfield and Glentoran, battled with each other for supremacy.

## Intra-community rivalry and the 'Big Two'

In the wake of Belfast Celtic's departure from the scene, Linfield won the league championship in 1950, after a play-off match with Glentoran, thereby setting the pattern for subsequent 'Big Two' dominance. In the absence of sustained competition from clubs outside the city, this intra-Belfast rivalry had now become a head-to-head struggle for supremacy in domestic football.[11]

In the period immediately following Belfast Celtic's withdrawal, some Celtic supporters attached themselves to Glentoran as, despite its being an overwhelmingly Protestant club, it had shown a 'continued willingness to employ Catholics, a policy fully accepted by most of the club's Protestant supporters' (Sugden and Bairner, 1993: 84). Glentoran's inclusiveness assisted the club in furthering its supporter and player base but was in direct contrast to Linfield's stance on Protestant exclusivity. Also Glentoran's club colours of green, red and black brought ridicule from Linfield supporters in the context of Ulster Protestantism as such colours provide little, if any, visual representation of a loyalist supporter base. For Linfield supporters, their 'Big Two' rivals were to be regarded as a lesser Protestant club with few, if any, discernible symbols of Ulster Protestantism. Linfield supporters' reading of the rivalry is summed up in the words of one of their favoured songs:

> We are Linfield, super Linfield
> No one likes us, we don't care
> We hate Glentoran, Fenian bastards
> And we'll chase them everywhere.

In response, however, and in apparent recognition of the intra-loyalist rivalry and the need to show overt symbols of loyalism, Glentoran supporters have been known to display Union Jack flags on which the club colours of green, red and black replace red, white and blue. To anyone doubting the Protestant identity of the club's supporter base this is an indication that, despite the successful recruitment of Catholic players and the attachment – in the immediate post-Celtic era at least – of some Catholic supporters, Glentoran is to be regarded as a Protestant club.

The 'Big Two' rivalry assumes a further, more sinister aspect when viewed in the context of 'territorial affiliations' (Bairner, 2002: 122) and in particular the battle for paramilitary supremacy that has developed in Protestant areas of Belfast since the 1970s. Linfield traditionally draws heavily on supporters from south Belfast but also from loyalist west Belfast and in particular the Shankill Road (Bairner, 1997). Protestant working-class Belfast is divided into specific areas that have been dominated by the Ulster Volunteer Force (UVF) paramilitary group and the rival Ulster Defence Association (UDA). Supporters of both clubs have, on occasion, displayed vocal support and flags / emblems for the paramilitary group familiar to them. Such actions have been commented on by Bairner (1997) as being part of the visible reinforcement of loyalist culture at Irish League matches as well as a display of *machismo* among a distinctly working-class group. The Glentoran–Linfield rivalry has at times replicated the struggles within loyalist paramilitarism, thereby increasing the quasi-political significance of 'Big Two' clashes (Bairner, 1997).

Unfortunately, though not unexpectedly, the intense rivalry of 'Big Two' matches has resulted in violence. This peaked in the early to mid-1980s with the seminal moment being the 1983 Irish Cup Final, an event focused on by Bairner (2002).[12] However it is necessary to consider in more detail this particular cup final in view of intra-community rivalry dynamics. Firstly, the Irish Cup Final is the last match of the season and as the showpiece traditionally attracts a larger than average crowd. The 1983 final had extra significance as it was only the third post-war 'Big Two' final,[13] but was also critical in deciding which club would finish the season with the most trophies. Linfield had already secured the league championship and the County Antrim Shield whilst Glentoran were looking to make the Irish Cup part of a hat trick of cup triumphs that included the Ulster and Gold Cups. Secondly, and in the absence of a national soccer or multi-sport stadium, the choice of Windsor Park – the premier soccer stadium – as a 'neutral' venue[14] added to the situation. Irish Cup finals are held at Windsor Park unless Linfield are involved when the venue switches to the Oval, but where finals involve both Linfield and Glentoran, either venue is chosen by the football authorities.[15] In choosing Windsor Park to host the 1983 final, the football authorities could have appeared to be favouring Linfield by essentially making them 'hosts' as well as finalists with Glentoran and their supporters assuming the 'visitors' tag in a 'neutral' final.[16] Therefore, given the territorial politics involved, allowing Windsor Park to host the final could have been another determining factor in the violence. To elaborate, a perceived sense of invasion of territory took place whereby the 'away' supporters of Glentoran entered the 'home' space of Linfield's ground. However, Linfield supporters took up their usual positions in the parts of the ground reserved to them for 'home' Linfield matches whilst Glentoran were allocated the 'away' parts reserved for visiting supporters at matches with Linfield. The defence of the 'stadium's symbolic meaning' (Bairner and Shirlow, 1998a: 160) by the Linfield supporters was required in light of the visit of supporters of a club which, to them at least, represented a 'lesser' Protestant institution.

The political context of the time also needs to be considered as the Unionist and loyalist communities were experiencing a sense of betrayal that was to be exacerbated by the 1985 Anglo-Irish Agreement. Given the importance attached to the cultural identity of soccer within the Protestant community, 'Big Two' soccer matches increasingly became sites of cultural resistance. Therefore, the political climate of the time added additional pressure to an already potentially volatile situation, with the final providing a cathartic experience for those who wished to express political dissatisfaction whilst still serving at the same time as an opportunity for rival fans to identify themselves as 'the main champions of loyalism' (Bairner, 2002: 124).

It is also worth noting that the major disturbances took place after the game had finished in a 1–1 draw, necessitating a replay.[17] With the outcome undecided, neither supporter group was able to claim victory and assume the superiority that comes with it; subsequently some supporters may have been left at a loose end. It is possible then that a number of Linfield supporters left their Spion Kop terracing to confront Glentoran supporters at the opposite end of the pitch as an alternative outlet for their aggression. This could have been perceived as an 'attack' by Linfield supporters on their opponents but also a 'defence' of their territory and Protestant space. The trespassing Linfield supporters acted as the catalyst for the violence and with Glentoran supporters also encroaching on the field of play to fight, 16 people were arrested. The next week the replay, whilst involving less violence between the supporter groups, was conducted in an equally hostile environment.[18]

Ultimately, disturbances at 'Big Two' matches, as typified by the 1983 Irish Cup Final, have more to do with intra-community rivalry and the Protestant 'other'. To be able to fully understand the tribal rivalry between the Big Two and how this exists despite, or arguably because of, the absence of the Catholic 'other', one needs to appreciate the iconic status assumed by Linfield as a 'supra-Protestant' club.

## Linfield's iconic status

There can be little doubt that Linfield is the most successful club in Northern Ireland. Whilst other clubs have experienced periods of success in their history, only Linfield has had this in constant measure. To date the club has won 45 Irish League championship titles and 36 Irish Cups.[19] The nature of soccer support is such that successful clubs attract supporters from outside their vicinity. The unparalleled success of Linfield has made some fans adopt them as their 'local' team, attracting province-wide support denied to other clubs. Glentoran also has supporters outside Belfast but not to the same extent as Linfield.[20] It is common for football fans from provincial towns like Bangor, Newtownards, Lisburn, Carrickfergus, Ballyclare, Larne, Coleraine and Ballymena – all towns with local Protestant dominated senior clubs – to support Linfield. Also towns that do not have local senior clubs like Newtownabbey, Kilkeel, Sion Mills and Antrim are important sources of support for Linfield. It is important, however, to note that support for Linfield in Lurgan and Portadown, two traditional Protestant towns with Irish League clubs, is almost non-existent.

A large supporter base has contributed greatly to Linfield's commercial success as the richest soccer club in Ireland. It should be said that there is more to Linfield's province-wide supporter base than an attraction to pure football success. Despite Protestant hegemony and widespread Protestant attachment to the majority of Irish League clubs, it is only Linfield that have been regarded as a 'Protestant symbol' (Sugden and Bairner, 1994: 131). Historic ethnic exclusivity is arguably the most significant factor in the iconography of the club. Protestant tradition at Linfield has been preserved by various management committees throughout the club's history, guaranteeing its status as a 'Protestant and Unionist club' (Bairner and Walker, 2001: 85). Bairner and Walker (2001: 87) point out that at the time of the 1921 partition 'Linfield's Protestant and Loyalist identity seems to have been well established'. The authors go on to provide a comprehensive account of Linfield's relationship with Ulster unionist politics and government patronage between 1920 and

1960, and in particular the actions of Harry Midgley.[21] The Protestant and unionist nature of the club is further supported by the depiction of the British royal family's Windsor Castle on the club badge.

Linfield has been described as 'well known for having appeared to have adopted a policy at various stages . . . of not signing Catholic players or, indeed, employing Catholics in any capacity' (Bairner and Walker, 2001: 83). It is clear that whilst other clubs with Protestant roots and supporter bases attracted – and welcomed – Catholics players and supporters, Linfield did not. Even though Sugden and Bairner (1993) point out that over seventy Catholics have played for Linfield during the club's history and Bairner and Walker (2001) profile the interesting case of Gerry Morgan,[22] the club has managed to maintain a reputation for being almost exclusively Protestant with a unionist ideology and a loyalist supporter base. Whilst the club rejects implications of sectarianism (Sugden and Bairner, 1993), Protestant ethnic exclusivity is a central feature of its iconic status and influences Linfield's ability to attract province-wide support superior to that of their rivals.

It is certain that many supporters are attracted to Linfield because following the club affords them the opportunity to display themselves as Ulster Protestants and in the process to celebrate their broader culture. The Linfield supporter can be anti-Catholic, openly sectarian, and is able to 'sing about being up to their knees in Fenian blood or chant the names of loyalist paramilitary organisations' (Bairner and Shirlow, 1998a: 161). Clearly Linfield are a 'Protestant club for Protestant people' (Bairner and Walker, 2001: 84) and it is unsurprising that their Windsor Park ground is regarded as Protestant territory.

As both Fulton and Hassan argue in this collection, the dual role of the ground as home to Linfield *and* Northern Ireland has helped to make it a hostile environment for Catholics who wish to enter. Yet this simply adds to the iconography of Linfield on two counts. Firstly, those Linfield supporters who attend international matches lay claim to the same parts of the ground that they use at Linfield matches. Thus it is well known, for example, that the South Stand is reserved for home supporters at Linfield matches but is also used by the same supporter group at international matches. Secondly, as the ground is home to Linfield, it has been relatively easy for many supporters to transfer their red, white and blue scarves between Saturday Linfield matches and Wednesday Northern Ireland matches (Sugden and Bairner, 1993). Thus, although for international matches the ground becomes a place for all Protestants, Linfield supporters seek to demonstrate that the ground is *their* Protestant space that has been temporarily borrowed. In this sense, the IFA is providing Linfield and its supporters with added justification for feeling 'special' as it is their ground and space that are chosen to host the national side. Displaying club colours is, to some Linfield supporters, a recognition that this is Linfield's ground first and foremost.

Linfield's appeal as a symbol of Ulster loyalist identity and culture is additionally enhanced by the club incorporating red into the traditional club colours of blue and white.[23] In doing so, Linfield became the only Irish League team to display colours so central to Ulster Protestantism and loyalist culture. This can be viewed as an additional reason for supporters, interested in reinforcing a visible loyalist culture through soccer support, to attach themselves to the club. Any criticism levelled at Linfield supporters for sporting such colours is suitably deflected as they can claim merely to be displaying their club colours, regardless of the obvious symbolism. Thus the iconography of Linfield as a Protestant symbol is enhanced, presumably as a consequence of a deliberate policy by the club's management committee who chose the team colours.

Beyond the cultural and ethnic symbolism attached to Linfield, one cannot dispute that in pure football terms Linfield deserves its exalted position but it is the broader symbolism of the club that further separates it from its rivals. Overt Protestant and loyalist imagery is critical in determining Linfield's iconic status, allowing the club to attract a certain supporter type who sees more in the club than soccer success. The sense of belonging felt by Linfield supporters is based upon the club's image as a Protestant symbol and the visible reinforcement of a broader loyalist culture that no other Irish League club can match. This goes some way to explaining Linfield's iconic status as a symbolic Protestant club but it also provokes a hostile response from Protestant supporters of other Irish League clubs.

## Linfield and intra-community hatred

Linfield's unrivalled success is as good a reason as any for fans of other teams to dislike the club. Pure soccer success, however, is not the only reason that the club has become a hated symbol. As Bairner and Walker (2001: 84) note, 'some fans of other Irish League clubs – particularly Glenavon and Portadown – actually hate Linfield as part of a wider struggle to be identified as the true football representatives of Ulster loyalist identity'.

As was pointed out earlier in the chapter, the majority of Irish League clubs are located in Protestant dominated areas and attract majority Protestant support. But it is only Linfield that has sought to maintain Protestant exclusivity and thus come to be seen as a 'Protestant symbol' (Sugden and Bairner, 1994: 131). Whilst the previous section justified the legitimacy of this mantle, citing Linfield as representatives of the whole Protestant (soccer) community is summarily dismissed by supporters of other Protestant-dominated clubs, especially those outside Belfast. This is well expressed by Bairner (2001a: 33) using the example of Lurgan club Glenavon in mid-Ulster:

in towns such as Lurgan, with a significant nationalist population, the character of support for the local team, Glenavon, has been so symbolically Protestant and loyalist as to dissuade all but the most thick-skinned nationalist to follow his or her local club.

In this case, which is not untypical, Lurgan Protestants regard Glenavon as a Protestant club which has as much right to this title as any other club, Linfield included.

The club's strong Protestant history and location within the loyalist Mourneview housing estate is sufficient to create and preserve the club's Protestant image among its supporter base. Glenavon command a predominantly Protestant support from the local area and whilst Catholic players have been successfully recruited, local Catholics have tended not to associate with the club. Thus like Linfield, albeit at a more localised level, Glenavon is a 'Protestant symbol' (Sugden and Bairner, 1994: 131) and, like Windsor Park, its ground is 'a Protestant place for Protestant people . . . [and] Catholics must require special dispensation to be there' (Bairner and Shirlow, 1998a: 160).

Related to this, Bairner (2001a) and Bairner and Walker (2001) note that Catholic players have become a more regular feature in recent Linfield teams, giving the team an ethnic composition similar to that of their rivals, including Glenavon. However, both sets of supporters deal with this by reinventing Catholic players as honorary Protestants for the time they represent the club. Whilst Linfield could be considered to be an example of a national Protestant symbol, in the eyes of many of their fans Glenavon should be considered as the local equivalent which allows them to display their own sense of Ulster Protestant identity.

Bairner and Walker (2001: 85) point out that Linfield 'fans have continued to sing Ulster loyalist songs, many of them offensive to and disparaging of Catholics, regardless of (or conceivably in response to) the presence of Catholics in their team'. However, if it were to take action against sectarian chants and attitude, the club could be seen as attacking its history and traditions. On the other hand, whilst the songs and chants could be viewed as a reinforcement of Linfield's iconography, it should be noted that Protestant supporters of other clubs are engaged in the same loyalist rhetoric.

A clear example of this was the 2002 Irish Cup Final where a 2–1 Linfield victory over mid-Ulster club Portadown saw all three goals celebrated with chants of the anti-Catholic song 'The Billy Boys'. Further pro-loyalist chanting was heard from both supporter groups, making a mockery of the IFA's 'Give Sectarianism the Boot' banners exhibited around the ground. Singing Ulster loyalist songs is therefore not the exclusive preserve of Linfield fans.

The presence of Catholic players in the Linfield team has also compromised the popular chant of 'No Fenians in our team' that Linfield supporters directed at those rivals who have dared to contest their club's iconic status. Lately, supporters of Glenavon and Portadown have inverted the relationship by making the same claim (contrary to objective reality) in order to draw attention to the transformation of Linfield. However, it is common for Linfield supporters also to chant the Protestant supremacist claim of 'We are the People', signifying again that the supporters regard their club to be above all others in the Protestant community. This is an antagonistic claim and causes consternation among supporters of clubs like Glenavon and Portadown who feel that Linfield supporters have no special Protestant status. This shows the depth of intra-loyalist rivalry in the Irish League and how the battle to be seen as representatives of Ulster loyalism is very much alive and kicking.

In terms of the rivalry between Linfield and Glenavon, it is also necessary to pay attention to the importance of contestation around club colours. Blue is undoubtedly the colour that symbolises Protestantism in the soccer worlds of Northern Ireland and Scotland. Linfield chronicler, Malcolm Brodie (1985: 1), in his introduction to the club's centenary publication, noted that 'it is the proud boast of many Linfield fans that theirs is the bluest of blue'. Brodie continues the blue connection by referring to Linfield not by name but as 'the Blues' and argues that the loyalty of former Linfield players is summed up by the adage 'once a Blueman always a Blueman' (Brodie, 1985: 2). The players' blue shirts led to the popular chants of 'One Blues in Ulster' and 'Come on ye Blues'. However, even this is given an internecine dimension when applied to Glenavon whose team colours are blue shirts and white shorts/socks, requiring the away side to wear alternative kits at matches with Linfield.[24]

Thus, supporters of each club regard themselves as 'the Blues' and, more importantly, as 'the Blues of Ulster'. This has obvious significance for the contest to be 'the true football representatives of Ulster loyalist identity' (Bairner and Walker, 2001: 84) but the response of Linfield in particular adds to the iconography of the club and also provides further reason to hate the club. Linfield's choice of alternative colours at away matches against Glenavon has included orange, purple, scarlet or white, all significant colours in Ulster Protestant imagery.[25] Orange/scarlet/purple (along with blue) are colours sacred to loyalism and the Orange Order whilst red/white can be matched with Linfield's home kit of blue to make up the colour scheme so central to Ulster Protestantism and British identity. For example, in the 1950s and 1960s Linfield could be seen at Mourneview Park wearing orange shirts, purple shorts and socks or scarlet shirts, white shorts, and blue socks with the club defending its the kit choices as donations from supporters clubs of the time.[26] If Linfield could not be seen as 'the Blues' when visiting Glenavon, the Protestant and loyalist image was displayed by drawing on a broader range of colours that still reinforced Protestantism symbolism. Linfield was still visibly recognisable as a 'Protestant club for Protestant people' (Bairner and Walker,

2001: 84), further disputing any challenges to the contrary. However, such overt use of colour, in the context of intra-Protestant rivalry on the soccer landscape, is additionally antagonistic to those clubs that seek a Protestant image similar to that of Linfield. Glenavon has continually refrained from using red as their alternative kit,[27] disappointing those supporters who would regard red in the team kit as (re)centralising the club as a Protestant symbol. Linfield on the other hand have much to thank Glenavon for in terms of (inadvertently) enhancing the iconography of the club in relation to overt loyalist symbolism, by making them change their blue shirts.

The rivalry between Linfield and Glenavon reached its peak when Glenavon beat Linfield 2–1 in the 1992 Irish Cup Final at the Oval. Prior to the game poor ticketing allocation led to supporters of both clubs fighting in the main stand,[28] whilst Linfield's goal was celebrated by some supporters climbing the perimeter fence and encroaching on to the playing surface and delaying the game for a period.

The status of Windsor Park is a further factor in the intra-Protestant rivalry that is provoked by Linfield's iconic status and, in this context, its perceived position of privilege with the IFA that is disputed. The most tangible outcome of the Linfield–IFA relationship is the ongoing redevelopment of Windsor Park at a time when other Irish League grounds remain under-developed. For example, Portadown continue to perform in their comparatively dilapidated Shamrock Park home and Glentoran await the opportunity to build a new stadium. Meanwhile, Glenavon have completed the £200,000 construction of a new 2,000 all seated stand, but at the club's own expense.

Much has been said elsewhere (by Fulton and Hassan in this volume for example) about how Windsor Park is an unwelcoming place for Northern Irish Catholics, an unsuitable venue for the national side and a constant reminder of Northern Ireland's location within the United Kingdom. Less well documented, however, is the extent to which some Protestant soccer supporters are also dissuaded from attending national team games for some of the same reasons, particularly the fact that home matches are played at Linfield's home ground.

Some supporters from rural clubs believe that paying to watch the national side at Windsor Park is effectively financing Linfield. By not attending, therefore, even though these supporters are missing out on the opportunity to support their national side and to be overtly sectarian in line with the much of the traditional behaviour of the Windsor Park crowd, they feel justified in their actions. They may also feel uncomfortable sitting alongside fans who prefer to wear the red, white and blue of Linfield in preference to the green and white of the national team. Of course, the red, white and blue symbolism attached to the national side by some supporters also affects those Protestants who do not wish to enter into anti-Catholic displays and also decline to attend.

Protestant supporters of other Irish League clubs are ambivalent towards Windsor Park. Most visits involve supporting an 'away' team but for international matches they form part of the 'home' support. Linfield supporters, however, never experience the feeling of being 'away' at Windsor Park and it is almost as if, like Catholics, Protestant supporters of other Irish League clubs attending national matches also 'require special dispensation to be there' (Bairner and Shirlow, 1998a: 160). Although some of these attitudes may seem petty, they testify to the hatred that is directed towards Linfield from within the Protestant community and the effect of local politics on national team support. Perhaps the problems would be less apparent if the Northern Ireland team were more successful. For the time being, though, the refusal of certain Protestant fans, as well as most Catholics, to attend Windsor Park adds support to those who argue for a national stadium that is welcoming to all and owned by none (Hamilton et al., 2001).

## Soccer, politics and paramilitarism

The ethno-sectarian differences and political wrangling between unionists and nationalists and loyalists and republicans that are played out in the soccer arena are well documented elsewhere (Sugden and Bairner, 1993; 1994; Bairner and Darby, 1999). However, as has been demonstrated, the politics of intra-community rivalry also find expression at football games in Northern Ireland. When Gerry Adams was elected MP for west Belfast in the 1980s, and as important matches involving the Belfast 'Big Two' and their mid-Ulster challengers increased due to the latter's improved performances, political chants became a regular occurrence. In Portadown, the chanting of:

> Gerry Adams, Gerry Adams
> Gerry Adams your MP
> Gerry Adams your MP

was directed at the Linfield support, the reference being to the fact that Adams's West Belfast constituency includes the Shankill Road, from which Linfield has drawn heavily for its support (Bairner, 1997). The Shankill Road is a key symbolic space in loyalist imagery but having an Irish republican as its MP was deemed to reduce its significance. Political chants of this sort increased the rivalry between Portadown and Linfield beyond normal tribal levels and assumed even greater significance a decade later when mid-Ulster became more central to the political debate. Following David Trimble's Drumcree U-turn after his appointment as First Minister, Linfield fans exacted their revenge at games with Glenavon and Portadown by re-wording the chant to become:

David Trimble, David Trimble,
David Trimble your MP
David Trimble your MP.

This development can be linked to broader disputes between Belfast and mid-Ulster unionists, with Trimble regarded by many as being to blame for the current perceived favourable political climate for Irish nationalism. By popularising the chant, it could be argued that Linfield supporters were not only goading their mid-Ulster rivals for their choice of elected representative, but also in effect blaming them for the unfavourable political climate by continuing to elect the modern day Lundy.[29] With working-class support for Trimble decreasing in mid-Ulster, any mention of his name can be sensitive for many Glenavon and Portadown supporters.

During this period loyalist graffiti on walls leading to the two mid-Ulster grounds added another dimension to the intra loyalist schism. One prominent slogan in the vicinity of Mourneview Park in Lurgan read 'Trimble Beware – the PUP won't save you'. This was a reference to Trimble's alleged association with the Progressive Unionist Party (PUP) in the build up to the Good Friday Agreement. Billy Hutchinson, a PUP figurehead and representative of the Shankill Road, is a lifelong Linfield supporter and this is enough for mid-Ulster soccer fans to consider all Linfield supporters pro-PUP. Thus the warning was of some significance to all Linfield supporters indicating that broader political trends have made them more unwelcome in Lurgan than before.

This example is also linked to loyalist paramilitary infighting between mid-Ulster and Belfast-based former associates. The mid-1990s saw a split within the loyalist paramilitary grouping, the UVF as a consequence of its ceasefire. A prominent Portadown loyalist, the late Billy Wright, formed his own organisation, the Loyalist Volunteer Force (LVF), and openly defied a UVF death threat imposed on him. Indeed Wright held his press conferences in the Shamrock Park Social Club at Portadown's ground and was known to hold court there with his supporters. Wright subsequently gained considerable support within mid-Ulster and also attracted into his LVF ranks disaffected or suspended UVF members as well some UDA outcasts.

Some of Wright's appeal to his local followers rested not only on his fearsome reputation as an elite gunman (McKay, 2000) but on his regular attendance at Shamrock Park during Portadown's most successful seasons in the early 1990s. LVF murals and flags became conspicuous in the vicinity of both mid-Ulster soccer grounds, laying claim to these locales as 'belonging' to the LVF and warning any Belfast UVF and UDA supporters travelling with Linfield and Glentoran that they are in alien territory. The town and the soccer ground that they entered was 'under the control' of the locally based but potent LVF.

It must be pointed out that neither of the soccer clubs has any paramilitary involvement. But, as outlined by Bairner (1997), certain types of fan behaviour are located at one end of a spectrum at the other end of which can be found paramilitarism. As matches between Glenavon / Portadown and Linfield (and to a lesser extent Glentoran) took place against the backdrop of this brutal paramilitary warfare, the football grounds in Lurgan and Portadown became implicated in intra-loyalist conflict and paramilitary rivalries.

## Conclusion

Analysis of relationships between various Irish League clubs shows that there are a number of intra-Protestant rivalries on display and not just the Linfield–Glentoran one.

Soccer in Northern Ireland, as elsewhere, has space for apolitical rivalries. As Bairner and Walker (2001: 83) point out, 'hatred for Linfield goes beyond the convention of sporting rivalry'. Exceptional on-field success, superior marketing and commercial potential together with a perceived favoured relationship with the IFA regarding Windsor Park, are justifiably forwarded by Bairner and Walker (2001) as factors that attract hostility from other clubs, Protestant and Catholic supported alike. In addition, given the cultural politics of Northern Ireland, specific opposition to Linfield is also understandable. However, in order to understand the additional reasons for unionist and loyalist dislike of the club, there is a need to reconsider Linfield's status as a 'supra-Protestant' club that represents the whole Protestant community. In fact, this iconic status is not endorsed by those Protestant soccer supporters who seek to reproduce their identity through the devotion to 'other' Protestant-dominated clubs.

This chapter has shown the extent to which some fans use soccer as a means of demonstrating loyalism and unionism. However, it is clear this is not a unilateral or harmonious process and has different meaning for supporters of various Protestant-dominated clubs. 'Criticized over many years for promoting an essentially sectarian message' (Bairner and Walker, 2001: 96), Linfield is loathed by supporters of other clubs that are located within the Protestant community purely for its ultra-Protestant image. On the other hand, many fans of other clubs are simply envious of Linfield's unquestionable Protestant image and Ulster loyalist identity. This hatred has become more intense in recent years with the changing scene within loyalism. As traditional routes around many provincial towns are denied to Orange marchers, the local football club takes on greater significance as a remaining yet isolated symbol of Protestant identity. Greater displays of intra-loyalist conflict can be expected within Northern Irish soccer if the political situation does not improve in the eyes of the working-class Protestant. These in turn will be important indicators of divisions within unionism and loyalism.

As Irish League clubs suffer economic hardship and dwindling attendances, principally owing to the perceived lowering of standards of play, the economic hangover from the Bosman case, and the ease with which the likes of Manchester, Liverpool and Glasgow can be accessed at the weekend, Irish League football remains politicised. The introduction of Donegal Celtic from west Belfast and Lurgan Celtic into the Irish League in 2002/3 offers hope to the large nationalist working class which so far has been lost to the local senior realm of the global game. But there is also fear that such moves could result in the demise of the game with a return to the familiar patterns of sectarian hatred that affected both Belfast Celtic and Derry City in the past. However, involving the Celtic clubs within the Irish League could also act as a lure to attract greater numbers of Protestants back to football grounds with the primary aim of retaining their hegemonic stranglehold in the face of significant and long overdue local working-class Catholic involvement. As a result, soccer and its grounds will be once again used by Protestants for the purposes of reactive defence, albeit for more traditional reasons. Whether or not this occurs will depend on whether one or both of the Celtics can emerge as challengers to Linfield and Glentoran, just as Belfast Celtic once did. However, as this chapter has shown, less difficult to predict is the extent to which local soccer will continue to be used for the purposes of expressing intra-Protestant rivalries of a variety of sorts.

Part 3
# Issues

Chapter 12

# The migration of sporting labour into Ireland[1]

Thomas Carter

## Introduction

The migration of athletes and coaches, particularly in the past thirty years, has virtually exploded both in the number of individuals involved and the breadth of sports and places that are implicated in the increasing movement of sport-related people, technology, capital, and ideology. While the migration of athletes across and between continents is not new (Lanfranchi and Taylor, 2001), it is increasingly apparent that both the number and diversity of routes taken by migrant athletes have increased (Bale and Maguire, 1994). Irish athletic migration, in general, has historically consisted of an exodus away from both the Republic and Northern Ireland. However, although any discussion about the movement of sport personnel in Ireland is usually located within the context of emigration (see for example chapter 6 above, in which Darby discusses the role of sport in the lives of Irish immigrants in Boston), there is also a historical basis for the arrival of foreign sport personnel in Northern Ireland. For most of the twentieth century, however, this immigration has occurred on an ad hoc basis, with the occasional individual arriving on a club-by-club basis in any given sport. All of this began to change in the last two decades of the twentieth century.

The increasing presence and roles of foreign athletes and coaches in Irish sport are indicative of the growing impact that the globalisation of sport has had on local practices and institutions. In this chapter, general patterns and issues that affect sport across the island are identified and discussed based primarily on a longitudinal study of the impact that sport migrants are having on local sport in Northern Ireland. The study examined six different sports as case studies (Carter et al., 2003) and, of those six case studies, all but one involved sports organised on the basis of cross-border competition – that is, regular structured competition between athletes in the Irish Republic and in

Northern Ireland leagues, overseen by encompassing 'All-Ireland' administrative bodies. Thus, statistical examples and other data provided in this
chapter are based upon the final report submitted to the Sports Council for
Northern Ireland (Carter et al., 2003). Although this study dealt only with the
migration into Northern Ireland, because all but one case study were involved
in sports organised under the aegis of 'All-Ireland' structures, those general
patterns of athlete migration into Northern Ireland can be safely extended to
permit comment on the whole of the island. These migrants are not random
occasional instances of cosmopolitan individuals deciding to come to Ireland
but rather are part of distinct patterns within the larger flow of sport migrants
around the world. Although the initial impetus for sport migrants coming to
Ireland has more to do with external changes in sport than any specific decision
on the part of any Irish administrator, local expectations and perceptions
frame who these migrants are and why they come. In short, specific kinds of
migrants come to Ireland and specific local individuals focus their own efforts
to bring certain kinds of sport migrants to Ireland.

## Globalisation, sport and Irishness

It is quickly becoming a truism that the world is fundamentally characterised
by accelerating objects in motion. Sports are all about bodies in motion and
these bodies are moving faster and further than ever before. This is true not just
on the pitch, in arenas and in stadia but across continents and hemispheres.
The increasing ability of athletes to cover distances more swiftly than ever before
is a reflection of the social reality that there are more sports bodies moving
around the globe than ever before. Sport appears to be but one example supporting David Harvey's (1989) assertion that the world itself experienced a
'time-space compression' over the last decades of the twen- tieth century in
which space became annihilated by time. This compression reflects the rapid
flows of capital, people, goods, images and ideologies, drawing more and
more of the world into increasingly complicated and interconnected webs.
However, this compression is nowhere near uniform. The world may be full
of complex interconnections but there are numerous peoples in various places
whose experiences are marginal to these movements and linkages. Not everyone participates equally in the circuitous interconnected flows that transverse
the globe. It is through local agency and meanings that the position of Ireland
within the various global movements of people, capital and ideologies needs
to be understood. Human agency and the production and negotiation of cultural meaning are vital to the impetus of globalisation. A model of globalisation that analytically defines the global as political and economic and the
local as cultural does not express the embedded nature of contemporary
cultural, social, and economic processes that stream across space.

It is the unequal participation and embedded relations between disparate locales that lead me to consider sport and the Irish as part of broader sportscapes. Drawing upon Appadurai's (1996: 33–7) notion of 'scapes', sportscapes are, in and of themselves, amorphous global cultural flows that illustrate both the conjunction of disparate locations and the disjunctures that occur when a cultural form, such as a sport, is introduced to a new area and the local interpretations create differences in its meanings, form and practices. These various flows are not coeval, convergent, or spatially consistent and exist in relations of disjuncture. That is, the flows are paths or vectors that have different speeds, axes, points of origin and termination, and varied relationships to institutional structures in different regions, nations, or societies (Appadurai, 2000). These disjunctures, characterising the world-in-motion, precipitate various kinds of problems and frictions in different local situations. Consequently, these disjunctures must be comprehended from the perspective of each specific locale and, yet, the local perspective must be understood in relation to forces that emanate from and affect these local understandings and practices. In short, globalisation produces problems that manifest themselves in intensely local forms but have contexts that are anything but local.

Local sporting structures have become increasingly immersed in the processes of sport globalisation. Much of this immersion is explicitly tied to expansive capitalist forms of organisation thereby altering how local sport institutions are structured which in turn leads to increasing professionalisation, spectacularisation and movement of personnel. While many athletes had previously moved on an individual basis, the efforts of professional organisations at exporting their particular vision of a given sport to audiences outside their 'indigenous' society has affected regions around the world in different ways and at different speeds. These globalisation processes are by no means straightforward civilising processes of sportisation (Elias and Dunning, 1986). Rather, these varying processes of intercultural contact are best understood as a balance between and a blend of 'diminishing contrasts and increasing varieties' (Maguire, 1994) that reflect the shifting relations of power between distinct social entities. The globalisation of sport then cannot be merely understood as the diffusion of British games intimately bound up with cultural imperialism (Bairner, 2001a). Instead, various localities that had been on the edge of the Empire now act as central nodes of sporting power in and of themselves, sending their own practices embodied in athletes and coaches out into the world along pathways that may have little to do with historical imperial connections. A consequence of these global flows is that areas previously unaffected by athletic immigration began to be affected. Ireland is no exception.

The relationships between sport and the Irish are necessarily and messily complicated by the relative position of the Irish within and with Britain during and after independence. For much of the British Empire's existence,

Ireland was situated as part of the imperial centre of the Empire yet remained marginal within that colonial centre of power. While sport was frequently used as a means of socially marking who was and who was not considered part of the colonial elite (Guttmann, 1996; Mangan, 1985), these self same sports became embodied performances of nationalist movements in the former colonies (James, 1993; Beckles and Stoddart, 1995; Stoddart and Sandiford, 1998; Darby, 2002). Competition against and defeat of English national teams, even more than British, still provide symbolic discourse of the changed power relations between the former colonial overlords and subjects. As numerous Irish rugby supporters have told me, 'Nothing is better than someone beating the English, even if it isn't us.' Yet the shift in symbolic power relationships evident in international competition in which former colonies regularly defeat England does not provide any real suggestion as to why so many athletes and coaches are coming to Ireland. In this light, the 'British Isles' cannot be taken as a unified whole. Different regions of the isles experience athlete immigration in wide-ranging patterns with Scotland, Wales, England and Ireland all experiencing different migration patterns owing to local circumstances rather than global forces. The reasons, motivations and social factors that influence migrants moving to Ireland are not necessarily the same as for those migrating to England or Scotland. Nor are they the same throughout the island of Ireland. Those who come to Northern Ireland may have different reasons and experiences from those who come to the Republic. It is abundantly clear that Ireland cannot be conceptually or intellectually marginalised as simply one part of the 'British Isles' when the manner in which such global movements of people, capital, and ideas are shaped and experienced are specific to each location.

The historical legacy of sport in Ireland is one of interaction with colonisation, resistance, and unremitting tension between Irish and English sport. Sugden and Bairner (1993) usefully describe the historical positioning of various sports in Ireland, identifying those historically associated with Irish nationalism, Britishness, and political neutrality in terms of identity politics. While the affiliated Gaelic sports feed a specific ethnic-based national identification of Irishness (Bairner, 1999a; Cronin, 1999), the fact that these games are virtually unique to the Irish and its diaspora means opportunities for international competition are severely limited (Bairner, 2001a). Such limitations also restrict transnational sport migration. The sports which have involved the greatest number of immigrants are part of the milieu that Sugden and Bairner (1993) identify as that of the historically British sports, in particular, rugby union and cricket.[2] Despite the perception that these are 'British games', these sports also evoke passionate expressions of Irishness, as Tuck details above in chapter 7 on Irish rugby. An individual's Irishness is certainly not lessened by practising any of these supposedly foreign games.

Furthermore, as Bairner reveals in chapter 10, when Irish national squads compete in international competition, even Protestants in Northern Ireland can and do give their support, although this is likely to wane for events such as the Olympics in which the United Kingdom competes as a totality and becomes the team of choice for many.

## On the move: migrants coming to Ireland

The majority of sport migrants fill one of three professional positions in a sport's hierarchy: athlete, coach or administrator. The greatest number of these migrants operate on the lowest rung of the professional sports' hierarchy – that of athlete. While athletes receive the greatest amount of publicity and status in the eyes of the wider public, they are the least empowered group, essentially the labourers, albeit well-paid labourers, of the sport industry. Invariably, the professional athletes who migrate to Ireland have enjoyed relative success in their home country before their departure. Indeed, in many of the sports, athletes cannot become migrants until they attain the status of 'internationally capped' player, meaning they must have competed for their 'home' country in an international competition before they can be hired by an Irish side. Furthermore, that 'cap' has to have been earned within a recent period of time (usually 18 to 24 months prior to migrating for the recognition to be considered contemporary). It is not enough for someone to have been capped for his national side at the age of 21 and then to decide seven or eight years later that he wants to play in another country. The 'cap' must be recent, although the rules set by international sporting administrations regarding what can be considered recent vary from sport to sport. However, there is normally some flexibility in such rules. For example, a player who misses extended periods of time owing to injury may still be considered recently capped even if he did not play in the previous year or two.

The second category into which migrants fall is coaching personnel. This comprises not just head coaches but also specialised staff such as physical trainers, strength and endurance trainers and position coaches. The increasing professionalisation of sport overall has created specialised position coaches who provide instruction for specific techniques and skills depending on where an athlete plays on the pitch. In interviews, several migrants suggested that they acquired their posts in Ireland because local infrastructures had not yet produced such specialisation of knowledge. Such specialised positions, however, are only available at the upper end of the sport hierarchy with professional sides, such as the provincial sides in Irish rugby and national set-ups in various sports. Besides these specialised, elite coaches, there are several coaches working at Irish clubs, especially in the top division of cross-border leagues.

The third category consists of sport administrators who are hired to develop a specific sports club, in effect professionalising the entire operations of that club. Most administrators who have been brought to Ireland have been hired by local clubs to serve as development officers with a mandate to develop the entire club, including such responsibilities as finances and funding, public relations, youth development, and also coaching in a particular sport, usually cricket or rugby. Unlike the specialised coaches, most club directors are not affiliated to any national or professional set up but are hired by clubs whose administrators decided that they needed to professionalise their every-day operations while remaining an amateur sport club. Many migrants fulfil more than one of these roles. Many administrators are also coaches. Several coaches below the provincial levels also play their respective sport for the squad they are coaching.

Some social trends can be discerned within this migration into Ireland, which reflect gender, racial, and economic patterns within the overall sportscape that penetrates the island. While these patterns reflect the larger movement of sports migrants across the globe, there are some unique currents in the flow of migrants coming to Ireland. To begin with, nearly all of the migrants, who are extending their playing careers by leaving their home country and coming to Ireland, are men. Ireland is not the first foreign stop for most of them. Indeed, at least two thirds of these men have worked somewhere else in the world other than their home country before their arrival on the island's shores. Consequently, in terms of the length of athletic careers, the majority of these male migrants are older, ranging in age from their late twenties to their mid thirties. Furthermore, almost all of them are past their athletic prime and are on the downward slope of their competitive careers. Coaches, for the most part, have also worked elsewhere before migrating to Ireland and, in many cases, have done so to continue their careers after finding their coaching ambitions blocked at home. Unlike athletes, most have not had illustrious coaching careers in their home countries and thus are often younger (in their 40s or 50s) than their colleagues who have stayed at home.

Secondly, the majority of the migrants coming into Irish sport are white. At least three out of every four sport migrants who come to Ireland are white. The non-whites who arrive are not soccer athletes from Latin America, Africa, and Asia as is commonly the pattern in European countries with major professional soccer leagues. Indeed, Irish soccer overall still tends to be an exporter of talent rather than an importer. Instead, non-white migrants are principally involved in the sports of basketball and cricket with a few Pacific islanders joining local rugby clubs. African Americans tend to dominate the foreign professional ranks in basketball across Europe and Irish basketball is no exception in this regard. South Asian cricketers are also prevalent in Northern Ireland but they are not the dominant group of foreign professionals across the island, with that distinction belonging to white professionals hailing from South Africa.

Indeed, one of the more surprising patterns to emerge is the prevalence of South African athletes and coaches in Irish sport. Over one third of all sport migrants who came to Northern Ireland in 2001–2 were of South African nationality. The majority and most visible are rugby and cricket players and coaches but there are also hockey and tennis coaches and players. A number of external factors suggest reasons for the numerical dominance of South African migrants in Irish sport. One is the long historical connection between Ireland and South Africa as regions of imperial cultural influence (McCracken, 1996). A second possible historical reason resides in the relatively similar social structures in South Africa and Northern Ireland, thereby creating a sense of familiarity among some South African migrants (Akenson, 1992; O'Malley 2001). Historical reasons aside, it is likely that recent socioeconomic difficulties in South Africa are more relevant for South African migrants. Although the recent global trend of professionalisation has affected South African sport structures (Black and Nauright, 1998), the devaluation of the Rand has led to a decrease in the value of domestic salaries. Migrants can earn quite modest salaries at Irish clubs that effectively double or treble their annual income for working five or six months in Ireland. The salaries involved may be considered high locally, but are reportedly lower than are paid for similar positions in England. Another reason for leaving that some South African migrants have cited is the increasing threat of crime in their country. This factor was especially prevalent among family men who brought their spouses and children with them rather than leaving them 'home alone' for the time that they would be away. Thus, the safety of one's family and the desire to avoid becoming a victim of violent crime also serve as an impetus for migration.

The South Africans' ability to augment their annual earnings by migrating is similar to the experience of all the other migrants. For many migrants, their ability to procure employment in Ireland is a means of expanding their income during a time when they would not be paid at home and/or to make more money than they would at home. Many professional athletes around the world are only paid during their sport's season. In other cases, migration is a career move that is perceived to be either essential to achieve necessary experience required for advanced posts in a migrant's home country or as a means to extend an athletic or coaching career that has either stagnated or started its decline. The relative strength of both the Euro and Sterling compared with other currencies on the global market makes migration to Ireland particularly attractive and lucrative from an economic standpoint.

## Migration patterns

The South African exodus into Ireland is part of one of the two broad flows of migration that affect Irish sport. One is a hemispheric migration current between the southern and northern hemispheres, and the other is trans-atlantic. Within these two currents, there is strong tendency for a particular sport to draw its migrants primarily from one source country. A combination of factors works to produce such patterned flows. One factor is the reputation a country's athletes have in a given sport. Canadians are renowned worldwide for playing top class ice hockey. Prior to 2003, the world champions in rugby union had been Australia, New Zealand and South Africa, the three major suppliers of foreign talent to Irish rugby clubs. South African and South Asian cricketers have also achieved international prominence. South Africans are also amongst the best hockey players in the world. Americans dominate inter-national basketball and African Americans dominate the professional ranks in the USA – and in Ireland. Thus, in each sport, a single migrant group numerically dominates.

A second factor that is evident in both major migrant patterns is the prevalence of English-speaking migrants. All of the countries that domi-nate migrants' numbers in Irish sport also happen to be societies with large English-speaking populations. The majority of migrants come from countries where English is the primary language. In those cases where the migrant's first language is not English, English is the second language of his country of origin. Particularly good examples of this are Indian and Pakistani pro-fessional cricketers.

The issue of language is one of several interrelated reasons for local interest in southern hemisphere athletes and coaches. The first reason is the simple geographic fact of the reversal of seasons in the southern hemisphere. The reversal of seasons means that any athlete coming to Ireland during that sport's season is, theoretically, already in playing condition and not missing any competition back in the home country. Migration, then, is a way for these athletes to maintain their fitness level and continue competing whereas back home, the 'off season' would consist of weight training and little else. Within the sport milieu, actual competition is valued more highly than weight training and aerobic workouts. Various coaches insist that athletes worked harder and stay in better shape through participation in competition than through intensive, non-competitive training.

Also embedded within this logic are negative local perceptions of English or Scottish professionals. Several club officials expressed reluctance to hire English, Scottish, Welsh or even Irish athletes who are 'free', i.e. not contracted to a specific club, because they felt that if such an athlete were any good, he would already have a contract with a club. Indeed, the few Scottish professionals who found positions in Northern Ireland in our study did so because they had extensive experience somewhere in the southern hemisphere prior to coming to Northern Ireland (Carter et al., 2003). Thus, the quality of athlete is considered more dubious where British talent is concerned. As one club official blithely remarked, 'After all, why would an English cricketer leave to come here? Since it is the same season, if he is worth anything at all he'll find a club on the mainland.'

A further factor in this pattern of hemispheric migration is the historical connection between Ireland and the various countries from which migrants hail, already mentioned specifically in relation to South Africa. All of the migrants originate from places that were once part of the British Empire. Moreover, all the migrants coming to Ireland from the southern hemisphere are involved solely in those sports that Sugden and Bairner (1993) identified as historically British games. Many of these countries have themselves experienced earlier Irish diasporas, resulting in historical familial connections that some migrants then use to return to Ireland.

Another factor is the perception that the athletes and coaches from the southern hemisphere are better trained than local athletes and coaches. While it can be argued that this is a misguided perception, it does exist in the region. Those who espouse such a view point to two different factors to support it. The first is the international sporting success that many of these countries have had. Australians, New Zealanders and South Africans have all excelled in rugby. Australians, Pakistanis, Indians and South Africans have all had international success in cricket. South Africa and Australia have two of the best field hockey sides in the world. Additionally, local authorities and supporters point out that many of these countries, especially Australia, New Zealand and South Africa, have established state-sponsored sports academies that have produced proven athletes and coaches, and not just in those three sports but overall, as their international records indicate. International success is used to support claims that local athletes can learn more from foreign athletes by playing with and against them in a form of bodily learning through osmosis. Additionally, it is argued that local athletes can also learn more from foreign coaches until local coaching structures meet similar standards. Several migrant coaches commented in interviews that the standard of play in Ireland is not as high as back in their home countries but that local athletes will close that gap in a relatively short time. Essentially, local coaches and athletes are simply considered not of the same standard as foreign ones by both migrant coaches and local officials and coaches. The presence of migrant athletes and coaches, then, is justified as a means to accelerate the development of Irish sport.

The transatlantic current differs from the hemispheric in that transatlantic migration involves sports that are themselves considered imports. They are also 'World Games' based on Sugden and Bairner's classificatory scheme

(1993), with their cultural origins not nearly as relevant as the historical antecedents of British games. Consequently, the history of migration related to these specific sports is a relatively new phenomenon. Basketball migrants only began coming to Ireland on a regular basis in the early 1980s while ice hockey migrants have only been coming regularly since the late 1990s. Thus, unlike the hemispheric current, the transatlantic current is relatively novel. Because of this current's relative novelty, transatlantic migrants number roughly one third compared to the hemispheric flow of migrants coming to Ireland for sport. Intriguingly, the transatlantic current can be narrowed to a north Atlantic flow in that migrants from the Caribbean or Latin America are nearly non-existent within the context of Irish sport. It is curious that no West Indian cricketers have been in Ireland for a number of years. There are, however, West Indian cricketers in Britain, which raises the question as to what local factors in Ireland, Britain and the Caribbean can be discerned to explain this difference. Unfortunately, this must remain a question for another time. Instead, nearly all of the migrants came from either the USA or Canada, and which country they came from depends on the sport. Americans are involved in basketball primarily and Canadians are involved predominantly in ice hockey with the advent of a professional ice hockey team in Belfast. Without that particular organisation, Canadians would be almost completely absent from local sport and would not enter the public eye in the way South Africans and New Zealanders have in other sports. A further difference between transatlantic migrants and hemispheric ones is that, with the exception of one ice hockey playing American, the majority of the Americans (as distinguished from Canadians) are black. Basketball is the only sport in which non-whites constitute the dominant numerical group. A further difference between the two is that basketball migrants are all athletes with a couple acting as player coaches. Irish coaches continue to hold the more prestigious positions in this particular sport. This differs from those hemispheric migrants who are or have been provincial and national coaches in several sports.

## Local control(s)

At first glance, the global forces propelling changes in local sport, such as the professionalisation and the overall commercialisation of sport in general, would appear inevitable and overwhelming. Local administrators do, however, have some tools they can use to control the impact that these outside forces will have on Irish sport. Two particularly useful tools are state-defined rules on citizenship and league-wide quotas that restrict the number of foreigners (i.e. non-citizens) per club. These tools facilitate the establishment and enforcement of limitations regarding who can and cannot immigrate to either

Ireland or the UK for work, and the roles and influence migrants can have in specific sports.

Citizenship regulations determine who is and who is not a member of any given state. By controlling membership within a particular state, a government can delineate who does belong ('citizen') and who does not ('foreigner'). Often these ideals are tied to notions of territoriality and/or blood. Quotas are set by a sport's governing body in a given country and are a major restraint on a migrant's ability to move from one place to another. The sports discussed here all have overseeing bodies based in Dublin, with the exception of ice hockey, which is administered by the British ice hockey organisation, Ice Hockey United Kingdom.

A necessary digression must be made here to discuss the complex case of Northern Ireland sport. The situation in Northern Ireland is complicated because it is constitutionally part of the United Kingdom of Great Britain and Northern Ireland. However, many of the governing sport institutions are controlled by sport associations and unions that are based in the Republic of Ireland. In most cases, a prospective migrant has to meet the qualifications of the UK's immigration laws, and also the standards of the Republic's administrative regulations for that sport. Consequently, the question of sport migration into Northern Ireland is necessarily complicated, since any migrant or organisation that wants to make use of migrants must meet criteria of not just one overseeing bureaucracy but sometimes two, three or more. For example, a rugby player desiring to migrate to Northern Ireland must have qualified as an international player within the last 18 months in his home country, be recognised as an international player by the International Rugby Board (IRB), and recognised by the British government as a skilled labourer such as cannot be found within the UK's borders. In addition, the Irish Rugby Football Union must vet the player as a legitimate, internationally skilled player who could improve local rugby. Various governing bodies, some of which are part of the United Kingdom while others are national sporting bodies of the Republic, also limit athlete migration into Northern Ireland.[3]

Whether a migrant is attempting to enter the Republic or the UK, he or she is not considered foreign if the individual in question somehow meets one of three criteria for national qualification in that sport. National qualification is tied to each state's definitions of citizenship, symbolically and practically defined through eligibility for a British or Irish passport. The three criteria (of which only one needs to be met) for a migrant to obtain citizenship and, consequently, not count against a club's quota of foreign players are *ancestry*, *birth*, or *residency*.

In general, a migrant meets the ancestry requirement in order to qualify for an Irish passport as long as one of his or her grandparents was born in Ireland. To highlight the arbitrariness of this delineation, consider the following. A migrant rugby player who played for a local club did not count against his club's quota because he qualified for an Irish passport even though the grandfather that made him eligible had never set foot on Ireland. His grandfather had been born on a ship sailing from England to New Zealand. Since his grandfather was born *en route*, the babe was legally considered to have been born on British soil (at a time when Ireland was still part of the United Kingdom) even though the man never actually left New Zealand during his lifetime. Nonetheless, his grandson was eligible for Irish citizenship. Had the grandfather been born twelve hours later, this athlete would not be Irish qualified and he would not be in Ireland at present.

The second way a foreign player can qualify for a British or Irish passport is through 'natural citizenship' or *birth*. Having been born in Ireland, an athlete's family may move during his or her childhood, even to the other side of the globe, but as long as the athlete has not played for another national side after turning 18 years of age, he or she is eligible to play for either the British or Irish national squads, depending on whether the individual in question was born in Northern Ireland or in the Republic.

The issue of 'natural citizenship', as being related to one's birthplace, is contentious. The controversy over Roy Keane's departure from the Republic's national soccer team and Yorkshire-born Mick McCarthy's 'Irishness' just prior to the 2002 World Cup Finals is but one publicly prominent example. Similar difficulties arise in Northern Ireland regarding ethnic identity and citizenship. Many athletes born in Northern Ireland who play for local clubs may be citizens of the United Kingdom, but they also qualify to represent Ireland in international competition by virtue of their place of birth and their right to dual citizenship. Indeed, it is assumed within many sports that athletes in Northern Ireland will play for Irish national sides. In such circumstances, these athletes' 'Irishness' is not questioned in the manner that McCarthy's was, yet they share citizenship with McCarthy and not with all of their team-mates. Many in Northern Ireland choose to represent Ireland because they consider themselves to be ethnically, culturally or politically Irish. More practically, from their perspective, there is less competition in most sports to make an Irish national squad than a British one. Nevertheless, some athletes from Northern Ireland have chosen to represent Britain because they have felt that they had better chances at earning medals in international tournaments because of the higher quality of British training, facilities and personnel. Even in those cases where athletes can choose which nationality they wish to represent, once the choice is made, they cannot switch back. This seems rather ironic considering that migrants coming to Ireland from elsewhere can eventually qualify for Ireland national squads through *residency* if by no other means.

Contrary to the regulations regarding *birth* and *ancestry*, a migrant can become eligible for his or her second national side if he or she establishes *residency* in the UK or Ireland and obtains a UK or EU passport, effectively becoming a transnational or 'flexible citizen' (Ong, 1999). *Residency* is established through an individual's continuous presence in either state for 36 consecutive months. One rugby player explained that establishing residency in the UK was part of his motivation for coming to Northern Ireland. He had played rugby in England for two seasons and had the option of either returning to his home country or going to Northern Ireland. His decision to come to Northern Ireland was influenced by the opportunity playing presented in establishing UK residency. Becoming eligible for a UK passport would ease his entry into the UK workforce later in life, if he so chose to return after his playing career was over. Such an option is open only to professional migrants who will be employed throughout that period and can obtain the work permits.

The irony is that for athletes to obtain work permits they must have represented their home country's national side within the previous 18 to 24 months in an international match recognised by that sport's international administrative board. Thus, a young, locally raised athlete has to decide if he or she will be British or Irish within the context of his or her sport even while that individual may be a citizen of the other country. Yet an athlete from the southern hemisphere could have represented his or her country as a youth and then emigrated to Ireland and qualified for national representation by establishing *residency* in Ireland. Migrant athletes can and do represent Ireland, Great Britain or Northern Ireland in international competitions even if they have represented their 'home country' earlier in their careers once they have establish *residency.*

The ability of a migrant to become 'naturalised', that is, to become a citizen of either the Republic or the UK, is an important distinction since the quotas most sporting bodies place on the number of migrants refer to the number of *foreign* migrants rather than *overseas* migrants permitted per club in each sport. Although there is no official distinction made between *foreign* and *overseas* migrants, distinctions between *overseas* and *foreign* migrants, however, are informally understood in various locales throughout Ireland. *Overseas* migrants, for specific reasons, are not marked in local sport's consciousness to the same degree as *foreign* migrants.

An *overseas* migrant is an individual who has not established *residency* but can claim either British or Irish citizenship through his *ancestry* or *birth.* There are local distinctions made regarding overseas migrants. While an *overseas* migrant is someone who is nationally qualified to represent either Ireland or a British squad, most locals involved in sport conceptually include anyone who comes from across water as an *overseas* migrant. In this cognitive framework, a British citizen who is English, Welsh or Scottish and, ostensibly, white, who crosses the Irish Sea or North Channel, is an *overseas* migrant. However, an individual crossing the border is not considered an *overseas* migrant even though that person may not share citizenship with many residents on the other side of the border. Thus, for many people, an *overseas* migrant is an individual whose ethnic identity is something other than Irish, even if the individual in question shares citizenship with the local athletes.

A *foreign* migrant, by contrast, is a migrant who cannot claim British or Irish citizenship. This means that, conceptually a *foreign* migrant is from somewhere other than the British Isles and is not qualified upon their arrival to represent the Republic, the United Kingdom, or Northern Ireland in international competitions. Consequently, unlike *overseas* migrants, a *foreign* migrant has no legitimate claim to citizenship through *birth* or *ancestry*. *Foreign* migrants can, however, become qualified through *residency*. However, a *foreign* migrant cannot 'disappear' from local consciousness in the way that *overseas* migrants can. Even if a *foreign* migrant settles permanently in a local community, perhaps marrying a local woman and raising a family, and becomes nationally qualified, thereby removing the criterion that would make him 'foreign', he remains a *foreign* migrant in local officials' eyes.

These distinctions are important to sports' administrators because of the quotas that exist on athletes who are not nationally qualified, that is qualified to represent either Great Britain or the Republic. An *overseas* migrant does not count against the quotas established by a given sport's ruling body because he can qualify through *ancestry* or *birth*. Thus, one can have two Australian migrants in the same squad, one an *overseas* migrant and the other a *foreign* migrant, because the former is Irish qualified whereas the latter is not. Only one counts towards any quota that may exist in the given sport. So on the one hand, citizenship determines whether one is an *overseas* or *foreign* migrant. In practice, locals think of sport migrants in terms of *ancestry* and *birth*, but these become conflated with ethnic identity in various cases as the distinctions between *foreign* and *overseas* migrant and professional and amateur athlete come into play. Because *overseas* migrants exist as a secondary category that does not readily come to mind, they are much more difficult to distinguish from natives than *foreign* migrants are. An *overseas* migrant, especially one who is an amateur athlete, playing for a local club fades into the background much more readily in local perceptions. It is in these instances, where an *overseas* migrant does not count against any quota, that ethnic identity rather than citizenship informs the distinction between local and migrant sports personnel.

## Conclusion

To summarise, the majority of sports migrants coming to Ireland are white, middle-class men. A significant proportion of these migrants are sports professionals who are older than many of the elite athletes found in most international-level competitions. Nonetheless, the professional athletes who come to Ireland have played at the international level – indeed, it is an immigration requirement to be eligible for work in the UK or the Republic of Ireland unless one can claim familial ancestry. The majority of these migrant athletes are now reaching what they consider the end of their athletic careers. Their situation in their countries of origin is such that they recognise that their careers are about to end. For some, this means coming to Ireland as an opportunity to extend their playing careers. Many also desire to continue their careers in their chosen sports but as coaches. They see migration to Ireland as providing an opportunity to play but also to gain valuable training and practice in coaching, thereby easing the career shift from athlete to coach. Thus, their arrival in Ireland signifies a personal transition not only in space but also in career.

The migrant's arrival in Ireland is, however, by no means a straight-forward process. There are numerous social, economic and political factors in a migrant's home country and on the island of Ireland that affect the outcome of any potential movement. Although there are powerful forces that push individuals to migrate within sport, these collide with local administrative barriers and resistance creating disjunctures between the larger patterns and the localised reactions to these strangers in their midst. Governments and sports' administrative bodies place barriers restricting the intake of migrants. The use of citizenship qualifications and arbitrary quotas serve to limit the impact migrants will have on local sport structures, ethos and practices.

Other factors affecting sport migrants' movement have little to do with actual sport. Currency stability, frequency of crime, and relative safety of one's family all act as motivators for sport migrants beyond any career incentives. Likewise, Ireland draws migrants because of historical, social or economic factors. The Irish diaspora and many migrants' ancestral ties to the island are one drawing factor. The similarities between migrants' home cultures and Irish culture can be another attraction for migrants. A third is the relative stability of either the Euro or of Sterling on the international monetary market thereby ensuring migrants a stable income when their own currency may be more volatile.

Finally, all of the remarks here are written in a context that is fluid and rapidly changing. There are local movements in several sports resisting the global trend towards the professionalisation of athletes and organisations. If successful, these potential regulations would also affect sport migration into Ireland. The tensions described here will continue in Irish sport. The issues of 'foreigners' in Irish teams and who is or is not qualified to play for the respective states on the island will continue as long as there are debates over what it means to be Irish.

Chapter 13

# Some reflections on women's sports in Ireland

Katie Liston

## Introduction

This chapter continues the discussion of themes already addressed in chapter 5 by Ryan, and focuses particularly on the role of sport in identity-formation, especially as it relates to the self-conceptions and social ranking of men and women. The various contributions to this volume highlight other important aspects of the sport–society relationship, such as the role that sport plays in the production and reproduction of a national identity in times of social conflict, as well as the historical emergence of Gaelic sports on this island. Besides that, all contributors share a common focus on a particular form of sports: the use of a physically active body capable of competing against another, often in close physical proximity and sometimes with the requirement that a competitor make direct physical contact with an opponent (as in combat sports such as ice-hockey, rugby football, association football or soccer, Gaelic football). I shall suggest, taking account of wider sociological arguments concerning sport and the body (e.g. Bourdieu, 1988; 1990), that sport is particularly important in the maintenance of visible differences between male and female bodies. This has significant implications for the development and organisation of sports generally, and women's sports specifically. Public and private financial investment in, and sponsorship of, sports depend on a high media profile, sporting success, public interest and support. Thus, what one might call 'the sporting body' can be said to stand at the centre of an inter-related nexus of commercial, cultural, state, regional, local and individual interests. Moreover, images and expressions of the body vary across time, space, culture and location and the 'ideal' Irish sporting body is contested by sports participants and supporters alike.

In the first section, Irish sports are presented as a fully functioning, self-regulating and dynamic social arena with their own set of rules or structuring principles – or, in Pierre Bourdieu's terms, as a social 'field' (1990: 156).[1] The discussion then moves on to examine the relationship between the field of Irish sports and the predominant systems of bodily preferences in that country, and their impact on the practices of male and female sportspeople. Using this framework, I examine empirical findings on sport and physical activity in the Republic of Ireland, particularly gendered differences in rates and perceptions of, and motivations for, participation in sports. I conclude with a reappraisal of the role of sport in identity-testing, particularly in relation to the physical expression of a gendered identity.

## The field of Irish sport

We can characterise the field of sports in the Republic of Ireland (Figure 13.1) in terms of prevailing discourses and ideologies that are consistently produced and reproduced within sporting institutions and specific social practices. The field of Irish sport[2] is generally dominated by discourses that emphasise the heroic and competitive elements of sporting achievements as well as the necessary physical strength, speed, instrumental aggression (which is an acceptable and expected feature of most sports) and sacrifices that are required in order to be successful. Examples of these discourses can be seen in media coverage of dominant amateur and professional sports such as Gaelic football, soccer and rugby. Over the past ten years, alternative – though not necessarily contradictory – discourses have emerged from interactions between participants in the field of sport and elsewhere (Bourdieu, 1990); the leisure sphere has grown, the increased productivity of the Irish economy has led to increasing commercial (and often private) interest and investment in sport, and some Irish sports such as rugby, soccer and athletics have undergone 'de-amateurisation'. Thus alternative discourses have emerged in the field focusing on health and the body, commercialisation and marketing interests, and the emergence of professional sporting practices that challenge the 'fair play' ethos traditionally associated with amateurism. A notable feature of prevailing ideologies is the absence of critical discourses concerning sport. There might be for example – but there is not – critical discussion of the physically and psychologically harmful effects of participation in sports, particularly at elite level and within contact sports; or a challenge to the 'sport is good for you' dictum that often prevails in political debate; or an acknowledgement that sport can help to perpetuate social divisions and conflict as well as play a part in softening them. The general absence of critical discourses is perhaps not surprising considering: the low status of sociology in Ireland generally (and the lack of sports researchers within Irish sociology, with the exception of some of the contributors to this volume); the fact that sport plays such a central role in the Irish Republic; and that the importance of sport as a mechanism of identity-formation and identity-testing, from the national to the local and individual levels, is simply taken for granted.

Dominant discourses are produced in the field of sport through the practices of specialist agents and powerful institutions, some directly engaged in the administration and organisation of sports, others engaged only indirectly. Dominant sporting bodies include the Gaelic Athletic Association, the Irish Rugby Football Union, the Football Association of Ireland and the Irish Sports Council, which is the formal umbrella body with responsibility for the organisation of Irish sports. Other important parts are played by the state, which plays an important role in the provision of sports facilities and policies as well as financial investment in the development of sports; by the Catholic Church, not only through its patronage of, and association with the GAA, but also its position within Irish society generally; and by the increasingly powerful mass media (print, radio and television) as a dominant interest group (Inglis, 2000). Debates and discussions about sport take place both in the public and the private spheres. The importance and value of these discussions generally depend on the position of institutions and specialists with investments in the field of sport, and they are both affect and are affected by transformations, such as de-amateurisation and commercialisation, in sporting values and practices. But in general, there is relatively little *public* debate and critical discussion in the field of Irish sport, except for specific incidents such as Michelle Smith's positive drug testing after the 1996 Olympics, Cathal Lombard's positive drug testing before the 2004 Olympics, and what has recently been labelled the 'Roy Keane saga', which generate an emotive national focus. While it is common to see and hear daily, weekly and weekend sports reports that focus on particular individual athletes and teams, most of these discussions converge on implicit assumption that sport is 'good', that sporting achievement is to be applauded, and that the sporting Irish are alive and well. Critical discussion of the development, organisation and future of Irish sports is generally confined to regular meetings of marginalised groups such as female sportspersons and those involved in minority-interest sports. The protagonists of minority sports are often forced to finance and publish their own publications to generate a public profile.[3] Thus the interests of traditionally powerful sports bodies, commercial sponsors and private groups are generally reflected in the everyday sports conversations in the *private* sphere – in public houses, homes and sports centres throughout the country. These discussions provide a focus for expressing and developing attitudes, individual beliefs and practices that are conveyed within the home, in local community activities, in the local and national media and in the physical education curriculum, which in turn reshape discourses on sport.

*Figure 13.1:* **The field of Irish sport and physical activity (adapted from Inglis, 1998: 121)**

**Discourses on sport** (drawing on prevailing ideologies)

heroism; achievement; competition; health; beauty; physicality; commercialisation; commodification; sex/erotic; fair play ethos

**are produced within**

state; media; church; dominant sporting bodies (GAA; IRFU; FAI etc.);

**debated and discussed in**

public sphere (very little); traditionally powerful interest and commercial groups; marginalised groups; e.g. women's sports

**giving rise to**

attitudes; beliefs; practices

**that are conveyed within**

education (first to third level); home; books; media; church; local, national and international community activities

**and filtered through**

parents; teachers; role models; friends; peers; sports; organisers; coaches

**creating**

a sporting habitus

**giving rise to**

attitudes, beliefs, practices

**which in turn reshape**

discourses on sport

# A Bourdieuian analysis of sport

If we apply Bourdieu's (1988, 1990) work on the body to the field of Irish sports, we can see that sports are partly organised on the basis of the type of 'body' that particular sports require or favour – whether a sport 'implies direct contact, hand-to-hand, such as wrestling or rugby, or whether on the contrary it excludes all contact, like golf, or authorises it only by the interposing of the ball, like tennis, or the intermediary of instruments, like fencing' (Bourdieu,

1990: 157). Sports can be understood within a system of bodily preferences that is associated with a particular 'experience of the physical and social world' (Bourdieu, 1990: 157) and social position. The relationship between sporting practices and social position can be characterised as a homology (or correspondence) and it is in the relation between these two spaces that the pertinent properties of every sporting practice are defined. And the very changes in practices can be understood only on the basis of this logic, in so far as one of the factors which determine them is the desire to maintain in practice the gaps which exist between different positions (Bourdieu, 1990: 158).

The field of sport is not only characterised by specialised activities, it is also constituted by people who have a stake in them and who share a passion for the central focus of the field – a love of and investment in sport. Relationships are established between people with differing resources, motives and sporting abilities within this field, and with people in other fields. These relationships generally constitute a hierarchy and, through the assertion of its own criteria, the field of sport can seem to operate according to its own social dynamics. However, this is not to suggest that hierarchical relationships external to the field such as those related to money and power do not affect internal processes within sport. While 'the two do not recognise the same merits and values and use a different hierarchy to speak of the various agents competing in the same field' (Defrance, 1995: 127), Bourdieu (1990: 156) suggests that 'one has to imagine the space of sporting practices as a system from which every other element derives its distinctive value'. In this way, the field of sport is a social activity with distinctive structuring principles and dynamics, and 'to understand a sport, whichever one it may be, one has to recognise the position it occupies in the space of sports' (Bourdieu, 1990: 156).

Figure 13.1 provides an illustration (though not an exhaustive one) of how the field of Irish sport is structured in terms of various discourses, practices and struggles between specialists in this field. Sport is a field in which individuals and representatives of sports institutions struggle to attain dominance over one another through the production and reproduction of relations of power and the acquisition of different forms of capital – social, economic and symbolic (Bourdieu, 1986). Individual and team sports can be understood within a system of bodily preferences that reflects a deep understanding of the physical and social world, and from which every other element in the sports field derives its value. Thus power struggles between male and female sportspersons are also (though not exclusively) part of struggles for access to, and dominance of, the meanings attached to particular sports and forms of physical expression. Furthermore, as Bourdieu suggests, various sports (e.g. women's rugby) can be understood from their position within the field of sports and their relationship to power struggles. The idea that some women can play rugby as successfully as their male counterparts implicitly challenges the idea that rugby is a male sport and what it means to be a sporting male in Irish society (Liston, 1999).

If, as Bourdieu suggests, the field of sport operates within a socially constituted order (as seen in discourses such as the practice of sport for sport's sake or a modern 'fair play' ethos), then the dominance of attitudes, values and beliefs is generally reproduced at an habitual level precisely because these attitudes are taken for granted. The homology between the field of Irish sports and an individual person's habitus, or embodied dispositions and stock of long-lasting knowledge about how sports 'work', can be explained as:

> the activity of an agent, an action that can be adjusted to the social world without the agent being aware of what is going on around him or her, without the agent understanding all or having an omniscient and perfectly just vision of the situation (Defrance, 1995: 128).

The 'logic' (or illusion of logic) of sports practice can be seen in 'the way things are', and it is such a logic that can be seen behind assertions that weight-lifting is not appropriate for women, that some female bodies are *too* muscular or that the emergence of a power game in women's tennis is unwelcome. The remainder of this chapter looks at the relationship between sport, gender and the body by exploring the role of sport in the construction and reproduction of cultural conceptions of gender, and also how our ideological notions about the body (and gender) structure sport. Evidence can be seen in rates of participation in sport, the relative popularity of sporting activities, and perceptions of sporting and physical activities as gender-appropriate. I shall also explore the hidden assumptions (what Bourdieu terms 'illusio') about 'natural' differences between male and female bodies which underpin the position of various sports and athletes within the field of Irish sports generally. As a social activity, sport both reflects and plays an active role in divisions, processes and changes in Irish society. The practice of sport thus has productive and reproductive effects throughout Irish society as well as the ability to generate processes of change, for example in the growth in popularity of women's Gaelic football (Liston, 2002).

## Sport and gender in contemporary Irish society

Research presented elsewhere (Department of Education, 1996, cited in Liston, 2001) found that 77 per cent of a sample of Irish men and 71 per cent of a sample of Irish women had participated in sport and physical activity on a regular basis in the preceding year.[4] Not surprisingly, the overall activity rate decreased as the age of participants increased. While only a slight gender difference was evident in overall rates of participation, gender differences became more apparent in motivation for participation and the popularity of activities. The health-related benefits of sports participation were the most commonly cited motivations for sports participation: 'maintenance of good health' and 'getting outdoors'. While the overall findings on motivation are consistent with other Irish and international studies, the gender differences were striking. Men cited 'making life more enjoyable', 'maintaining good health' and 'getting outdoors' as their three main motivations. Women ranked health benefits as their main motivation followed by 'getting outdoors' and 'relaxation'. Where men tended to cite 'competition' and 'occupying spare time' as important motivation, women were more apt to mention 'weight', with very few citing 'competition'. Gender differences in relation to spare time (what it constitutes and how it is used), appearance and competitive nature were also evident.

Differences in motivation are also reflected in findings on the relative popularity of activities (Liston, 2001). Women listed walking as their most popular activity,[5] followed by swimming and aerobics. In contrast, men cited soccer, followed by walking and golf. While walking and swimming were equally popular with men and women, clear gender differences were apparent in the popularity of dancing, soccer, golf, aerobics, snooker and Gaelic football.

Three years later, in the 1999 National Health and Lifestyles Survey, 42 per cent of the sample of adults engaged in some form of physical activity on average three times per week; 24 per cent reported doing mild forms of physical activity up to four times a week; 31 per cent did moderate forms of activity up to three times per week. Only nine per cent reported doing strenuous exercise three times weekly. As in the previous national survey (Department of Education and Health Promotion Unit, 1996), an age effect was apparent with activity levels decreasing with age. The 1999 study also examined children's activity levels and found that 53 per cent of children exercised four or more times each week, while six per cent exercised less than weekly. Apart from giving rise to concern about low levels of activity relative to European and international standards, the survey revealed a significant gender difference among children. Sixty-two per cent of boys exercised four or more times weekly while only 45 per cent of girls participated in similar levels of exercise. Only 26 per cent of 15–17 year-old girls exercised four or more times each week. In addition, 13 per cent of this age group did not participate in any form of physical activity.

Little substantial change levels of physical activity among Irish males and females is evident in the 2003 National Health and Lifestyles Survey. Just over half of all adults (51 per cent) reported some form of activity compared with 52 per cent in 1999. As before, marked differences remained in levels, types and rates of participation in sports and physical activity by gender, with men more likely to be strenuously active than women.[6] Numbers of those reporting no physical activity at all have increased among both males (from 21 per cent to 30 per cent) and females (from 20 per cent to 25 per cent). While these differences could simply be the outcome of gender differences in choice (between men and women, and between boys and girls), a closer look at the cultural dynamics of sports education and sports participation reveals a more complex picture.

## Sport and the physical education curriculum

Men and women are socialised into the field of sport from a young age, generally through the physical education curriculum and community-organised sporting activities for young males and females. Lynch and Lodge (2002) provide an in-depth analysis of the ways in which Irish schools work in the production, management and recognition of gender differences. They argue, perhaps not surprisingly, that schools play a key role in gender identity-formation and identity-testing, since a large number are single-sex (at primary and second level), the gender-segregated nature of many Irish schools being part of the legacy of the denominational origin and control of education since the nineteenth century (Lynch and Lodge, 2002: 89). There were differences between the various types of school. For example, single-sex girls' schools were characterised by high academic attainment, control of physical appearance and personal demeanour as well as active resistance to a gender order 'albeit often in a covert, timid manner' (Lynch and Lodge, 2002: 106). Single-sex boys' schools were characterised by an emphasis on sporting achievement and physical prowess, with one exception: 'While the culture of this school differed considerably from the others and especially from the two sports-focused schools, nevertheless the prevailing culture was still one that held students who were successful in sports in high regard' (Lynch and Lodge, 2002: 117).

Earlier Irish research (Jones et al., 1991) also found sex stereotyping in Irish physical education. 'Gaelic football, hurling, weight training, soccer, golf and karate were perceived as being "male" activities [while] yoga, dance, gymnastics and netball were strongly associated with females' (Jones et al., 1991: 2). These patterns tended to be reinforced by males and females and are borne out in my interviews with elite-level Irish female athletes.[7] During one interview Catherine (name changed) described one teacher's attitude towards females' interest in Gaelic football and the Combined Rules series as follows:

> Me and Bernie hid at the back of the bus and went to the Combined Rules game anyway. We knew we could get into loads of trouble, and we did, but we wanted

to make a point. Why were three or four boys' classes getting the day off to go the match and none of the girls were even given the option? It was just assumed by someone – the male teacher who coached Gaelic football – that the girls couldn't go, either because we weren't interested or we shouldn't be interested anyway. I ended up getting the gloves of one of the top Australian players and detention the following day but I also had the satisfaction of seeing some teachers squirm when confronted by parents who heard we weren't even given the option to go to such an important game.

Existing survey and interview data show that the content and practice of the physical education curriculum play a key role in the inculcation of gender identities. In particular, the 2003 National Health and Lifestyles survey shows that rates of vigorous exercise are higher among boys than girls at all ages. Moreover, as in the 1999 findings, the gender gap in physical activity doubled by the age of 15–17, with an increasing number of girls reporting no partici-pation in physical activity. Crucially, Bourdieu argues that the predispositions or 'habituses' of individual people (in this case those involved in sports) are central to the practice of sports. Gendered bodily processes have deep-reaching consequences in the physical education curriculum, and practitioners' assumptions about perceived differences in the 'natural' abilities of males and females play an important role in the maintenance of gendered divisions in sport practices. For example, Waddington et al. (1998) highlighted how the attitudes and actions of many PE teachers in the UK continued to reflect gender stereotyping of what have traditionally been considered male- and female-appropriate activities. There were 'marked tendencies for male PE teachers to perceive dance as a female-appropriate activity and female PE teachers to per-ceive outdoor education as a male-appropriate activity' (Waddington et al., 1998: 34). Similarly, young Irish males associated physical prowess, sporting ability and achievement with masculinity, while young females were socialised to control their physical appearance and personal demeanour (*Sunday Tribune*, 5 Nov. 2000; Lynch and Lodge, 2002). One of my respondents' comments regarding female PE teachers shows that what Jones et al. found in 1991 is still relevant today: that patterns of gender-appropriate sports practice tend to be reinforced by males and females most strongly within their own sex:

> We went through a phase of having a number of female PE teachers in our school, and if one more said that we were going to do dancing or trampolining I would have walked out and complained. I don't know who to, mind you, because the school principal wasn't exactly encouraging us to break the mould. But luckily we ended up getting a PE teacher who felt that women could equally participate in team sports, could use the school gym and weren't afraid to get their nails dirty (Anne).

The dominance of traditional and sex-segregated team sports in the Irish PE curriculum (e.g. Gaelic sports, rugby, soccer, hockey) reflects and reinforces existing discourses about sport and the gendered body. We can therefore understand the dynamics of the physical education process (in terms of the effects of teachers' gendered predispositions; the gendered segregation of education generally and physical education in particular; the organisation and content of PE; and the peer values of recipients in the educational system) as generally reproducing gender stereotypes in the field of Irish sports. This is not surprising when international research shows that sport is a 'male preserve' (e.g. Dunning, 1986, 1994, 1999; Birrell and Cole, 1994; Hargreaves, 1986, 1994, 2000; Lenskyj, 1986, 1994; Scraton and Flintoff, 2002).

## The gendered dynamics of sports participation

Although the relationship between sport and gender has been examined in international sociological research, there has been little critical analysis in Ireland. One problem with existing research is that the idea that certain sports (if not most) are 'suitably' masculine or feminine is treated as an *a priori* assumption. In other words, writers argue that sport is a male preserve without drawing on empirical research. Survey research findings presented here (Table 13.1) and elsewhere (Liston, 2001) regarding cultural perceptions of the gender-appropriateness of sports and physical activities provide empirical evidence for this assumption. They also highlight the importance of sport to the main-tenance of visible differences between Irish male and female bodies, as well as to the maintenance of hierarchical power relations between the sexes (Birrell, 1983; Dunning, 1999, Liston, 2002).

*Table 13.1* **Gender-appropriate sports**

| | |
|---|---|
| Female Appropriate | Yoga, Skipping, Netball, Aerobics, Dancing, Ice Skating, Synchronised Swimming, Camogie, Tennis, Jogging, Volleyball, Badminton, Equestrian, Orienteering, Hill, Walking, Gardening, Hockey, Gymnastics, Walking, Croquet |
| Neutral | Swimming |
| Male Appropriate | Pool, Track Athletics, Cricket, Diving, Horseracing, Water sports, Surfing, Cross-Country Skiing, Chess, Sub Aqua, Darts, Golf, Snooker, Parachuting, Basketball, Sailing, Aikido, Downhill Skiing, Field Athletics, Squash, Tai Chi, Bowls, Archery, TaeKwonDo, Cycling, Canoeing, Water Polo, Angling, Ski Jumping, Gaelic Football, Bodybuilding, Rowing, Hurling, Mountaineering and rock climbing, Motor Racing, Hunting, Ice Hockey, Soccer, Weightlifting, Judo, Boxing, Handball, Rugby,Wrestling |

Three hundred respondents[8] were asked to rank a diverse list of 67 sports and physical activities into what they considered to be appropriate gender categories: hyper-feminine, feminine, neutral, masculine and hyper-masculine. While there were some minor differences between males and females in the categorisation of hyper-feminine *versus* feminine, and hyper-masculine *versus* masculine (for example, males categorised camogie as hyper-feminine while females felt it was feminine and similarly females categorised hurling as hyper-masculine while males felt it was masculine), it was striking that male and female respondents did not differ in which sports they regarded as masculine or feminine overall. In other words, all respondents agreed on the gender appropriateness of sports for males and females. Table 13.1 is a summary of the overall categorisation of sports and physical activities as male- or female-appropriate. Swimming was the only activity to be perceived as gender-neutral. A deeper analysis of female-appropriate sports reveals an 'exercise' or 'health' orientation in sports that are commonly regarded as predominantly individual rather than team-based, involving little or no competition or physical contact and, emphasising the 'aesthetic' – for example, synchronised swimming, yoga, skipping, tennis, jogging, hill walking, hockey and croquet. In contrast, male-appropriate sports are predominantly associated with physical strength, aggression (reactive and instrumental), speed, a team environment and a culture of risk – for example wrestling, hurling, surfing, rowing, aikido, cycling and Gaelic football.

Interestingly, male and female respondents generally agreed on the gender-appropriateness of sports despite an imbalance in gender membership. The categorisation of Gaelic sports such as football, hurling and camogie warrants further explanation. Camogie appears to be an anomaly in the female-appropriate category, being a physical contact sport that demands strength, competitiveness, skill and aggression.[9] The Camogie Association (Cumann Camogiochta na nGael – CCnG) has been in formal existence since 1904 and has responsibility for the segregated organisation of the game. Thus it is not sociologically surprising that it was categorised as feminine while hurling was perceived as masculine. Camogie players still find their perceived femininity, or lack thereof, to be the subject of social commentary (Liston, 1999; 2001), precisely because of the levels of physicality required to participate in the sport. However, the categorisation of Gaelic football is slightly different (male-appropriate) and hides the growth in profile and participation levels of women's football, particularly over the last ten years. Because women's football is not a distinct category, it is assumed that respondents included both male and female players in the category 'Gaelic football' despite the formal existence of the Ladies Gaelic Athletic Association since 1974 and its recent elevated status. Indeed, a pilot scheme was established on 25 February 2003 with the aim of finding a successful framework for the integration of the LGAA and

CCnG within the GAA itself. In addition, the Dáil Committee on Arts, Sport, Tourism, Community, Rural and Gaeltacht Affairs will be publishing a report on women's involvement and participation in sport.[10]

**Sport and the 'idealised' body**

As well as ranking 67 sports and activities, respondents were asked to define five prescribed gender categories – hyper-feminine, feminine, neutral, masculine and hyper-masculine. An in-depth analysis of these five categories reveals ways of thinking, including conscious and unconscious ideas, about what men and women do, and should do, with their bodies. They also help to explain the relationship between gendered perceptions of sports and motivations for participation, that is manifested in gendered rates of participation.

> *Hyper-feminine sports* were characterised as:
>> all female (M)[11]
>> grace and attitude (F)
>> the highest point at which female sports people can achieve (M)
>> not for boys, very female characteristics (F)
>> these are sporting extremes where in the feminine case there is a lack of physical activity and masculinity (M)
>> geared towards the female physical make-up(F)
>> futile sports mainly pursued by females (F)
>> not for boys, very female in characteristics (M).
>
> *Feminine sports* were characterised as:
>> not intense enough for men and they'd rather do something else (M)
>> sports where great stamina and strength [are] not required, an art form, based on suppleness (M)
>> sports . . . suited to females and the lack of physical contact in the sport makes it lack masculinity (F)
>> mild pursuits, aesthetic (F)
>> enjoyed by women in most cases (F)
>> can be achieved best by female sportspeople (M).
>
> *Neutral sports* in some ways seemed to represent the idealised notion of an androgynous sport:
>> designed for either sex (M)
>> women and men can participate in them together as a group, they have no contact or brutality (M)
>> participation in these sports is open to both genders – both men and women can compete and sports don't show particular masculine or feminine traits (F)
>> more equally pursued by both genders (F)
>> sports that can be achieved at a high standard by both male and female (M).

*Masculine sports* were believed to be more appropriate for men because:
> most of them require high levels of endurance, strength and mental
> abilities (M),
> they only take the interests of the male (M)
> although some women participate in these, they are predominantly
> masculine in attitude (F)
> most of them require high levels of endurance, strength and mental
> abilities (F)
> maybe [they are] a bit too physical for some women, maybe not (M)

*Hyper-masculine sports* – the physicality of sport was most evident here:
> the physical demands can be achieved best by males (M)
> Hyper-masculine sports are those sports which favour men and which
> men participate in more than women. (F)
> they are very male orientated, for stronger tough men, all action and,
> heavy physical contact (F)
> levels of aggression [are] high (M)
> sports that are geared towards the masculine physical make-up (M)
> extremely physical sports including physical risk (M)
> these sports are dominated by men as in media coverage (F)
> you rarely see females playing (F).

While it is important to acknowledge there are problems with attitudinal studies as well as quantitative ranking scales, Balvanes and Caputi (2001) and Oppenheim (1992) argue that these problems can be addressed through the integration of attitudinal data within a broad and varied research framework that draws on interpretivist and positivistic paradigms. An integrated research framework can address the complexity and subtlety of attitudes by situating them within the various interactive forces that shape conscious and unconscious behaviour. Although it is difficult to generalise from a sample of 300 respondents to the field of Irish sports generally, it is possible to argue that the combination of in-depth interview data and various survey findings provide a strong indication that both males' and females' ideas about sports converge on bodily characteristics. We can say that Irish sports are perceived as gender appropriate and that the majority involving physical strength, physical contact and overtly competitive attributes are regarded as male appropriate. In most cases, males and females participate in the same sports but perceptions of participation (as indicated in respondents' definitions of gender categories) do not always reflect the reality of participation. Therefore rates of participation in sports, or the perception of these, need to be situated within an in-depth study of what athletes and spectators think about sports, how they feel and what ideas form the basis for their understandings of the logic of sports practice.

The characteristics of male-appropriate sports listed in Table 13.1 include physical contact, physical strength, aggression, speed and competition, which Dunning (1986) refers to as a 'mock battle' (in combat sports) and a culture of risk. Most are also team sports. In contrast, female-appropriate sports are characterised by grace, a fitness and exercise culture, little or no physical contact, a lack of aggression and physical strength, an aesthetic form and are largely (though not exclusively) individual sports. While sports psychologists (for example Moran, 2001) emphasise the importance of mental and cognitive skills, particularly in elite-level sports, only one respondent referred to mental attributes as a criterion in the gender-assessment of sports. Similarly, few respondents referred to technical skills as being a requirement for sports participation by either sex. Sports psychological research shows that although males and females *may* differ on inherent levels of aggression, a focus on the social conditions under which 'appropriate' responses to aggression are learned provides us with a clearer understanding of the expectation that aggressive behaviour would be a part of some sports and not others (Birrell, 1983).

## Sport, habitus and capital

Taking into account the many facets of the sport–gender relationship in Ireland (gendered rates of participation as well as perceptions of participation, motivations for participation as well as individuals' gendered understandings of how sports 'work'), we could argue that the field of sport reflects an 'affinity with the interests, tastes and preferences of a determinate social category' (Bourdieu, 1990: 157). Irish sports are organised within a system of bodily preferences that shape how, where and why we put male and female bodies into action. This is closely associated with a deep experience of the social and physical world, and the values espoused through wider systems of knowledge towards physical size, appearance, shape, difference and strength. The field of Irish sport is an expression and generator of social distinction, and similar to other social practices. Bourdieu argues that 'the principle of this construction is the system of structured, structuring dispositions, the habitus, which is constituted in practice and is always oriented towards practical functions' (Bourdieu, 1990: 52). Research data presented here reflect that habitus is constituted in 'moments of sports' and that the field of sport is a site of power struggles for access to, and dominance of, the meanings attached to particular sports and forms of physical expression. Habitus is a logic of sporting practice that conforms with, and confirms, perceptions of the sporting world and physical activities as male- and female-appropriate, generally on the basis of physical difference. The development of women's sports in the Olympics is a good example of how beliefs about the inappropriateness of 'flexing female muscles' have changed over time. The 200 metres was the longest women's race in the Olympics until the 1970s (following the collapse of several women at the end of the 800 metres in 1926), while the women's marathon was first run at the 1984 Olympics (Blue, 1987).

Sports such as rugby, soccer, gymnastics and all codified physical activities are cultural products shaped by those who practise them. Knowing how to be 'a soccer player' on and off the field of play is a physical, psychological and social activity and it is a defining factor in acquiring forms of capital. For Bourdieu, the body has become an important expression of status and power in society and it can be used as a form of capital, 'like the aces in a game of cards . . . powers that define the chances of profit in a given field' (Bourdieu, 1985: 24). The cultural emphasis on sporting success in Ireland can therefore be understood as the struggle for capital or the strategies and tactics used by athletes and those with an 'investment' in sport, to attain power. As has been argued elsewhere, the more or less 'feminised' or 'masculinised' sporting body carries social capital (Liston, 2002). Social capital can be defined as the forms of power held by athletes such as achievement, ability, 'sportsmanship' and competitiveness. These characteristics are also structuring principles of the field of sports (see Figure 13.1) and indicate the homology that exists between sporting practices and the social position of sports. Social capital is socially constructed. It can lead to rewards based on other forms of capital such as economic capital (e.g. corporate sponsorship) or symbolic capital (e.g. social status and prestige), and it has different consequences for male and female sportspersons. For example, interviews with leading Irish international female rugby players indicate a wider lack of acceptance of their cultural capital as elite-level athletes with the consequence that they often engage in 'apologetic' behaviour (Felshin, 1974) in order to attain capital: 'We're like rugby players on the pitch but once we step off we're 100% ladies' (*Backpacker*, 2002: 36). Similarly, a recent newspaper report on the 'violent image' of female rugby stressed that 'skill is the main element of the game' and '(women's) rugby is not as rough and tough as people think':

> In fact, it's all about skill, speed, agility, strength and the ability to think on your feet and women of all shapes, sizes and levels of fitness can get involved [. . .] The sense of camaraderie is palpable and they're the furthest thing from the butch stereotype you can imagine – girly, giggly, fun and fit (*The Star*, 9 Apr. 2003).

Interestingly, most female rugby players stress the skill and fitness elements of women's rugby which correspond to what are generally acceptable characteristics of female-appropriate sports. Few openly refer to the physical strength and aggression also required to participate in the sport. In contrast, men's rugby is headlined with titles such as 'Richards still fiercest Tiger' and

'Wounded giants promise day of thunder' (*The Sunday Times*, 13 Apr. 2003). However, that is not to suggest that female athletes receive little media coverage. Anna Kournikova's participation in an appropriately feminine sport (tennis) facilitates her attainment of cultural, symbolic and economic capital, despite the relative lack of sporting success that she achieved in competition.

Our understanding of sports in Ireland can therefore be usefully situated within the context of cultural conceptions of gendered differences, which shape our ideological notions of sport. It is important to understand how our habitualised ideas about male and female bodies affect the organisation, financing and administration of sport-participation for men and women. Birrell (1983: 49) argues that 'the female athlete is a special case in two senses. Because of her sport interests, she is considered a special kind of female; because she is female she is considered a special kind of athlete'. In particular, Johns and Farrow (1990) argue that married women receive conditional acceptance as athletes and are judged on a different set of criteria from male athletes. Cultural factors, such as the active discouragement of female participation in sport from a young age and the subtle socialisation of preconceived ideas about how males and females *should* act, are embodied at a physical and psychological level. Taking a long-term view, a reconceptualisation of sport as androgynous would involve both an examination of the gendered factors in motivation and participation in sport as well the outcomes of gendered participation, e.g., the psychological and sociological consequences of sports participation as well as an analysis of the determinants of future involvement. However, many examples highlight that social criteria and notions of 'physical suitability' continue to determine the relative acceptability of various sports to men and women (for example Metheny, 1965, 1972; Colley et al., 1987; Csizma et al., 1988).

## Sport and power relations between the sexes

Besides their role in the demarcation of male and female bodies, team sports (as well as some individual sports), also offer participants the opportunity to exercise their power and see the immediate effects of their actions. They also offer the opportunity to satisfy a need for power, when it exists. Power motivations are inherent in most, if not all, codified sports and an individual person's power or 'social position in society depends on the volume and structure of the different forms of capital they have accumulated' (Inglis, 1998: 66). Cultural capital 'is fundamental to being socially acceptable and respected . . . and is institutionalised in the form of accepted social awards' (Inglis, 1998: 66), such as conferring honorary degrees on Roy Keane and Sonia O'Sullivan or the social prestige attached to prominent rugby players such as Keith Wood and Brian O'Driscoll. 'Sports for males tend to enhance their chances of success in the world outside of sport and it is common practice for sportsmen to endorse products and services' (Duffy, 1994: 20).[12] 'Anyone in doubt that O'Driscoll has made an impression on the world outside of rugby need only look at the type of products our top rugby players are being asked to endorse' (*Evening Herald*, 28 Mar. 2003). These examples also indicate that basic forms of capital such as cultural capital can be traded for other forms such as symbolic capital through the strategic manipulation of habitualised ideas about 'the way the world works' (Liston, 2001). Empirical findings presented here also support Dunning's (1999) contention that sports, particularly combat sports, are one of the few remaining social arenas which actively encourage the expression of a particular kind of masculinity and the maintenance of a male-dominated prestige hierarchy between the sexes. This has specific consequences for female athletes in that their femininity is often compromised in the eyes of others (for instance, from 'mild' labelling as tomboys to relatively 'extreme' labels as butch and/or lesbian), as well as in their own eyes. Females also still encounter obstacles towards their participation in sport that are not generally experienced by males. While women's increasing participation in sports is a consequence of equalising and civilising tendencies and an example of their relative empowerment, males' and females' capacities to use physical violence remain relatively unequal and can be characterised as a 'civilised tolerance of difference' (Dunning, 1999).

## Conclusion

Thompson (1988: 209) argues that 'sport symbolises an idealised version of . . . social order'. Duncan and Hasbrook (2002: 86) also suggest that:

> sport tells us, through its lopsided distribution of women into female-appropriate individual sports, men into team sports and certain manly individual sports, how this power is withheld from women and how it is accorded to men.

Discourses and practices of sport pose important questions about how we understand sport and leisure as well as how we 'idealise' male and female sporting bodies. Sport is deeply embedded in the social fabric of Irish society. It enshrines the value of achievement in surpassing a standard of excellence and depicts an achievement-motivated 'national Irish character'. It carries emblems of recognition and identity whether at individual, parish, club, team, county, national or international level. The role of sport in shaping bodily processes and expectations about how we should act has many implications for levels of role conflict and stigmatisation experienced by male and female athletes. Prevailing and often hidden ideas about the appropriate development of the male and female body, in and through sports, play a key role in the maintenance of social divisions that already exist within the field of sports. A Bourdieuian analysis of the field of Irish sport raises a number of important questions for sports practitioners, administrators and governing bodies alike. Do elite-level female athletes have volumes and compositions of capital comparable with those of elite male athletes? Do the volume and composition of various forms of capital differ in individual and team sports as Birrell (1983) implies? Do elite female athletes embody gendered forms of capital with less social value? And why do some women and some female athletes in particular often comply with dominant practices and what Bourdieu (1988) refers to as symbolic violence? As Shilling (1992: 147) suggests, this may reflect the fact that 'many women have far fewer opportunities than men to turn any participation they may have in physical activities into social, cultural or economic capital'. Irish females are still under-represented as participants, coaches, officials and decision makers in the field of sports. Gaelic and other codified sports provide a powerful lens through which we can clearly see the value that Irish society places on the development of male and female sporting bodies, and bodies in general, as well as the struggles 'over which part most truly represents or embodies the field (of Irish sport) and its values' (Webb et al., 2002: 30).

Chapter 14

# Sport, leisure and territory in Belfast

Peter Shirlow

## Introduction

This chapter focuses upon the practices of ordering and the discursive differentiation between ethno-sectarian groups as seen through the lens of spatial bordering.[1] Many sporting and leisure facilities within Belfast are ordered via spatial routines and the link between location and ethno-sectarian belonging (Anderson and Shuttleworth, 1998; Bairner and Shirlow, 1998b). Those that are not explicitly ordered in such a way are seen to dilute boundary demarcations and in so doing undermine the impact of established ethno-sectarian practices. As a result, there are also 'shared' arenas within which sporting activities are undertaken by both Catholics and Protestants.[2]

The inter-community support received by the Belfast Giants ice hockey team is heralded as an example of how sports fans have begun to share sporting loyalties after several decades of violence and political confrontation. Other examples of mixing are to be found in sports such as cycling, swimming and basketball. There are also golf, rugby and cricket clubs which enjoy 'mixed' memberships. Yet at the same time these 'examples' of togetherness are not without social and political complication. Rugby and cricket clubs tend to be both middle class and predominantly Protestant owing to the link between these sports and the grammar school system that pertains in Northern Ireland. In Belfast only one Catholic school, St Malachy's Grammar, has played rugby at competitive level. None plays cricket. Catholics who play or have played these sports should therefore be considered as individuals and not as a representation of their 'home' community. The same applies to Gaelic sports and the handful of Protestants who both play and support them. More crucially, the recent out-movement of rugby and cricket clubs in Belfast to new stadia has come about owing to the areas within which they were once located becoming more 'Catholic' through population shifts. The North of Ireland Rugby and Cricket club's recent move from the Lower Ormeau is the most recent example of this trend. The strong cross-community links that are to be located in other sports such as cycling and swimming are relatively enduring and more likely than not transcend more obvious ethno-sectarian practices. However, such sports lack any meaningful support and are not a threat to the dominance of football and Gaelic games (Bairner, 2001a; Sugden and Bairner, 1993). Furthermore, the fact that Catholics and Protestants go to the Odyessy Arena to watch ice hockey or are members of the same golf club should also be understood as examples of mixing and not of inter-community integration. There is a distinct difference between both communities using an arena as consumers and both communities using space as a purposeful act of inter-community solidarity.

Football is undoutedly a game that is supported and played by both communities in significant numbers. Football clubs both at amateur and semi-professional level are firmly rooted in and reflect the ordering of ethno-sectarian relationships. Many amateur league teams, for example, usually conform to some degree of ethno-sectarian separation. Gaelic sports are more firmly rooted within the Catholic community. The spatial bordering that takes place between the two main sporting codes presents a series of acute and at times rigified territorial processes. Sport and devotion to codes and distinct clubs are also sourced from within wider categories of loyalty and sectarianised fandom. This latter point leads on to the recognition that processes of spatial bordering are parallelled by issues of immmobility (Adair et al., 2000; Belfast Interface Project, 1999; Burton, 1978; Downey, 2000). Belfast's highly segregated environment and the ethnicisation of space creates borders that not only endorse loyalty but which also rebut the entrance both theoretically and at times physically to those from the 'other' side. This chapter looks at two examples of the processes of identity formation and bordering through an examination of the construction and meaning of support for Linfield Football Club and the ethno-sectarian use of public-funded leisure centres.

## Bordering, segregation and the construction of space

The boundaries between Catholics and Protestants in Belfast do not begin or stop at the demarcation lines between segregated areas. Moreover, boundaries between each ethno-sectarian group do not merely represent a fixed point in space or time. Rather they symbolise a set of social practices that reaffirm spatial differentiation. Northern Ireland's home matches at Windsor Park provide a clear example of how a sectarian place has undergone a process of becoming more unattractive to the minority Catholic community. As Fulton and Hassan have revealed in earlier chapters, Catholics attend international matches at Windsor Park in smaller numbers than they did in previous years due, amongst other things, to the growth in sectarian chanting, the treatment of players such as Neil Lennon and the swapping of loyalties to the Republic

of Ireland's national team. In this context the borders between Protestants
and Catholics have, in relation to Northern Ireland's home matches, been
intensified. The making of place, in this and other instances, must be
understood as an act of purification, as it is the desire to justify and encourage
separation by ethno-sectarians that is of crucial concern (Douglas and
Shirlow, 1998; Feldman, 1991).

Designing place-centred sporting communities, which actively resist an
ethno-sectarian 'other', has been achieved via symbolic practice and the
perpetuation and reproduction of religious segregation (Adair et al., 2000).
Political and religious segregation within the Northern Irish context have
been accomplished through regulating social contact between communities
and in turn directing political logic by way of encouraging spatial enclosure.
In Northern Ireland's most visibly politicised arenas, the images and discourses
used in the reproduction of segregation have followed propaganda condi-
tioning perspectives which have directed the figurative milieu of place (Bale,
1994). Segregation has aided the reproduction of interlinked spatial devices,
which have enacted both violence and conflict. These devices include the
reproduction of sporting loyalties, the sociology of deviance and the articulation
of discourses of defence. Without doubt the disquisition which constitutes
ethno-sectarianism and the main sporting identities in Northern Ireland is
reproduced through what are essentially 'lived experiences'.

Determining and understanding the complexities of sporting loyalties are
important in that they aid an appreciation of community diversity and support
a more valid explanation of extensive violence, self-imposed spatial restrictions
and the attempt to avoid inter and intra-community based harassment
(Anderson and Shuttleworth, 1998; Bairner and Shirlow, 1998b; Shirlow,
2003). Ethno-sectarian fandom has been tied to those behaviours that have
been both eulogised and censured in the ideological struggle over 'truth' and
political legitimacy within the Northern Ireland conflict. Sporting allegiances
within Northern Irish society have also been paralleled by multifarious forms
of felon setting which present the opposing communities' sports and sporting
loyalties as dangerous, aberrant and irrational. Sporting loyalties thus
contribute to the constitution and appearance of the 'imagined' community
(Anderson, 1991).

Spatial relationships and sporting practices are conditioned by a series of
factors that in turn are conditioned by experience, perception and imagination.
Experience suggests to those who follow ethno-sectarian discourses that there
is a need to appropriate the use of sporting spaces. Sites and arenas of sporting
practice thus become 'owned' by the home community. Such spaces are sanc-
tified as ontological and uncontaminated by the political and ideological
practices of the 'other' community. 'Knowledge' also provides spatial practices
that respond to the threat of ethno-sectarian 'occupation'. The recent closure,

as noted above, of cricket and rugby grounds in areas that have become more 'Catholic' creates spatial discourses that are tied to 'transgressive' acts by the 'other' community and a sense of loss on the part of the communal 'self'. The actual occupation of certain GAA grounds by the British army provided the most obvious form of loss and external domination. The loss of such sporting arenas suggests that the reproduction of sectarianised space is based upon both celebration and defence. Experience thus provides for spatial practices that are exclusive to community and neighbourhood and within which social control is based upon eulogised ethno-sectarian loyalties.

In a society within which political discourses are highly fragmented and contested, it is not surprising that perception influences the representation of space. Spatial separation is not merely physical but conditioned by social and psychological boundaries. As such, sports arenas are both 'permitted' to the communal 'self' and 'forbidden' to the communal 'other'. This is further reinforced by the marking of space within Belfast by paramilitary regalia and wall murals. Thus sporting arenas are imagined as part of the socio-political landscape of ritualised political meaning. Sport also influences the system of mapping within Belfast's most ethno-sectarian places. Muralists in several republican communities have used images of Gaelic games to encourage notions of Irish nationalism. Graffiti announcing support for Celtic and Rangers as well as making threats against the 'other' community next to sporting venues are also important features in ethno-sectarianised spatial practices.

Sporting arenas and loyalty to particular clubs are also tied to spaces of representation. Certain places such as football and Gaelic grounds come to be sites that both attract and repulse. Vociferous ethno-sectarianists, who are Protestants, would view Catholic-supported football clubs and Gaelic sites (especially those named after IRA volunteers) as places that are transgressive and within which the ideological forces to which they are opposed are 'actively' encouraged and promoted. In contrast, the home site is familiar, open, ideologically friendly and popular. Home sites are 'pure' and uncontested as such sporting arenas provide spaces within which to articulate what are seen as rational rituals and symbolic practices.

Sporting arenas are not merely sites of physical demarcation between Catholics or Protestants; they are also locations within which wider imagined discourses can be subsumed into celebrating cultural practices and desires. In political and cultural terms the ability to obliterate the sporting allegiances of the 'other' community is impossible. Thus sporting allegiances are tied to articulating dissimilar political and cultural systems. Intensified ethno-sectarian logic finds within sport and leisure a series of arenas within which to employ the wider tactics of political homogenisation and the sanctioning of social and cultural separation. Due to the primacy of sectarian argument around a unidimensional logic, it is clear that sporting differences exclude any rational understanding or sympathy for those with alternative sporting commitments (Jarman, 1998).

A central goal in the exploration of segregation is the capacity to determine not only the nature of contact between spatially separate populations but also to designate how ideas, beliefs and behaviours are reinforced by their social milieu (Shirlow, 2001, 2003). More recent work, which explores city environments, has advanced the theme of fear within spatial analyses. Much of this work has examined the fear of crime, domestic and sexual violence and racially motivated attacks. Within the Northern Irish context, fear has also been spatialised in relation to the impact of violence, societal corrosion and ethno-sectarian practice. A significant body of work has indicated how violence is linked to the perpetual defence and violation of ethno-sectarian space (Boal et al., 1991; Douglas and Shirlow, 1998). However, work within the Northern Irish arena, which has evaluated the link between religious segregation, victimisation, security-consciousness and ultimately the impact of fear upon mobility, has been generally absent. This omission is peculiar given that the establishment of residential segregation has synchronised harm and fear via intricate spatial devices. Visiting sporting or leisure arenas that are controlled by the 'other' community is in many instances simply not undertaken for fear of physical attack. To go to such places can also provide visitors with a sense that they are defying any threat that exists. Fear can thus mobilise some as well as immobilising others (Jarman, 1998).

## Kill all 'taigs'

Graffiti discouraging the visits of those from the other ethno-sectarian group is commonplace in Belfast. 'Taigs Keep Out' has long been a familiar piece of graffiti outside Windsor Park, home of Linfield Football Club and the Northern Ireland national football team. In more recent times the abbreviations KAT (Kill all Taigs) and KAH (Kill all Huns)[3] have also appeared close to stadia throughout Northern Ireland. Such graffiti are an obvious sign of a desire to repel and resist the location of the other community within those sites dominated by the collective 'self'. Windsor Park is an interesting example of a sporting arena becoming a symbol of resistance to Irish nationalism and the demographic growth of Catholics within the city. In many ways it is a site that has shifted from being a place of unionist confidence to a place of unionist intransigence and uncertainty. Like many football stadia in Britain the ground is located within a maze of terraced streets that once housed local mill and other industrial workers. The neighbourhoods closest to the ground, such as the Village, were not only areas tied to traditional industries but also places that were overwhelmingly Protestant. In more recent years there has been a growth around the ground of a transient population of students and young professionals, many of whom are Catholics. Thus Windsor Park is 'losing' its historical connection with the local population. In addition, social mobility and re-housing schemes have dispersed the local Protestant support throughout the city and beyond. Even though Windsor Park's location within a predominantly Protestant place is likely to endure for some time to come, the certainties of Protestant/unionist hegemony are less secure. Within such a climate of political and demographic decline, it is evident that Windsor Park takes on the role of becoming both a cultural and political 'fortress' and a place that must be protected against the political and cultural growth of the 'other' community. Clearly there is a complex interplay between sport and politics within which Windsor Park remains one of the few places that many Protestants feel they have control over despite wider cultural and political shifts. The inability of the Orange Order to parade where it wishes, the reality of sharing political power with nationalists and republicans and the obvious decline in traditional industries encourage many sections of the Protestant community to seek out places of less diminished control.

The more recent outbreaks of sectarianism, at international matches, against Catholic supporters and players at Windsor Park, highlight how socio-political 'decline' has produced a clear desire to purify this particular arena. The national soccer team is important in that it is the only obvious one to which Protestants can owe loyalty given that most other national teams are based at Great Britain or even all-Ireland level. Sectarian chanting and the presentation of loyalist emblems and symbols within Windsor Park illustrate how spectators use the arena in order to display 'civil liberties' and 'tradition' that are being 'denied' to them by a political and peace-building process that is based upon inclusion and pluralism. It is an arguably more sinister example of what took place at the Camp Nou where Catalans found a site within which to openly practise their language and other customs (Burns, 1999). Windsor Park thus emerges, especially during international matches, as a site within which to symbolically assert Northern Ireland's constitutional status within the United Kingdom. Yet the overall relationship between fans and their political and cultural loyalties has shifted from the certainties of yester-year to a more difficult present and an even more problematic future.

As with Northern Ireland matches, a similar set of cultural and political relationships are displayed at Linfield games. As has already been noted by Magee in chapter 11 above, unlike most other Irish league clubs, Linfield draws its support from throughout Northern Ireland. As a result of this, Linfield matches, like Northern Ireland ones, become the stage upon which various sections of the dispersed 'Protestant' family can be brought together. Windsor Park thus acts as a site of 'unified' resistance. The imagined community of unionist 'solidarity' becomes 'real' as Linfield and Northern Ireland fans express their shared loyalty at Windsor Park and, in so doing, struggle to resolve at the level of the imaginary, the real contradictions confronting the Protestant working class, those being their constitutional and political uncertainty. In their own way, Linfield and Northern Ireland fans are attempting to defend their home turf and its allied traditions, which make Windsor Park what they want it to be. This reactive defensiveness is part of a more general 'siege' mentality (Aughey, 1989). Defence and the protection of territory, in this case Windsor Park, thus emerges as the primary discourse defining the mediating practice between the 'self' and the 'other' through the conceptual ordering of inter-communal relations.

## Ethno-sectarianism and leisure centre usage

Henderson and Frelke (2000: 18) have noted that 'researchers studying leisure with a few notable exceptions . . . have been slow to examine the meanings of space and place in people's everyday leisure lives'. Most of the literature on the use of leisure facilities, with a few notable exceptions, has concentrated on issues concerning social class, age and gender. Much less evidence has been produced in relation to leisure use and issues such as racism and ethno-sectarian practice. As noted above ethno-sectarian practices influence the use of facilities among those living within some of Belfast's most segregated communities. This is of course particularly ironic given that one of the central aims of leisure provision is to reach out to sections of the community which might have few other outlets for engaging in sport or other forms of healthy physical recreation. The building of leisure centres in Belfast was linked to 'challenging' socio-economic exclusion. However, it was also tied to a somewhat peculiar behaviourist notion that the provision of leisure centres would take the para-militaries off the street and into the gym – that young men who were involved in political violence could be 'cured' through expending excess energy in publicly funded leisure facilities (Bairner and Shirlow, 2003).

The location of leisure facilities in Belfast generally followed sectarian lines with most centres being firmly located within highly segregated communities. As Knox (1987: 260) suggests, 'it is tempting to portray the pattern of leisure provision (mainly leisure centres) as politically motivated in a province where few government and local authority functions are perceived as apolitical'. At the same time, it could be argued that decisions makers were merely 'cognizant of the political/sectarian geography of Northern Ireland in locating leisure and community centres' (Knox, 1987: 253). If anything the location of leisure centres merely reflected spatial patterns of sectarian division and in so doing created more arenas within the built environment that could be claimed as either Catholic or Protestant. The flying of the Irish national flag on top of

Andersonstown leisure centre in west Belfast in the 1980s was an example of territorial claiming. Similarly, the 'No Taigs Here' graffiti that were for many years displayed outside the Shankill leisure centre was another example of the sectarian claiming of public property.

The evidence, presented below, on how ethno-sectarianism motivated fear has reduced mobility and cross-community contact, illustrates how social practice still engenders different imaginings of community and the production of community-based and eclectic forms of political identification, fear and violent enactment. The evidence indicates that ethno-sectarianised fears of the 'other' community play a decisive role in the choice of arenas within which to undertake leisure centre based activities. This information, when combined with interviews with leisure centre users, highlights the disturbing factors which encourage ethno-sectarianised forms of spatial interaction.

For the purposes of a quantitative study, 1800 adults aged 16 and above, were surveyed in six interface areas. These consisted of (Catholic district first):

Whitewell/White City
Ardoyne/Upper Ardoyne
Manor Street/Oldpark
Lenadoon/Suffolk
Short Strand/Ballymacarrett
New Lodge/Tiger's Bay

The survey was based upon the respective demography of each area. In relation to basic spatial statistics, the survey aimed to measure interaction in relation to consumer and recreational behaviour. Given that paired communities are adjacent to one and other and have similar socio-economic profiles, it was predicted that utility maximisation would be very similar in terms of interaction levels. It would be expected, given that only 36 per cent of respondents had access to private transport and that Belfast has a relatively poor public transport system, that the closest leisure facilities would be those most likely to be relied upon.

Out of the 1800 respondents, 52 per cent stated that they did not use public leisure centres at all. Around two thirds of the 864 respondents who used leisure centres, in the year prior to being surveyed, stated that they 'would not use leisure facilities in areas dominated by the "other" religion'. Survey respondents who did not use leisure centres in areas dominated by the 'other' religion provided two main reasons for their refusal to do so. The vast majority, 84 per cent, stated that they did not do so for fear of being attacked, mistreated or harassed. Twelve per cent stated that they did not wish to interact with the 'other' community. The remaining four per cent would not provide a reason. Seven per cent stated that they used facilities in areas dominated by the 'other' ethno-sectarian group but preferred to use facilities located in arenas dominated by their 'own' community. Fewer than six per cent of the respondents who used leisure centres irrespective of their ethno-sectarian location did so due to a desire to access specialist facilities such as fitness suites and swimming pools. Around one in five stated that they used facilities located in both communities.

Table 14.1 highlights two important relationships between the community studied and the use of leisure centres. Firstly, it is evident that the share of those who use leisure centres falls when the nearest facilities are located in areas dominated by the 'other' religious group. Secondly, it is evident that those who refrain from using their nearest facility, which is located in an area dominated by the 'other' religion, undergo a considerable distance penalty. Within this sample, Catholic communities in north Belfast (Whitewell, Ardoyne, Manor Street and New Lodge) are most affected by the location of public leisure centres. The main facilities in North Belfast, including Ballysillan, Grove, Loughside and Valley, are each located in markedly Protestant communities. The average percentage share of those who reside in Whitewell, Ardoyne, Manor Street and New Lodge and who use leisure centres is 24.7 per cent. This compares to a use rate of 49.4 per cent in the Protestant communities (White City, Upper Ardoyne, Oldpark and Tiger's Bay) located in north Belfast. The average distance travelled to leisure centre services by those in Catholic areas in north Belfast, was 6.8 km compared to 2.2 km for respondents from predominantly Protestant districts of north Belfast.

In Whitewell, for example, the nearest facility, Valley Leisure Centre, is merely 1 km away. However, the average distanced travelled to leisure facilities is 9.8 km. Within the north Belfast sample a mere 16 per cent of those who live in predominantly Catholic areas use leisure facilities positioned in largely Protestant areas. The key destinations, among those who reside in predominantly Catholic areas in north Belfast, are located in the chiefly Catholic communities of west (Falls, Andersonstown and Whiterock) and central Belfast (Maysfield).

The use of leisure centres within the Protestant sample in north Belfast is less intricate. In White City and Upper Ardoyne the use of facilities is highly influenced by the location of leisure centres within or beside each community. However, in the case of Oldpark the number using leisure centres is lower than the average for Protestant communities in north Belfast and virtually all leisure centre usage is based upon the Shankill Centre. The uniformly close Ballysillan Centre, located in a Protestant community, is not commonly used by respondents from Oldpark due in part to having to journey past or through largely Catholic areas to reach that facility.

Table 14.1 **Percentage use of leisure centres by location and distance travelled in study areas**

| Mainly Catholic areas | % of respondents in mainly Catholic areas who use leisure centres | Mainly Protestant areas | % of respondents in mainly Protestant areas who use leisure centres | Mean distance per visit (km) | |
|---|---|---|---|---|---|
| | | | | Catholic areas | Protestant areas |
| Whitewell | 26.1 | White City | 58.5 | 9.8 | 1.8 |
| Ardoyne | 28.1 | Upper Ardoyne | 58.2 | 6.2 | 1.9 |
| Manor Street | 21.2 | Oldpark | 33.1 | 6.8 | 2.9 |
| Lenadoon | 56.3 | Suffolk | 24.1 | 2.0 | 6.8 |
| Short Strand | 52.1 | Ballymac'tt | 46.0 | 1.4 | 1.3 |
| New Lodge | 43.4 | Tiger's Bay | 58.1 | 4.4 | 2.3 |

A similar pattern to that found amongst Catholic communities in North Belfast was apparent in Suffolk, the only Protestant enclave in west Belfast. Around 12 per cent, most of whom are pensioners, use the nearby Andersonstown Centre which is located in a predominantly Catholic district. In general, however, residents in Suffolk travel on average over three times further to access facilities than their nearest neighbours in Lenadoon. Among respondents in Suffolk, the Olympia and Shankill centres are those used most frequently. Only one pair of communities share similar use levels and distance profiles. Short Strand and Ballymacarrett, which are located in East Belfast, are serviced by two centres. Virtually all respondents in Short Strand use Maysfield (recently designated for closure), which is positioned adjoining the Markets, a sizeable Catholic neighbourhood. Within the Ballymacarret sample, the centre at Avoniel, which is located in Protestant territory, is highly used. Given the proximity of each community to a safe location it is evident that leisure centre usage is less problematic. Without doubt the ethno-sectarian position of services plays an overriding role in choice. The bulk of leisure centre use, as shown in table 14.1, links points of origin and destinations of the same religion. Ethno-sectarianism appears to direct leisure centre choice and has in turn fashioned a misshapen model where the majority of residents from one community choose one set of destinations and residents from the other community another, with very little sharing.

Among those interviewed who engaged in the use of leisure facilities which stretched beyond the sectarian divide, the reasons given for doing so were largely based upon a desire to maintain cross-community relationships. As noted from the survey findings, most tended to be in and around pensionable age. Reasons for accessing leisure facilities in areas dominated by the 'other' religion were tied to a strong conviction that members of the 'other' community could be trusted and to apparent lived social histories, within which there has been an extensive form of cross-community linkage. As noted by a Catholic respondent from Ardoyne:

> I have no problems going up to Ballysillan. I have friends up in Glenbryn (location of leisure centre) and we have always been keen on the weight lifting. We used to box when we were young and just made an attempt to keep our friendship. No hassle just men who are friends and have been since we were wee lads. They keep an eye out for me and when things are a bit dicey they know I won't be up.

Among those who refrained from using leisure facilities located in areas dominated by the 'other' community a series of reasons were presented for not doing so. A problem identified by some was that of forenames and surnames. Given that Catholics tend to have Irish names and Protestants do not, the potential exists to denote a person's religion when hearing their names. This fact of sectarian labelling affected leisure centre use. Sectarian tattoos are also problematic given that they are likely to be viewed in changing areas. However, the main responses in relation to leisure centre usage invoked the sense of peril and the environment of implied threat. In such instances, imagined and told harm represented the nature of most people's refusal to use centres located in areas dominated by the 'other' religious group.

There were also those who believed that segregated use is not a reflection of a repressive relationship but should be witnessed as an articulatory process that should positively enshrine spatial segregation. Wanting or keeping the 'other' side out of your leisure space was seen by some as a valid politicisation of space. Among those who advance sectarian discourses, the materialisation of residential segregation into spatial constructs is imperative in order to functionalise and advance topographic conflict. At every point of conversation, among those who maintain sectarian narratives, it is acknowledged that all social space should be coded by way of a sectarian analysis. Virtually all members of the sectarian group understood their community via utopian discourses of integrity, loyalty, kinship and symbolic purity. In comparison, non-sectarians were more likely to denote that 'their' communities contained multiple forms of impurity, transgression and deviant behaviour. The interviews conducted among the sectarian group produced fervent sectarian narratives and the most visible belief that the 'other' community was abnormal, aggressive and untrustworthy. As noted by one respondent, the perception of leisure centres as unsafe places is intensified by wider sectarian dimensions:

> But, like the changing rooms aren't safe places. Like you go in there and there are lots of places to give you a hiding. You know like at the school. The scary places, at school, were the toilets and changing rooms. No one about see. Slippery floors

too. Even in my own centre you are always careful. Even looking out for razor blades on the floor and the like. So you are wary in your own place. But go over there. You slip they give you a hiding. You see leisure centres they're big places, lots of empty rooms and most of all scary places. Dark corners. They get you in there and the only way out is in a box.

The general sense of menace was most commonly promoted in the interviews by those who displayed sectarian narratives, conditioned by wider displays of sectarian rhetoric. As noted by a Protestant respondent aged 32:

How could we go there? They would attack us just because we are Prods. Look it's also this way. Go to the leisure centres in Catholic areas and what do you see? Nothing but filth. Their centres aren't the cleanest. Their places are like them. They could do with a good wash.

A similar response came from a Catholic male aged 35:

Go up there. Are you mad? Like why? Like why go up there? They would have you for their supper. You just couldn't. Like imagine being in the showers and seeing them with their big fat guts and tats [tattoos]. Like they are scum. Not right in the head. Dangerous people even.

Such evidence implies that telling, violence and the reproduction of fear are centred upon sectarianised relationships which intend not only to reproduce segregation but also to contain any belief system which views ethno-sectarian decency as a socially constructed and imagined set of relationships. It is indisputable that maintaining the ability to control the cant of ethno-sectarian belonging is facilitated through disseminating the belief that the 'other' community is to be feared, despised and avoided.

## Conclusion

In many instances the political instability that still exists reflects the limitations of the current peace process and the ability of devolution to substantially alter the nature of inter-community conflict. The central goal of the Irish and British states is to be seen to promote 'parity of esteem' and 'mutual consent' through the promotion of political structures that underline pluralism. However, as evidenced by the information presented in this chapter, sectarian actions are still in certain arenas more voluminous than constitutional and pluralist words.

Despite the cessation of most paramilitary violence, we are left with a situation within which the creation of territorial division and rigidified ethno-sectarian communities mean that fear and mistrust are still framed by a desire to create communal separation. Without doubt residential segregation still regulates ethno-sectarian animosity by way of complex spatial devices. Indeed the reproduction of violence and fear is still achieved through linking ethno-sectarian affiliation and residence through the spatial confinement of political and cultural identity. The narratives and reality of constantly protecting place and religious segregation continue to be interlinked devices in the whole enactment of discord and conflict. More importantly, the capacity to reconstruct identity and political meaning is obviated by political actors who mobilise fear in order to strengthen unidimensional classifications of political belonging. Furthermore, community-based self-representation assumes the form of a mythic reiteration of purity and self-preservation. As a result, the potential to create cross-community understandings of sport and sporting loyalties is, in terms of politics, marginalised by wider ethno-sectarian readings. Indeed, for political actors the capacity to win political support has been based upon delivering a singular narrative of victimhood and exclusion. To accept now that such political vocabularies and actions victimise the 'collective other' would be politically unwise. If anything sport has become an even more important symbol of separation than in the past. It is clear that the type of conflict that existed between the late 1960s and early 1990s has been replaced by a more proxy-based set of inter-community tensions. The more visible wearing of Celtic and Rangers replica shirts is not merely an example of the impact of the mass marketing of football merchandise but is also a reflection of wider desires to adopt signs of sectarianised fandom. Together with issues such as housing, marching and decommissioning, sport has filled the void left by more violent ethno-sectarian acts.

As evidenced here, intra-community divisions testify to the reality that conflict resolution is not merely undermined by inter-community based sectarianism. Wider senses of powerlessness are responsible for the failure of inter-community based sporting practices to emerge. In relation to these points, this essay conveys a sense of the localised nature of territorial control and resistance, where the imperatives of communal and intra-communal difference, segregation and exclusion still predominate over the politics of shared interests, integration and assimilation.

Sport and the 'topophobia' associated with it are reproduced through the representation and reproduction of ethno-sectarian places. Places such as Windsor Park or Casement Park (the main GAA ground in Belfast) are not simply benign sites of sporting practice but are part and parcel of the act of territorial building. Sporting and leisure choices within such a climate are at times malign especially when fandom and sporting practices are read as assertions of ethno-sectarian choice. In a peculiar way those devoted to ethno-sectarian practice see the outplaying of territorial control as an expression of fear and the location of safe places. But, in reality, safety consciousness reaffirms spatial bordering and in so doing undermines the capacity for meaningful inter-community interaction. In effect sport provides another medium within which to assert the passionate desire, by many, to remain separated from the 'other' community. The impurity of ethno-sectarian allegiance is attached to the imagined purity of sporting and spatial allegiances.

Chapter 15

# Sport and community relations in Northern Ireland and Israel

John Sugden

## Introduction

The first fortnight of April 2003 was an interesting time to be thinking about sport and peace. The US and British-led military machine disarmingly known as the coalition (somebody in Washington had been watching too many Star Wars movies) was in the process of crushing Baghdad, hurling tons of high velocity munitions into the heart of the beleaguered Iraqi capital. Relations between the Arab world and the West had not been so low since the time of the Crusades.

This was not the best of times either for England to be playing Turkey in a crucial European Nations qualifying football match at Sunderland's Stadium of Light. As the British stood shoulder to shoulder with the Americans in Gulf War II, Turkey, the gateway to the East, a country with a largely Moslem population, and with a recent history of bad blood between groups of English and Turkish supporters (Sugden, 2002), is the last team the English FA had wanted to host. But the fateful outcome of the Euro 2004 draw required them to do so. Predictably, both off and on the field, surrogate war broke out. Outside the stadium, baying revengefully for Turkish blood, England's most wanted hooligan generals led their troops into battle with one another and the police, while in the stands the Turkish national anthem was drowned by a cacophony of boos and racist chants. On the pitch, the players kicked, cursed and spat at one another, augmenting the vitriol and bile of the English fans.

In the midst of all this, US President, George W. Bush, flew to Northern Ireland to take part in a peace and/or war summit with UK Prime Minister, Tony Blair. During Bush's address at Hillsborough Castle high prominence was given to linking events in Iraq with the search for a peaceful resolution to the conflict in the Holy Land and the progress that had been achieved in the journey towards a lasting peace in Northern Ireland. Now we get closer to understanding the rationale for including this chapter in a book about sport in Ireland.

One of the main reasons that I had managed to carve out the time and space to write this piece – and that I was around to see the England versus Turkey game – was that on Foreign and Commonwealth Office and British Council advice, I had cancelled a trip to Israel. The purpose of this visit was to have been to take part in a series of planning meetings in Nazareth with a view to setting up football-based community relations camps for Arab and Jewish children in the country's Galilee region. Quite rightly, as the local population shored up their blast and gas proof shelters, organising a football project could not be a high priority. Whatever the outcome of Gulf War II, it is universally acknowledged that the search for some form of lasting settlement in what is currently and rather accurately termed by the FCO as 'Israel and the Occupied Territories' must be given the highest of priorities by the international community. The main dimensions of the Bush and Blair endorsed 'road map to peace' will of course be political, territorial, economic and military. Nevertheless, if the peoples of the region are to accept a new status quo, social and cultural initiatives will be needed to support any the peace process. It is in this context that this chapter examines the role of sport, real and potential, in Israel and the Occupied Territories. Its relevance in terms of the rest of the book lies in the fact that the study of the role of sport in Israel draws comparatively and extensively upon lessons learned from the use of sport in Northern Ireland's search for peace and reconciliation. However, with the damaging diplomatic circumstances of the England versus Turkey game still relatively fresh in the mind, it is important to question from the outset and in general the role of sport in situations of peace and conflict.

## Sport: peacemaker or warmonger?

What then, if anything, is the value of sport to processes of peace and reconciliation? Throughout the world, in places such as Northern Ireland, South Africa, the Balkans and the Middle East, there have been one-off initiatives and more lengthy programmes that have aimed to use sport as a tool for engineering peaceful co-existence in otherwise deeply divided societies. More often than not, however, ideology, sentiment, hope and sometimes self-interest, as opposed to hard, empirical evidence, are the rationale behind such interventions (Sugden and Bairner, 1999).

The mythology of the social and political healing powers of sport can be traced back to the fabled ancient Olympic truce, when the warring city states of ancient Greece laid down their weapons for the duration of the Olympic festival (McIntosh, 1993). Likewise, the reputed soccer match played between

British and German soldiers in no-man's-land on Christmas Day 1914 during an impromptu cessation in hostilities during the Great War, is used to exemplify the capacity of sport to divert warring factions. Scenarios such as these are invoked to argue the case for sport as a temporary refuge from war. In making such a case, the fact that once the ancient Olympics were over internecine tribal wars rapidly rekindled, and that at full-time on the Western Front the intrepid footballers of the Great War returned to the trenches to participate in mutual mass slaughter are conveniently airbrushed out of history.

Other arguments, made mainly by sports administrators, allied politicians, and others who have career-vested interests in sport development, are even more optimistic about sport's ongoing and incremental capacity to promote peace and understanding. Such sports evangelists preach that sport offers more than a temporary haven for the suspension of conflict. For this group sport, both locally and globally, can solve those problems that politicians and militarists palpably cannot. Most of these people will have been long-time sports participants and enthusiasts. If sport was good for them, their thinking goes, then it must be good for others and the intrinsic value of sport as a social good is rarely questioned. They believe in the fraternal and character-building qualities of sport and in its capacity to bring diverse people and peoples together in global festivals, such as the modern Olympics or the World Cup Finals. The promotional literature of the International Olympic Committee (IOC) and other national and world sports governing bodies reflects this and is littered with the rhetoric of sports evangelism (Hill, 1992). In their hands sport is offered as a vehicle through which to resolve community conflict and to end war permanently.

There is some support in the academic community for an amalgamation of these positions. According to Elias and Dunning (1986) and their followers, the experience of sport has a progressively moderating effect on social behaviour beyond the playing field itself and as such makes a positive contribution to peace and harmony. It is a long game. Nevertheless, by offering opportunities for the socially approved arousal of moderate excitement, sport leads people to exercise stricter control over their public behaviour in society in general. In short, sport is a civilising influence, both within and between nations.

George Orwell's statement that sport is 'war minus the shooting' (Orwell, 1970: 63) is often quoted by those who would use sport as a servant of peace. They invoke Orwell to help demonstrate that sport can serve as a cathartic alternative to war. In this vision, the playing of competitive sports provides distinctive communities (nations, regions, towns and so forth) with opportunities to express distinctiveness and rivalry without threatening the wider social order – in other words, sport instead of war (Goodhart and Chataway, 1968). It is this optimistic reading of sport that dominates the thinking of sports administrators and politicians. In an interview in 1998, João Havelange, then the outgoing President of FIFA, the governing body of international football, spoke eloquently of his last great ambition:

> One day during the World Cup (USA '94) I had a telephone call from Al Gore (vice president of the United States). At that time Gore was involved in negotiating for a peaceful settlement in the Middle East. Mr Gore said he really had no experience of football before, but he was amazed that the World Cup could be so perfectly organised and that so many people could become so passionately involved. He was greatly inspired by this and asked would it not be possible to have a match between Palestine and Israel, organised by FIFA? The project is now indeed to have such a match, Palestine versus Israel, ideally in New York – New York being the seat of the United Nations – just to show the politicians football can do things that they cannot! (Sugden and Tomlinson, 1998: 240).

This vision would not have been shared by Orwell himself, who harboured bitter memories of his experiences of sports at public school. He observed that sport was a training ground for elitist bullies who would go on to use their experiences within sport to promote violence and conflict in later life. He coined the phrase 'war minus the shooting' in an essay about the Moscow Dynamo soccer team's post-war tour of Britain in 1945. In it Orwell argued that far from helping to improve international relations between the West and the Soviet Union, by providing opportunities for public and collective displays of aggressive nationalism, tours such as this made the Cold War even icier and the threat of global nuclear war greater.

Few sports optimists/evangelists quote the first half of Orwell's statement when he states, 'it (sport) is bound up with hatred, jealousy, boastfulness, disregard of all rules and sadistic pleasure'(Orwell, 1970: 63). He continues:

> If you wanted to add to the vast fund of ill-will existing in the world at this moment, you could hardly do it better than by a series of football matches between Jews and Arabs, Germans and Czechs, Indians and British, Russians and Poles and Italians and Jugoslavs, each match to be watched by a mixed audience of 100,000 spectators (Orwell, 1970: 64).

Today Orwell's list of fixtures from hell would need some modification (at the time of writing we would certainly want to add England and Turkey and maybe even the USA and France!). Despite Havelange's optimism, it is interesting to note that the prospect of Jews playing Arabs continues to be for many a game too far. In the same week that England defeated Turkey, Israel were defeated 1–2 by France in a home leg of a Euro 2004 qualification fixture. Geographically Israel is in Asia and should play its international football within the confines of the AFC (Asian Football Confederation). In its wisdom the world football governing body FIFA argued that it would be far too risky to have Israel competing with its Asian–Arab neighbours and determined instead that it should be assigned to membership of UEFA, the European confederation. What is more, Israel's home game with France was played in Sicily's capital Palermo as it had been deemed to be too dangerous to play international football matches inside Israel itself.

Who then is right, Orwell or Havelange? Can sport make a significantly positive contribution to peace processes in deeply politically divided regions such as the Middle East or does it make matters worse? What, if any, is the empirical evidence that sport can make a positive difference? To help to answer these questions the chapter continues with an examination of the case of Northern Ireland.

## The Northern Ireland experience

From 1982 until 1996, when I moved to the University of Brighton, I lived and worked in Northern Ireland. As an academic, I was and still am interested in the theme of sport and politics. In the early 1980s the most outstanding regional exemplar of the lived relationship between the two could be found in South Africa. One morning while I was lecturing on this topic at the University of Ulster a huge bomb exploded in an adjacent wing of the building buckling the blast-proof windows of my classroom. The bomb had targeted a group of policemen undertaking a criminology examination and killed three people and injured many more. While not exactly a Damascene moment, it did cause me to resolve to turn my attention away from global issues and discover more about what was going on in what was then my own back yard.

This new focus overlapped with the interests of the editor of this book and between us, based upon systematic research and argument in a variety of books, articles, conference presentations and related media work, we developed and presented a critical map of the socio-political presence of sport in that deeply divided society. The most coherent statement of this came with the publication of the first book on the subject, *Sport, Sectarianism and Society in a Divided Ireland* (Sugden and Bairner, 1993). The essential message was that rather than helping to resolve cross-community conflict, sport was doing more harm than good. While there was a sustainable academic rationale for undertaking such work there was also an applied dimension as our efforts were in part devoted towards helping to influence and change policy in Northern Ireland in the overlapping areas of sports development and community relations. To achieve this, we argued, sport in Northern Ireland needed to change its ways.

At another level there was my engagement with a variety of grass roots and hands-on sport and community relations projects. Chief among these was Belfast United, a programme that provided opportunities for young Protestants and Catholics to play and learn together in a politically neutral environment. The peak experience of Belfast United came when integrated football and basketball teams spent time in the United States, coaching and being coached and playing in competitions with and against the American hosts. While this was going on pairs of Protestant and Catholic youngsters lived together with US families. At the end of these projects, it was clear that under such carefully managed conditions the participants did in fact experience positively changed perceptions about the nature of 'the other' and equally positively altered views about the potential for mutual co-existence (Sugden, 1991; McLaughlin, 1995). At the same time, follow-up research revealed that, because of the institutionalised depth of sectarianism and its geographical consequences, it was virtually impossible for those youngsters who went through the Belfast United experience to build on cross-community friendships once they returned home from the US. Indeed a criticism of such projects is that no matter how much the participants may enjoy their shared experiences abroad, taking young people temporarily out of the context of conflict can achieve little long-term impact once they return home. The persistence of such obstacles has been highlighted and theorised by Shirlow in chapter 14.

Taking account of this, eventually, the Belfast United project became the foundation for the development of the Scholar Athlete Games. This was an international residential youth summer camp held in Belfast that brought together Protestant and Catholic teenagers from Northern Ireland and the Irish Republic along with young people from the USA and continental Europe. As well as participating together in sports, this multi-national audience took part in lectures, seminars and debates around the theme of conflict resolution.

Meanwhile throughout the rest of the Province a wide variety of sport and activity-based community relations projects ensued. The detailed, case by case, impact of such hands-on projects is notoriously difficult to gauge. However, they certainly provided a context for and momentum towards change within the policy community for sport in Northern Ireland. Some of the people who were researching Northern Irish sport and lobbying for political change and policy development in terms of sport and community relations were also actively engaged in this grassroots work. At a number of levels, simultaneously there were and continue to be a wide-ranging series of interventions that have led to significant and ongoing changes in the way sport is considered and provided for in Northern Ireland.

In 1998, for example, the Sports Council for Northern Ireland published a policy for sport and community relations and announced the appointment of a Community Relations Officer for sport who subsequently oversaw a Province-wide programme of sport-based community relations initiatives. In addition, some of the region's governing bodies of sport recruited community relations specialists and advisers. Now, almost all of Northern Ireland's 26 district councils have sport and community relations officers working for them. Whilst by no means wishing to take credit for any of this, taken altogether it is clear that two decades after the bomb disrupted my lecture on sport in South Africa,[1] sport in Northern Ireland is now making a small but nonetheless significant contribution to the peace process there. In this regard, is there anything that can be learned from the role of sport in Northern Ireland that can make a contribution to the 'road map' to peace in Israel and the Occupied Territories? It is to this question that I now turn.

## The World Sport Peace Project in Israel

In 2000 the University of Brighton agreed to take part in a three-year pilot scheme that set out to use football as a means of promoting improved community relations in the Galilee region of Northern Israel. What follows draws upon the author's thoughts and reflects upon his experience of being engaged with this ongoing project up until spring 2003.

While the idea of researching sport, conflict and community in the Middle East was something that I had contemplated for some time, there was an element of serendipity in how I first became practically involved in the region. The WSPP (World Sport Peace Project) was the idea of a small group of like-minded individuals based in the south of England who, like many others, had become sick and tired of the images of violence and death in Israel and Palestine broadcast into their living rooms on a daily basis. Unlike most others, however, they decided to try to do something about it and set up WSPP. The broad aims of this small organisation were dedicated to finding ways of using sport to help bring peace to troubled societies with a specific remit to develop projects in the Middle East. Initially it was financed through sponsorship raised by generous and determined people running the London Marathon.

At the outset there was nobody on WSPP's co-ordinating committee who had undertaken sport-related community relations work before. I had moved to the University of Brighton in 1996 and was brought on board in late 2000 when one of WSPP's founder members learned of my Northern Ireland sports pedigree. This was timely as, for personal reasons, another founder member of WSPP withdrew from the project. Amongst other things he had responsibility for recruiting volunteer soccer coaches. The University of Brighton has dedicated undergraduate programmes in Physical Education,

Sport Science, and Sport Studies and because of this we were able to fill the coaching void by recruiting some of our own students who were also well-qualified soccer coaches.

It is naïve to think that, like flat-pack furniture, projects designed to achieve reconciliation in one country can simply be transported and reassembled to work in regions with vastly different social and political histories. I had learned from Northern Ireland that in situations of deep-seated social and political conflict everything is politicised, including community relations projects. Before embarking on such endeavours it is essential to learn as much as possible about the nature of the political milieu into which one is entering and adapt one's ideas accordingly. It is especially important that those actually engaged in the facilitation of these kinds of projects appreciate this. In this particular case, before leaving for Israel it was vital to equip the student coaches with a summary profile of the place and peoples with and alongside whom they would be working. There have been countless volumes written about this subject (Elon 2000; Said, 2000) and while there is no room here to provide a critical summary, in the context of project design and process it is nevertheless worth noting some key observations that were drawn from such a review and passed on to the student coaches:

1   The Middle East conflict is thousands of years old. Its current manifestation has certain unique features, but it can only be fully comprehended with an appreciation of its history, ancient and modern.

2   Given the scale and depth of the conflict it is unrealistic to claim that sport alone can achieve what politicians have spectacularly failed to do. But it can have a small and nonetheless important part to play.

3   Israel is an intensely politically sensitive place and everything is subject to political interpretation. It is wrong to assume that sport and sports people are automatically neutral in this regard.

4   Sport has its own political history and political legacy in Israel and, like all other economic, social and cultural resources, it, too, is contested terrain.

5   The participants in such a contest are not simply monolithic blocks of Arabs and Jews. Each category has multiple sub-groups that are often antagonistic within a supposed shared religious and/or ethnic identity. Understanding the subtleties of this situation and how it feeds into the political process is vital to the success of any peace work.

6   Even if Palestine achieves full and separate statehood, community relations issues will remain between Jewish and Arab (and Christian) citizens who live within Israel's boundaries.

With this contextual information to hand, the primary task for WSPP volunteers in the region was to provide an opportunity, through football and social education, for children from Arab and Jewish communities to meet and participate together in teams and groups. Football was the obvious choice as the medium through which to pursue a community relations agenda because it is a popular team game with young people throughout the country, irrespective of ethnicity, national identity or religious affiliation (Johnson, 2001). It was hoped that by setting up coaching and playing camps and having children from different communities playing in the same teams, trust and support, personal development, friendship and an appreciation of the perspective of 'the other' could be facilitated in order to begin to establish communities that are more inclusive.

## Ibillin 2001

The project was scheduled to run over three years. One member of the project development team had been working in the region for many years and had particularly strong links with the town of Ibillin which was in the centre of the province of Galilee and about forty miles from Israel's northern frontier with Lebanon. It was agreed that, because of existing connections, the first phase of the project should be based in this town. Like the rest of Israel, Galilee's social geography is sectarian. The bigger cities and towns have clearly and sharply delineated Jewish and Arab quarters while smaller towns, villages and settlements tend to be almost exclusively either Arab or Jewish. Ibillin is essentially an Arab town and, in order for the basic aims of the project to be met, it was necessary to establish relations with a nearby Jewish community. This proved to be extremely difficult as, at the time, the country was enduring one of its more destructive periods of cross-community hostility. At a political level peace negotiations had broken down completely. The Israeli Prime Minister, Ariel Sharon, was on the warpath whilst Yasser Arafat, the veteran leader of the Palestinian Liberation Organisation (PLO), was sounding equally uncompromising from his bunkered headquarters in Ramala. The Palestinian *intifada*, or uprising, was intensifying with a growing number of suicide bombings aimed at Jewish civilian targets and Israeli Defence Forces (IDF). The re-occupation of large tracts of the Palestinian Authority by the IDF with ensuing violence and death was a regular occurrence and the construction of Jewish settlements on Arab land in the West Bank and Gaza continued apace. It was the worst, or perhaps best, of times to launch yet another peace initiative.

It was, therefore, no small achievement that, in the nearby town of Tivon, we managed to secure a partner Jewish community that agreed to provide children pro-rata to participate in the Ibillin-based initiative. The project development team was under no illusions, however, that this was anything more than a very tenuous partnership that could be caused to collapse by events beyond our control in the broader political landscape. With this in mind, back in the UK, the organisers set about selecting student coaches and providing them with a crash-course in the politics of the Middle East, while, at the same time, preparing them to do both the coaching and the team-building exercises that were to be the practical centrepieces of the first project in Galilee.

At one level the first project in the summer of 2001 was a spectacular failure; at another, in terms of learning, it was a huge success. It was a failure because, at the eleventh hour, the Jewish partners pulled out, citing fears about the security of their children. A car bomb had exploded in the region killing passengers on a bus, and the parents of the children from Tivon, not unreasonably, had decided that it was too risky to transport their loved ones into the heart of an Arab community. Even at the earliest stages of our planning we had realised that, given the volatile nature of the region and the contingent nature of the security situation, the project may have to be cancelled at the last minute. Thus, even before we got going, our primary aim of bringing young Jewish and Arab children together was defeated. Nevertheless, it was too late to cancel flights and other logistical deployments so we decided to go anyway.

The venture was successful to the extent that, from a practical point of view, we proved to ourselves that we could mount a project such as this: raise the money; recruit the coaches; transport them and their equipment to the site of the project; and coach children. It was also successful in an unforeseen way in that hitherto we had not realised the extent of the divisions within the Arab town between Muslim Arabs and Christian Arabs. Approximately 20 per cent of Israeli citizens are Arabs and of them less than ten per cent are Christians, most of whom live in the north of the country close to the Lebanese boarder. Ibillin, the site of the 2001 and 2002 projects, is roughly fifty-fifty Muslim Arab and Christian Arab and the town betrays the same sectarian geography that can be found in parts of Belfast. Most of Ibillin's children live in neighbourhoods differentiated by religion and attend separate schools. There is little or no opportunity for the kind of fun-filled socially inclusive activity promoted by WSPP. In this regard we believe our decision to carry on regardless of the Jewish withdrawal was a good one.

Learning about the depth of division and potential antagonism amongst the Arabs of Ibillin would also serve us well for future project development. In addition, we learned that we would have to do a lot more work with local partners if a further project in 2002 was not to suffer the same fate. In particular, helped by our own evaluations and the observations of an official from Olympic Aid (a branch of the IOC), who accompanied the 2001 project team, it was recognised that there was a need for more Jewish involvement in the planning stages and for a wider range of feeder communities.

## Galilee 2002

For the 2001 project the vast majority of the planning and co-ordination had taken place from London. Our evaluations showed that the length of lines of communication had been one factor that contributed to the loss of the Jewish partners. For the 2002 project development we decided that we needed a neutral broker to work on the ground on our behalf in Israel to help us identify partner communities and work with them with regard to local planning. To this end, three of the WSPP's co-ordinating committee visited Israel in early spring 2002 and met with a variety of agencies that were involved in peace-related work and had bases in the Galilee region. Our most productive contacts were with representatives of the British Council who supported our objectives and proved eager to help. Working with them we managed to persuade two Jewish communities to join with Ibillin and pro-vide children for the 2002 event. The identification of a second Jewish partner was important: should one pull out there would still be a chance that we could work with Jewish children from the remaining town. In the event, all three communities stayed on board, which was extremely reassuring since the political situation had dramatically deteriorated from that which was already considered to be dire a year earlier.

The local co-ordinating work of the British Council worked on several levels. It helped to arrange a series of regular planning meetings so that the representatives of the three partner communities were much more likely to fulfil their commitment to seeing the project through. It also operated as a vital medium through which the planning decisions of the WSPP coordinating committee could be disseminated, considered and adapted to local conditions. Finally, and most importantly, it facilitated the establishment of a network of Arab and Jewish sport and community development workers who otherwise would never have worked together. This is of vital significance for the long-term aims of the WSSP initiative.

After months of exhaustive planning and preparation, eight trainee physical education teachers from the University of Brighton embarked on the peace mission in August 2002. The students were escorted by their university lecturers/coaches and a former university chaplain. In 2001 all of the coaching and competitions had taken place in Ibillin. For 2002, after consulting our local partners, it was decided to rotate the football-peace camp around the three participating communities of Ibillin, Misgav and Tivon. First, the children were to be split into two age categories so that the numbers for the coaching sessions would be manageable within the facilities available. The children were then to be organised in groups mixed according to religious/ethnic affiliation. Each group would be assigned two British coaches and two coaches (one Arab and one Jewish) drawn from the participating communities. This helped to overcome the language difficulties associated with English-speaking coaches instructing children who, for the most part, knew little English and spoke only Hebrew or Arabic. More importantly, by allowing these local coaches to get to know each other and work co-operatively, another layer of cross-community contact was established.

On the first morning of the first day of the project, the teams of British and local coaches were introduced to one another and spent some time discussing the day-to-day project plans. The first three days were to be spent taking the children through a basic soccer skills coaching programme. On the fourth day the children would be re-mixed into teams according to ability as well as religious affiliation/ethnicity. This was to ensure that teams would be evenly matched on the day of the tournament. The rest of the fourth day was spent engaging the groups with a series of team-building games and activities. We believed that the community-relations dimension of the programme would be best served by emphasising the sport team-building process. This was to be supplemented by a series of recreational activities organised by local volunteers that would take place alongside the football programme as the different age groups were rotated.

The final day consisted of a six-a-side tournament which was a huge success, with children mixed in teams and competing for trophies and prizes. A Jewish child passes the ball to an Arab team mate to score a goal before sharing happy high-fives in celebration. It was an unlikely image in a country devastated by religious conflicts, political turmoil and suicide bombings but it happened and it happened many times. Throughout the day the children competed against each other for a place in a play-off game which culminated in a dramatic penalty shoot-out. As each child received commemorative awards, t-shirts and other gifts from the British deputy ambassador in front of a large crowd of parents and community representatives, there were handshakes, hugs and embraces between team members and opposition.

The student coaches were in little doubt that the project had been an enjoyable and progressive experience for the participants. As one commented:

At the start of the week the kids were really apprehensive, you could see the division. You had Muslim and Jewish kids at separate ends of the training grounds. But as time went on they would go straight into their teams with no hassle. You could feel the tension between the different communities. Once we got into the football that disappeared. They were just like children anywhere –

they just wanted to play and didn't care who with. By the end of the week during the tournament they were happily chatting and playing together.

There are several other indicators that have led us to believe that our work had a positive impact. Whilst we acknowledge that it may not be possible to reflect fully on how successful it has been, the 2002 event brought together more than 100 Jewish, Muslim Arab and Christian Arab children (boys and girls) who mixed together and shared a very harmonious inclusive experience. As with the situation in Northern Ireland two decades earlier, given Israel's sectarian geography and high levels of community polarisation, it is too much to hope that friendships formed across religious/ethnic boundaries would last for long after we left. It was, however, a potentially significant and formative experience for many of these youngsters and the memory of it may linger much longer. This may, in the long run, make a small contribution to community reconciliation.

Of course any impact is likely to be enhanced by embedding such projects in locally developed and collectively owned initiatives. There is a doubtful value in fly-by-night operations that zoom in for a spectacular show once a year, then leave without any follow-up. The planning for and practice of this project necessitated the establishment of cross-community networks of local administrators and coaches and related facilitators. Indeed, one of the most poignant moments of the 2002 trip was the sight of a Jewish groundsman and his Arab counterpart sitting in the shade of an olive grove eating ice cream together and sharing stories and ideas about the upkeep of their respective playing fields: grass roots diplomacy at its best perhaps. Even as we prepared to leave we were privy to animated discussions between Jewish and Arab coaches about things such as more cross-community sports camps and the setting up of a regional cross-community soccer league. The fact that these networks will be built upon in the planning and development of the 2003 expedition leads us to hope that more lasting cross-community links are being forged.

## Conclusion

Even as we began our planning for what is to be the third and final phase in the summer of 2003, there were strong indications that the project would be extended and expanded. Impressed by the success of the 2002 event, the British Council approached WSPP and asked if they could have more involvement and eventually adopt the project's aims, objectives and practices within their own cultural programme for the region and, eventually, throughout Israel. This would mean the involvement of more Jewish and Arab villages and towns and an expansion in the numbers of children, coaches and leaders. This expansion has been facilitated by inviting other UK universities to join WSPP,[2] thus allowing more British trainee teaches and coaches to share in some of the positive experiences outlined herein. Further, it was agreed that in 2003 UK coaches would work in tandem with small groups of local young coaches and community leaders who will themselves become active as sport-community relations animators in the future.

Thus, what started as a noble idea of a few well-minded individuals, funded by personal donations and voluntary fundraising, promises to make a progressive contribution to the cultural dimension that must necessarily accompany any movement toward any political peace in 'Israel and the Occupied Territories'.

Faced by what can seem to be massive and intractable global political problems such as the Middle East, there is a temptation to do nothing. But as Edmund Burke reminds us, 'It is necessary only for the good man to do nothing for evil to triumph'. For those of us who might seek to make a difference we should do what we can and I believe that in both the Northern Ireland case and in Israel it can be demonstrated that sport, if handled sensitively, can make some proportionate contribution to peace. Havelange and Orwell, quoted at the beginning of this chapter, are both wrong about sport. Sport is neither essentially good nor bad. It is a social construct and its role and function depends largely on what we make of it and how it is consumed. Sport alone will definitely not change the world. Neither will it be a key factor in any Middle East peace settlement, but as Baghdad smoulders, doing nothing may no longer be an option.

# Notes

*Chapter 1   'Sport' and Ireland in 1881*

1     For further information on the birth of the modern sporting world in Britain and its subsequent spread across the globe, see, for example, R. Holt (1989), *Sport and the British: A Modern History.* Oxford: Clarendon; N. Tranter (1998), *Sport, Economy and Society in Britain, 1750–1914.* Cambridge: Cambridge University Press; D. Brailsford (1992), *British Sport: A Social History.* Cambridge: Lutterworth Press; W. Vamplew (2002), *Pay Up and Play the Game, Professional Sport in Britain 1875–1914.* Cambridge: Cambridge University Press; N. Elias and E. Dunning (1986), *Quest for Excitement: Sport and Leisure in the Civilizing Process.* Oxford: Blackwell; J. Hargreaves (1986), *Sport, Power and Culture: A Social and Historical Analysis of Popular Sport.* Cambridge: Polity; W. J. Baker (1982), *Sports in the Western World.* Totowa, NJ: Rowman & Littlefield; A. Guttmann (1995), *Games and Empires: Modern Sports and Cultural Imperialism.* New York: Columbia University Press; R. Holt (1981), *Sport and Society in Modern France.* London: Macmillan; R. Guha (2002), *A Corner of a Foreign Field: The Indian History of a British Sport.* London: Picador; J. A. Mangan (ed.) (1991), *The Cultural Bond: Sport, Empire, Society.* London: Frank Cass; and J. Lowerson (1993), *Sport and the English Middle Classes 1870–1914.* Manchester: Manchester University Press.

2     Between 1845 and 1910 the number of rural labourers fell from at least 700,000 to less than 300,000. Further, in that same timeframe, the number of cottiers working farms of less than five acres of land fell from 300,000 to 62,000, while the number of farmers holding between five and 15 acres fell from 310,000 to 154,000. By 1916, 64 per cent of agricultural holdings in Ireland were owner-occupied as compared with a mere three per cent in 1870. See P. Rouse (2000), *Ireland's Own Soil: Government and Agriculture in Ireland, 1945–1965.* Dublin: Irish Farmers Journal.

3     For wider social and economic change in Ireland, see, for example, T. Guinnane (1997), *The Vanishing Irish: Households, Migration, and the Rural Economy in Ireland, 1850–1914.* Princeton, NJ: Princeton University Press; and J. J. Lee (1973), *The Modernisation of Irish Society, 1848–1918.* Dublin: Gill & Macmillan. For studies of the initial development of modern sporting organisations in Ireland, see J. S. Donnelly and K. S. Miller (eds) (1998), *Irish Popular Culture, 1650–1850.* Dublin: Irish Academic Press; O. MacDonagh, W. F. Mandle and P. Travers (eds) (1983), *Irish Culture and Nationalism, 1750–1950.* London: Macmillan; T. West (1991), *The Bold Collegians: The Development of Sport in Trinity College, Dublin.* Dublin: Lilliput; P. Meenan (1997), *St Patrick's Blue and Saffron: A Miscellany of UCD Sport since 1895.* Dublin: Quill Print; W. F. Mandle (1987), *The GAA and Irish Nationalist Politics, 1884–1924.* Dublin: Gill & Macmillan; P. Griffin (1990), *The Politics of Irish Athletics, 1850–1990.* Ballinamore, Co. Leitrim: Marathon Publications; A. Ó Maolfabhail (1973), *Camán: Two Thousand Years of Hurling in Ireland.* Dundalk: Dundalgan Press; M. de Búrca (1999), *The GAA: A History,* 2nd edn. Dublin: Gill & Macmillan; L. P. Ó Caithnia (1980), *Scéal na hIomána.* Dublin: An Chlóchomhar Tta; B. Ó hÉithir (1991), *Over the Bar.* Swords, Co Dublin: Poolbeg; S. O'Riain (1998), *Maurice Davin (1842–1927). First President of the GAA.* Dublin: Geography Publications; J. J. Barrett (1997), *In the Name of the Game.* Bray, Co. Wicklow: The Dub Press; T. McElligott (1984), *The Story of Handball: The Game, the Players,*

*the History*. Dublin: Wolfhound; N. Garnham (ed.) (1999), *The Origins and Development of Football in Ireland*. Belfast: Ulster Historical Foundation; T. S. C. Dagg (1944), *Hockey in Ireland*. Tralee, Co. Kerry: The Kerryman; N. Mahony and R. Whiteside (1997), *Cricket at the King's Hospital, 1897–1997*. Dublin: King's Hospital; N. Mahony and R. Whiteside (1992), *Hockey at the King's Hospital, 1892–1992*. Maynooth, Co. Kildare: Cardinal Press; W. H. Gibson (1988), *Early Irish Golf: The First Courses, Clubs and Pioneers*. Naas, Co. Kildare: Oakleaf; W. P. Hone (1956) *Cricket in Ireland*. Tralee, Co. Kerry: The Kerryman; and F. A. D'Arcy (1991), *Horses, Lords and Racing Men: The Turf Club, 1790–1990*. Curragh, Co. Kildare: Turf Club.

4   The *Freeman's Journal* was founded in September 1763 and ran until 19 January 1924.

5   See Roy Foster (1993), *Paddy and Mr Punch: Connections in Irish and English History*. For his part, Joe Lee (1973) wrote *The Modernisation of Irish Society 1848–1918* without a single mention of sport. These are but two examples of a tendency repeated across the historiography of modern Ireland.

*Chapter 2    The early years of Gaelic Football and Cricket in County Westmeath*

1   References to NA, CBS, DICS, Midland Division, 1887–94 are given in the text thus: (CBS, S/2452).

2   NLI, MS 9515. Account book of Kilruane football club, 1876,

*Chapter 3    Rugby's imperial connections, domestic politics and colonial tours to Ireland*

1   Report of the inter-departmental committee on physical deterioration, BPP (1904), xxxii, CD 2175: 1–48.

2   Minute book of the Irish Rugby Football Union (Northern Branch), 2 Dec. 1902–5 Nov. 1907. PRONI, ref: D/3867/A/3.

*Chapter 4    The Irish Free State and Aonach Tailteann*

1   For a further explanation of Aonach Tailteann, especially its governmental and financial organisation, see Cronin (2003).

2   NA, Department of Finance, FIN 1/379.

3   Ibid., FIN 1/293.

4   Ibid., FIN 1/741.

5   NA, Cabinet Minutes, 7 July 1922.

6   'Draft Invite, 1924 Aonach Tailteann'. NLI, Yeats Papers, MS 1078,

7   For details of Ranji's visit to the Tailteann games, see Anne Chambers, *Ranji: Maharajah of Connemara* (Dublin: Wolfhound, 2002: 113–18). Thanks to Margaret Ó hÓgartaigh for this reference.

8    'Memo from S. Ua Broin to Ernest Blythe, 7 November 1924'. NLI, Brennan Collection, MS 26,221,

9    'Letter Walsh to Blythe, 21 August 1924'. NLI, Brennan Collection, MS 31,707 (3),

10   Ibid.

11   NA, Department of Finance, S200/0002/28.

12   NA, Department of Taoiseach, S8 369

*Chapter 5    The Aonach Tailteann, the Irish press and gendered symbols of national identity*

1    The extent to which women in both India and Ireland have engaged with and negotiated these nationalist symbols has been discussed by Thapar-Bjorkert and Ryan (2002).

2    I would like to thank Mike Cronin for this interesting piece of information.

*Chapter 6    Gaelic games and the Irish immigrant experience in Boston*

1    Personal observations, Irish Cultural Centre, Canton, MA, Sept. 2000.

2    Details of the complement of GAA clubs in Boston in this period were found in the club histories of Boston Galway Hurling Club and The Young Ireland's Hurling Club which were published as part of the North East Gaelic Athletic Association publication, *A Century of Boston GAA.*

3    For example, the two units came into conflict over the financial and logistical arrangements in connection with the 1927 tour of All-Ireland football champions, Kerry, to America. The tour was only sanctioned by the GAA when the American organising committee agreed to demands for the tour to be directed by a professional American sports promoter who subsequently disappeared without paying the Kerry touring party the monies owed to them. Further conflict arose in the following year when an American team was granted permission to play a number of exhibition games to make up a financial shortfall caused by their early expulsion from the Tailteann games. In their preparations for these games the American team had broken one of the GAA's cardinal rules of the time by using the facilities of a soccer club to train. The Central Council immediately withdrew permission to play any further games in Ireland and the American team departed shortly afterwards. Tensions between the GAA in Ireland and North America have persisted into the modern era. For example, clubs based in Ireland are often resentful when their players make use of the Sanctions system to play for North American teams during the summer months because this can effectively deprive these clubs of important human resources. The payment of substantial sums of money to high profile county players who travel to the US in the summer months is also at odds with the amateur ethos of the GAA and is often the cause of discontent.

4    The camogie clubs, Eire Og, Celtics, Claddagh and St. Bridget's were formed in 1978, 1981 and 1982 respectively. The other clubs founded in this period were the football clubs Shannon Blues, St. Patrick's, Columbkilles, Jamaica Plain Shamrocks and Charlestown whilst Tipperary were added to the roster of Hurling clubs.

5   For those not formally affiliated to a club, attending Gaelic football, hurling or camogie matches in Boston as a spectator has also afforded individuals with the opportunity to wear their county-based identity on their sleeves through the donning of replica county shirts. This is a common occurrence at GAA matches and events in Boston (personal observations during training sessions for the Notre Dame Gaelic Football Club at Soldiers Field, Brighton and during matches at Canton, MA, July–September, 2000).

6   There are a large number of Irish contractors involved in the building trade in Boston and suburbs, many of whom are involved in the GAA as officials and/or benefactors. It is predominantly through these that opportunities for work come. Clubs in Boston will also rent accommodation on short-term leases for players who fly out to the city for the season.

7   During the author's fieldwork in Boston between July and September 2000, it was clear that the practice of paying top-level players for their services was widespread.

8   Some of these venues included, Boston Common, Victory Field, Tech Field, Hormel Stadium, Smith Field, Cleveland Circle, Foxboro Stadium, Columbia Park and more recently Dilboy Field.

9   The opening also involved a hurling match between All-Ireland Champions Cork and the 1998 All Star select team and a re-run of the 1999 All-Ireland football final between Meath and Cork. This provided an opportunity to watch at first hand the cream of Gaelic sportsmen and undoubtedly provided a fresh injection of interest in Gaelic games in Boston

10   This observation is based on conversations with GAA members in Boson during fieldwork between July and September 2000. Northern Aid (NORAID) collects money in the USA which it claims is used to support the families of Republican prisoners in Northern Ireland. However, the American, British and Irish Governments insist that its primary function is to raise funds to arm the IRA.

11   The 18-year-old Grenadier Guardsman charged with the unlawful killing of Aidan McAnespie claimed that he had been cleaning his weapon when his finger had slipped discharging three shots, one of which ricocheted and hit McAnespie in the back killing him instantly. The official inquiry into the incident has proved inconclusive and the McAnespie family suspect a conspiracy and cover-up.

12   It should be noted that Rule 21 has since been rescinded from the Association's rule book.


*Chapter 7   Rugby union and national identity politics*

1   See Cronin (1999: 26–7) and Maguire et al. (2002: 148–62) for a fuller elaboration of theories of nationalism.

2   This research was part of a longitudinal study taking in the period between the Rugby World Cups of 1995 and 1999. Firstly, a series of semi-structured interviews was carried out with a representative sample of the 1995 Irish Rugby World Cup squad. This was then supported with the administering of semi-structured questionnaires to every member of the 1999 Irish Rugby World Cup squad. In addition, findings from other research into the perceptions of English, Scottish and Welsh rugby players (of the Irish) are referred to in order to provide some alternative 'outsider' views on Irish rugby. All players are referred to by pseudonyms to protect anonymity.

3    It is interesting to note that Ireland have now established themselves as the second strongest team in the northern hemisphere (finishing second to England in the 2001, 2002 and 2003 Six Nations Championships). In addition, Irish provincial sides have had some success in European competition since the advent of the first Heineken (European) Cup in 1999–2000. Munster have been losing finalists in two Heineken Cups and were one of the semi-finalists along with Leinster in the 2002/3 competition, and semi-finalists again in the 2003/4 competition.

4    A far more detailed analysis of the GAA can be found in Bairner (2001a) and Cronin (1999).

5    The Barbarians (or 'Baa-Baas') represent the British-based 'united nations of rugby'. Formed in 1890 by William Percy Carpmael, they are an 'occasional invitational' team established to spread good fellowship through playing entertaining and adventurous rugby. The Baa-Baas usually play touring teams who are touring the British Isles and always endeavour to field a multi-national selection of exceptional rugby talent in their line-up.

6    The mostly short-lived, and not always homogeneous, 'feel-good' national identity provided by international sporting success is discussed further by Maguire et al. (2002). In addition, Jarvie and Walker's (1994) work makes reference to the transitory nature of a sport-induced national identity by exploring the notion of the Scottish public as 'ninety minute patriots' (a phrase coined in 1992 by Jim Sillars, an ex-Member of Parliament for the Scottish National Party).

*Chapter 10    Sport, Irishness and Ulster unionism*

The interviews from which this material is taken were conducted between January 2000 and February 2002 by two of my former students and have been referenced as Gibson (2001) and Mason (2000)

1    It is worth noting that in Ireland, as in the United States and for the same basic reason, association football is often referred to as soccer. Many rugby union enthusiasts would use the word to distinguish the game from their own chosen football code. However, the word 'soccer' is used even more frequently to distinguish association football from Gaelic football. Ulster unionist football fans are unlikely to use the word 'soccer' since they feel no particular need to differentiate their favoured code. In this chapter, both 'soccer' and 'football' are used, without it is hoped causing any confusion for the reader.

2    The Edinburgh-based club Hibernian is the other. It predated Celtic and was the original 'Irish' club in Scotland. Increasingly, though, it began to draw its support from throughout the east end of the city and from the neighbouring burgh of Leith. Celtic's fan base, on the other hand, remains closely interwoven with the club's Irish, Catholic origins.

3    The author was provided with graphic evidence of the intense hatred felt towards Manchester United in some sections of the Protestant community whilst teaching a group of loyalist inmates in the Maze Prison in the 1990s. A number of the prisoners, members of the Ulster Volunteer Force and Red Hand Commando, arrived for the class wearing Manchester City shirts. When asked about their reasons for supporting the other Manchester club, the men proceeded to rhyme off a series of 'facts' that proved conclusively, at least to them, that United was still a Catholic club.

*Chapter 11   Football supporters, rivalry and Protestant fragmentation in Northern Ireland*

1   Following regular violence at matches between Belfast Celtic and Linfield, Belfast Celtic withdrew from the Irish League at the end of the 1948–9 season partly in response to the abandonment of the Boxing Day fixture with Linfield earlier that season.

2   Portadown is a town located in north Armagh whilst Glenavon are based in Lurgan, a neighbouring town to Portadown.

3   In Scotland it was Hibernian FC in Edinburgh and Glasgow Celtic FC that were attractive to the local Catholic population.

4   Glasgow Celtic sent a donation to assist with the establishment of Belfast Celtic (Kennedy, 1989).

5   Sugden and Bairner (1993) report violent incidents at Belfast Celtic matches between and Glentoran and Linfield during 1986–7, Celtic's first season in the Irish League.

6   Cliftonville were established in a middle-class Protestant area in north Belfast but managed to steer clear of ethno-sectarian problems until the 1970s when demographic changes attracted a nationalist following to the club (Sugden and Bairner, 1993).

7   Jimmy Jones, the Belfast Celtic centre forward, was a particular target for the on-rushing Linfield crowd that had stormed the pitch at half time and was badly injured in fleeing for the safety of the changing rooms. The irony here is that Jones was a Protestant from Lurgan and, though the broken leg he received was to hinder his career, he still went on to play for his home town team Glenavon, itself a Protestant dominated club.

8   Belfast Celtic toured the United States in the summer of 1949, even defeating the Scotland national side, but never again featured in the Irish League.

9   Only until Donegal Celtic were accepted into the Second Division of the Irish League in season 2002–3 did senior soccer return to west Belfast giving the local Catholic community a local Irish League team to support once more.

10   In 1985 Derry City were accepted into the League of Ireland and, despite some tentative suggestions regarding their return to the Irish League, remains there. This is a graphic indicator of the complexities of soccer and its politics on the island of Ireland.

11   It was not until 1952 that Lurgan club Glenavon became the first non-Belfast club to win the Irish League championship, a feat their near neighbours Portadown did not manage until 1990.

12   The 1985 Irish Cup Final between the Big Two also contained spectator disorder with a pig painted red, white and blue and a cockerel (the Glentoran club emblem) surreally wandering around the perimeter of the pitch throughout the game.

13   Glentoran had won the previous two Big Two finals, in 1966 and 1973.

14   The last time Linfield was in the final, in 2002, the IFA chose Windsor Park as the venue with Linfield defeating Portadown at their home ground. Linfield's previous appearance in the final, however, saw them beat Carrick Rangers in 1995 at The Oval, indicating a new IFA policy regarding Irish Cup Final venues.

15   This has not always been the case as The Oval was not the preferred venue for the 1961, 1970 and 1975 finals involving Linfield with Cliftonville (twice) and Ballymena United's grounds being used.

16   The reverse situation was also the case in 1966 when Glentoran defeated Linfield at the Oval and again in 1985 when a draw at The Oval saw Glentoran win the replay at Windsor Park.

17  Glentoran won the replay 2–1.

18  Glentoran had a player sent off whilst in a separate incident a Linfield player fractured his leg.

19  Glentoran are the next successful club with, in comparison to Linfield, a mere 21 league titles and 19 Irish Cup successes.

20  Outside Linfield and Glentoran support for Irish League clubs is rather localised.

21  Midgley was Chairman of Linfield at the time of the 1948 Boxing Day clash but also a Stormont MP for the Northern Ireland Labour Party and vocal anti-Catholic (Bairner and Walker, 2001).

22  Morgan was a Linfield player during the 1920s and 1930s and trainer of the team in the 1940s and 1950s.

23  At the time of any club's inception officials had only to nominate their shirts and shorts as club colours. Hence Linfield's colours were entered as blue and white in the club rules of 1886. The precise introduction of red into the playing kit is unknown but certainly it has been a regular feature of post-war Linfield teams.

24  This is the only time in the season until very recently that either club had to wear an alternative kit.

25  More recently Linfield have adopted yellow shirts and blue shorts / socks as an away kit which might indicate a watering down of loyalist imagery until one sees the continued mix of red, white and blue in the home kit.

26  At the time it was common for supporters' clubs to donate a playing kit to the club, something that was common to both Linfield and Glenavon, but was no longer necessary once sports manufacturing companies became more modernised and replica kits became more popular.

27  Recently Glenavon has adopted yellow shirts and blue shorts/socks as an away kit.

28  I attended this match in the capacity of a Linfield player who had not made the final squad and was hence in very close proximity to the fighting that took place. As a Lurgan-born Linfield player, the fighting took place between Lurgan friends of mine and Linfield supporters whom I knew.

29  Lundy was an infamous Protestant traitor of 1688 with the phrase 'Lundyism' substituting for treachery in popular Protestant terminology.

*Chapter 12    The migration of sporting labour into Ireland*

1    For the purposes of this chapter, 'Ireland' refers to the entire island. When distinguishing between the two political states, I use the Republic of Ireland or Northern Ireland as is appropriate. There are instances where I use the adjective "Irish" in which it should be abundantly clear that I am discussing an individual's citizenship (that is, relationship with a particular state) and thus affiliation with the Republic in contrast to a British citizen who has a specific relationship with the United Kingdom.

2    Indeed, all six case studies are either British or World games by Sugden and Bairner's

classifications with rugby union, cricket and hockey as British games and basketball, ice hockey, and tennis all considered World games. The world game of association football (soccer) also attracts some migrants but nowhere near the amount the professional leagues in England or continental Europe do. All of the case studies are politically neutral or said to be 'Protestant' practices in Northern Ireland with the exception of basketball which has become 'Irish',

3    The exception is soccer in Northern Ireland. Northern Ireland has its own internationally recognised national soccer administration and competes in World Cup competitions as a national side.

*Chapter 13    Some reflections on women's sports in Ireland*

1    Norbert Elias and Pierre Bourdieu have both used the term 'social field' and it is likely that they adapted it from Kurt Lewin's work in the 1930s.

2    'Irish' refers to the Republic of Ireland throughout this chapter.

3    For example, see the launch of *Fairplay: Sport and Leisure* as a publication specifically orientated towards minority and women's sports – www.fairplay.ie.

4    This sample was controlled to be representative of the national population in respect of all key socio-demographic variables including gender, age, socio-economic background, marital status and regional distribution. A 'seasonality monitor' was also conducted to assess to what extent if any, seasonal differences in participation levels emerged.

5    Sociologists would regard walking as a physical activity and not a 'sport'.

6    The most strenuously active category is males in the 18–35 year age group.

7    Twelve in-depth interviews were conducted between 1999 and 2000 with elite Irish female athletes. Interviews focused on their sporting careers and life histories, including participation in sport during their school years.

8    The demographic breakdown of respondents was as follows: 83 pr cent were aged 17–28 years, 94 per cent were Irish and the remainder European; all were undergraduate students in University College Dublin (12 per cent part-time); 92 per cent categorised themselves as sports participants (including being a sports supporter) while only one respondent had 'no interest or involvement whatsoever in sport'; 52 per cent were female while 48 per cent were male.

9    Dunning suggests that the development of field hockey in England is also an anomaly in that 'females who chose to play hockey in the late nineteenth century were probably fully aware of the then-dominant beliefs in its "masculinising" implications and (they) were probably deliberately setting their stall out against then-contemporary ideals of femininity and female habitus' (1999: 233).

10    The author of this chapter is editor and consultant for this report, published by the Joint Oireachtas Committee in July 2004.

11    M = Male respondent, F = female respondent.

12    See *Evening Herald*, 28 Mar. 2003, for an example of the celebration of the male body in sport as well as the ability of an elite male athlete (such as Brian O'Driscoll) to transform 'cultural capital' from the field of sport into other forms of capital such as economic capital.

*Chapter 14    Sport, leisure and territory in Belfast*

1    Spatial bordering can be defined as the creation of boundaries, both physical and symbolic, which divide separate communities.
2    The term Catholics and Protestants is used even though political divisions in Northern Ireland are more complex given the divisions between nationalists and republicans and loyalists and unionists.
3    Taigs and Huns are derogatory terms for both Catholics and Protestant respectively.


*Chapter 15    Sport and community relations in Northern Ireland and Israel*

1    While the context is vastly different, there is a similar story to be researched and told about the progressive role being played by sport in the reconstruction of post-apartheid South Africa.
2    St Mary's College Twickenham, Brunel University, Southampton Institute of Higher Education.

# References

Adair, A. S., J. N. Berry, W. S. McGreal, B. Murtagh and C. Paris (2000) The local housing system in Craigavon N. Ireland: ethno-religious residential segregation, socio-tenurial polarisation and sub-markets, *Urban Studies*, 37 (2): 1079–92.

Adelman, M. L. (1990) *A Sporting Time: New York City and the Rise of Modern Athletics, 1820-1870*. Urbana and Chicago: University of Illinois Press.

Akenson, D. (1992) *God's Peoples: Covenant and Land in South Africa, Israel and Ulster*. Ithaca: Cornell University Press.

Amery, L.S. (ed.) (1900–9) *The Times History of the War in South Africa 1899–1902*, 5 vols. London: The Times.

Anderson, B. (1983) *Imagined Communities: Reflections on the Origin and Spread of Nationalism*. London: Verso.

Anderson, B. (1991) *Imagined Communities: Reflections on the Origin and Spread of Nationalism*, 2nd edn. London: Verso.

Anderson, J. and I. Shuttleworth (1998) Sectarian demography, territoriality and political development in Northern Ireland, *Political Geography* 17 (2): 187–208.

Anthias, F. and N. Yuval-Davis (1993) *Racialised Boundaries: Race, Nation, Gender, Colour and Class*. London: Routledge.

Appadurai, A. (1996) *Modernity At Large: Cultural Dimensions of Globalization*. Minneapolis: University of Minnesota Press.

Appadurai, A. (2000) 'Grassroots globalization and the research imagination', *Public Culture* 12 (1): 1–19.

Aughey, A. (1989) *Under Siege: Ulster Unionism and the Anglo-Irish Agreement*. Belfast: Blackstaff.

Aughey, A. (1995) Tracing Arguments in Conservatism and Unionism, unpublished DPhil thesis. Jordanstown: University of Ulster.

*Backpacker* (2002) 'Adventure sports: Lorna Connelly comes to grips with women's rugby', 14, Nov./Dec. www.backpacker.ie.

Bairner, A. (1996) 'Sportive nationalism and nationalist politics: a comparative analysis of Scotland, the Republic of Ireland, and Sweden', *Journal of Sport and Social Issues* 20 (3), Aug.: 314–34.

Bairner, A. (1997) '"Up to their knees?" Football, sectarianism, masculinity and Protestant working-class identity', pp. 95–113 in P. Shirlow and M. McGovern (eds), *Who are 'The People?' Unionism, Protestantism and Loyalism in Northern Ireland*. London: Pluto.

Bairner, A. (1999a) 'Civic and ethnic nationalism in the Celtic vision of Irish sport', pp. 12–25 in G. Jarvie (ed.), *Sport in the Making of Celtic Cultures*. Leicester: Leicester University Press.

Bairner, A. (1999b) 'Soccer, masculinity and violence in Northern Ireland: between hooliganism and terrorism', *Men and Masculinities* 1 (2): 284–301.

Bairner, A. (2001a) *Sport, Nationalism and Globalisation. European and North American Perspectives*. Albany, NY: State University of New York Press.

Bairner, A. (2001b) Sport, politics and society in Northern Ireland: changing times, new developments, *Studies* 90 (359): 283–90.

Bairner, A. (2002) 'The dog that didn't bark? Football hooliganism in Ireland', pp. 118–30 in
    E. Dunning, P. Murphy, I. Waddington and A. E. Astrinakis (eds), *Fighting Fans: Football
    Hooliganism as a World Phenomenon* (Dublin: University College Dublin Press).

Bairner, A. (2003) 'Political unionism and sporting nationalism: an examination of the
    relationship between sport and national identity within the Ulster unionist tradition',
    *Identities: Global Studies in Culture and Power* 10 (4): 517–35.

Bairner, A. (2004) 'Creating a soccer strategy for Northern Ireland: reflections on football
    governance in small European countries', *Soccer and Society* 5 (1): 27–42.

Bairner, A. and P. Darby (1999) 'Divided sport in a divided society: Northern Ireland',
    pp. 51–72 in J. Sugden and A. Bairner (eds), *Sport in Divided Societies*. Aachen: Meyer
    & Meyer.

Bairner, A. and P. Shirlow (1998) 'Loyalism, Linfield and the territorial politics of soccer
    fandom in Northern Ireland', *Space and Polity* 2 (2): 163–77.

Bairner, A. and P. Shirlow (1999) 'The territorial politics of soccer in Northern Ireland',
    pp. 152–63 in G. Armstrong and R. Giulianotti (eds), *Football Cultures and Identities*.
    London: Macmillan.

Bairner, A. and P. Shirlow (2001) pp. 43–60 in G. Armstrong and R. Giulianotti (eds), *Fear
    and Loathing in World Football*. Oxford: Berg.

Bairner, A. and P. Shirlow (2003) 'When leisure turns to fear: fear, mobility, and ethno-
    sectarianism in Belfast', *Leisure Studies* 22 (3): 203–21.

Bairner, A. and G. Walker (2001) 'Football and society in Northern Ireland: Linfield Football
    Club and the case of Gerry Morgan', *Soccer and Society* 2 (1): 81–98.

Bale, J. (1986) 'Sport and national identity: a geographical view', *British Journal of Sports History*
    3 (1): 18–41.

Bale, J. (1994) *Landscapes of Modern Sport*. Leicester: Leicester University Press.

Bale, J. and J. Maguire (eds) (1994) *The Global Sports Arena: Athletic Talent Migration in an
    Interdependent World*. London: Frank Cass.

Balvanes, M. and P. Caputi (2001) *Introduction to Quantitative Research Methods: An investigative
    approach*. London: Sage.

Beckles, H. and B. Stoddart (eds) (1995) *Liberation Cricket: West Indies Cricket Culture*.
    Manchester: Manchester University Press.

Belfast Interface Project (1999) *Belfast Interface Project Report*. Belfast: Belfast Interface Project.

Best, G. (with R. Benson) (1991) *The Good, the Bad and the Bubbly*. London: Pan.

Best, G. (with R. Collins) (2002) *Blessed: The Autobiography*. London: Ebury Press.

Best, A. (with N. Pittam) (2001) *George Best and Me: My Autobiograohy*. London: Virgin.

Billig, M. (1995) *Banal Nationalism*. London: Sage.

Birley, D. (1999) *A Social History of English Cricket*. London: Aurum.

Birrell, S. (1983) 'The psychological dimensions of female athletic participation', pp. 49–92 in
    M. Boutilier and L. SanGiovanni (eds), *The Sporting Woman*. Champaign, IL: Human
    Kinetics.

Birrell, S. and C. Cole (eds) (1994) *Women, Sport, and Culture*. Champaign, IL: Human Kinetics.

Black, D. and J. Nauright (1998) *Rugby and the South African Nation: Sport, Cultures, Politics
    and Power in the Old and New South Africa*. Manchester: Manchester University Press.

Blain, N., R. Boyle and H. O'Donnell (1993) *Sport and National Identity in the European
    Media*. London: Leicester University Press.

Bloom, W. (1990) *Personal Identity, National Identity and International Relations.* Cambridge: Cambridge University Press.

Blue, A. (1987) *Grace Under Pressure: The Emergence of Women in Sport.* London: Sidgwick & Jackson.

Boal, F., J. Campbell and D. Livingstone (1991) 'The Protestant mosaic: a majority of minorities', pp. 99–129 in P. Roche and J. Barton (eds), *The Northern Ireland Question: Myth and Reality.* Aldershot: Avebury.

Borrows, B. (2002) *The Hurricane. The Turbulent Times of Alex Higgins.* London: Atlantic.

*Boston Irish Reporter* (1999a) 'GAA, cultural centre sign deal for athletic fields', 10 (4), Apr.

*Boston Irish Reporter* (1999b) 'Irish sports youth league seeks new players', 10 (7), July.

*Boston Irish Reporter* (1999c) 'Irish cultural centre marks decade of progress, eye to the future', 10 (10), Oct.

*Boston Pilot* (1879a) 'Field sports at the Boston Irish Athletic Club picnic', 42 (40), 4 Oct.

*Boston Pilot* (1879b) 'Irish games: the ancient sports introduced into America', 42 (40), 4 Oct.

*Boston Pilot* (1886a) 'Irish games: the coming exhibition at Oak Island June 17', 49 (24), 12 June.

*Boston Pilot* (1886b) 'Irish games', 49 (24), 12 June.

*Boston Pilot* (1950a) 'Shamrock camogie interest increases', 121 (29), 29 July.

*Boston Pilot* (1950b) 'Camogie game Sunday', 121 (43), 4 Nov.

Bourdieu, P. (1977) *Outline of a Theory of Practice.* Cambridge: Cambridge University Press.

Bourdieu, P. (1985) 'The genesis of the concept of habitus and field', *Sociocriticism, Theories and Perspectives,* 2 (2): 11–24.

Bourdieu, P. (1986) 'The forms of capital', pp. 241–58 in J. Richardson (ed.), *Handbook of Theory and Research for the Sociology of Education.* New York: Greenwood.

Bourdieu, P. (1988) 'Program for a sociology of sport', *Sociology of Sport Journal* 5 (2): 153–61.

Bourdieu, P. (1990) *In Other Words: Essays Towards a Reflexive Sociology.* Cambridge: Polity.

Bourdieu, P. (1993) 'How can one be a sportsman', *Sociology in Question.* London: Sage: 117–31.

Bourdieu, P. (2001) *Masculine Domination.* Cambridge: Polity.

Boyce, D. G. (1990) *Nineteenth-century Ireland: The Search for Stability.* Dublin: Gill & Macmillan.

Boyce, D.G. (1995) *Nationalism in Ireland,* 3rd edn. London: Routledge.

Bradley, J. (1998) 'Sport and The contestation of cultural and ethnic identities in Scottish society', pp. 127–50 in M. Cronin and D. Mayall (eds), *Sporting Nationalisms: Identity, Ethnicity, Immigration and Assimilation.* London: Frank Cass.

Brodie, M. (1980) *100 Years of Irish Football.* Belfast: Blackstaff.

Brodie, M. (1985) *Linfield: 100 Years.* Belfast: The Universities Press.

Brown, T. (1987) *Ireland a Social and Cultural History.* London: Fontana.

Bryan, D. (2000) *Orange Parades: The Politics of Ritual, Tradition and Control.* London: Pluto.

Buckley, A. D. and M. C. Kenney (eds) (1995) *Negotiating Identity: Rhetoric, Metaphor, and Social Drama in Northern Ireland.* Washington: Smithsonian Institution Press.

Burchill, J. (2002) *Burchill on Beckham.* London: Yellow Jersey Press.

Burns, J. (1999) *Barça: A People's Passion.* London: Bloomsbury.

Burton, F. (1978) *The Politics of Legitimacy: Struggles in a Belfast Community.* London: Routledge.

Calhoun, C. (ed.) (1994) *Social Theory and the Politics of Identity.* Oxford: Blackwell.

Calhoun, C. (1995) *Critical Social Theory: Culture, History and the Challenge of Difference.* Oxford: Blackwell.

Carter, T., H. Donnan, S. Ogle, and H. Wardle. (2003) *Global Migrants: The Impact of Migrants Working in Sport in Northern Ireland.* Belfast: Sports Council for Northern Ireland.

*Celtic Monthly* (1879) 'John Boyle O'Reilly: The story of his eventful career', II (1): 76–82.

Cochrane, F. (1997) *Unionist Politics and the Politics of Unionism since the Anglo-Irish Agreement.* Cork: Cork University Press.

Colley, A., J. Nash, L. O'Connell and L. Restorick (1987) 'Attitudes to the female sex role and sex-typing of physical activities', *International Journal of Sports Psychology* 18: 19–29.

Coughlan, B. (1983) *The Irish Lions 1896–1983.* Dublin: Ward River Press.

Coulter, C. (1994) 'Class, ethnicity, and political identity in Northern Ireland', *Irish Journal of Sociology* 4: 1–26.

Coulter, C. (1999) *Contemporary Northern Irish Society: An Introduction.* London: Pluto.

Coyle, P. (1999) *Paradise Lost and Found: The Story of Belfast Celtic.* Edinburgh: Mainstream and Belfast: Blackstaff..

Crick, B. (ed.) (1991) *National Identities: The Constitution of the United Kingdom.* Oxford: Blackwell.

Cronin, M. (1997) 'Which nation? Which flag? Boxing and national identities in Ireland'. *International Review for the Sociology of Sport* 32 (2): 131–46.

Cronin, M. (1998a) 'Enshrined in blood: the naming of Gaelic Athletic Association grounds and clubs', *The Sports Historian* 18 (1), May: 90-104.

Cronin, M. (1998b) 'Fighting for Ireland: playing for England? The nationalist history of the Gaelic Athletic Association and the English influence on Irish sport', *International Journal of the History of Sport* XV (3): 36–56.

Cronin, M. (1999) *Sport and Nationalism in Ireland: Gaelic Games, Soccer and Irish Identity Since* 1884. Dublin: Fours Courts.

Cronin, M. (2003) 'Projecting the nation through sport and culture: Ireland, Aonach Tailteann and the Irish Free State, 1924–32', *Journal of Contemporary History* 38 (3): 395–411.

Csizma, K., A. Wittig and T. Schurr (1988) 'Sport stereotypes and gender', *Journal of Sport and Exercise Psychology* 10 (1): 62–74.

Cullinane, J. (1997) *Aspects of the History of Irish Dancing in North* America. Cork City: Central Remedial Clinic.

Cunningham, P. J. (2001) *A. N. Other.* Bray, Co. Wicklow: Dub Press.

Curtis, L. P. (1971) Apes and angels: the Irishman in Victorian caricature. Newton Abbot: David & Charles.

Darby, P. (2002) *Africa, Football and FIFA: Politics, Colonialism and Resistance.* London: Frank Cass.

Davies, N. (2000) *The Isles. A History.* London: Papermac.

De Búrca, M. (1980) *The GAA: A History of the Gaelic Athletic Association.* Dublin: Gill & Macmillan.

De Búrca, M. (1999) *The GAA: A History*, 2nd edn. Dublin: Gill & Macmillan.

Defrance, J. (1995) 'The anthropological sociology of Pierre Bourdieu: genesis, concepts, relevance', *Sociology of Sport Journal* 12 (2): 121–32.

Department of Education and Health Promotion Unit (1996) *A National Survey of Involvement in Sport and Physical Activity.* Dublin: Government of Ireland Official Publication.

Department of Health and Children and Health Promotion Unit (1999) *The National Health and Lifestyles Survey.* Dublin: Stationery Office.

Diffley, S. (1973) *The Men In Green: The Story of Irish Rugby.* London: Pelham.

Dineen, M. (1901) 'The game of hurling', *The Gael,* Sept.

*Donohoe's Magazine* (1886) 'Parliamentary Fund', XV (4), Apr.

*Donohoe's Magazine* (1888) 'Irish Athletes', XX (5), Nov.

*Donohoe's Magazine* (1890) 'Death of John Boyle O'Reilly', Oct.: 359–70.

Dougan, D. (1972) *The Sash He Never Wore.* London: Allison & Busby.

Douglas, N. and P. Shirlow (1998) 'People in conflict in place: the case of Northern Ireland', *Political Geography* 17 (2): 125–28.

Downey, O. (2000) *Glory tales of violence.* Belfast: Red Button.

Doyle, P. (2002) 'Putting the bigoted boot in for the sake of "Irishness"', *Sunday Tribune,* 7 Apr.

Duffy, P. (1994) 'The role and function of the National Coaching and Training Centre in the promotion of women in sport', pp. 18–26 in N. Murphy, N. and C. Woods (eds), *Proceedings of National Forum for Girls and Women in Sport.* Limerick: Physical Education Association of Ireland.

Duke, V. and L. Crolley (1996) *Football, Nationality and the State.* Harlow: Longman.

Duncan, M. and C. Hasbrook (2002) 'Denial of power in televised women's sports', pp. 83–94 in S. Scraton and A. Flintoff (eds), *Gender and Sport: A Reader.* London: Routledge. (Also published in *Sociology of Sport Journal* 5 (1) 1988: 1–21.)

Dunning, E. (1986) 'Sport as a male preserve: notes on the social sources of masculine identity and its transformations', pp. 267–84 in N. Elias and E. Dunning (eds), *Quest for Excitement: Sport and Leisure in the Civilizing Process.* Oxford: Basil Blackwell.

Dunning, E. (1994) 'Sport as a male preserve: notes on the social sources of masculine identity and its transformations', pp. 163–92 in S. Birrell and C. Cole (eds), *Women, Sport, and Culture.* Champaign, IL.: Human Kinetics.

Dunning, E. (1999) 'Sport, gender and civilization', pp. 219–39 in E. Dunning, *Sport Matters: Sociological Studies of Sport, Violence and Civilization.* London: Routledge.

Egan, S. (1980) 'The Aonach Tailteann and the Tailteann Games: origin, function and ancient associations', *CAPHER Journal:* 3–5, 38.

Elias, N. (1978) *What Is Sociology?* London: Hutchinson.

Elias, N. (1991) *The Society of Individuals.* Oxford: Basil Blackwell.

Elias, N. (1994) 'Introduction: a theoretical essay on established and outsider relations', pp. xv–lii in N. Elias and J. L. Scotson (eds), *A Sociological Enquiry into Community Problems.* London: Frank Cass.

Elias, N. (1996) *The Germans: Power Struggles and the Development of Habitus in the Nineteenth and Twentieth Centuries.* Cambridge: Polity.

Elias, N. and E. Dunning (1986) *Quest for Excitement: Sport and Leisure in the Civilizing Process.* Oxford: Blackwell.

Elliott, M. (2000) *The Catholics of Ulster.* London: Penguin.

Elon, A. (2000) *A Blood Dimmed Tide: Dispatches from the Middle East* London: Penguin.

*Evening Herald* (2003) 'The man who made rugby sexy', 28 Mar.

Fahy, D. (2001) *How the GAA Survived the Troubles.* Dublin: Wolfhound.

*Fairplay: Sport and Leisure.* London: Fairplay Sport Leisure Lifestyle Ltd. www.fairplay.ie

Feldman, A. (1991) *Formations of violence: the narrative of the body and political terror in Northern Ireland.* Chicago: University of Chicago Press.

Felshin, J. (1974) 'The triple option . . . for women in sport', *Quest* 21: 36–40.

Fenton, R. (2000) 'Clubs apply for senior status', *Belfast Telegraph*, 28 Mar.

Finn, G. (1994) 'Sporting symbols, sporting identities: soccer and intergroup conflict in Scotland and Northern Ireland', pp. 33–55 in I. Wood (ed.), *Scotland and Ulster.* Edinburgh: Mercat.

Fletcher, J. (1997) *Violence and Civilization: An Introduction to the Work of Norbert Elias.* Cambridge: Polity.

Foster, R. F. (1989) *Modern Ireland 1600–1972.* Harmondsworth: Penguin.

Foster, R. F. (1993) *Paddy and Mr Punch: Connections in Irish and English History.* London: Allen Lane.

Free, M. (1998) 'Angels with drunken faces? Travelling Republic of Ireland supporters and the construction of Irish migrant identity in England', pp. 219–32 in A. Brown (ed.), *Fanatics! Power, Identity and Fandom in Football.* London: Routledge.

*The Gael* (1882) 1 (1), Jan.

*The Gael* (1887) 'An Irish hurling green: a ballad for the Gael', 6 (3), May.

Garnham, N. (1999) 'Introduction', pp. 1–33 in N. Garnham (ed.), *The Origins and Development of Football in Ireland,* (reprint of R. M. Peter's *Irish Football Annual*, 1880). Belfast: Ulster Historical Foundation.

Gaughran, M. B. (1999) 'Football's fighting Irish', *Boston Globe*, 26 May.

Gibbons, L. (1996) *Transformations in Irish Culture.* Cork: Cork University Press.

Gibson, A. (2001) 'Irish When It Suits? An Examination into Identity Issues within Rugby in Northern Ireland'. Unpublished BSc (Hons) dissertation, University of Ulster at Jordanstown.

Giulianotti, R. (1996) 'All the Olympians: A thing never known again? Reflections on Irish football culture and the 1994 World Cup Finals', *Irish Journal of Sociology* 6: 101–26.

Goldring, M. (1993) *Pleasant the Scholar's Life: Irish Intellectuals and the construction of the nation state.* London: Serif.

Goodhart, P. and C. Chataway (1968) *War Without Weapons.* London: W. H. Allen.

Graham, B. (1997) 'Ireland and Irishness: place, culture and identity', pp. 1–15 in B. Graham (ed.), *In Search of an Ireland: A Cultural Geography.* London: Routledge.

Gray, B. and L. Ryan (1998) 'The politics of Irish identity and the interconnections between feminism, nationhood and colonialism', pp. 121–38 in R. Roach-Pierson and N. Chaudhuri (eds), *Nation, Empire, Colony.* Bloomington: Indiana University Press.

Greeley, A. M. (1981) *The Irish Americans: The Rise to Money and Power.* New York and Cambridge: Harper & Row.

Griffiths, J. (1994) *The Five Nations Championship 1947–93.* London: Methuen.

Guinnane, T. (1997) *The Vanishing Irish: Households, Migration, and the Rural Economy in Ireland, 1850–1914.* Princeton, NJ: Princeton University Press.

Guttmann, A. (1996) *Games and Empires: Modern Sports and Cultural Imperialism.* New York: Columbia University Press.

Hall, S. (1992) 'The question of cultural identity', in S. Hall, D. Held and A.McGrew (eds), *Modernity and its Futures.* Cambridge: Polity.

Hamilton, B et al.(2001) *Creating a Soccer Strategy for Northern Ireland.* Belfast: Department of Culture Arts and Leisure.

Hanna, F. (1999) 'The Gaelic Athletic Association', in M. Glazier (ed.), *The Encyclopedia of the Irish in America*. Notre Dame, IN: University of Notre Dame Press.

Hargreaves, J. (1986) *Sport, Power and Culture*. New York: St Martin's Press.

Hargreaves, J. (1994) *Sporting Females: Critical Issues in the History and Sociology of Women's Sports*. London: Routledge.

Hargreaves, J. (2000) *Heroines of Sport: The Politics of Difference and Identity*. London: Routledge.

Harvey, D. (1989) *The Condition of Postmodernity*. Oxford: Blackwell.

Hassan, D. (2001) 'A people apart: soccer, identity and Irish nationalists in Northern Ireland', *Soccer and Society* 3 (3): 65–83.

Healy, J. (1997) *Proceed to Banteer*. Dublin: Jerimiah Healy.

Hehir, J., (2000) 'Boston and North East Gaelic Athletic Association 1884–2000', pp. 2–3 in North East Gaelic Athletic Association, *A Century of Boston GAA*. Boston: Woburn Printing Inc.

Henderson, K. A. and C. E. Frelke (2000) 'Space as a vital dimension of leisure: the creation of place', *World Leisure Journal* 42 (3): 18–24.

Hewitt, J. (1974) 'Clash of identities', p. 4 in P. Craig (ed.), *The Rattle of the North: An Anthology of Ulster Prose*. Belfast: Blackstaff.

Hill, C. (1992) *Olympic Politics*. Manchester: Manchester University Press.

Hoberman, J. (1986) *Sport and Political Ideology*. London: Heinemann.

Hobsbawm, E. J. (1983) 'Mass-producing traditions: Europe, 1870–1914, pp. 263–307 in E. Hobsbawm and T. Ranger (eds), *The Invention of Tradition*. Cambridge: Cambridge University Press.

Hobsbawm, E. J. (1992) 'Introduction: inventing traditions', pp. 1–14 in E. Hobsbawm and T. Ranger (eds) *The Invention of Tradition*, Cambridge: Cambridge University Press.

Hobsbawm, E. J. and T. O. Ranger (eds) (1992) *The Invention of Tradition*. Cambridge: Cambridge University Press.

Holmes, M. (1994) 'Symbols of national identity and sport: the case of the Irish football team', *Irish Political Studies* 9: 91–8.

Holt, R. (1990) *Sport and the British: A Modern History*. Oxford: Oxford University Press.

Houlihan, B. (1997) *Sport, Policy and Politics: A Comparative Analysis*. London: Routledge.

Hunt, T. (2002) 'Mullingar Sport in the 1890s: communities at play', in M. Farrell (ed.), *Mullingar: Essays on the History of a Midlands Town in the 19th century*. Mullingar: Westmeath County Library

Inglis, T. (1998) *Lessons in Irish Sexuality*. Dublin: University College Dublin Press.

Inglis, T. (2000) 'Irish civil society: from church to media domination', pp. 49–68 in T. Inglis, Z. Mach. and R. Mazanek (eds), *Religion and Politics: East–West Contrasts from Contemporary Europe*. Dublin: University College Dublin Press.

Innes, C. L. (1993) *Woman and Nation*. Hemel Hempstead: Harvester Wheatsheaf.

Irish Cultural Centre (1999) 'Boston and the North East Gaelic Athletic Association 1884–1999', pp. 8–9 in *Commemorative Program, Irish Cultural Centre Grand Opening – Phase I*. Boston: Irish Cultural Centre.

*Irish Echo* (1888a) 'Ireland's games and pastimes: The national Irish Athletic Association to the fore', II (7) July.

*Irish Echo* (1888b) 'Irish athletic champions', II (10) Oct.

*Irish Independent* (2001) 'GAA repeal Rule 21', 19 Nov.

*Irish News* (1999) 'McLaughlin congratulates City of Derry', 25 Oct.

Irish Sports Council (2003) *Statement of Strategy 2003–2005.* Dublin: Irish Sports Council. www.irishsportscouncil.ie

Jackson, A. (1996) 'Irish unionists and the Empire, 1880–1920: classes and masses', pp. 124–36 in K. Jeffery (ed.), *'An Irish Empire'? Aspects of Ireland and the British Empire.* Manchester: Manchester University Press.

James, C. L. R. (1993 [1963]) *Beyond a Boundary.* Durham: Duke University Press.

Jarman, N. (1998) *Material conflicts: parades and visual displays in Northern Ireland.* London: Berg.

Jarvie, G. and Walker, G. (eds) (1994) *Scottish Sport in the Making of the Nation: Ninety Minute Patriots?* Leicester: Leicester University Press.

Jenkins, R. (1997) *Rethinking Ethnicity: Arguments and Explorations.* London: Sage.

Johns, D. and A. Farrow (1990) 'Gender difference in role accumulation in parent athletes'. Paper presented at the annual conference of the North American Society for the Sociology of Sport, Denver, CO.

Johnson, P. (2001) 'Sport and The Reconciliation Process in Israel. A Case Study of Ibillin'. Unpublished MA dissertation. Eastbourne: University of Brighton.

Jones, T., P. Duffy, G. Murphy and J. Dinneen (1991) *Girls and Boys Come Out To Play.* Limerick: Physical Education Association of Ireland.

Keating, F. (1999) 'Ulster unites for "Our Boys"', *Guardian,* 29 Jan.

Kennedy, J. (1989) *Belfast Celtic.* Belfast: Pretani.

Klein, A. M. (1997) *Baseball On the Border: A Tale of Two Laredos.* New Jersey: Princeton University Press.

Knox, C. (1987) 'Territorialism: leisure and community in Northern Ireland', *Leisure Studies* 6 (4): 251–63.

Lanfranchi, P. and M. Taylor (2001) *Moving with the Ball: The Migration of Professional Footballers.* Oxford: Berg.

Layder, D. (1994) *Understanding Social Theory.* London: Sage.

Lee, J. J. (1973) *The Modernisation of Irish Society 1848–1918.* Dublin: Gill & Macmillan.

Lennon, J. (1997) *The Playing Rules of Football and Hurling, 1884–1995.* Gormanstown: Northern Recreation Consultants.

Lenskyj, H. (1986) *Out of Bounds: Women, Sport and Sexuality.* Toronto: The Women's Press.

Lenskyj, H. (1994) 'Sexuality and femininity in sports contexts: issues and alternatives', *Journal of Sport and Social Issues* 18: 358–76.

Liston, K. (1999) 'Playing the masculine/feminine game . . . so he plays harder and she plays softer' in *PaGes: Postgraduate Research in Progress.* University College Dublin, Faculty of Arts (6): 133–47.

Liston, K. (2001) 'Sport, gender and commercialization', *Studies* 90 (359): 251–66.

Liston, K. (2002) 'The gendered field of Irish sport', pp. 231–47 in M. Corcoran and M. Peillon (eds), *Ireland Unbound: A Turn of the Century Chronicle.* Dublin: Institute of Public Administration.

Lovejoy, J. (1999) *Bestie: A Portrait of a Legend.* London: Pan Macmillan.

Lovesey, P. (1979) *The Official Centenary History of the Amateur Athletic Association.* Enfield: Guinness Superlatives.

Lynch, K. and Lodge, A. (2002) *Equality and Power in Schools: Redistribution, Recognition and Representation.* London: Routledge.

MacDiarmid, H. (1987) *A Drunk Man Looks at the Thistle*, ed. K. Buthlay. Edinburgh: Scottish Academic Press.

MacDougall, C. (2001) *Painting the Forth Bridge: A Search for Scottish Identity*. London: Aurum.

Maginness, A. (2001) 'Redefining Northern nationalism: a political perspective', pp. 1–5 in *Redefining Northern Nationalism*, Working Paper No. 3. Dublin: University College Dublin, Institute for British–Irish Studies.

Maguire, J. (1993) 'Globalization, sport and national identities: "The Empire strikes back"?', *Loisir et Société* 16 (2): 293–322.

Maguire, J. (1994) 'Sport, identity politics, and globalization: diminishing contrasts and increasing varieties', *Sociology of Sport Journal* 11 (4): 398–427.

Maguire, J. (1996) 'Blade runners: Canadian migrants, ice hockey, and the global sports process', *Journal of Sport and Social Issues* 20: 335–60.

Maguire, J. (1999) *Global Sport. Identities, Societies, Civilizations*. Cambridge: Polity.

Maguire, J., G. Jarvie, L. Mansfield and J. Bradley (2002) *Sport Worlds: A Sociological Perspective*. Champaign, IL: Human Kinetics.

Maguire, J. and E. K. Poulton (1999) 'European identity politics in Euro 96: Invented traditions and national habitus codes', *International Review for the Sociology of Sport* 34 (1): 17–29.

Maguire, J., E. K. Poulton and C. Possamai (1999) 'Weltkrieg III? Media coverage of England versus Germany in Euro 96', *Journal of Sport and Social Issues* 23 (4): 439–54.

Maguire, J. and D. E. Stead (1996) 'Far pavilions?: Cricket migrants, foreign sojourns and contested identities', *International Review for the Sociology of Sport* 31 (1): 1–24.

Maguire, J. and J. Tuck (1998) 'Global sports and patriot games: rugby union and national identity in a United Sporting Kingdom since 1945', pp. 103–26 in M. Cronin and D. Mayall (eds), *Sporting Nationalisms: Identity, Ethnicity, Immigration and Assimilation*. London: Frank Cass.

Mandle, W.F., (1977) 'The Irish Republican Brotherhood and the beginnings of the Gaelic Athletic Association', *Irish Historical Studies* XX: 418–38.

Mandle, W. F. (1987) *The Gaelic Athletic Association and Irish Nationalist Politics, 1884–1924*. Dublin: Gill & Macmillan.

Mangan, J. A. (1985) *The Games Ethic and Imperialism: Aspects of the Diffusion of an Ideal*. London: Frank Cass.

Mason, S. (2000) 'The History of Irish Rugby: A Transition from Amateurism to Professionalism'. Unpublished MSc thesis, University of Ulster at Jordanstown.

Mason, T. (1993) 'All the winners and all the half-times', *Sports Historian* 13: 3–10.

Mayer, T. (ed.) (1999) *Gender Ironies of Nationalism*. London: Routledge.

McCaffrey, L. J. (1992) *Textures of Irish America*. Syracuse, NY: Syracuse University Press.

McCaffrey, L. J. (1997) *The Irish Catholic Diaspora in America*. Washington, DC: Catholic University of America Press.

McClintock, A. (1995) *Imperial Leather: Race, Gender and Sexuality in the Colonial Context*. New York: Routledge.

McClintock, A. (1997) 'No longer in a future heaven: gender, race and nationalism', pp. 89–112 in A. McClintock, A. Mufti and E. Shohat (eds), *Dangerous Liaisons: Gender, Nation and Post-Colonial Perspectives*. Minnesota: Minnesota University Press.

McCracken, D. P. (ed.) (1996) 'Ireland and South Africa in modern times', *South African-Irish Studies*, vol. 3. Durban: Atlas.

McCracken, D. P. (1989) *The Irish Pro-Boers, 1877–1902*. Johannesburg: Perskor.

McCrone, D. (2002) 'Scotland, small? Making sense of nations in the 21st century'. Seminar on 'New Politics: New Governance: the experience of Scottish Devolution', Scotland in Sweden, Stockholm, 18 Oct.

McDevitt, P. F. (1997) 'Muscular Catholicism; nationalism, masculinity and Gaelic team sports, 1884–1916', *Gender and History* IX (2): 262–84.

McGarry, J. and B. O'Leary (1995) *Explaining Northern Ireland: Broken Images*. Oxford: Blackwell.

McGrew (eds) *Modernity and its Futures*. Cambridge: Polity.

McIntosh, P. (1993). 'The sociology of sport in the ancient world', pp. 19–38 in E. Dunning et al. (eds), *The Sports Process: A Comparative and Developmental Approach*. Champaign, IL: Human Kinetics.

McKay, S. (2000) *Northern Protestants: An Unsettled People*. Belfast: Blackstaff.

McLaughlin, J. (1995) 'An Evaluation of Sport's Contribution to Community Relations in Northern Ireland'. Unpublished DPhil thesis, Jordanstown: University of Ulster.

Mennell, S. (1989) *Norbert Elias: Civilization and the Human Self-Image*. Oxford: Blackwell.

Mennell, S. (1990) 'The globalization of human society as a very long-term social process: Elias's theory', *Theory, Culture and Society* 7: 359–71

Mennell, S. (1994) 'The formation of we-images: a process theory, in C. Calhoun (ed.), *Social Theory and the Politics of Identity*. Oxford: Blackwell.

Metcalf, A. (1988) 'Football in the mining communities of east Northumberland, 1882–1914', *International Journal of the History of Sport* 5 (3): 269–91.

Metheny, E. (1965) *Connotations of Movement in Sport and Dance*. Iowa: Wm. C Brown.

Metheny, E. (1972) 'Symbolic forms of movement: the feminine image in sport', pp. 277–90 in M. Hart (ed.), *Sport In The Socio-Cultural Process*. Iowa: Wm. C. Brown.

Minute book of the Irish Rugby Football Union (Northern Branch), 2 December, 1902–5 November, 1907 (Public Record Office of Northern Ireland) ref: D/3867/A/3.

Moore, C. (1999) *United Irishmen: Manchester United's Irish Connection*. Edinburgh: Mainstream

Moran, A. (2001) 'What makes a winner', *Studies* 90 (359): 266–76.

Mosse, G. (1985) *Nationalism and Sexuality*. Madison: University of Wisconsin Press.

Nairn, T. (1981) *The Break-Up of Britain*, 2nd edn. London: Verso.

Nally, T. H. (1922) *The Aonach Tailteann and the Tailteann Games: Their Origin, History and Ancient Associations*. Dublin: Talbot Press.

Nash, C. (1993) 'Remapping and renaming: new cartographies of identities, gender and landscape in Ireland', *Feminist Review* 44: 39–57.

Nauright, J. (1990) 'Myth and reality: reflections on rugby and New Zealand historiography', *Sporting Traditions* 6 (2): 219–30.

Nauright, J. (1991) 'Sport, manhood and empire: British responses to the New Zealand rugby tour of 1905', *International Journal of the History of Sport* VIII (2): 240–55.

Nauright, J. (1996a) 'A besieged tribe'?: nostalgia, white cultural identity and the role of rugby in a changing South Africa', *International Review for the Sociology of Sport* 31 (1): 69–90.

Nauright, J. (1996b) 'Colonial manhood and imperial race virility: British responses to post-Boer War colonial rugby tours', pp. 121–43 in J. Nauright and T. J. L. Chandler (eds), *Making Men: Rugby and Masculine Identity*. Manchester: Manchester University Press

Nauright, J. (1997) *Sport, Cultures and Identities in South Africa.* London: Leicester University Press.

Nauright, J. and T. J. L. Chandler (eds) (1996) *Making Men: Rugby and Masculine Identity.* London: Frank Cass.

NicCraith, M. (2001) *Cultural Diversity in Northern Ireland and the Good Friday Agreement,* Working Paper No. 7. Dublin: University College Dublin, Institute for British–Irish Studies.

North American County Board (1998) *Official Programme for the NACB Finals.* Washington: NACB.

North East GAA (2000), *A Century of Boston GAA.* Boston: Woburn Printing Inc.

O'Brien, G. (ed.) (2000) *Playing The Field: Irish Writers on Sport.* Dublin: New Island.

O'Connor, F. (1993) *In Search of a State: Catholics in Northern Ireland.* Belfast: Blackstaff.

O'Connor, K. (1985) 'Ireland: A nation caught in the middle of an identity crisis', *Irish Independent,* 20 June.

O'Leary, B. and J. McGarry (1993) *The Politics of Antagonism: Understanding Northern Ireland.* London: Athlone.

O'Malley, D. (2001) 'Redefining southern nationalism: a political perspective', pp. 1–3 in *Redefining Southern Nationalism,* Working Paper No. 1. Dublin: University College Dublin, Institute for British–Irish Studies.

O'Malley, P. (1983) *The Uncivil Wars: Ireland Today.* Belfast: Blackstaff.

O'Malley, P. (2001) 'Northern Ireland and South Africa: "Hope and history at a crossroads"', pp. 276–308 in J. McGarry (ed.), *Northern Ireland and the Divided World: Post-Agreement Northern Ireland in Comparative Perspective*

O'Riain, S. (1998) *Maurice Davin (1842–1927), First President of the GAA.* Dublin: Geography Publications.

Official GAA Website (2001). 22 Nov.

Ong, A. (1999) *Flexible Citizenship: The Cultural Logics of Transnationality.* Durham: Duke University Press.

Oppenheim, A. (1992) *Questionnaire Design, Interviewing and Attitude Measurement.* London: Pinter.

Orwell, G. (1970) *In Front of Your Nose: The Collected Essays, Journalism and Letters of George Orwell,* vol. 4. Harmondsworth: Penguin.

Parker, A. et al. (1992) *Nationalism and Sexualities.* New York: Routledge.

Parkinson, M. (1975) *Best: An Intimate Biography.* London: Arrow.

Paseta, S. (1998–9) 'Trinity College, Dublin and the education of Irish Catholics, 1873–1908', *Studia Hibernica* XXX: 7–20.

Phoenix, E. (1994) *Northern Nationalism: Nationalist Politics, Partition, and the Catholic Minority in Northern Ireland 1890–1940.* Belfast: Ulster Historical Foundation.

Porter, N. (1996) *Rethinking Unionism.* Belfast: Blackstaff.

Rao, S. (1999) 'Woman-as-symbol: the intersections of identity politics, gender, and Indian nationalism', *Women's Studies International Forum* 22 (3): 317–28.

Reiss, S. A. (1992) 'Sport, race and ethnicity in an American City, 1879–1950', pp. 191–219 in M. D'Innocenzo and J. P. Sirefman (eds), *Immigration and Ethnicity: American Society – 'Melting Pot' or 'Salad Bowl'?* Westport, CN and London: Greenwood.

Roche, J. J. (1891) *The Life, Poems and Speeches of John Boyle O'Reilly.* New York.

Roche, M. (2000) *Mega-Events and Modernity: Olympics, Expos and the Construction of Global Culture*. London: Routledge.

Rouse, P. (1993) 'The politics of culture and sport in Ireland: a history of the GAA ban on foreign games 1884–71. Part one: 1884–1921', *International Journal of the History of Sport* X (3): 41–60.

Rouse, P. (2003) 'Why Irish historians have ignored sport: A note', *History Review*, XIV.

Ruane, J. and J. Todd (1996) *The Dynamics of Conflict in Northern Ireland: Power, Conflict and Emancipation*. Cambridge: Cambridge University Press.

Ryan, G. (1993) *Forerunners of the All Blacks: the 1888-89 New Zealand Native Football Team in Britain, Australia and New Zealand*. Canterbury (NZ): Canterbury University Press.

Ryan, L. (1998) 'Negotiating tradition and modernity: newspaper debates on the "modern girl" in the Irish Free State', *Journal of Gender Studies* 7 (2): 181–98.

Ryan, L. (2002) *Gender Identity and the Irish Press, 1922–1937: Embodying the Nation*. New York: Mellen Press.

Sack, D. (1993) *Place, Modernity, and the Consumer's World: A Relational Framework for Geographical Analysis*. Baltimore: Johns Hopkins University Press.

Said, E. (2000) *The End of the Peace Process*. London: Granta.

Scally, J. (1998) *Simply Red and Green: Manchester United and Ireland*. Edinburgh: Mainstream.

Schwarz, B. (1992) 'England in Europe: Reflections on national identity and cultural theory', *Cultural Studies* 6: 198–206.

Scraton, S. and A. Flintoff (eds) (2002) *Gender and Sport: A Reader*. London: Routledge.

Shannon, W. V. (1966) *The American Irish: A Political and Social Portrait*. New York: Macmillan.

Sharkey, S. (1994) *Ireland the Iconography of Rape*. London: University of North London Press.

Sheehan, J. (1987) *Worthies of Westmeath*. Wellbrook Press and Jeremiah Sheehan, Moate, Co. Westmeath.

Shilling, C. (1992) 'Schooling and the production of physical capital', *Discourse* 13 (1): 1–19.

Shilling, C. (1993) *The Body and Social Theory*. London: Sage.

Shirlow, P. (2001) 'The geography of fear in Belfast', *Peace Review* 43 (1): 12–28.

Shirlow, P. (2003) 'Ethno-sectarianism and fear in Belfast', *Capital and Class* 80: 46–67.

Smith, A. D. (1991) *National Identity*. Harmondsworth: Penguin.

Smith, A. D. (1995) *Nations and Nationalism in a Global Era*. London: Polity.

Smith, C. G. (1919), *Scottish Literature*. London: Macmillan.

*The Star* (2003) 'Plucky players tackle violent image of female rugby', 9 Apr.

Stoddart, B. and K. A. P. Sandiford (eds) (1998) *The Imperial Game: Cricket, Culture and Society*. Manchester: Manchester University Press.

Stoddart, B. (1998) 'Sport, cultural imperialism, and colonial response in the British Empire', *Comparative Studies in Society and History* 30 (3): 649–73.

Sugden, J. (1989) 'As presently constituted, sport at an international level does more harm than good', in G. Cohen (ed.) 'Peace and understanding through sport', *Journal of the Institute for International Sport* 2 (1): 63–8.

Sugden, J. (1991) 'Belfast United: encouraging cross-community relations through sport in Northern Ireland', *Journal of Sport and Social Issues* 15 (1): 59–80.

Sugden, J. (2002) *Scum Airways: Inside Football's Underground Economy*. Edinburgh: Mainstream.

Sugden J. and A. Bairner (1993) *Sport, Sectarianism and Society in a Divided Ireland.* Leicester: Leicester University Press.

Sugden, J. and A. Bairner (1994) 'Ireland and the World Cup: "two teams in Ireland, there's only two teams in Ireland . . ."', pp. 119–39 in J. Sugden and A. Tomlinson (eds), *Hosts and Champions: Soccer Cultures, National Identities and the USA World Cup.* Aldershot: Arena.

Sugden, J. and A. Bairner (eds) (1999) *Sport in Divided Societies.* Aachen: Meyer & Meyer.

Sugden, J. and S. Harvie (1995) *Sport and Community Relations in Northern Ireland.* Coleraine: University of Ulster.

Sugden, J. and A. Tomlinson (1998) *FIFA and the Contest for World Football: Who Rules the Peoples' Game?* Cambridge: Polity.

*Sunday Tribune* (2000) 'New male order', 5 Nov.

Sutton, P. P. (1900) 'The ancient games of Ireland at Tailten and Carman', *The Gael* Aug.–Sept.

Thapar-Bjorkert, S. and L. Ryan (2002) 'Mother India/ Mother Ireland: Comparative gendered dialogues of colonialism and nationalism in the early twentieth century', *Women's Studies International Forum* 25 (3): 301–13.

Thomas, C. (1996) *The History of the British Lions.* Edinburgh: Mainstream.

Thompson, K. (1988) 'Challenging the hegemony: New Zealand women's opposition to rugby and the reproduction of a capitalist patriarchy', *International Review for the Sociology of Sport* 23 (3): 205–12.

Todd, J. (1987) 'Two traditions in Unionist political culture', *Irish Political Studies* 2: 1–26.

Todd, J. (1990) 'Northern Irish nationalist political culture', *Irish Political Studies* 5: 31–44.

Todd, J. (1999) 'Nationalism, republicanism and the Good Friday Agreement', pp. 49–70 in J. Ruane and J. Todd (eds), *After the Good Friday Agreement.* Dublin: University College Dublin Press.

Todd, J. (2001) 'Redefining northern nationalism – an academic perspective', pp. 6–16 in *Redefining Northern Nationalism,* Working Paper No. 3. Dublin: University College Dublin, Institute for British–Irish Studies.

Tranter, N. (1990) 'The chronology of organised sport in nineteenth century Scotland: a regional study', *International Journal of the History of Sport* 7 (2): 188–203.

Tsigdinos, Karl (2003) 'A lark in the park', *Cara* Mar.: 64.

Tuck, J. and J. Maguire (1999) 'Making sense of global patriot games: rugby players' perceptions of national identity politics', *Football Studies* 2 (1): 26–54.

Turner, V. (1974) *Dramas Fields and Metaphors: Symbolic Action in Human Societies.* New York: Cornell University Press.

Turpin, J. (2000) *Oliver Sheppard, 1865–1941: Symbolist Sculptor of the Irish Cultural Revival.* Dublin: Four Courts.

Van Esbeck, E. (1974) *One Hundred Years of Irish Rugby: The Official History of the Irish RFU.* Dublin: Gill & Macmillan.

Van Esbeck, E. (1986) *The Story of Irish Rugby.* London: Stanley Paul.

Van Esbeck, E. (1999) *Irish Rugby 1874–1999: A History.* Dublin: Gill & Macmillan.

Waddington, I., Malcolm, D. and Cobb, J. (1998) 'Gender stereotyping and physical education', *European Physical Education Review* 4 (1): 34–46.

Webb, J., T. Schirato and G. Danaher (2002) *Understanding Bourdieu.* London: Sage.

Whyte, J. (1990) *Interpreting Northern Ireland.* Oxford: Clarendon.

Wilcox, R. C. (1992) 'Sport and the nineteenth century immigrant experience', pp. 177–89 in M. D'Innocenzo and J. P. Sirefman (eds), *Immigration and Ethnicity: American Society – 'Melting Pot' or 'Salad Bowl'*? Westport, CN and London: Greenwood.

Williams, G. (1985) 'How amateur was my valley?: Professional sport and national identity in Wales, 1890–1914', *British Journal of Sports History* 2 (3): 248–69.

Williams, G. (1988) 'From popular culture to public cliché: image and identity in Wales 1980–1914', in J. A. Mangan (ed.), *Pleasure, Proselytism: British Culture and Sport at Home and Abroad, 1700–1914.* London: Frank Cass.

Williams, G. (1991) *1905 And All That: Essays On Rugby Football, Sport and Welsh Society.* Llandysul: Gomer.

Wilson, T. W. (1993) 'Frontiers go but boundaries remain: the Irish Border as a cultural divide', pp. 167–87 in T. W. Wilson and M. Estellie Smith (eds), *Cultural Change and the New Europe: Perspectives on the European Community.* Oxford: Westview.

Yuval-Davis, N. (1993) 'Gender and nation', *Ethnic and Racial Studies* 16 (4): 621–32.

Yuval-Davis, N. (1997) *Gender and Nation.* London: Sage.

# Index